302933 D1758794

The publisher and the University of California Press Foundation gratefully acknowledge the generous support of the Atkinson Family Foundation Imprint in Higher Education.

Education and Society

EDUCATION AND SOCIETY

An Introduction to Key Issues in the Sociology of Education

Edited by Thurston Domina,
Benjamin G. Gibbs, Lisa Nunn, and
Andrew Penner

UNIVERSITY OF CALIFORNIA PRESS

University of California Press, one of the most distinguished university presses in the United States, enriches lives around the world by advancing scholarship in the humanities, social sciences, and natural sciences. Its activities are supported by the UC Press Foundation and by philanthropic contributions from individuals and institutions. For more information, visit www.ucpress.edu.

University of California Press
Oakland, California

Cataloging-in-Publication Data is on file at the Library of Congress.

ISBN 978-0-520-29558-2 (pbk. : alk. paper)
ISBN 978-0-520-96830-1 (ebook)

Manufactured in the United States of America

27   26   25   24   23   22   21   20   19
10   9   8   7   6   5   4   3   2   1

Contents

Illustrations

Editors' Introduction

Education is a vast institution in contemporary societies. Virtually every child on earth today will be exposed to some form of formal schooling. And that child's education will likely play a central role in organizing her development and social identity. As she grows, her education will likely influence her labor market experiences, where and how she lives, her marriage and family-formation decisions, and even her health and life expectancy.

If you're reading this book, you no doubt have a strong personal understanding of schooling as an institution and of its profound social importance. After all, if your educational experience is typical, you spent some fifteen thousand hours in school between the ages of five and eighteen. In the process, you likely worked your way through reams of photocopied worksheets, bubbled in the answers to thousands of multiple choice questions, and negotiated countless complex social encounters in locker-lined hallways and lunchroom lines. And, if you're reading this book as a college student, you likely experienced some measure of success in the process. Like nearly 90 percent of contemporary young people, you earned a high school diploma; and like more than half of those high school graduates, you made the leap into postsecondary education.

Because your experience gives you considerable expertise on education as an institution, this textbook works a little differently from most of the textbooks you encounter. Rather than trying to introduce you to an established and settled body of knowledge (as an anatomy textbook might), or training you in a set of skills (as a computer science textbook might), this book invites you into an ongoing conversation about education and society.

This conversation takes place across a range of venues, including academic journals, conferences, research talks, and—increasingly—social media. One venue that has been particularly important for the development of this book is a relatively small and informal conference that occurs every spring at a state park in Northern California. Over two days, at the Sociology of Education Association's annual meetings, some seventy to eighty experts on the sociology of education think through dozens of papers and talk and laugh through a handful of meals together. In the process, we share both the excitement of scientific discovery and the entirely different excitement of intense debate. We poke at one another's ideas and explore one another's data in an attempt to broaden our understanding of education—an institution about which we all care deeply.

We have tried to capture some of the spirit of those meetings in this book. Each of the book's chapters and case studies is meant as an introduction to the ideas and evidence that have been formative to the authors' ongoing understanding of education as a social institution. As such, each chapter and case study has a viewpoint and an argument to make. You'll likely find it easier to agree with some than others. And in fact, if you read carefully, you'll likely find places in which the authors of chapters or case studies disagree with one another. That is, we think, as it should be.

Education is an incredibly complex, and indeed contradictory, institution in contemporary life. We expect schools to provide opportunities to all, even as they prepare students for highly unequal adult societies and legitimate that inequality. We want schools to teach students how to cooperate even as we ask them to structure hugely influential social competitions. We ask schools to establish and reinforce a shared body of social knowledge, even as they recognize and respect a pluralistic society's diversity of views and experiences. Given the contradictions inherent in contemporary mass education, it is our view that it's appropriate that the sociology of education should also be a contentious and multifaceted field of study.

That said, you will also notice three common threads that run through each of the chapters and case studies. First, central to the sociology of education—and, indeed, all sociology—is the assumption that the social world is knowable. While at any given moment each of us has a limited view of our social setting, sociologists have developed a wide range of qualitative, quantitative, and historical methods that make it possible to subject the interactions, structures, and interpersonal relationships that we collectively describe as *society* to empirical scrutiny. By applying this social scientific view to education, we seek to understand the complex relationship between education and social inequality, the ways in which schools change, and the ways in which changing schools then change society.

Second, the authors of all these chapters and case studies are motivated by the belief that the act of collecting and interpreting information about the world has the potential to make a more just and equitable society. As a result, the authors dedicate considerable attention to providing an accurate empirical representation of schools and their social role in contemporary societies. The word *empirical* is important here. Sociology thinks of itself as a social science. Consequently, sociologists are committed to producing knowledge that is reproducible and transferable across time and space. We draw upon theory—and indeed our own experiences—to articulate hypotheses. But we also work hard to collect data and subject our hypotheses to rigorous tests. Thinking carefully about the evidence assembled here can shed light on your own educational experiences, the social processes that explain them, and how they compare to those of your peers.

Third, you will notice the concept of *inequality* cropping up repeatedly across chapters and case studies. Questions about why some people have more resources, power, and or status than others, and about the implications of that unequal distribution, are important throughout all aspects of sociology. But they are particularly important in the sociology of education. Schools are egalitarian institutions by their conception, dedicated to the principle that all people have worth and thus deserve opportunities to learn. At the same time, the production and legitimation of inequality is one of education's central roles in contemporary societies. When you graduate from college, your school will give you a degree that is intended to signify all of the work and learning that you did over the course of your college career. That degree will likely confer advantages that students who stopped their schooling before enrolling in college won't be able to access. If it didn't, you'd likely wonder if college was worth the time, money, and effort. In this way and many others, schools create unequal categories and sort youth among them. These categories are templates that influence the contours of inequality throughout contemporary societies.

Each of the chapters and case studies that follow consists of a summary of sociological thinking and research on pressing issues in contemporary schools, written by trail-blazing researchers in the sociology of education. While each of the scholars you read here has a viewpoint, each is also dedicated to producing and thinking through new knowledge.

In the book's first section, two leading authorities in the sociology of education provide broad overviews of the field and its development. In chapter 1, Evan Schofer offers an overview of the field from a global perspective, drawing attention to the ways in which educational systems differ, as well as to the important similarities that exist among educational systems worldwide. In chapter 2, Doug Downey considers the complex relationship between education and social inequality in the contemporary world.

The chapters and case studies in the book's second section take a closer look at student experiences within educational institutions. These chapters and case studies investigate how these school experiences vary with students' *ascriptive* characteristics—including their gender, race, immigration status, and sexual orientation. In addition, they investigate the informal social processes that occur among students in schools, including interactions between students and teachers and the construction of cliques and other student peer groups.

Two case studies in the book's second section take a closer look at the way schools shape students' identities and the ways those identities, in turn, shape students' educational experiences. The concluding case study uses the example of Asian American students to explore how ethnic stereotypes and other social expectations shape students' school experiences. This case study is structured differently from the rest of the chapters in the section. While the others provide you with a broad introduction to the issues and research in a given area, this case study is designed to "go deep" on a single social setting and the sociological questions it raises. As a result, it is structured much more like a scholarly paper in the field of sociology and includes an abstract, an introduction, a methods section, and a set of results. We hope that reading this case study gives you a context in which to explore the ideas that you've encountered elsewhere in *Education and Society.*

The book's third section takes on more formal social *structures* that define contemporary education and its place in society. Our chapters and case studies consider the ways these structures shape the internal organization of schools, influencing what is (and isn't) taught, the ways in which schools sort students into academic tracks and special education categories to facilitate instruction, and school disciplinary processes. In addition, the chapters and case studies in this section address how schools are situated in broader social structures, and how residential and legal arrangements lead to racial and class-based segregation between schools. They also examine the recent policy efforts to introduce market pressures to K–12 education via school choice, and the ways in which colleges and universities interact with the labor market.

The third section also includes two case studies. One illustrates the diffusion of the school's organization form to a new realm, "life skills" classes offered to poor parents by social service agencies. We think this case sheds light on the many ways in which the social structures that we associate with "schooling" permeate contemporary societies.

As you read and discuss your way through this book, we encourage you to take time to connect the ideas and facts reported here to your own educational experiences and to the broader educational debates that you see in the news. We aim to help you think more broadly about the central place that schools occupy in contemporary societies; about why societies organize schools and other institutions the way they do, and the implications of those organizational decisions; and about why some students experience success in schools while others fall behind, and how those disparate experiences contribute to social inequality.

THEORETICAL ORIENTATIONS IN THE SOCIOLOGY OF EDUCATION

The Growth of Schooling in Global Perspective

EVAN SCHOFER, UNIVERSITY OF CALIFORNIA, IRVINE

EDITORS' NOTE

Having grown up in and around schools, we all have a considerable store of firsthand knowledge about education. We likely also have strong ideas about the various ways in which schools interact with the societies in which they are located. For example, many of us behave in a way that's consistent with **human capital theory**—studying because we believe that the knowledge and skills we accumulate in school will make us more employable, more productive, and better-paid members of the labor force.

What we already know and believe about education and society is a valuable resource to draw upon as you begin your study of the sociology of education. But it's also important to acknowledge that our firsthand knowledge is limited in important ways. The sociology of education is all about taking a broader view of schooling. We hope that, as you read this book, you'll reflect on the remarkably different ways that diverse students experience school and the many different ways that societies might organize the education of their youth.

This chapter by University of California, Irvine, sociologist Evan Schofer is a good place to start. Schofer reminds us that "school" is a relatively new invention, and that the idea that schools should be open to virtually all youth is newer still. You'll repeatedly encounter the word **institution** in this chapter. You surely know this word, but unless you've spent a lot of time in a sociology classroom, you may not have thought hard about what it means. In this chapter, Schofer is using institution to mean a set of ideas about how to accomplish broad social goals. In this sense, education is an institution.

As you read this chapter, think about why the institution of education became central to societies around the world during the twentieth century. Can you imagine a world without schools? How different might your life be in such a world?

KEY POINTS

- Schooling has grown tremendously over time, at every level, and in every corner of the globe. Scholars refer to this as the rise of the schooled society.
- It is commonly assumed that schools emerge and expand because people need human capital (skills) in order to get jobs.
- Sociologists offer alternative views about the growth of schooling. Some believe it reflects the efforts of elites to maintain their advantages.
- Other sociologists believe that the growth of schooling reflects the spread of ideas and cultural norms, such as a belief in the scientific method and in universal human rights, that make schooling seem particularly important and valuable.
- Some evidence can be found for each perspective. Historical evidence often supports the two sociological arguments. Quantitative studies of global trends tend to support the latter view.

INTRODUCTION

School is a universal experience for children growing up in wealthy countries like the United States. In fact, school is so commonplace, so utterly taken for granted, that we rarely question its existence. But why do we have schools in the first place? And why is there more schooling now than in the past?

This chapter describes and explores the tremendous growth of schooling over the past two centuries. Several important theories developed by sociologists of education are discussed, as well as evidence sociologists have used to evaluate these perspectives. Finally, the chapter briefly reflects on the consequences of the hyperexpansion of schooling.

THE OVERWHELMING SUCCESS OF MODERN SCHOOLING

Educators and scholars often proclaim a state of crisis in schooling, because schools do not accomplish all that we hope and desire. Yet in an important sense, schools are fantastically successful. Two centuries ago, schooling was rare around the world, mainly limited to affluent men in a handful of countries.

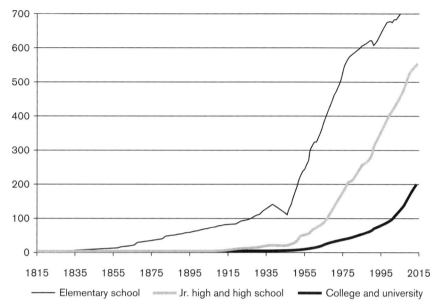

Figure 1. Worldwide school enrollments in millions, 1815–2015. Source: adapted and updated from E. Schofer and J. W. Meyer, "The Worldwide Expansion of Higher Education in the Twentieth Century," *American Sociological Review* 70, no. 6 (2005): 898–920.

Even fifty years ago in Europe, university matriculation was fairly uncommon. In poor countries, few children continued beyond elementary school, and hardly anyone went on to college. Now, most of the world's children get at least a basic education. College is the norm for people growing up in rich countries, and college enrollment is expanding quickly everywhere else. Schooling has also become more inclusive over the past century. Women were excluded from many kinds of education in the past, but they now attend school at higher rates than men in most parts of the world. Enrollment trends among members of disadvantaged minority groups have also improved in many places. This is not to say that all inequalities have been solved, but the overall trends in school enrollments are encouraging.

Figure 1 presents historical trends in school enrollments for the last two centuries, pieced together from different sources (adapted and updated from Schofer and Meyer 2005).[1] As is evident, mass education expanded during the course of the nineteenth century, with a sharp acceleration after 1945, when

1. Sociologists usually examine enrollments as a proportion of the population of children who might attend school, called an *enrollment ratio*, to correct for population growth. Enrollment ratios don't grow quite as dramatically, but the overall trend is similar.

World War II ended. Participation in junior high and high school took off at the end of the nineteenth century and followed a similar trajectory. College and university enrollments accelerated starting around 1960.

The sheer scale of modern schooling around the world is something to behold. Upward of 700 million children now attend elementary school, 550 million attend junior high or high school, and another 200 million are enrolled in college or graduate school.[2] All told, something like 1.4 billion people are students at this very moment, or nearly 20 percent of humanity.

The world's incredible commitment to education is also reflected in budget numbers. Most wealthy countries spend around 5 percent of their economic resources on education.[3] The US economy produces about eighteen trillion dollars' worth of goods and services each year, and about 5.7 percent of that amount is spent on education—roughly a trillion dollars! The figure for the globe is harder to estimate but certainly exceeds five trillion dollars and is probably closer to ten trillion. Sociologist David Baker (2014) refers to this as the educational revolution and describes our world, in which education has such centrality and importance, as "the schooled society."

Opposition to schooling was common in the past. Elites feared education would lead to rebellion: peasants filling their heads with new ideas might become discontent with their place in the social order. Families and religious groups worried that secular public schools would undermine traditional values and authority over their children. These forms of opposition still exist. For instance, radical religious groups have intimidated and even attack schoolchildren in Afghanistan and Nigeria. But opposition to schooling is now very much the exception rather than the rule.

THE RISE OF MODERN SCHOOLING

All human societies provide some form of education to their young, but the forms have varied throughout history (see Collins 2000). Children are taught knowledge and skills directly by their parents. A craftsperson may learn a trade by apprenticing with a master for many years. Workers may gain job skills from training programs run by their employers. Or religious groups may create schools focused solely on theology and religious tradition. These can all be observed today, but they are not the main story.

---

2. These figures derive from 2014 data supplied by UNESCO, a part of the United Nations that attends to educational issues. UNESCO Institute of Statistics, *UIS.Stat* database, 2016, http://data.uis.unesco.org.
3. This is according to data from the World Bank's *World Development Indicators* database, 2016, https://datacatalog.worldbank.org/dataset/world-development-indicators.

The huge expansion of schooling primarily involves a particular form of education, often called modern schools, which have their origins in western Europe. The features are familiar, as most of us have experienced them. Modern schooling takes place outside the home, in age-graded groups, taught by professional teachers and organized by governments or sometimes private or religious groups. Modern schools generally emphasize reading and writing, math, and social studies at the lower levels. The higher levels of schooling tend to be more diverse and sometimes include job skills or professional training. Universities have a longer history in Europe, dating back to the medieval era, and elements of modern schooling are derived from them. Ultimately universities became linked to rapidly growing systems of mass schooling, producing the stages of education we are familiar with today.

COMPARATIVE VARIATIONS: BRIEF EXAMPLES

Modern school systems have many similarities around the world, a point that will be taken up later. That said, there are plenty of differences in schools around the world, variations on a common theme. The United States happens to be one of the more atypical countries when it comes to the organization and funding of schools. American education is unusually decentralized. Schools are mainly funded by states and local communities, rather than by the central government in Washington, DC. Consequently, US schools are particularly unequal in terms of funding, as poor communities have few tax dollars for education. State or local groups have relatively greater control over the curriculum than does the federal government. This can be seen as ensuring valuable flexibility: schools can cater to local values and concerns. But this control can create an opportunity for controversy and conflict if, for example, some local communities would prefer to gloss over the injustices of slavery or teach creationism rather than evolution.

In contrast to the US approach, a more typical approach is for countries to establish a ministry of education (a high-level branch of the government), which plans and funds schooling throughout the country. This tends to produce greater consistency in funding and in what schools teach. Another difference is that many countries have different *types* of schools at the higher levels. In Germany, for instance, some students might go to academic high schools to prepare for college, while others may attend specialized vocational schools devoted entirely to teaching job skills like metalworking or car repair. Finally, high-stakes examinations are a common feature in many countries. To graduate from one level of schooling to the next, or to avoid being forced into vocational training, one has to pass a challenging test. In South Korea and China, for example students may study for years, often spending long hours in after-school tutoring programs ("shadow education"), to gain access to the best high schools and colleges.

Another huge difference in schooling worldwide is the amount of resources schools have. In most wealthy countries, schools have lavish buildings, computers, and many highly trained teachers. In the poorest parts of the world, schools may have dirt floors, crude chalkboards, and a teacher with very little training. And many schools fall in between. To get a sense of the range, consider the fact that Cambodia has an economy that produces about fifteen billion dollars per year, and the country spends about 1.6 percent of that on education. After taking population into account, the United States is over fifty times wealthier than Cambodia and spends roughly two hundred times more on schooling. We tend to think of American inner-city schools as poverty stricken, but many rural schools in parts of Africa, Asia, and Latin American are vastly poorer.

EXPLAINING THE EXPANSION OF SCHOOLING

What is the relationship between schools and society? Why do societies have schools in the first place? And why has schooling grown so much?

It is useful to start by reflecting on the kinds of arguments that sociologists avoid. People sometimes proclaim that humans pursue knowledge or create schools because we are naturally curious or have an innate drive to learn and explore the world. While we know that human behavior is affected to some extent by genetics and psychology, sociologists tend to be skeptical of efforts to explain highly complex human behavior—such as the emergence of modern schools—as the result of our DNA or psychological impulses. Throughout history, human societies have had radically different customs and beliefs regarding education. We should be very cautious about assuming that our schools reflect "human nature."

FUNCTIONALISM AND HUMAN CAPITAL THEORY

Functionalism

One classic sociological perspective argued that schooling was natural for the kind of society we have. The functionalist perspective holds that social institutions—such as governments or religions or schools—arise because they serve an important purpose (a "function"), that societies require them in order to work properly. The perspective draws on the analogy of a living organism: each body part, such as the heart or lungs, must surely perform some essential function needed to survive. So, the task for sociologists is to figure out what essential purpose schools fulfill.

Functionalist scholars argue that schools are needed to socialize children (teach them society's rules), to train people for jobs, and sort people into the right jobs. Society needs specially trained people, like engineers and surgeons, and schools arose to produce them. But only so many engineers or surgeons are needed. School grades and degrees are thought to reflect merit (skill and hard work), which employers and professional schools can use to decide who is suited to professional work, and who should do menial farm labor or scan items at a cash register.

So, why did schooling grow? Functionalist sociologists focus on the major economic shifts of the eighteenth and nineteenth centuries, such as the Industrial Revolution. European countries went from agriculture-based economies to having complex industrial economies, a process referred to as *modernization.* In agricultural societies, most people were farmers and didn't need much education. By contrast, modern industrial societies needed skilled workers to fill rapidly expanding jobs in factories, corporations, and governments. This necessitated the growth of modern schooling.

Classic functionalism has gone out of style in the field of sociology. Sociologists have largely abandoned the idea that society and its components naturally evolve over time like an organism. But many outside of sociology continue to assume that schools exist to teach necessary skills and are fundamentally meritocratic, meaning that they evaluate and reward people based on talent and hard work.

Human Capital Theory

Economists have developed a similar argument, using their own distinct language. Economists explain the world as a consequence of individual choices in a market economy. Schools will exist if people think schooling is more valuable than alternative activities such as earning a paycheck at work. But why would anyone spend years and years working hard in school, not earning a penny? The answer, according to economists, is that schools teach valuable skills that will pay off in the future. These skills are called human capital (Schultz 1961). People may choose to spend years in medical school and even pay lots of tuition to obtain skills needed to land an extremely high-paying job, which will generate greater income over one's lifetime.

Human capital theory views schools as the handmaidens of the economy, producing workers needed to fill the jobs in the labor market. If this is true, why would schooling expand over time? The answer is similar to the functionalist argument above: societies shift from agriculture to industry, and now increasingly to a high-tech postindustrial economy. In particular, economists focus on "skill-biased technological change," which refers to the rise of technologies that depend on highly skilled workers (see Goldin and Katz 2008). An example of one such technology is computers, which produce huge leaps in efficiency for those with the skills to use them. Such technologies create demand (and thus high salaries) for skilled workers, which in turn propels more and more people to seek out schooling.

CONFLICT THEORIES OF EDUCATION

Conflict theories explore ways that schools may either benefit some people at the expense of others or serve as a way for the powerful to exclude or exploit others. Scholars in this tradition have mainly argued that schools are *not* meritocratic, that they instead maintain or even exacerbate social inequalities.

Marxism

Marxist sociologists such as Samuel Bowles and Herbert Gintis (1976) developed one version of this story, arguing that schools are a tool of industrial capitalists, who need docile workers to fill their factories. They pointed out that schools—especially those that serve poor students—focus on obedience and punctuality. Children are trained to show up on time, follow rules, and work quietly for long periods of time. By contrast, the children of the wealthy often attend lavish private schools that teach a much broader set of skills, producing the next generation of lawyers, doctors, and capitalist elites.

In terms of explaining the growth of schooling, this perspective parallels the prior arguments: schools expand when the economy shifts from agriculture to industrial capitalism. But whereas modernization scholars believe that schools benefit society as a whole, Marxists think schools mainly benefit business owners, who profit from the large supply of obedient workers.

Reproduction and the Credential Society

Sociologists such as Randall Collins and Pierre Bourdieu offer a more complex story, proposing that schooling is an arena in which elites struggle to reproduce their advantage through the success of their children. Collins (1979) argued that white Protestant American elites use schooling as a way to establish their culture as dominant in the face of widespread immigration and to create hurdles that lock other groups out of elite jobs and professions (for instance, law and medicine). He suggested that American schools in the 1950s and 1960s were not necessarily focused on teaching useful job skills but, instead, reproduced a white Protestant status culture, from which employers then selected workers for top positions. Collins (1971: 1010) wrote, "The main activity of schools is to teach particular status cultures, both in and outside the classroom[:] . . . vocabulary and inflection, styles of dress, aesthetic tastes, values, and manners. The emphasis on sociability and athletics found in many schools is not extraneous but may be at the core of the status culture propagated by the schools." Obviously, white Protestant children would fare very well in such schools. Many others have pursued this line of argument. For instance, Pierre Bourdieu developed the concept of cultural capital and explored the ways that schools reward those with elite cultural tastes, ultimately reproducing social class differences.

Collins argued that competition among social groups would create pressures for educational expansion. Once education was established as the main way to get elite jobs in a society, all sorts of individuals and groups would have incentive to compete in schooling. As more people began to attend school and earn degrees (also referred to as "credentials"), elites would have to establish even higher educational hurdles to preserve the best jobs for their offspring. This would produce a cycle in which people acquire ever more schooling and the educational requirements for jobs keep going up, what Collins referred to as *credential inflation.* How does the story end? Collins has pointed to episodes in history where expansions of schooling and credential inflation were followed by crashes, in which people could not sustain further investments in schooling and became disillusioned with the value of schools and degrees. Perhaps the growing cost of college and the incredible burden of student loans in the United States will eventually undermine faith in higher education. But for the moment at least, the appetite for credentials is still growing.

Institutional Theory

Neo-institutional theorists such as John Meyer and Francisco Ramirez claim that society is governed not by functional needs, market forces, or powerful elites, but by culture, ideas, and norms that are widely accepted and built into important institutions such as government policy and law. We *believe* in the importance of education, and as a result we have built a world in which schools are everywhere, and where attendance for many years is required by law. Like Collins, neo-institutional scholars do not assume that schools teach useful knowledge, though the theory does not preclude that possibility. Nor does it argue that it is rational or advantageous for governments to build schools or for people to attend them, though things might work out that way. After all, if everyone in your society believes education is important, and everyone has lots of education, it may become hard to get through life without it.

Education plays a dual role in neo-institutional theory. On the one hand, scholars have explored how particular ideas, institutionalized in Europe and disseminated across the world, made education seem so important. On the other hand, scholars argue that education is now a key institution in modern society, one that profoundly shapes our culture by defining key stages of the life course, by establishing some kinds of people and some kinds of knowledge as important, and by transmitting culture via the curriculum (e.g., Meyer 1977; Baker 2014; Patricia Bromley and Daniel Scott Smith, this volume).

Why did schooling expand? According to neo-institutional theorists, it did so because of changing ideas and norms, built into institutions like the state, that made schooling seem appropriate and valuable to an ever-growing set of people.

To understand why we have schools now, it helps to think about why we didn't have schools in the past. Imagine European feudal lords and peasants in the Middle Ages. The most important European institution, by far, was the Holy Roman Empire, which sustained a culture centered on medieval Christianity. It is not surprising that such a society produced lots of churches and cathedrals and didn't focus on schooling. The few schools that could be found in the medieval world, such as early universities, were in large part focused on religion. Theology and canon (church) law were primary subjects. The question isn't whether schools might have had utility in that era (which is actually hard to evaluate) but whether they made *sense,* given the way people viewed the world at the time. It would be centuries before society's elites would even begin to debate whether peasants (and women and people of other races), who were seen as inferior to noblemen, were capable of advanced reasoning. People certainly didn't view every individual as a potential vessel of human capital, capable of greatly augmenting his or her skills and productivity. Societies that view most people as incapable of imbibing knowledge will not create schools for the masses.

Neo-institutional scholars point to features of European culture that ultimately created space for mass education to be imaginable and, later, valued (Ramirez and Boli 1987; Schofer and Meyer 2005). For one thing, European society was relatively individualistic and became more so as it was wracked by the Reformation and the Enlightenment. Many of the early impulses toward mass schooling were linked to Protestantism, an individualistic religion which emphasizes that each person should have a direct relationship to God. This provided one early rationale for mass literacy: people should be able to read the Bible themselves. Western science expanded and, with it, the idea that we live in an orderly world that could be understood and mastered through the acquisition of knowledge. Knowledge increasingly seemed important and useful. Ramirez and Boli point out that the religious roots of European societies gave rise to a strong belief in progress, the idea that individuals and society as a whole could improve over time. We take these views for granted now, but each was radical at the time, and each helped make schooling seem more possible, sensible, and valuable to pursue. At the same time, European states (governments) became stronger and more independent from the church. As they became increasingly democratic and concerned with national development and progress, they provided an important site of potential support for mass education.

Neo-institutional scholars have focused much of their attention on the spread of Western schooling around the globe. In fact, neo-institutional theory was partly born out of efforts to understand the puzzle of why poor countries in Africa, Asia, and Latin America appeared to be importing and expanding Western-style schooling, even though they didn't have high-tech economies to employ skilled workers. To explain this, Meyer proposed that our world has a shared global culture that celebrates the virtues of education and establishes the strong norm that governments should provide schools to their citizens.

Leaders around the world tend to conform to such global norms and pressures and to expand schooling.

Neo-institutional theory offers a twist, by pointing out that our culture and beliefs are increasingly shaped by science and experts (Drori et al. 2003). The very ideas and theories articulated by Enlightenment thinkers, and later by sociologists and economists (discussed above), whether they are right or wrong, represent powerful beliefs that infuse our culture and propel our society. The notion that schooling drives economic modernization led leaders around the world to invest in education to accelerate the transition from agricultural to industrial society. Human capital theory, likewise, has become widely accepted and propels further investment in schooling.

Neo-institutional scholars further argue that ideas and norms about schooling get built into major international organizations like the United Nations and the World Bank. People in the United States and Europe tend not to think much about international organizations, but the United Nations and World Bank strongly influence policy among poor nations in the global South. For instance, the United Nations Education Science and Cultural Organization propagates the idea that schooling is a panacea for problems of poverty and underdevelopment, and more recently the organization proclaimed education to be an essential human right. Countries that don't provide schooling to all are increasingly seen as backward and even as violating the rights of their citizens. These ideas, embedded in the culture of world society, encourage the growth of schooling.

RESEARCH AND EVIDENCE

Why does schooling expand? The question receives relatively little attention from sociologists, presumably because of the dominance of human capital thinking. If we assume that schools arise because of a demand for skills, we don't look for other possible answers to the question. In her historical study of the origins of schooling in western Europe, Mary Jo Maynes (1985: 135) warns, "Contemporary assumptions (whether founded in fact or not) about the social functions of schools . . . cloud our vision of their function in the past."

Historical Research on the Origins of Schooling in Europe

Historians have carefully examined the early rise of mass schooling in eighteenth-century Europe, and their observations raise questions about conventional human capital arguments. Mass education emerged from a series of reform movements and progressive initiatives put forth by elites rather than a demand for skills by peasants or workers (Maynes 1985). Moreover, the elites involved in early schooling were motivated by a diverse set of religious, moral, and progressive concerns, rather than simply aiming to train workers.

While eighteenth-century opponents of mass schooling thought that education would confuse peasants and disrupt the existing social order, proponents argued that schooling was a source of moral improvement, which would uplift peasants and potentially improve society as a whole. The debates varied across Europe and sometimes addressed practical benefits of education for farming or early industry, but the emphasis on moral development was central (Maynes 1985). Early efforts to develop schools were often propelled by religious orders or individual noblemen; but following the reform debates of the late eighteenth century, governments began to get involved, again invoking discourses of moral development, which were increasingly linked to ideas of citizenship and nation building (Ramirez and Boli 1987).

The historical literature is too large and diverse to summarize here. My goal is simply to give the flavor of the kinds of historical evidence that bear on the question at hand. History is complex, and one can find specific examples that fit nearly any theory; but generally speaking, historical accounts tend to depart from functional, human capital, and Marxist arguments. The strong moral and religious dimensions of early school reform movements fit with neo-institutional arguments. A number of historical episodes, discussed below, fit Collins's conflict theory of educational expansion.

Research on Wages and Jobs

It is well established that highly educated workers tend to earn more than less-educated workers. Indeed, this is one of the strongest empirical findings in sociology and economics, based on extensive statistical analysis of people's earnings over their lifetimes. For some, that is sufficient to conclude that human capital theory is correct. Why would companies pay for skilled workers, if cheaper, uneducated workers could get the job done?

However, conflict theorists have an alternative account of why education is valued and rewarded: credential requirements are a way to exclude the masses, preserving the best-paying jobs for children of elites, who are advantaged in schools. If school were really about job skills, why do children study Shakespeare and trigonometry in high school, which almost nobody ever uses at work? Credential inflation also explains why many jobs now have higher educational requirements than in the past.

One way to get at the issue is to study the relationship between education and job skill requirements. For instance, studies of workers in the United States describe a trend toward overeducation: people often have more schooling than their jobs require, and this has become more common over time (e.g., Vaisey 2006). The debates about human capital theory are too complex to resolve here, but a consistent trend toward overeducation suggests that school expansion does not solely reflect the needs of the labor market.

Reproduction and Maintained Inequality

The lion's share of sociological research addresses educational reproduction, so not much needs to be added here (see chapters 2, 4, 6, 10, 11, and 13 of this volume). Children from more elite backgrounds, in terms of class, race, immigration status, and so on, have numerous advantages that accrue in school and later in occupational success and earnings. Moreover, several important studies observe a tendency for inequalities to be *maintained* to the extent possible as schooling expands (e.g., Raftery and Hout 1993; Lucas 2001). That is, elites are always the first to fill higher levels of education (first high school, then college, now graduate programs) as more and more people go to school. This scholarship does not directly answer the question of *why* schooling expanded, but it is certainly consistent with the logic of conflict and reproduction theories of education.

Explorations of Competitive Expansion

Collins (2000) draws on a broad range of historical evidence and cases—including early schooling in China and Japan, as well as in medieval universities—to support his argument that school expansion is driven by competition. He found repeated examples, including the infamous Chinese imperial exam systems, where competition for elite jobs propelled credential inflation, forcing aspiring elites to pursue schooling into their twenties, thirties, or sometimes even longer.

Paul Windolf (1997) examines the growth of education over time with quantitative data on university enrollments in several countries. His analysis of the timing of university expansion raises questions about functional and economic modernization arguments: the growth of universities does not consistently follow economic shifts such as industrialization. Indeed, whereas human capital theorists expect job opportunities to drive people to attend college, Windolf found that enrollments often grew fastest in historical periods when jobs were scarce. He interprets this as evidence for Collins's conflict perspective: economic scarcity intensifies competition for jobs and status, leading people to acquire more and more schooling.

Schools in World Society

Neo-institutional scholars have done most of the research on school expansion across the world. The perspective faces an interesting challenge: how do you demonstrate that schooling is driven by ideas and culture spreading through world society, as opposed to economic necessity?

First, neo-institutional scholars looked at the timing and scope of expansion. If schools were driven by the economy, they should grow mainly in industrialized countries and not in agricultural ones. But in recent decades, schooling suddenly began to expand *everywhere,* even in countries where high-skilled jobs were rare. Also, these newly created schools didn't seem particularly oriented toward local labor markets but, rather, followed a common blueprint and curriculum (see Bromley and Smith, this volume). From this, scholars inferred that schooling diffused around the world much like a fad or meme, rather than arising in response to local economic circumstances or needs.

More recently, neo-institutional scholars have used quantitative methods to measure cultural change and its effects. Schofer and Meyer (2005) measured important cultural shifts, including the rise of individualism, science, and democratization, and observed that they correlate with school expansion. Moreover, institutional scholars point out that ideas and norms about the importance of schooling have become institutionalized in international organizations such as the United Nations and the World Bank. Education is increasingly depicted as a critical goal of all nations, a solution to pressing issues such as poverty and underdevelopment. Schofer and Meyer show that countries most strongly tied to international organizations tend to expand schooling the fastest, suggesting a pattern of influence across world society.

Implications: School Expansion and Society

Functionalist sociologists and economists argue that education serves the modern society and economy, training individuals and sorting them into jobs. The existence of schooling—and the availability of human capital skills—should help the economy work better. For instance, it has been observed that educational enrollments are correlated with improved economic growth. Thus, modernization and human capital theorists have often advocated greater societal investments in education, in hopes of boosting the economic potential of societies, especially in countries where skilled workers are in short supply.

Conflict theorists assume that the growth of schooling will benefit elites, reproducing existing class-based or group-based inequalities. Collins, in particular, suggests that school knowledge and credentials have little relevance for jobs. Thus, the great expansion of schooling is largely a waste of time. Education should be theoretically linked to greater (or at least continuing) inequality and limited social mobility. This line of reasoning animates most sociological research on schools, and many specific policy interventions have been proposed to reduce educational reproduction (see other chapters in this volume). I will not elaborate here, other than to note that policy interventions that directly reduce economic inequality—such as raising taxes on the wealthy to help the poor—are the most obvious remedy (Jenks et al. 1982). However, if such reforms are not politically feasible, tinkering with schools is one alternative.

In contrast to functionalism, neo-institutional theory does not assume that education fulfills any necessary purpose for the economy or society's elites. But this doesn't mean schools are unimportant. To the contrary, neo-institutional scholars offer the most radical view: schools are fundamentally transformative of our society. For instance, schools deeply define how we organize and even think about childhood. Right or wrong, schools and their credentials define categories of knowledge, personnel, expertise, and status (Meyer 1977).

Neo-institutional theory is a theory of social construction, which argues that culture fundamentally defines the world in which we live. Cultural beliefs often create self-fulfilling prophesies, which have real-world consequences. If we believe that schooling is valuable, and especially if we institutionalize such beliefs—for instance, in laws that make schooling compulsory and in practices that reserve the best jobs for the highly educated—then education will become absolutely necessary for people to succeed.

David Baker (2014) explores the consequences of schooling in his book *The Schooled Society*. He takes on conventional human capital thinking: schools don't simply create workers that the economy needs. Rather, the expansion of schools *created new kinds of people,* and their entry into the labor force ultimately transformed the nature of work. In a schooled society, companies begin to see individuals in a new light, as a potential storehouse of advanced skills that can be mobilized and deployed in new and innovative ways. Thus, the rise of schooling helped produce what is now called the knowledge society, a world in which much of the economy now involves high-skilled, knowledge-based work.

Now that schooling has become entrenched globally, it may have important consequences for our culture and beliefs. As Bromley and Smith point out in chapter 9, schools around the globe now transmit a common set of themes via curricula and textbooks. For instance, contemporary curricula increasingly address environmental issues. Each year, hundreds of millions of children are taught about the importance of protecting the natural environment—something that was not done in the past. The potential effects are staggering: over a series of generations, people are likely to think, act, and vote differently regarding environmental issues. Likewise, Bromley and Smith show that curricula increasingly stress individual empowerment, gender equality, and human rights. Thus, Schofer and Meyer (2005) suggest that the expansion of education strengthens global culture, knitting different national societies together into a world society.

According to neo-institutional theory, the more that schooling is celebrated and institutionalized as a central feature in modern societies, the greater its effects on stratification will be. The rise of schooling enshrines certain kinds of knowledge, skills, and credentials as important and valuable. Baker (2014: 3) writes, "Increasingly, individuals with a less-than-average education see themselves as failures—less than fully actualized persons—and assume that only more educational attainment will make them successful." Whether this is good or bad is somewhat hard to say; and even if one had a preference, it is hard to imagine policy interventions to alter this state of affairs.

CHAPTER 1 REVIEW

Discussion Questions

1. What does the author mean when he says that ours is a schooled society? What other institutions have, in earlier societies, played the roles that schools currently play?
2. How does schooling contribute to the construction of a global culture? Can you think of an example in your own life in which common educational experiences have facilitated cross-cultural communication?

Suggestions for Further Reading

Baker, David P. 2014. *The Schooled Society: The Educational Transformation of Global Culture.* Stanford, CA: Stanford University Press.

Collins, Randall. 1979. *The Credential Society: An Historical Sociology of Education and Stratification.* New York: Academic Press.

Goldin, Claudia, and Lawrence F. Katz. 2008. *The Race between Education and Technology.* Cambridge, MA: Harvard University Press.

Ramirez, Francisco O., and John Boli. 1987. "The Political Construction of Mass Schooling: European Origins and Worldwide Institutionalization." *Sociology of Education* 60 (1): 2–17.

Schofer, Evan, and John W. Meyer. 2005. "The Worldwide Expansion of Higher Education in the Twentieth Century." *American Sociological Review* 70 (6): 898–920.

References

Baker, David P. 2014. *The Schooled Society: The Educational Transformation of Global Culture.* Stanford, CA: Stanford University Press.

Bourdieu, Pierre, and Jean-Claude Passeron. 1977. *Reproduction in Education, Society, and Culture.* London: Sage.

Bowles, Samuel, and Herbert Gintis, 1976. *Schooling in Capitalist America: Educational Reform and the Contradictions of Economic Life.* New York: Basic Books.

Collins, Randall. 1971. "Functional and Conflict Theories of Educational Stratification." *American Sociological Review* 36 (6): 1002–19.

———. 1979. *The Credential Society: An Historical Sociology of Education and Stratification.* New York: Academic Press.

———. 2000. "Comparative and Historical Patterns of Education." In *Handbook of the Sociology of Education,* edited by Maureen T. Hallinan, 213–39. New York: Kluwer Academic / Plenum Publishers.

Drori, Gili, John W. Meyer, Francisco O. Ramirez, and Evan Schofer. 2003. *Science in the Modern World Polity: Institutionalization and Globalization.* Stanford, CA: Stanford University Press.

Goldin, Claudia, and Lawrence F. Katz. 2008. *The Race between Education and Technology.* Cambridge, MA: Harvard University Press.

Jencks, Christopher, Marshall Smith, Henry Acland, Mary Jo Bane, David Cohen, Herbert Gintis, Barbara Heyns, and Stephan Michelson. 1972. *Inequality: A Reassessment of the Effect of Family and Schooling in America.* New York: Basic Books.

Lucas, Samuel. 2001. "Effectively Maintained Inequality: Education Transitions, Track Mobility, and Social Background Effects." *American Journal of Sociology* 106 (6): 1642–90.

Maynes, Mary Jo. 1985. *Schooling in Western Europe: A Social History.* Albany: SUNY Press.

Meyer, John. 1977. "The Effects of Education as an Institution." *American Journal of Sociology* 83 (1): 55–77.

Raftery, Adrian, and Michael Hout. 1993. "Maximally Maintained Inequality: Expansion, Reform, and Opportunity in Irish Education, 1921–1975." *Sociology of Education* 66 (1): 41–62.

Ramirez, Francisco O., and John Boli. 1987. "The Political Construction of Mass Schooling: European Origins and Worldwide Institutionalization." *Sociology of Education* 60 (1): 2–17.

Schofer, Evan, and John W. Meyer. 2005. "The Worldwide Expansion of Higher Education in the Twentieth Century." *American Sociological Review* 70 (6): 898–920.

Schultz, Theodore W. 1961. "Investment in Human Capital." *American Economic Review* 51 (1): 1–17.

Vaisey, Stephen. 2006. "Education and Its Discontents: Overqualification in America, 1972–2002." *Social Forces* 85 (2): 835–64.

Windolf, Paul. 1997. *Expansion and Structural Change: Higher Education in Germany, the United States and Japan, 1870–1990.* Boulder, CO: Westview.

A Contextual Understanding of Schools' Role in the Stratification System

Are Schools a Compensatory, Neutral, or Exacerbatory Institution?

DOUGLAS DOWNEY, OHIO STATE UNIVERSITY

EDITORS' NOTE

One claim that often accompanies efforts to expand formal schooling is the claim that education is an antidote to social inequality. Horace Mann, the nineteenth-century American educator who argued for schools to be freely available to all youth (known as the common schools movement), famously called school "the great equalizer." Mann's idea was consistent with the **human capital hypothesis**. If schools confer valuable skills that students can convert into higher pay in the workplace, then making those skills more widely available should level the playing field, thereby helping everybody, regardless of family background, have a fair shot at social and economic success.

While undoubtedly appealing and widely held, Mann's idea remains the subject of ongoing debate in the sociology of education. As Evan Schofer notes in chapter 1 of this volume, scholars in the **social reproduction tradition** question the assumption that schools convey the same skills to youth regardless of their backgrounds, hypothesizing instead that unequal educational opportunities **reinforce** and **legitimate** inequality.

Ohio State University sociologist Doug Downey reports on an innovative empirical approach for testing the link between schooling and social inequality. Are schools being held responsible for inequalities that emerge when students aren't in school? To see, Downey compares students' test-score growth rates during the school year with their growth rates during the summer months. While Downey stops short of endorsing Mann's "great equalizer" claim, he argues that, all else being equal, schools compensate for existing social inequalities.

KEY POINTS

- The 1966 Coleman Report concluded that variations in children's math and reading skills were mostly a product of children's families, not their schools.
- Many sociologists of education have disputed Coleman's conclusion, but because children's development is a product of both families and schools, understanding how schools matter raises significant methodological challenges.
- The kind of research best positioned to contribute to this discussion has three characteristics. It (1) rigorously isolates school effects, (2) carefully weighs the magnitude of exacerbatory and compensatory mechanisms, and (3) places school effects in the context of broader society.
- Seasonal comparison studies (comparing how gaps in skills change when children are in school versus not), while imperfect, provide one way of meeting these three criteria.
- Seasonal comparison studies suggest that inequality in skills would be greater if not for schools.

INTRODUCTION

One of the big questions in the sociology of education is the role that schools play in the stratification system. Do schools provide an avenue for social mobility, allowing youth from relatively disadvantaged backgrounds to rise above their parents' socioeconomic status (SES)? If they do, then in this way they would be a compensatory institution. Or do schools reproduce existing inequality, legitimating it through unfair practices that are thought of as meritocratic but which really favor the advantaged? If they do, then from this perspective schools would be an exacerbatory institution. Or are schools mostly neutral—largely reflecting existing inequalities without changing them much?

Scholarship on this question is heavily influenced by the 1966 Coleman Report (the *Equality of Educational Opportunity Study*), which famously concluded that variations in children's reading and math skills are mostly influenced by their family conditions and only weakly related to school characteristics. The report, which is more than seven hundred pages long, carried tremendous weight because its main author, sociologist James Coleman, was widely respected and the study was massive, including information about nearly six hundred thousand children in four thousand schools. It remains one of the largest survey efforts ever undertaken in American schools. The main conclusion of the report—that inequalities in children's skills were only weakly related to the kinds of schools they attended—was a surprise to many.

But after the report was released, sociologists energetically critiqued it. The notion that schools had little to do with inequality seemed wrong. Schools serving advantaged children enjoy substantially better resources—better curricula, better teachers, smaller classrooms, and a wider range of extracurricular activities. Parents know this. It is why affluent parents seek out neighborhoods with "good" schools. And it is why poorer parents are often eager to withdraw their children from the local school and enroll them in a charter school. Anyone who has entered both a well-financed suburban school serving mostly advantaged white children and an inner-city urban school serving mostly poor black or Hispanic children cannot help but see the difference. Coleman's report acknowledged that some of these disparities in resources existed across schools serving advantaged and disadvantaged children, but it suggested that they did not matter much. This conclusion did not match people's gut instinct about schools.

In addition to its puzzling conclusion, there were methodological reasons for doubting the Coleman Report. The study had significant weaknesses. One problem was that the survey data was collected at just one point in time, making it difficult to know if the report was simply discussing correlations or causal relationships. Another limitation was that Coleman could only look at how differences *between* schools mattered. He lacked the kind of data needed to understand how within-school processes might contribute to inequality. For example, suppose one of the main ways that schools advantage children from high-income families is by providing them with easier access to college-track courses while pushing children from low-income families toward vocational tracks. Coleman would have observed little difference between schools, but this kind of within-school process was overlooked. As critics pointed out later, within-school variation in math and reading skills outweighs between-school variation, and so the Coleman Report missed a large source of information about how schools might reproduce inequality even when children attend the same schools. Processes like ability grouping, tracking, and cultural mismatches with teachers are all within-school processes that the Coleman Report overlooked.

There were many credible reasons for doubting the conclusions of the Coleman Report, but this debate raises bigger questions for the sociology of education. It prompts us to consider: "What constitutes good evidence?" What kinds of methods provide the best estimate of causal relationships? And this line of inquiry also forces us to think about how we frame our questions. For example, if we want to know schools' role in the stratification system, should we focus primarily on how school quality varies, or should we think more about what things would be like if we did not have schools? Frame the question too narrowly, and we will see only trees, not the forest. To understand how schools matter within the stratification system requires a lens broad enough to see how schools fit within the system.

THE CRITICAL VIEW OF SCHOOLS

The response to Coleman's report within the sociology of education was energetic and critical. Indeed, some prominent members of the American Sociological Association tried to have Coleman expelled for his conclusions, a move that eventually failed. Coleman continued to defend his conclusions and, despite the continued controversy, was elected president of the association in 1991.[1]

In most cases, the disputes were addressed with reasonable discourse. At Harvard a group of well-known intellectuals formed a yearlong seminar to reanalyze the data and critique Coleman's methods. Others assembled a body of evidence showing that schools favor the advantaged. For example, Jonathan Kozol's well-known 1991 book *Savage Inequalities* skillfully described the differences in resources available to schools serving wealthy, white children and those serving poor, black children. Because American schools are primarily funded on the basis of local property taxes, children of the wealthy enjoy better-funded schools than children of the poor.

Others criticized schools for the way they supported capitalism. Samuel Bowles and Herb Gintis (1976) argued that schools provide capitalism with the kinds of workers it needs. And because the economy needs only a modest number of managers and a much larger number of docile workers, the school system trains only some (the children of the wealthy) to become leaders (see chapter 15 in this volume). Schools serving these students emphasize skills that leaders need, like communication skills and independent thinking. But schools also train a large number of workers to follow orders. In these schools, children are rewarded for rote memory skills and obedience to authority.

Another strain of critique emphasized how status cultures control the schools and reward the arbitrary knowledge of elites. Bourdieu discussed what he called "cultural capital"—the ability to signal affiliation with elite groups through speech, style, and dress—as critical to success in school. Some scholars found evidence that teachers allocate grades on more than just students' performance, that grades are partly based on children's knowledge of elite culture (e.g., symphonies, museums, art; DiMaggio 1982). Along these same lines, many scholars noted how challenging it is for children from disadvantaged families to overcome the cultural mismatches they face with teachers from mostly white, middle-class backgrounds (see chapter 7).

In addition, schools may reproduce inequality by what is referred to as curriculum differentiation, or grouping children based on skill level. Ability grouping, for example, combines children of similar skills on the assumption that each group will make more progress if the members are exposed to material in their "sweet spot"—that is, material that is appropriately challenging (see

---

1. See "Obituary: James Coleman, Sociology," *University of Chicago Chronicle*, 14, no. 14 (March 30w, 1995), http://chronicle.uchicago.edu/950330/coleman.shtml.

chapter 10). This concept is often employed in elementary school classes for reading groups, and it may promote wider skill gaps (Condron 2008; Gamoran and Mare 1989). In addition, among middle- and high-school students, schools often begin to "track" students toward different kinds of programs—academic or vocational. The concern with these practices is that students in the "lower" tracks are exposed to lower-quality material, less-motivated teachers, and a more disruptive peer group (Oakes 1982).

In sum, the critical perspective has identified a wide range of both between- and within-school mechanisms that may favor children from advantaged families.

UNDERSTANDING HOW SCHOOLS MATTER: THE METHODOLOGICAL CHALLENGE

The critical view of schools, while valuable in identifying characteristics of schools that may exacerbate inequality, does not describe schools' *overall* effect on inequality. While many school processes exist that may favor children from advantaged families, there are likely other processes that favor the disadvantaged, and these compensatory processes have been mostly overlooked. The result is an imbalanced perspective. To understand schools' overall effect on inequality, we need to know whether the magnitude of exacerbatory school processes outweighs the magnitude of the compensatory processes.

One reason scholars have made little effort to gauge the magnitude of compensatory processes is that few come to mind. What might these compensatory school processes be? One potential compensatory mechanism is the way that schools organize children. The default mechanism is by chronological age, a practice that results in groupings of students with widely disparate skills. These children are then exposed to roughly similar curriculums, a practice that likely works toward equalizing their skill levels. In addition, teachers report spending most of their time with struggling children. Although there may exist cultural mismatches between teachers and some disadvantaged students, there is also the tendency for many teachers to provide the most help to the students most in need. Eighty percent of teachers say that they spend most of their time with struggling students. To understand how schools matter, we need to find a method that gauges the magnitude of both exacerbatory and compensatory school processes and to determine which is more powerful.

In addition, we would then need to compare the way schools affect inequality with the way nonschool environments affect it. As figure 2 illustrates, schools could allow inequality to grow, yet still be an equalizing force, if achievement gaps grow more slowly when school is in session versus out. In this way, schools may not be able to reduce inequality in the absolute sense, but they may reduce the level of inequality we would observe in their absence.

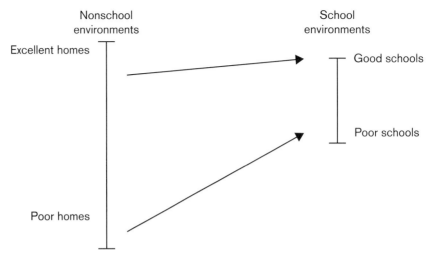

Figure 2. A contextual view: variations in nonschool and school environments.

SEASONAL COMPARISON AND EARLY CHILDHOOD STUDIES

The best method for identifying causal mechanisms is to conduct random assignment experiments. By randomly assigning children to treatment and control groups, researchers can confidently assign causality to differences in outcomes to schools. Many experiments have been performed in schools, but most of these have targeted a single school characteristic, such as class size. For example, in the Tennessee Star Project, children were randomly assigned to classrooms of varying size, which helped the researchers determine that children learn more in smaller classes. But note that this approach tells us little about the *overall* magnitude of all school characteristics that favor the advantage, and it tells us nothing about the magnitude of school processes that may favor the disadvantaged. In addition, experiments typically entail only small, local samples, limiting their generalizability.

Fortunately there is a quasi-experimental approach, seasonal comparisons, that maintains many advantages of the experimental design while also being applicable to nationally representative survey data. The seasonal comparison method takes advantage of the fact that most American students do not attend school in the summer. Scholars observe how achievement gaps between high- and low-socioeconomic children, for example, change when school is in session versus out. Methodologists have praised this strategy for identifying school effects, in part because it captures the overall consequence of all mechanisms (both exacerbatory and compensatory) by observing how inequality changes when school is in session versus out.

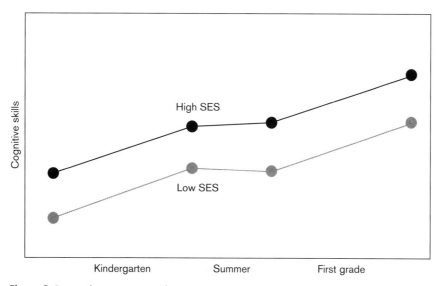

Figure 3. Seasonal comparison studies: SES gaps in cognitive skills.

Most education studies lack seasonally collected data—that is, data on children at both the beginning and the end of each school year—but the handful of studies that have performed seasonal comparisons are revealing. The first seasonal studies used data from a small number of cities, such as New Haven, Atlanta, and Baltimore. Later, two nationally representative data sets, the Early Childhood Longitudinal Study of 1998 and 2010, provided the highest-quality seasonally collected data on children. While these various seasonal studies produced somewhat different outcomes, one pattern is consistent—socioeconomic gaps in children's math and reading skills grow faster during the summer months, when school is out, than in the fall, winter, and spring months, when school is in. In other words, if we lived in a world without schools, inequality would be worse than it is. Karl Alexander (1997: 12) explains the ramifications of the seasonal comparison patterns: when it comes to inequality, "schooling is more 'part of the solution' than 'part of the problem.'" Figure 3 reports the results of some of my own work using seasonal comparisons to understand the role schools play in the production of educational inequality.

Other empirical patterns are consistent with the notion that inequality is largely driven by inequalities outside of schools. Socioeconomic-based achievement gaps are mostly formed before the onset of formal schooling. Sean Reardon (2011) has examined these gaps by income (the "income achievement gap" refers to income differences between a child from a family at the ninetieth percentile of family income distribution and a child from a family at the tenth percentile). He finds that the income gap in reading grew about 12 percent between kindergarten and eighth grade, and the math gap actually narrowed (Reardon 2011; see also Duncan and Magnuson 2011). If socioeconomic-based achievement gaps form primarily before kindergarten and then increase only modestly (and sometimes even narrow) once children are in school, then most of the action regarding achievement gaps occurs in early childhood.

In addition, differences among countries in terms of international test scores may have less to do with schools than we thought. Each year new international tests are revealed, and Americans lament their mediocre showing. But these studies mix school and nonschool conditions in unknown ways. It is especially useful, therefore, to compare gaps in skills among children who have yet to start school. A study of US and Canadian children's reading skills highlights this point. Merry (2013) documented that Canadians are ahead of US children by a sizeable .30 standard deviation units (nearly a year's worth of learning) in the Programme for International Student Assessment reading test given to fifteen-to sixteen-year-olds. Merry also compared similar-cohort Canadian and US children on the Peabody Picture Vocabulary Test reading test at the ages of four to five, before formal schooling had started, and found that a similar gap of .31 standard deviation units was already in place at that age.

UNANSWERED QUESTIONS

The seasonal comparison and early childhood results present a formidable challenge to the critical view of schools, but many issues merit further discussion. First, do schools also reduce racial/ethnic gaps in achievement? The evidence here is less clear. Heyns (1978) found that black/white gaps grew faster in the summer than in the school season in Atlanta, suggesting that schools are compensatory with respect to race; but black/white patterns were less clear in Baltimore (Entwisle and Alexander 1992). And in nationally representative data from the Early Childhood Longitudinal Study—Kindergarten Class of 1998–99, the black/white gap grew faster during kindergarten and first grade than during the summer in between, consistent with the view that schools generate inequality (Downey, von Hippel, and Broh 2004). There is also evidence that schools may undermine the performance of Asian Americans (Downey, von Hippel, and Broh 2004; Yoon and Merry 2018). Overall, it appears that white children may benefit more from school than do black or Asian children, but the patterns are not definitive. (See chapter 4 in this volume for a more detailed discussion of race in education and case study 2 for a discussion of Asian Americans' educational experiences.)

Second, how can schools be compensatory when children with low SES endure both poorer home and poorer school environments? It is difficult to understand how schools serving low-SES children manage to produce learning gains on par with schools serving high-SES children despite the obstacles they face. One would expect schools serving high-SES children to consistently produce more math and reading gains; but in models that carefully isolate schools' contributions to learning, there is little evidence of this pattern (Downey, von Hippel, and Hughes 2008; Lubienski and Lubienski 2013).

To examine this point further, consider one study in which colleagues and I evaluated school quality in three different ways: (1) achievement: reading skills at one point in time; (2) growth: gains in reading between the end of kindergarten and the end of first grade; and (3) impact: the degree to which schools improve students' learning from summer to school year. We argued that achievement scores are weak measures of school quality because they mix school and nonschool effects in unknown ways. Growth scores are better measures, but they, too, are biased against schools serving disadvantaged children, because they include the summers, when children's skills diverge for reasons unrelated to schools. We posited that impact scores more persuasively isolate school effects from nonschool effects and compared children's observed learning with what that learning would have been had they not been in school.

Interestingly, ideas of which schools are "failing" change in important ways when we move across achievement scores (weak measure), growth scores (better measure), and impact scores (even better measure). In figure 4, my colleagues and I plotted the average reading score for children in 287 schools and then identified the worse-performing schools—those in the bottom 20 percent were the ones vulnerable to the "failing" label. But the schools we typically think of as failing look much better when evaluated via a growth model, and even better when evaluated by impact. Indeed, three-quarters of the schools deemed failing according to achievement are not considered failing when evaluated by impact, and 17 percent of the schools performing well on achievement look like poor-performing schools when evaluated via impact. Finally, the correlation between the number of poor children attending a school (measured by their eligibility for free lunches) and the achievement measure is strong and negative, as expected; but when impact is the measure of school quality, the correlation is zero (Downey, von Hippel, and Hughes 2008).

Schools serving disadvantaged children are doing substantially better than they are given credit for, but why? How do they produce learning that is on par with that produced by schools serving children from advantaged backgrounds? We need to know more about schools' compensatory mechanisms.

Third, what are the nonschool factors that shape large SES gaps at the beginning of kindergarten? There are many obvious culprits, such as the extent to which parents talk to their children and the complexity of the language they use (Hart and Risley 1995), maternal depression, stress, family structure, and access to health care. And middle and upper-class parents tend to use authoritative parenting (explaining boundaries and encouraging independence) while working-class parents tend to use authoritarian parenting (emphasizing rules

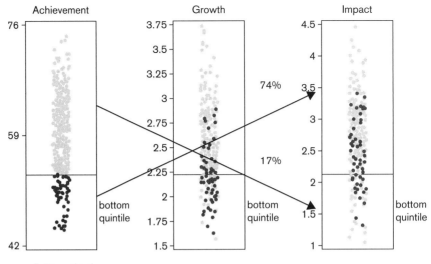

Figure 4. Are "failing" schools really failing? Source: adapted from D. B. Downey, P. T. Von Hippel, and M. Hughes, "Are 'Failing' Schools Really Failing? Using Seasonal Comparison to Evaluate School Effectiveness," *Sociology of Education* 81, no. 3 (2008): 242–70.

and obedience). While all of these factors may be at play, it is difficult to know which are the most salient.

Fourth, what school reforms would help reduce inequality? Some view the seasonal comparison patterns as reason for eliminating summer vacation. Perhaps the long summer break is the problem because that is when low-SES children lose skills. But analysis of schools that distribute their days more evenly across the calendar year suggests that simply redistributing the number of days would do little to change patterns of inequality. What would benefit low-SES children is exposure to more school. The current school calendar, based on an agrarian economy in which children left school to work on the farm during the summer months, should be replaced with one according to which children attend more school. All children would benefit from greater exposure to school, and disadvantaged children would benefit the most.

Finally, would it be possible to significantly reduce gaps via other school reforms? Haven't some schools succeeded in doing this? Can we scale these up to a national level? For example, black children who were chosen via lottery for the Harlem Children's Zone and experienced several years in the program demonstrated, in eighth grade, skills on par with those of white children in New York City, while their counterparts who were not chosen continued to lag behind (Dobbie and Fryer 2009). The Knowledge Is Power Program charter schools also have raised disadvantaged children's skills, in part by increasing the amount of time children spend in school and perhaps by attracting high-quality teachers (Tuttle et al. 2010). It is important to note that these occasional "high-flying" or "no-excuses" schools probably succeed by providing disadvantaged children with substantially *better* schools than their advantaged peers attend. An obstacle to reducing inequality via school reform, therefore, is that doing so would require scaling up similar efforts and, importantly, making them available to low-SES children while denying them to high-SES children. Or, at the least, low-SES children would need to enjoy greater benefits than high-SES children from the school treatments provided.

Of course, schools are imperfect and could be better, but I argue that the real problem lies outside of schools. Why are Canadian children already ahead of American children in reading before kindergarten begins? Merry's (2013) study raises the possibility that international differences in test scores among adolescents may have little (or maybe nothing) to do with schools. Perhaps Finland's impressive test scores, which have prompted great interest in that nation's teachers and schools, are mostly a product of its successful social welfare programs. SES-based gaps in reading and math are mostly formed before kindergarten. What reforms would reduce those gaps? What is different about Canada? Some possibilities are the different decisions Canadians have made regarding access to health care, public housing, rules regarding organized labor, mass incarceration, the real value of the minimum wage, unemployment benefits, and family leave options. If we could determine which of these larger, societal-level characteristics is most important for shaping children's cognitive skills, we could target that broader reform.

DISCUSSION

Sociologists are especially skilled at demonstrating how human behavior is shaped by context. For sociologists of education, this has mostly meant an emphasis on how school context shapes student outcomes. But the field would benefit from pushing this perspective further, contextualizing schools in broader society. The average eighteen-year-old American spends just 13 percent of his or her waking hours in school (Walberg 1984), and so if we really want to understand how schools matter we cannot ignore the other 87 percent. Understanding how schools influence children in a world where children mostly are not there is a significant challenge. That means employing methods that take seriously the fact that schools operate within a context and serve children from very different home environments. Those home environments shape kindergarten readiness in important ways and then continue to influence children's receptiveness to learning as they progress through school. Acknowledging this context is critical to understanding how schools really matter.

During the growth of schooling in American society over the last century, we have come to expect more and more from schools and to see them as a key social policy lever. It turns out that this lever is working the way we want when it comes to inequality—schools are part of the solution more than part of the problem. Without them, inequality would be much worse. Perhaps schools could do more—that is a discussion worth having—but any conversation about schools and inequality should start by noting that schools' overall effect is an equalizing one.

But schools cannot resolve social problems by themselves, and to continue to focus the majority of our attention on school-based solutions is a distraction from the more central sources of inequality. It might feel more comfortable to fiddle with school levers, but that does not make them the right policy levers. We need to understand why young American children are so far behind in reading skills before they even begin formal schooling. And we need to know how our growing economic inequality is shaping children's ability to learn. Rather than providing the answer to those questions, school reform may be a distraction.

If achievement gaps are formed primarily outside of school, why is there so much focus on school-based solutions to inequality? Americans tend to view schools as a legitimate policy tool for reducing inequality, while they are skeptical (more so than people in other countries) of reducing inequality via other means (e.g., raising the minimum wage, passing federal-level family leave policies). This is unfortunate, because it turns out that achievement gaps in school are largely formed by outside-of-school differences in children's lives. The focus on school-based solutions means that we end up "tinkering toward utopia" (to borrow a phrase from Tyack and Cuban 1995) rather than addressing the more fundamental causes of inequality. School reform keeps us busy, and it helps rub the rough edges off inequality, but it fails to address the core source.

Of course, if there are political problems in creating the kind of school reform that would reduce societal-level achievement gaps, the political challenges to broader social policy are likely even greater. The American public is more amenable to school reform than broader social reform. Economist Eric Hanushek explains the focus on schools: "While family inputs to education are indeed extremely important, the differential impacts of schools and teachers receive more attention when viewed from a policy viewpoint. This reflects simply that the characteristics of schools are generally more easily manipulated than what goes on in the family" (Hanushek 1992: 106).

This American emphasis on schools as the legitimate policy arena in which to shape the opportunity structure is unique. Americans are exceptional in the way they view school reform as an appropriate action of the welfare state, a view that is relatively nonpartisan (McCall 2013), yet they are skeptical of state involvement via other means. Americans are more reluctant to help families via nonschool policies than are people in Canada or Europe (Katz and Rose

2013; McCall 2013). Relative to European countries, the United States led the way in developing mass education yet lagged behind in developing the broader elements of the modern welfare state (e.g., social security), historical patterns that may explain the American emphasis on education as the legitimate tool of the welfare state (Flora and Heidenheimer 1981).

Pamela Walters (1995: 201) provides insight into this pattern. She notes that Americans have historically looked to schools as the mechanism by which to address social problems. For example, schools were seen as the problem when German industrial power threatened the United States in the early part of the twentieth century, and then again when *Sputnik* was launched and prompted concerns about our education system's ability to keep pace with the success of the Soviet Union's space program. Walters writes, "One reason why we have often turned to education to solve persistent social problems is that a philosophy of individualism runs very deep in American society. Taking the example of poverty, we tend to believe that high rates of poverty occur because the poor have limitations which keep them from moving out of poverty. If we can only 'fix' the individuals who are poor, poverty as a social phenomenon can be greatly reduced. Since it is difficult to intervene directly into families, we can turn to education as the primary means of 'fixing' the poor."

My concern, however, is that Americans' receptivity to school reform encourages researchers to look there while de-emphasizing the role of broader social conditions. It may be that researchers do not explore the relationship between broader social policies and achievement gaps simply because they perceive little chance that these broader social reforms are likely to be enacted. This is unfortunate. We may be dismissing the most plausible avenue to reducing achievement gaps because we assume it will not garner sufficient political support. I recommend that academics damn the political torpedoes and pursue this research path more vigorously. Perhaps if the voices of enough researchers explain to the public when and why achievement gaps develop (before school and not because of school), public sentiment might be more receptive to reforms aimed at improving children's early nonschool lives. And if the evidence that broader social conditions shape the size and malleability of achievement gaps is strong, political support for broader social reform might increase.

We need to start thinking about education policy more broadly. It needs to be about more than just teachers and resources (Rothstein 2004). Allowing inequality to increase in the nonschool environment—as we have done in the last several decades—is a decision inextricably linked to achievement gaps, though rarely discussed in that way. The link between what happens in children's lives outside of school, and their performance in school, is just too strong. Growing income inequality presents a major obstacle to reducing achievement gaps, yet education scholars have hardly noticed. They've been distracted by schools.

CHAPTER 2 REVIEW

Discussion Questions

1. Aside from what the author discusses here, in what other ways might schools reduce inequality?

2. If schools are already compensatory, why not continue to emphasize school reform as a way of reducing inequality even more?

3. What broader social reforms would most successfully reduce achievement gaps at kindergarten entry?

4. If schools serving high-SES children do not produce more learning than schools serving low-SES children, why do high-SES parents go to great efforts to place their children in these schools?

5. Is it possible that schools reduce achievement gaps yet exacerbate inequality in other ways?

6. How does schools' compensatory power change as inequality outside of school becomes greater?

Suggestions for Further Reading

Alexander, K. L. 1997. "Public Schools and the Public Good." *Social Forces* 76 (1): 1–30.

Alexander, K. L., D. R. Entwisle, and L. S. Olson. 2007. "Lasting Consequences of the Summer Learning Gap." *American Sociological Review* 72 (2): 167–80.

Downey, Douglas B., Paul T. von Hippel, and Beckett Broh. 2004. "Are Schools the Great Equalizer? Cognitive Inequality during the Summer Months and the School Year." *American Sociological Review* 69 (5): 613–35.

Downey, Douglas B., Paul T. von Hippel, and M. Hughes. 2008. "Are 'Failing' Schools Really Failing? Using Seasonal Comparison to Evaluate School Effectiveness." *Sociology of Education* 81 (3): 242–70.

Reardon, S. F. 2011. "The Widening Academic Achievement Gap between the Rich and the Poor: New Evidence and Possible Explanations." In *Whither Opportunity: Rising Inequality, Schools, and Children's Life Chances,* edited by G. J. Duncan and R. J. Murnane, 91–116. New York: Russell Sage.

Rothstein, R. 2004. *Class and Schools: Using Social, Economic, and Educational Reform to Close the Black-White Achievement Gap.* New York: Teachers College, Columbia University.

References

Alexander, K. L. 1997. "Public Schools and the Public Good." *Social Forces* 76 (1): 1–30.

Alexander, K. L., D. R. Entwisle, and L. S. Olson. 2007. "Lasting Consequences of the Summer Learning Gap." *American Sociological Review* 72 (2): 167–80.

Bowles, Samuel, and Herbert Gintis. 1976. *Schooling in Capitalist America: Educational Reform and the Contradictions of Economic Life.* New York: Basic Books.

Coleman, James S., Ernest Q. Campbell, Carol J. Hobson, James McPartland, Alexander M. Mood, Frederic D. Weinfeld, and Robert L. York. 1966. *Equality of Opportunity.* Washington, DC: Government Printing Office.

Condron, D. J. 2008. "An Early Start: Skill Grouping and Unequal Reading Gains in the Elementary Years." *Sociological Quarterly* 49 (2): 363–94.

DiMaggio, P. 1982. "Cultural Capital and School Success: The Impact of Status Culture Participation on the Grades of U.S. High School Students." *American Sociological Review* 27 (2): 189–201.

Dobbie, W., and R. G. Fryer Jr. 2009. "Are High Quality Schools Enough to Close the Achievement Gap? Evidence from a Social Experiment in Harlem." NBER Working Paper No. 15473. National Bureau of Economic Research.

Downey, Douglas B., Paul T. von Hippel, and Beckett Broh. 2004. "Are Schools the Great Equalizer? Cognitive Inequality during the Summer Months and the School Year." *American Sociological Review* 69 (5): 613–35.

Downey, Douglas B., Paul T. von Hippel, and M. Hughes. 2008. "Are 'Failing' Schools Really Failing? Using Seasonal Comparison to Evaluate School Effectiveness." *Sociology of Education* 81 (3): 242–70.

Duncan, G. J., and K. Magnuson. 2011. "The Nature and Impact of Early Achievement Skills, Attention Skills, and Behavior Problems." *Whither Opportunity: Rising Inequality, Schools, and Children's Life Chances,* edited by G. J. Duncan and R. J. Murnane, 47–69. New York: Russell Sage.

Entwisle, Doris R., and Karl L. Alexander. 1992. "Summer Setback: Race, Poverty, School Composition and Math Achievement in the First Two Years of School." *American Sociological Review* 57 (11): 72–84.

Flora, P., and A. J. Heidenheimer. 1981. "The Historical Core and Changing Boundaries of the Welfare State." In *The Development of Welfare States in Europe and America,* edited by P. Flora and A. J. Heidenheimer, 17–36. New York: Routledge.

Gamoran, A., and R. D. Mare. 1989. "Secondary School Tracking and Educational Inequality: Compensation, Reinforcement, or Neutrality?" *American Journal of Sociology* 94 (5): 1146–83.

Hanushek, E. A. 1992. "The Trade-Off between Child Quantity and Quality." *Journal of Political Economy* 100 (1): 84–117.

Hart, Betty, and Todd R. Risley. 1995. *Meaningful Differences in the Everyday Experience of Young American Children.* Baltimore: Paul H. Brookes.

Heyns, Barbara. 1978. *Summer Learning and the Effects of Schooling.* New York: Academic Press.

Katz, M. B., and M. A. Rose, eds. 2013. *Public Education under Siege.* Philadelphia: University of Pennsylvania Press.

Kozol, J. 2012. *Savage Inequalities: Children in America's Schools.* New York: Broadway Books.

Lubienski, C. A., and S. T. Lubienski. 2013. *The Public School Advantage: Why Public Schools Outperform Private Schools.* Chicago: University of Chicago Press.

McCall, L. 2013. *The Undeserving Rich: American Beliefs about Inequality, Opportunity, and Redistribution.* Cambridge: Cambridge University Press.

Merry, J. J. 2013. "Tracing the US Deficit in PISA Reading Skills to Early Childhood: Evidence from the United States and Canada." *Sociology of Education* 86 (3): 234–52.

Oakes, J. 1982. "The Reproduction of Inequity: The Content of Secondary School Tracking." *Urban Review* 14 (2): 107–20.

Reardon, S. F. 2011. "The Widening Academic Achievement Gap between the Rich and the Poor: New Evidence and Possible Explanations." In *Whither Opportunity: Rising Inequality, Schools, and Children's Life Chances,* edited by G. J. Duncan and R. J. Murnane, 91–116. New York: Russell Sage.

Rothstein, R. 2004. *Class and Schools: Using Social, Economic, and Educational Reform to Close the Black-White Achieve-* ment Gap. New York: Teachers College, Columbia University.

Tuttle, Christina Clark, Bing-ru Teh, Ira Nichols-Barrer, Brian P. Gill, and Philip Gleason. 2010. *Student Characteristics and Achievement in 22 KIPP Middle Schools.* Washington, DC: Mathematica Policy Research.

Tyack, D., and L. Cuban. 1995. *Tinkering toward Utopia: A Century of School Reform.* Cambridge, MA: Harvard University Press.

Walberg, Herbert J. 1984. "Families as Partners in Educational Productivity." *Phi Delta Kappan* 65:397–400.

Walters, P. B. 1995. "Crises of Excellence and Social Order in American Education: A Historical Perspective. In *Educational Advancement and Distributive Justice: Between Equity and Equality,* edited by Reuven Kahane and Chaim Adler, 187–205. Jerusalem: Magnes Press, Hebrew University.

Yoon, A. J., and J. J. Merry. 2018. "Understanding the Role of Schools in the Asian-White Gap: A Seasonal Comparison Approach." *Race Ethnicity and Education* 21 (5): 680–700.

STUDENT EXPERIENCES IN EDUCATION

3

Gender Inequality in Education

Outcomes and Experiences

CATHERINE RIEGLE-CRUMB,
UNIVERSITY OF TEXAS, AUSTIN

EDITORS' NOTE

The evidence that Doug Downey and his colleagues have assembled suggests that schools help compensate for socioeconomic inequalities. But as is often the case in social science, this conclusion comes with many important qualifications: this evidence seems to hold for socioeconomic inequality, in American elementary schools, in the early elementary grades, in regard to the sorts of basic academic skills that standardized tests measure. It is, in other words, just the beginning of a long conversation about education and inequality in the contemporary world.

The chapters in this section continue that conversation.

In this chapter, Catherine Riegle-Crumb, a sociologist and education scholar at the University of Texas at Austin, takes on the connection between education and gender inequality. It's remarkable to note that American schools were coeducational long before women could vote or participate fully in the labor market. As Riegle-Crumb notes, girls' educational outcomes arguably continue to outpace women's social status in the contemporary United States. Why might that be? And how might subtle gender differences in schools still contribute to gendered structures in society at large?

Riegle-Crumb also draws our attention to the notion of **intersectionality,** noting that the relationship between your gender and your educational experiences may differ according to multiple factors, including your race, socioeconomic background, religion, and the sort of community in which you live.

KEY POINTS

- Male and female students generally have very similar educational outcomes, and differences that do exist are small in scope, particularly during the K–12 years.
- At the postsecondary level, gaps in college attendance and graduation favor female students, while male students are more likely to obtain degrees in computer science and engineering, two lucrative and in-demand fields.
- Research shows evidence that male and female students are exposed to different kinds of bias in schools, and that male and female students sometimes respond differently to the same educational environment. Therefore, it is too simplistic to argue that schools are more or less beneficial for one gender than the other.

INTRODUCTION

Sociologists of education are typically concerned with examining and understanding educational inequality or stratification between different groups within society. Unlike other main axes of social stratification, such as race/ethnicity or social class, that are characterized by students from different backgrounds residing in different communities and attending different schools, this is not the case for gender. In other words, male and female students come from families with the same characteristics, live in the same communities, and attend the same schools. And yet, despite these similarities in circumstances, the educational experiences and outcomes of male and female students sometimes diverge in important ways. Thus, in this chapter, I discuss two important questions about, and related empirical results of, gender differences in education that have been addressed by sociological research.

First, to what extent are there gender differences in educational outcomes?

Second, to what extent are there gender differences in educational experiences? Specifically, is there evidence that either male or female students are subject to bias within schools, and/or is there evidence that male and female students respond differently to factors within the educational environment?

In reviewing research that addresses these two questions, I limit the discussion to the United States because educational systems sometimes differ markedly across countries and cultures. Additionally, I focus on formal education in the K–12 years (kindergarten through high school), as well as the postsecondary level. After discussing the critical empirical findings of researchers addressing these questions, I also consider what questions remain to be answered.

INTELLECTUAL ROOTS: SOCIOLOGICAL
THEORIES OF GENDER INEQUALITY

Sociologists have been focusing on gender inequality in education for many decades. In an effort to understand why male and female students sometimes have different outcomes and experiences, several theories have been advanced. *Gender socialization* is a theory which argues that girls and boys are raised to engage in different behaviors and develop different attitudes and priorities in accordance with social norms about what is appropriate for each gender and, in doing so, to prepare to fulfill their expected future adult roles (Eccles 1994). Gender stereotypes play a prominent role in this theory, as boys are expected to be assertive, aggressive, independent, and strong, and girls are expected to be more docile, submissive, and social. Parents and teachers are critical players in this process, since they both establish expectations and enforce sanctions if children violate expected norms. For example, a boy who wants to play with dolls may be chastised by a parent. This is a broad theory with wide applicability, but it has also been critiqued for not acknowledging individual agency and for viewing girls and boys as passive to the control of others. With regard to education specifically, gender socialization is often invoked to explain why girls get better grades in school (as discussed below)—that is, they are socialized to want to please others (e.g., teachers) and earn their approval.

Similarly, theories of gender essentialism argue that cultural beliefs that women and men are fundamentally and innately different from one another underlie the maintenance of gender inequality in education (Charles and Bradley 2002). Researchers with this perspective argue that while the United States and many other advanced industrial societies value egalitarianism (including the belief that males and females should generally have access to the same educational resources), cultural beliefs about essential differences between men and women remain strong and, at the same time, drive the continued gender segregation of fields of study. Thus, while it is culturally acceptable for women to receive the same amount of education as men (and even a little more), this progress toward equality is circumvented by social forces that continue to define some subjects (e.g., math and science) as "naturally suited" for men, and other subjects (e.g., humanities, social sciences) as "naturally" suited for women.

From a slightly different perspective, many sociologists theorize that gender is a social construction (Ridgeway and Correll 2004), arguing that it is a social category or schema created and reinforced by interactions and institutionalized through systems at the macro level. This theory acknowledges both the maintenance of gender inequality and the potential to disrupt it, arguing, for example, that local environments have the potential to subvert larger social stereotypes about gender and, in doing so, promote change. As a result, this theory acknowledges that individuals have agency, that they are not simply passive recipients of stereotypes and norms. Peering through the lens of gender as a social construction, researchers call explicit attention to the interplay between individual expectations and behaviors in local settings, such as classrooms, where, for example, female and male students might have very different interactions and experiences. For example, a female student who performs well in a math class might not receive the same recognition from either teachers or peers as a comparable male student, owing to the continued salience of gender stereotypes.

Finally, some sociologists and gender scholars emphasize the importance of theories of intersectionality, which point to the multiple axes of inequality in society beyond gender, including race/ethnicity and social class (Andersen 2005; Andersen and Collins 1995; Browne and Misra 2003). For example, theorists who focus on the intersection of gender and race/ethnicity caution that considering differences between males and females in the aggregate ignores the unique histories and experiences of each group at each point of intersection—for example, black females—and therefore risks making inferences that are too broad or inaccurate (Collins 1998). Examining intersectionality is particularly important for research on education, as it is not the case that one set of academic experiences and outcomes applies generally to all females, while another applies to all males.

Although not contradictory, these various theories nonetheless apply somewhat different lenses to gender inequality. As a result, some pertain more directly to understanding certain instances of inequality than others.

RESEARCH FINDINGS ON GENDER INEQUALITY IN EDUCATION

Gender Differences in Educational Outcomes

Perhaps the most logical place to start when discussing gender differences in education is to address the question of who does better in school? The answer varies somewhat based on the educational outcome being considered. When examining gender differences in the letter grades that students earn in school, there is consistent evidence from the past several decades that girls score higher than boys (Buchmann, DiPrete, and McDaniel 2008; Entwisle, Alexander, and Olson 1994; Mickelson 1989). This female advantage in grades is apparent from kindergarten through high school (and even continues into college), and it exists across all academic subjects. Sociologists often attribute females' higher grades to gender socialization, noting that girls are raised to follow rules set by, and meet expectations of, adults, and are more likely to want to please others and get their approval (e.g., that of teachers).

Of course, grades are not the only indicator of who does well in school. Test scores are another important educational outcome and are sometimes viewed as more objective or reliable indicators of academic achievement than grades, since they are not assigned by an individual (e.g., a teacher). While there are certainly reasons to believe that standardized tests can themselves be biased in terms of privileging certain kinds of content or knowledge, nevertheless they represent another key measure of academic performance. In general, research shows that male and female students have similar test scores; this is particularly the case for accountability exams administered by states (Hyde and Linn 2006). On national tests designed by the US Department of Education to track student knowledge across time and place, the results are somewhat mixed. While some researchers found no differences (DiPrete and Jennings 2012; Hyde et al. 2008), others reported evidence of small average differences favoring female students in reading and favoring male students in math and science (Penner and Paret 2008; Robinson and Lubienski 2011). To further complicate things, some studies show that the strength of these subject-specific gender differences diminishes over time (Robinson and Lubienski 2011; Quinn and Cooc 2015), while others show that these disparities grow slightly larger over time (Penner and Paret 2008). Beyond focusing on average differences, some studies have also revealed more variability in male students' scores, so that boys are more likely than girls to have scores at either the top or the bottom of the distribution, while female students' scores tend to cluster more around the mean (Penner and Paret 2008, Robinson and Lubienski 2011). Finally, some research has pointed to variation in the size of gender differences across racial/ethnic groups, as gaps appear smaller among minority students than among white students (Hyde and Linn 2006).

Despite the sometimes conflicting evidence within this research literature on test score gaps, it is nevertheless clear that, overall, any differences that do exist are small in scope. Additionally, it is important to point out that biological/genetic explanations for males' small advantage on some math tests fall short of explaining the ambiguity of results discussed above, and such explanations have been primarily discredited for other factors as well (Ceci, Williams, and Barnett 2009; Halpern 2013; Hyde and Mertz 2009). Instead, researchers have offered varying theories for any test-score gaps that do exist in relation to gender. Arguments regarding gender socialization point out that, consistent with stereotypes of natural ability, girls are raised to like reading and dislike math (Eccles 2011). Theories of gender construction take a different perspective, arguing that the salience of gender stereotypes in a math classroom can lead girls to underperform relative to their actual capability (McGlone and Aronson 2006).

Within K–12 education, but particularly in high school, the level of courses that students take can also be considered an important educational outcome. For example, advanced-course-taking at least partly captures the degree to which students engage with demanding curriculum and is visible to others (colleges, employers) on academic transcripts, just like test scores and grades. Much as in the patterns discussed above regarding test scores, there are few gender differences in advanced-course-taking, and those that are apparent are both small in scope and subject-specific. For example, my research has shown that while male and female students take advanced math classes at the same rate, male students are more likely than their female peers to take physics (Riegle-Crumb and Moore 2014). Additionally, other researchers have found that female students are more likely than their male peers to take both advanced English and advanced biology courses (Xie and Shauman 2003). While small in magnitude, gender differences in course-taking are most consistent with theories of gender socialization and of gender essentialism, as boys and girls exhibit what might appear to be "natural preferences" for different subjects that fall in line with prevailing norms and stereotypes. Yet my research has also shown that gender gaps in course-taking vary across local contexts, and that, for example, schools in communities with more adult women employed in science, technology, engineering, and mathematics (STEM) occupations have gender parity in physics enrollment (Riegle-Crumb and Moore 2014). Such patterns are consistent with theories of gender construction that point to the potential for messages within local environments to subvert larger social stereotypes.

Regarding two additional key educational outcomes, high school graduation and college attendance, female students hold a substantial advantage. Specifically, young women are much more likely to complete high school and subsequently matriculate to college, compared to their male peers (DiPrete and Buchmann 2013). This female advantage is present across racial/ethnic groups, although it is greater in size among black and Hispanic youth than among white youth. Yet males generally retain important advantages within the postsecondary realm, as they are overrepresented at the most selective institutions and overrepresented in several STEM fields. For example, men comprise approximately 80 percent of the bachelor degree recipients in engineering and computer science, two of the most financially lucrative and in-demand fields in contemporary times (Snyder and Dillow 2013). Importantly, researchers have demonstrated that men and women have equal persistence within these fields in college; thus women's underrepresentation is due to their much lower relative likelihood of choosing to enter such majors in the first place (Xie and Shauman 2003). Stepping back, similar to patterns in K–12 education, patterns of gender disparities in the postsecondary landscape are mixed, with different genders tending to experience different gaps; yet the magnitude of differences tends to be larger than that observed in K–12. Furthermore, disparities here at the tail end of formal education have implications for larger patterns of inequality in the labor market, as men's lower rates of high school and college completion are linked to their higher relative representation in low-wage or blue-collar employment, while at the same time women's lower rates of representation in STEM fields are linked to gender gaps in income favoring males among those in professional occupations (Shauman 2006). Overall, gendered postsecondary patterns are best explained by theories of gender essentialism, which argue that women's access to college is encouraged within modern industrial societies at the same

Figure 5. Although many gender inequalities in contemporary schools have narrowed, girls continue to face barriers in science and mathematics. Source: Proctor Academy, 2013, via Creative Commons license.

time that men retain their high social status via overrepresentation in the most elite schools and majors (Charles and Bradley 2002).

Gender Differences in Educational Experiences

Beyond gender disparities in educational outcomes, sociological research has focused on whether and how male and female students may have different experiences within the educational system. Here I distinguish between evidence that male and female students are sometimes systematically treated differently (either intentionally or not) by others within the educational system (including teachers and peers), and evidence that male and female students sometimes experience or react to the same educational environment in different ways (see figure 5). Both differential treatment and differential reactions are important to consider in order to shed light on the complexity of gender inequality within education. Importantly, research on these issues within the sociology of education often diverges from research on gender differences in educational outcomes in several ways: first, it gives greater emphasis to social-psychological factors (e.g., students' attitudes or feelings); second, it gives greater attention to intersectionality and, in doing so, highlights the experiences of minority males and females; and third, it is more qualitative in nature, as researchers focus on documenting students' experiences within classrooms rather than quantitatively measuring their performance.

Gender Bias in the Classroom

Given the continued prevalence of gender stereotypes about boys' greater "natural" aptitude for math, it is perhaps not surprising that researchers find evidence that teachers, and to some extent peers, often have biased views or engage in discriminatory behavior toward female students in STEM fields. For example, my research has found that teachers rate high school girls' math ability lower than that of their male peers who have the same grades and test scores and who are taught in the same classroom; interestingly, this bias was restricted to teachers' ratings of their white students, but not their minority students (Riegle-Crumb and Humphries 2012). At the postsecondary level there is also evidence of bias toward female students in STEM fields in the form of a "chilly climate." Researchers have found that female students are often viewed negatively by STEM faculty and are less likely to be called on or given recognition in class; at the same time, male students are less likely to include female students in study groups and discussions and more likely to disparage their contributions (Ecklund, Lincoln, and Tansey 2012; Heyman, Martyna, and Bhatia 2002; Seymour and Hewitt 1997; Starobin and Laanan 2008; Grunspan et al. 2016).

Yet at the same time, researchers have also found evidence of bias toward male students. For example, while it is true that boys have higher rates of acting out in class and breaking rules, a recent study found that the negative consequences of such behavior were greater for boys than for girls with disruptive behavior (Owens 2016). Specifically, teachers were more likely to retain boys than girls during the early years of elementary school even when both exhibited the same behavioral problems. This study is consistent with others which show that teachers and administrators treat male students' transgressions more harshly than those of female students, resulting in higher rates of suspension or expulsion (Skiba et al. 2014). Furthermore, research finds that minority boys are disproportionately subject to the most severe punishments (Ferguson 2001).

Therefore, researchers have documented how gender continues to be constructed within schools. Specifically, teachers (and others) have gendered expectations of performance that are largely shaped by dominant gender norms and stereotypes, and this has clear implications for their everyday assessments of and interactions with their students. In treating students in highly gendered ways, they create and maintain differences in attitudes as well as outcomes; for example, female students exposed to low teacher expectations regarding their math skills are likely to become less confident, which may in turn influence their desire to pursue math-related college majors. And male students who are constantly reprimanded and punished for minor transgressions (which occurs disproportionately for black and Hispanic males compared to white males) may begin to view themselves as unable to do well in school, contributing to their greater likelihood of dropping out. In this way, daily interactions and experiences can accumulate and contribute to the maintenance of gender inequality.

Gendered Reactions to Educational Environments

Yet gender differences in school experiences are not always the result of the biased actions or attitudes of others. Rather, there are instances where the same environment is experienced differently by female students and by male students. Regarding gender and STEM fields, research shows that female students' confidence can be undermined by high-stakes testing environments in math, while male students are undeterred (Good, Aronson, and Harder 2007; McGlone and Pfeister 2007; Spencer, Steele, and Quinn 1999). Similarly, researchers have suggested that the competitive norms within many STEM college classrooms, where grading is done exclusively on a curve and students are constantly compared to one another, are off-putting to female students and much less so for male students (Gasiewski et al. 2012).

Returning to the theme of behavior in school, researchers who point to boys' difficulty obeying classroom requirements that they sit still, remain quiet, and so on, suggest that boys find the school environment much less comfortable than their female peers do (Entwisle, Alexander, and Olson 2007). This is the case even if teachers expect the same behavior from both genders and sanction them similarly for transgressions (DiPrete and Jennings 2012). On a related note, researchers find that girls report liking school and being engaged in school much more than boys, again pointing to the notion that boys' and girls' psychological responses to the same school environments may diverge (Crosnoe, Johnson, and Elder 2004). Moreover, boys and girls may respond differently to the information and resources they receive in school. For example, my research shows that girls' decisions to take advanced courses in math and science in high school are influenced by having same-gender friends who are high-achieving in these areas, while boys' course-taking decisions are unrelated to peer performance (Riegle-Crumb, Farkas, and Muller 2006). In another study, researchers found that while high school girls' self-confidence was impaired (and their subsequent course-selection was negatively influenced) when they received a lower grade than expected, boys were negatively affected when labeled as having a learning disability (Crosnoe, Riegle-Crumb, and Muller 2007).

Thus, researchers have uncovered many instances of gender differences in reactions to various aspects of the schooling environment. As before, theories of gender socialization and gender construction can help us make sense of why this is so. Specifically, cultural beliefs about appropriate gender behaviors and preferences shape what happens in the classroom. If girls are raised to be, on average, less competitive than boys, then spending time in a highly competitive STEM classroom will be much less comfortable for girls than for boys. Similarly, if boys are raised to be more aggressive and physically active than girls, then they will find the expectations of appropriate classroom behavior much more restrictive and difficult to follow. And because stereotypes continue to paint math-related fields as the natural domain of males, girls may benefit from the presence of peers who help defy this stereotype. In short, the gendered scripts that male and female students bring with them into the classroom can greatly influence the roles they play there and, subsequently, influence many of the educational outcomes.

UNANSWERED QUESTIONS AND RESEARCH FRONTIERS

As can be seen from this discussion, there is a wealth of previous studies on gender inequality in education. Yet many important questions still remain. Regarding research examining gender differences in educational outcomes, the majority of extant research continues to focus on mean differences between genders, thereby obscuring heterogeneity within each gender. For example, we know very little about the girls who perform at the highest end of the math-test-score distribution—how do their backgrounds, attitudes, and resources differ from those of other girls, and do these high-achieving girls differ from high-achieving boys? The need to consider more heterogeneity is also apparent in the shortage of research that considers intersectionality. Although this chapter highlights some examples that do so, currently the quantitative literature within the sociology of education needs more studies that critically examine how and why gaps in educational outcomes often vary across groups.

Relatedly, in regard to research on the second major theme of this chapter, gender differences in educational experiences, there is a similarly limited body of research that considers the intersection of gender and race/ethnicity (see, for example, Holland 2012; Ispa-Landa 2013; Wilkins 2014). Further, the extent to which gender interacts with social class in the classroom remains mostly unexamined. Given the rising rates of poverty within the United States, and the extent to which schools are segregated, and to which poor youth tend to be concentrated in specific schools, this is an area that needs more attention.

Additionally, there is a critical need to move beyond research that considers gender as a binary category, and to instead consider how young people choose to identify their gender. Despite the fact that gender theorists have argued that the salience of individuals' gender membership and the manner in which they define it can vary widely (Ridgeway and Correll 2004), there is nonetheless, within the sociology of education, a dearth of research that examines the subsequent implications for educational inequality. Furthermore, given contemporary debates about how schools can and should accommodate the needs of transgender youth, it is vital that sociologists contribute to this conversation.

Finally, while this chapter has highlighted examples of research that consider how schools are locations of gender construction, more research is needed to further unpack some of the complexity hinted at here: we also need to consider whether and how this complexity shapes individuals' futures. For example, we know little about whether and how the beliefs and attitudes of young women and men that are shaped in school have consequences for their choices after school, including those related to labor force choices but also relationship and family choices. For example, are certain school contexts more likely to foster gender-egalitarian beliefs? While research currently focuses somewhat on the long-term impacts of gender differences in certain measures of educational achievement, such as measures demonstrating how females' advantage in academic performance in high school contributes to their greater rates of college attainment, there is a lack of research considering how schools may also contribute to gender differences in nonacademic outcomes (or a lack of gender differences) that have subsequent implications for individuals' futures.

IMPLICATIONS FOR POLICY AND PRACTICE

As I have argued, there is a need to move beyond a discussion of mean differences in outcomes between male and female students and to instead consider variations across different school contexts, as well as to further consider how gender intersects with race/ethnicity and social class. Only by understanding the complexity of gendered educational experiences can we design educational policies that are equitable in both their enactment and their consequences. For example, the fact that an educational practice may disproportionately harm minority male students may not be revealed if educational agents focus only on aggregate gender differences.

Additionally, given the evidence of different forms of teacher bias toward male and female students, there is clearly a need for further conversation about bias in the classroom. As teachers are, of course, themselves members of society, they are subject to the same cultural pressures to enforce gender norms and stereotypes. Explicit attention to this issue in the form of teacher training and professional development could help make classrooms more equitable places for all students.

CHAPTER 3 REVIEW

Discussion Questions

1. Do you think gender differences in test scores are important—why or why not? And why do you think researchers continue to study them?

2. Women are underrepresented in computer science and engineering college majors, but are equally represented in biology and math majors, as well as in other previously male-dominated majors, like business. Do you think computer science and engineering fields will eventually have as many women as men? Why or why not?

3. Researchers sometimes argue that focusing on average differences between males and females is not worthwhile, given the amount of heterogeneity within each gender. Do you agree? Why or why not?

4. The chapter offers different examples of teacher bias toward one gender or the other. Do your own experiences in school echo some of these findings?

Suggestions for Further Reading

DiPrete, T., and C. Buchmann. 2013. *The Rise of Women: The Female Advantage in Education and What It Means for American Schooling.* New York: Russell Sage Foundation.

Ridgeway, C. 2011. *Framed by Gender: How Gender Inequality Persists in the Modern World.* New York: Oxford University Press.

References

Andersen, M. L. 2005. "Thinking about Women: A Quarter Century's View." *Gender & Society* 19 (4): 437–55.

Andersen, M. L., and P. H. Collins, eds. 1995. *Race, Class, and Gender: An Anthology.* 2nd ed. Belmont, CA: Wadsworth.

Browne, I., and J. Misra. 2003. "The Intersection of Gender and Race in the Labor Market." *Annual Review of Sociology* 29:487–513.

Buchmann, C., T. DiPrete, and A. McDaniel. 2008. "Gender Inequalities in Education." *Annual Review of Sociology* 34:319–37.

Ceci, S., W. Williams, and S. Barnett. 2009. "Women's Underrepresentation in Science: Sociocultural and Biological Considerations." *Psychological Bulletin* 135:218–61.

Charles, M., and K. Bradley. 2002. "Equal but Separate? A Cross-National Study of Sex Segregation in Higher Education." *American Sociological Review* 67:573–99.

Collins, P. H. 1998. "Intersections of Race, Class, Gender, and Nation: Some Implications for Black Family Studies." *Journal of Comparative Family Studies* 29:27–34.

Crosnoe, R., M. K. Johnson, and G. H. Elder. 2004. "Intergenerational Bonding in School: The Behavioral and Contextual Correlates of Student-Teacher Relationships." *Sociology of Education* 77 (1): 60–81.

Crosnoe, R., C. Riegle-Crumb, and C. Muller. 2007. "Gender, Self-Perception, and Academic Problems in High School." *Social Problems* 54 (1): 118–38.

DiPrete, T., and C. Buchmann. 2013. *The Rise of Women: The Female Advantage in Education and What It Means for American Schooling.* New York: Russell Sage Foundation.

DiPrete, T., and J. Jennings. 2012. "Social and Behavior Skills and the Gender Gap in Early Educational Achievement." *Social Science Research* 41:1–15.

Eccles, J. 1994. "Understanding Women's Educational and Occupational Choices: Applying the Eccles et al. Model of Achievement-Related Choices." *Psychology of Women Quarterly* 18:585–609.

———. 2011. "Gendered Educational and Occupational Choices: Applying the Eccles et al. Model of Achievement-Related Choices." *International Journal of Behavioral Development* 35:195–201.

Ecklund, E. H., A. E. Lincoln, and C. Tansey. 2012. "Gender Segregation in Elite Academic Science." *Gender & Society* 26 (5): 693–717.

Entwisle, D. R., K. Alexander, and L. S. Olson. 1994. "The Gender Gap in Math: Its Possible Origins in Neighborhood Effects." *American Sociological Review* 59:822–38.

———. 2007. "Early Schooling: The Handicap of Being Poor and Male." *Sociology of Education* 80:114–38.

Ferguson, A. 2001. *Bad Boys: Public Schools in the Making of Black Masculinity.* Ann Arbor: University of Michigan Press.

Gasiewski, J. A., M. K. Eagan, G. A. Garcia, S. Hurtado, and M. J. Chang. 2012. "From Gatekeeping to Engagement: A Multicontextual, Mixed Method Study of Student Academic Engagement in Introductory STEM Courses." *Research in Higher Education* 53:229–61.

Good, C., J. Aronson, and J. A Harder. 2007. "Problems in the Pipeline: Stereotype Threat and Women's Achievement in High-Level Math Courses." *Journal of Applied Developmental Psychology* 29 (1): 17–28.

Grunspan, D. Z., S. L. Eddy, S. E. Brownell, B. L. Wiggins, A. J. Crowe, and S. M. Goodreau. 2016. "Males Under-Estimate Academic Performance of Their Female Peers in Undergraduate Biology Classrooms." *PLoS ONE* 11 (2): e0148405.

Halpern, D. F. 2013. *Sex Differences in Cognitive Abilities.* New York: Psychology Press.

Heyman, G. D., B. Martyna, and S. Bhatia. 2002. "Gender and Achievement-Related Beliefs among Engineering Students." *Journal of Women and Minorities in Science and Engineering* 8:41–52.

Holland, M. 2012. "Only Here for the Day: The Social Integration of Minority Students at a Majority White High School." *Sociology of Education* 85 (2): 101–20.

Hyde, J., S. Lindberg, M. Linn, A. Ellis, and C. Williams. 2008. "Gender Similarities Characterize Math Performance." *Science* 321:494–95.

Hyde, J., and M. Linn. 2006. "Gender Similarities in Mathematics and Science." *Science* 314 (5799): 599–600.

Hyde, J., and J. Mertz. 2009. "Gender, Culture, and Mathematics Performance." *Proceedings of the National Academy of Science* 106 (22): 8801–7.

Ispa-Landa, S. 2013. "Gender, Race and Justifications for Group Exclusion: Urban Black Students Bussed to Affluent Suburban Schools." *Sociology of Education* 86 (3): 218–33.

McGlone, M. S., and J. Aronson. 2006. "Stereotype Threat, Identity Salience, and Spatial Reasoning." *Journal of Applied Developmental Psychology* 27:486–93.

McGlone, M. S., and A. Pfeister. 2007. "The Generality and Consequences of Stereotype Threat." *Sociological Compass* 1: 174–90.

Mickelson, R. A. 1989. "Why Does Jane Read and Write So Well? The Anomaly of Women's Achievement." *Sociology of Education* 62:47–63.

Owens, J. 2016. "Early Childhood Behavior Problems and the Gender Gap in Educational Attainment in the United States." *Sociology of Education* 89 (3): 236–58.

Penner, A. M., and M. Paret. 2008. "Gender Differences in Mathematics Achievement: Exploring the Early Grades and the Extremes." *Social Science Research* 37:239–53.

Quinn, D., and N. Cooc. 2015. "Science Achievement Gaps by Gender and Race/Ethnicity in Elementary and Middle School: Trends and Predictors." *Educational Researcher* 44:336–46.

Ridgeway, C. L. 2011. *Framed by Gender: How Gender Inequality Persists in the Modern World.* New York: Oxford University Press.

Ridgeway, C. L., and S. J. Correll. 2004. "Unpacking the Gender System: A Theoretical Perspective on Gender Beliefs and Social Relations." *Gender & Society* 18 (4): 510–31.

Riegle-Crumb, C., G. Farkas, and C. Muller. 2006. "The Role of Gender and Friendship in Advanced Course Taking." *Sociology of Education* 79 (3): 206–28.

Riegle-Crumb, C., and M. Humphries. 2012. "Exploring Bias in Math Teachers' Perceptions of Students' Ability by Gender and Race/Ethnicity." *Gender and Society* 26 (2): 290–322.

Riegle-Crumb, C., and C. Moore. 2014. "The Gender Gap in High School Physics: Considering the Context of Local Communities." *Social Science Quarterly* 95:253–68.

Robinson, J., and S. Lubienski. 2011. "The Development of Gender Gaps in Mathematics and Reading during Elementary and Middle School: Examining Direct Cognitive Assessments and Teacher Ratings." *American Educational Research Journal* 48:68–302.

Seymour, E., and N. M. Hewitt. 1997. *Talking about Leaving: Why Undergraduates Leave the Sciences.* Boulder, CO: Westview Press.

Shauman, K. A. 2006. "Occupational Sex Segregation and the Earnings of Occupations: What Causes the Link among College-Educated Workers?" *Social Science Research* 35 (3): 577–619.

Skiba, R., C. Choong-Geun, M. Trachok, T. Baker, A. Sheya, and R. Hughes. 2014. "Parsing Disciplinary Disproportionality: Contributions of Infraction, Student, and School Characteristics to Out-of-School Suspension and Expulsion." *American Educational Research Journal* 51:640–70.

Snyder, T. D., and S. A. Dillow. 2013. *Digest of Education Statistics 2012.* NCES 2014–015. Washington, DC: National Center for Education Statistics, Institute of Education Sciences, US Department of Education.

Spencer, S. J., C. M. Steele, and D. M Quinn. 1999. "Stereotype Threat and Women's Math Performance." *Journal of Experimental Social Psychology* 35 (1): 4–28.

Starobin, S. S., and F. S. Laanan. 2008. "Broadening Female Participation in Science, Technology, Engineering, and Mathematics: Experiences at Community Colleges." *New Direction for Community Colleges* 142:37–46.

Wilkins, A. C. 2014. "Race, Age and Identity Transformations in the Transition from High School to College for Black and First-Generation White Men." *Sociology of Education* 87 (3): 171–87.

Xie, Y., and K. Shauman. 2003. *Women in Science: Career Processes and Outcomes.* Cambridge, MA: Harvard University Press.

4

Hidden in Plain Sight

Rethinking Race in Education

ROB ESCHMANN, BOSTON UNIVERSITY

CHARLES M. PAYNE, RUTGERS UNIVERSITY NEWARK

EDITORS' NOTE

Race, like gender, clearly influences students' educational experiences in a myriad of ways, both big and little. In schools, as Downey notes in chapter 2, racial inequalities appear to behave differently than socioeconomic inequalities, and there is some evidence to suggest that schools may exacerbate racial inequalities in education. This finding may not be all that surprising in the context of the United States, where racial inequality—in the form of slavery—is sometimes referred to as the nation's "original sin," and where pronounced racial inequalities in wealth, social status, and power persist.

It also shouldn't be surprising, therefore, that sociologists of education are profoundly interested in racial inequality in schools. Boston University sociologist Rob Eschmann and Rutgers University sociology and African American studies professor Charles Payne argue that before we seek the sources of racial inequality, we need to think carefully about what it is we mean by "race" in the first place. Race is, in their words, a **"social construct."** This doesn't mean that race isn't real or that it doesn't matter. After all, the idea that paper money carries value is also a social construct, but that doesn't make the twenty-dollar bill in your pocket any less valuable. What it means is that we define and redefine race on an almost daily basis through our laws, social norms, expectations, and actions.

As you read this chapter, as well as the discussions of race and educational inequality in chapters 5, 8, and 10–13, think about how you've seen schools help construct race and give it meaning in your own life.

KEY POINTS

- While the idea of race seems to hold a central place in the sociology of education, it could be argued that race is frequently conceptualized at a fairly low level, perhaps because of the lingering effects of the race-relations paradigm.
- Disconnected studies about the effects of race in particular aspects of schooling fail to convey a sense of race as a fundamental organizing principle of schooling and educational processes more broadly.
- At the same time, sociological discussions tend to underestimate the degree to which race can be used to leverage positive development among youth from racially stigmatized groups.
- Drawing upon Omi and Winant's notion of a "racial project," we argue for putting race and white supremacy at the center of the sociology of education.

INTRODUCTION

Race, as a social construction, is a central concept in the discipline of sociology. We feel that within the sociology of education, however, the analysis of race is too often shorn of historical and structural complexity; meanwhile, research that illuminates the deep, complex, and long-lasting ways in which race determines educational processes and outcomes is often presented piecemeal, obscuring the reality of widespread, structural racism within our educational system. In this light, it is difficult to develop a robust understanding of how racial categories reproduce themselves in schools. This, is turn, makes it more difficult to challenge the replication of structural racism within the educational sphere. We are getting it wrong.

This analytical blind spot characterizes one of the foundational studies in the field, the so-called Coleman Report; though it's more than fifty years old, the report can help us understand the "hiddenness" of race in some sociological research. For the 1966 *Equality of Educational Opportunity* survey (see chapter 2 for further discussion of the Coleman Report). James S. Coleman and his team set out to examine how school segregation and associated resource disparities—overt forms of racial discrimination—led to academic underperformance among minority communities. When the data failed to support the causal link as strongly as expected, Coleman suggested that family background—the skills, values, and attitudes passed from parents to children *outside* of school—determine academic achievement or failure within school. Coleman was not primarily concerned with how race operated within schools or how the experience of racism shaped families' attitudes toward school. More recent research, however, has tackled the historical context that Coleman's report lacked, including the dramatic underinvestment in African American education in the South for most of the twentieth century and the way nation-wide commitment to segregated schools undermined the trust of black communities (Neckerman 2010).

THE PROBLEM OF SUBJECTIVITY

Racial Bias in Teacher Expectations

We now know much more about the racialized character of teacher-student interactions than when Coleman wrote. We know, for example, that one of the most ambitious school reforms in recent memory—the standards-based movement of the nineties—failed to account for teachers' assumptions about student capacity. In their nine-city study, David and Shields (2001: p. i) concluded, "Promoting teaching practices designed to help *all* students reach ambitious standards runs counter to widely held shared beliefs about the nature of learning and about the abilities of many students, especially poor and minority students." We know now that even controlling for student ability, minority students are half as likely to be classified as gifted as white students; and black teachers are three times more likely than white teachers to recommend black students for honors (Grissom and Redding 2016). Gershenson and colleagues (2016) found that when black and white teachers are asked to comment on the same black student, white teachers are almost 40 percent less likely to believe the student will graduate high school. White teachers are particularly pessimistic when asked to predict black boys' graduation chances. Dee (2005), using the National Educational Longitudinal Survey, found that when teachers and students share racial background, teachers are significantly less likely to perceive those students as disruptive, inattentive, or disengaged; this effect is particularly strong among low-income students and students in the South. Students who are perceived negatively by teachers fare less well on important academic indicators. Given that 50 percent of public school students are students of color, as compared to 19 percent of teachers, we begin to see how students of color often confront structural barriers to success.

Tracking, Race, and Discipline

Arguably, grouping students by ability is the most important way to institutionalize expectations. Debates continue over how large a role race and class bias play in assignment to ability levels, or academic "tracks" (see chapter 10). There is no doubt, however, that, as tracking is normally practiced, black and Latinx students are disproportionately likely to be assigned to lower tracks. Within these lower tracks, research shows, these students receive poorer instruction than other students and develop low expectations of academic success. Evidence suggests that students who are placed for low-track reading instruction learn substantially less than their higher-tracked peers; and higher-grouped students learn slightly more (Lleras and Rangel 2009: 279). Some evidence suggests that even the best-prepared black students are much less likely to be assigned to upper tracks than comparable white students (Tyson 2013). Recently, many researchers have found evidence of racial disproportionality in the meting out of discipline, with much of the evidence coming from the Department of Education (see chapter 12). Black students are three and a half times more likely to be suspended than white students (Adams, Robelen, and Shaw 2012); and black and Latinx students receive harsher punishments for the same offenses (Gregory, Skiba, and Noguera 2010). Whereas white students tend to perceive disciplinary disparities as unintentional, students of color view such disparities as conscious and deliberate acts of discrimination (Skiba, Michael, and Nardo 2000: 17). Furthermore, skin color appears to play a role above and beyond simple categories of "black" and "white." Research shows that black women with darker complexions are three times more likely to be suspended than those with lighter complexions (Hannon, DeFina, and Bruch 2013).

THE PROBLEM OF INVISIBILITY: RACE AND CURRICULUM

How are minority communities represented in school curricula and textbooks, and why does this matter? Here, stigma arises from invisibility as much as visibility. Analyses show that, while social science and history textbooks took up themes and rhetoric of multiculturalism in the 1980s and 1990s, these changes were largely superficial. As Sleeter (2011: 2) has argued,

> Whites continue to receive the most attention and appear in the widest variety of roles, dominating story lines and lists of accomplishments. African Americans, the next most represented racial group, appear in a more limited range of roles and usually receive only a sketchy account historically, being featured mainly in relationship to slavery. Asian Americans and Latinos appear mainly as figures on the landscape with virtually no history or contemporary ethnic experience. Native Americans appear mainly in the past, but also occasionally in contemporary stories in reading books. Immigration is represented as a distinct historical period that happened mainly in the Northeast, rather than as an ongoing phenomenon. . . . Texts say little to nothing about contemporary race relations, racism, or racial issues, usually sanitizing greatly what they mention.

Thus, by the time they are ten years old, many black children feel tension between their everyday social realities and the world portrayed in textbooks. For example, while white fifth graders surveyed in one study believe that the Bill of Rights applies to all, about half of black students were skeptical of this supposition. By the time they are in high school, many students of color are able to critique curriculum bias in some detail, and they see this bias as contributing to their disengagement (Sleeter 2011). (See chapter 9 for a discussion of textbook content in an international perspective.)

THE PROBLEM OF SEGREGATION IN CONTEMPORARY SCHOOLING

Today's housing and school segregation results largely from more or less openly racist practices and policies at local and national levels (Massey and Denton 1993; Rothstein 2017). Massey and Denton (1993) have pointed out that the ghetto has become naturalized. Geographic concentrations of disadvantage by race/ethnicity, class, gender, and social capital are taken for granted, and we no longer "see" them; they have fallen completely out of the national discourse on public policy. Beyond the direct damage ghettoes do to those imprisoned there, their very existence may symbolize the lack of social honor among whatever population is identified with the ghetto, even for those individuals who don't actually live there. It is certain that the distinctive social and physical isolation of Latino and African American students ensures that they will not have the resources that should be available to all citizens. Notwithstanding decades of public policy since *Brown v. Board of Education,* the Government Accountability Office determined that the proportion of schools serving mostly (75 percent or more) black or Hispanic low-income students rose from 9 percent of all K–12 schools to 16 percent between 2000 and 2014 (see chapter 13). Segregated schools offer fewer math, science, and college preparatory courses. They also exhibit higher rates of student retention, suspensions, and expulsions (GAO 2016).

Segregation and Teacher Quality

Teacher quality may be the most fundamental building block of good education, and we know that the racial composition of the student body consistently predicts the quality of its teaching force. Presley, White, and Gong (2005) found that, across the state of Illinois, teacher quality declined as the percentage of minority enrollment rose. In low-minority schools, almost a third of teachers came from the top quartile on the quality index that these researchers compiled. In schools that were virtually all-minority, only 2 percent of teachers came from the top quartile and fully 61 percent came from the lowest-ranking decile of teachers. In those cases where minority schools had more high-quality teachers, they demonstrated higher achievement.

According to the 2010 census, 45 percent of blacks and 41 percent of Hispanics, compared to just 10 percent of whites, lived in high-poverty neighborhoods. Concentrating racial minorities in often under-resourced and dangerous communities—again, a matter of public policy to a considerable extent—has important consequences for how well youth develop, including their physical and mental health. Sampson and Winter (2016), examining over a million blood tests from Chicago youngsters, found a consistent relationship between elevated levels of lead and the racial composition of neighborhoods. Elevated lead levels are associated with significant reductions in academic performance. As for mental health, we have strong evidence that the kind of exposure to violence that typifies too many urban neighborhoods leads to increased aggressive behavior, emotional and psychological distress, and, at the extremes, an uncaring attitude toward others (Miller 2008: 34).

STUDENT REACTIONS TO RACIAL DISCRIMINATION IN EDUCATION

We can't say how students of color systematically react to the stigmas that come with racial bias in education, but their relegation to the least-respected educational spaces seems to contribute to disengagement in one form or another. It appears that a common reaction to academic failure is to devalue formal learning (Steele 2010). Wong and colleagues (2003), interviewing black students at the start of seventh grade and then again at the end of eighth grade, found that perceived discrimination predicted declines in grades, academic self-concepts, self-esteem, and psychological resiliency; increases in depression and anger; and increases in the proportion of reported friends who were not interested in school and who had problem behaviors. These findings are consistent with a body of research which shows that the experience of racial discrimination is associated with a lower sense of psychological well-being (Schmitt et al. 2014), poorer health outcomes (Williams and Mohammed 2013), delinquency (Brody et al. 2006), and diminished life satisfaction (Broman 1997).

Race is so deeply embedded in the fabric of social life that discrimination can be implicit rather than explicit. It's reasonable to say that the educational system in its totality, historically and in the contemporary context, protects and propagates white supremacy. This language, however, is almost never used by sociologists of education. This is presumably, because sociologists of education tend to focus not on the totality of the system but on discrete parts of the educational process, rendering the process itself invisible. Discussions about discipline disparities, for example, are seldom combined with discussions of funding inequities or the allocation of teachers. Looking at just one piece of the process of the reproduction of racial inequality at a time protects white supremacy and helps naturalize disparity. This testifies to the enduring power of the race relations paradigm (Steinberg 2007), in which racial "discrimination" is largely understood to be (in essence) deliberate, invidious acts by identifiable individuals. For example, if Latinx children at a given school were intentionally and explicitly excluded from afterschool programming, we would hear protest from all quarters. Yet the reality is that these children are often under-enrolled because they live in areas where property taxes don't support such programming, where staff aren't equipped to navigate cultural barriers, and where students don't know if they will be welcomed in certain programs. The reproduction of white privilege is thus hidden in plain sight. White supremacy can be hidden in plain sight, obscured by the fragmentation and implicit biases that reproduce stratification.

RESEARCH ON RESILIENCE AS A RESPONSE TO RACIAL DISCRIMINATION IN SCHOOLS

In light of hidden biases and structural racism in schools, do students exhibit agency in how they respond to discrimination and inequality? Some of the most promising responses to stigmatizing social forces can also be hidden in plain sight. Families, communities, and schools can buffer youngsters against unsupportive environments. Wong and associates (2003), discussed earlier, illustrated this point. Not all students in their study reacted to discrimination in the same way. Those who had a stronger and more positive attachment to their racial identity did not experience the same negative academic, social, and psychological consequences when exposed to racial discrimination as their peers with weaker racial identities.

Similarly, Hughes and colleagues (2006) found that helping young people think positively about their racial/ethnic group can lead them to exhibit greater psychological resilience, greater academic success, and higher attendance in school. Graves (2014) found that students who have higher measures of critical racial awareness—that is, greater recognition of current forms of racism and the challenges one faces by virtue of being black—are more likely to be high achievers. An experiment by Walton and Cohen (2011) suggests, too, that students of color can mitigate the role of bias by means of critical racial awareness. They told first-year students that feelings of alienation were normal for students of any racial/ethnic background, and instructed them to write a letter to incoming students about how their feelings of belonging changed over time. Compared to a randomly assigned comparison group, participants had higher GPAs for three years, cutting the black-white grades gap in half. One experimental study of Latino and white middle-school students asked participants to reflect on and write about their core values (Sherman et al. 2013). While the intervention had no impact on white students, the treatment boosted Latino student grades for at least three years.

These beneficial outcomes do not seem to be associated with mainstream socialization, either silence about race or the idea that individual characteristics are more important than race. In fact, this type of socialization is associated with lower self-esteem for black children and higher rates of depression for Korean American youth (Choi et al. 2014). And when children report that they do not receive racial/ethnic socialization from their parents, discrimina-

Figure 6. Mixed-race group of children protesting for equitable educational opportunities, 1950s. Source: New York Public Library, Schomberg Center for Research in Black Culture, Photographs and Prints Division.

tion has a greater negative impact on their mental health. The underlying message here seems to overlap with that from the racial socialization literature: if young people can be given healthy ways to process their differences from others—by means of normalizing those differences or reminding students what's good about who they are—that can help them more effectively navigate environments where they feel vulnerable. The available evidence suggests these effects may be strongest for students of color and may be robust and enduring. Developing a sense of belonging and competence in young people may do more for them than other, much more elaborate, interventions.

POLICY INTERVENTIONS IN SCHOOL PRACTICES

Though schools replicate structural racism in practice—if not in intention—perhaps schools can ultimately serve as a means of dismantling systemic inequality. Given what we know about the central significance of curricula in shaping and conveying normative experience, for example, schools might think of ways to reveal and redress hidden biases within curricula and establish substantively inclusive practices. There is good reason to think it would make a difference. Sleeter's (2011) review of the literature finds overwhelmingly that well-designed and well-taught courses that grapple explicitly with the subject of race are associated with positive changes in academic engagement, academic achievement, and personal empowerment for minority students. Such programs go beyond mere representation of minorities—the "heroes and holidays" approach—and raise critical and challenging questions about inequality. The most common finding about courses designed for diverse student constituencies is that they positively shape the democratic attitudes of white students, as emotionally challenging as these courses may be at first.

Why don't schools embrace these types of curricular interventions more readily? Obviously, such courses call for pedagogical knowledge and strategies for which few teachers are trained. Almost certainly, though, the larger problem is that conversations of this sort make white educators—and sometimes white parents—profoundly uncomfortable, raising issues they find divisive and threatening (Singleton 2012). For example, Pollock's (2004) ethnography on "racetalk" in schools shows that teachers and administrators use what she terms *colormute* language to describe race-related incidents or patterns in race-neutral terms. The racialized nature of problems facing students of color in schools is often ignored simply because it is deemed too problematic to acknowledge the persistent influence of race in the schoolhouse. Another example of how discomfort with race in schools can influence student educational experiences comes from the closing of an apparently successful Mexican American studies program in Tucson because officials thought it was teaching resentment of white people (Depenbrock 2017). This pattern illustrates what critical race theorists would call *interest divergence*. Changing the curriculum in ways that would almost certainly help some students of color find schooling less alienating runs the risk of alienating the white educators who dominate the teaching profession. In a very real sense, schools remain "white" spaces.

We can think of curricular change as one part of a larger racial project, what Omi and Winant (1994: 56) define as "simultaneously an interpretation, representation, or explanation of racial dynamics, and an effort to reorganize and redistribute resources along particular racial lines. Racial projects connect what race *means* . . . and the ways in which both social structures and everyday experiences are racially *organized*, based upon that meaning." From the meting out of discipline to the teaching of the Civil War, schools tend to reflect the privileges and worldviews of those in power. From the funding of neighborhood schools to the assignment of students to academic tracks, the educational system distributes more resources to some groups than others. In its modern guise, white supremacy has very little to do with explicit racism. Rather, white supremacy functions when (white) people with social power, whose interests diverge from those of underserved minorities, protect their own interests. Even if, theoretically, the vast majority of educators *as individuals* wish to support all children and see them flourish, the current system systematically works to disadvantage some children. It is in this sense that social structures cannot be understood as merely the accumulation of individual attitudes and desires.

Why does it matter that we understand race as one of the fundamental organizing principles of American education? For one thing, recognizing this reality changes the intellectual agenda for the sociology of education. For decades, we've been asking the question "Why do some disadvantaged children perform poorly academically?" The question looks different if one begins with the assumption that schools systematically disadvantage students of color. Taking the idea of white supremacy seriously means paying much more attention to how racialized minorities experience schooling, including the ways race intersects with other marginalized identities. It means paying much more attention to the racialized distribution of resources, from dollars to good teachers. At the level of policy, it means rethinking how and why to reform schools.

CHAPTER 4 REVIEW

Discussion Questions

1. What are the important differences between a theory that emphasizes structural racism and what the authors refer to as the "race relations paradigm"?
2. How have the expectations of teachers or others affected your development?
3. How would you describe your own racial or ethnic socialization? How has this been different at home, at school, or with your friends?
4. Was there a tracking system in your high school? How did it work? Did it benefit some students more than others? Were there students in your high school who didn't feel they belonged?
5. What values do you associate with your racial/ethnic identity? What values do you associate with other racial/ethnic groups?
6. How does the history of discrimination in education influence the educational experiences of students of color today?

Suggestions for Further Reading

Gershenson, Seth, Stephen B. Holt, and Nicholas W. Papageorge. 2016. "Who Believes in Me? The Effect of Student-Teacher Demographic Match on Teacher Expectations." *Economics of Education Review* 52:209–24.

Omi, M., and H. Winant. 2014. *Racial Formation in the United States*. New York: Routledge.

Pollock, Mica. 2004. *Colormute: Race Talk Dilemmas in an American School.* Princeton, NJ: Princeton University Press.

Rothstein, Richard. 2017. *The Color of Law: A Forgotten History of How Our Government Segregated America.* New York: Liveright.

Steele, Claude. 2010. *Whistling Vivaldi: And Other Clues to How Stereotypes Affect Us.* 1st ed. Issues of Our Time. New York: W. W. Norton.

Steinberg, Stephen. 2007. *Race Relations: A Critique.* Stanford, CA: Stanford University Press.

References

Adams, Caralee J., Erik W. Robelen, and Nirvi Shaw. 2012. "Civil Rights Data Show Retention Disparities." *Education Week* 31 (23): 1–18.

Brody, Gene H., Yi-Fu Chen, Velma McBride Murry, Xiaojia Ge, Ronald L. Simons, Frederick X. Gibbons, Meg Gerrard, and Carolyn E. Cutrona. 2006. "Perceived Discrimination and the Adjustment of African American Youths: A Five-Year Longitudinal Analysis with Contextual Moderation Effects." *Child Development* 77 (5). https://doi.org/10.1111/j.1467–8624.2006.00927.x.

Broman, Clifford L. 1997. "Race-Related Factors and Life Satisfaction among African Americans." *Journal of Black Psychology* 23:36–49.

Choi, Yoonsun, Kevin Poh Hiong Tan, Miwa Yasui, and Dina Drankus Pekelnicky. 2014. "Race-Ethnicity and Culture in the Family and Youth Outcomes: Test of a Path Model with Korean American Youth and Parents." *Race and Social Problems* 6 (1): 69–84. http://dx.doi.org.proxy.uchicago.edu/10.1007/s12552–014–9111–8.

David, Jane L., and Patrick M. Shields. 2001. "When Theory Hits Reality: Standards-Based Reform in Urban Districts; Final Narrative Report." http://eric.ed.gov/?id=ED480210.

Dee, Thomas S. 2005. "A Teacher Like Me: Does Race, Ethnicity, or Gender Matter?" *American Economic Review* 95 (2): 158–65.

Depenbrock, Julie. 2017. "Federal Judge Finds Racism behind Arizona Law Banning Ethnic Studies." National Public Radio. www.npr.org/sections/ed/2017/08/22/545402866/federal-judge-finds-racism-behind-arizona-law-banning-ethnic-studies.

Gershenson, Seth, Stephen B. Holt, and Nicholas W. Papageorge. 2016. "Who Believes in Me? The Effect of Student-Teacher Demographic Match on Teacher Expectations." *Economics of Education Review* 52:209–24.

Government Accountability Office (GAO). 2016. *K–12 Education: Better Use of Information Could Help Agencies Identify Disparities and Address Racial Discrimination.* GAO-16-345. Washington, DC: US Government Accountability Office.

Graves, Daren. 2014. "Black High School Students' Critical Racial Awareness, School-Based Racial Socialization, and Academic Resilience." *Berkeley Review of Education* 5 (1): 5–32.

Gregory, Anne, Russell J. Skiba, and Pedro A. Noguera. 2010. "The Achievement Gap and the Discipline Gap: Two Sides of the Same Coin?" *Educational Researcher* 39 (1): 59–68.

Grissom, Jason A., and Christopher Redding. 2016. "Discretion and Disproportionality." *AERA Open* 2 (1): 2332858415622175.

Hannon, Lance, Robert DeFina, and Sarah Bruch. 2013. "The Relationship between Skin Tone and School Suspension for African Americans." *Race and Social Problems* 5 (4): 281–95.

Hughes, Diane, James Rodriguez, Emilie P. Smith, Deborah J. Johnson, Howard C. Stevenson, and Paul Spicer. 2006. "Parents' Ethnic-Racial Socialization Practices: A Review of Research and Directions for Future Study." *Developmental Psychology* 42 (5): 747–70. https://doi.org/10.1037/0012–1649.42.5.747.

Lleras, Christy, and Claudia Rangel. 2009. "Ability Grouping Practices in Elementary School and African American / Hispanic Achievement." *American Journal of Education* 115 (2): 279–304.

Massey, Douglas S., and Nancy A. Denton. 1993. *American Apartheid: Segregation and the Making of the Underclass.* Cambridge, MA: Harvard University Press.

Miller, Jody. 2008. *Getting Played: African American Girls, Urban Inequality, and Gendered Violence.* New York: NYU Press.

Neckerman, Kathryn M. 2010. *Schools Betrayed: Roots of Failure in Inner-City Education.* Chicago: University of Chicago Press.

Omi, Michael, and Howard Winant. 1994. *Racial Formation in the US: From the 1960s to the 1990s.* New York: Routledge.

Pollock, Mica. 2004. *Colormute: Race Talk Dilemmas in an American School.* Princeton, NJ: Princeton University Press.

Presley, Jennifer B., Bradford R. White, and Yuqin Gong. 2005. "Examining the Distribution and Impact of Teacher Quality in Illinois: Policy Research Report; IERC 2005–2." Online submission. http://eric.ed.gov/?id=ED493170.

Rothstein, Richard. 2017. *The Color of Law: A Forgotten History of How Our Government Segregated America.* New York: Liveright.

Sampson, Robert J., and Alix S. Winter. 2016. "The Racial Ecology of Lead Poisoning." *Du Bois Review: Social Science Research on Race* 13 (2): 261–83.

Schmitt, Michael T., Nyla R. Branscombe, Tom Postmes, and Amber Garcia. 2014. "The Consequences of Perceived Discrimination for Psychological Well-Being: A Meta-Analytic Review." *Psychological Bulletin* 140 (4): 921–48. https://doi.org/10.1037/a0035754.

Sherman, David K., Kimberly A. Hartson, Kevin R. Binning, Valerie Purdie-Vaughns, Julio Garcia, Suzanne Taborsky-Barba, Sarah Tomassetti, A. David Nussbaum, and Geoffrey L. Cohen. 2013. "Deflecting the Trajectory and Changing the Narrative: How Self-Affirmation Affects Academic Performance and Motivation under Identity Threat." *Journal of Personality and Social Psychology* 104 (4): 591–618. https://doi.org/10.1037/a0031495.

Singleton, Glenn E. 2012. *More Courageous Conversations about Race.* Thousand Oaks, CA: Corwin Press.

Skiba, Russell J., Robert S. Michael, and Abra Carroll Nardo. 2000. *The Color of Discipline: Sources of Racial and Gender Disproportionality in School Punishment.* Bloomington, IN: Education Policy Center.

Sleeter, Christine E. 2011. *The Academic and Social Value of Ethnic Studies: A Research Review.* Washington, DC: National Education Association.

Steele, Claude. 2010. *Whistling Vivaldi: And Other Clues to How Stereotypes Affect Us.* 1st ed. Issues of Our Time. New York: W. W. Norton.

Steinberg, Stephen. 2007. *Race Relations: A Critique.* Stanford, CA: Stanford University Press.

Tyson, Karolyn. 2013. "Tracking Segregation, and the Opportunity Gap." In *Closing the Opportunity Gap: What America Must Do to Give Every Child an Even Chance,* edited by P. L. Carter, K. G. Welner, and G. Ladson-Billings. New York: Oxford University Press.

Walton, Gregory M., and Geoffrey L. Cohen. 2011. "A Brief Social-Belonging Intervention Improves Academic and Health Outcomes of Minority Students." *Science* 331 (6023): 1447–51.

Williams, David R., and Selina A. Mohammed. 2013. "Racism and Health I: Pathways and Scientific Evidence." *American Behavioral Scientist* 57 (8): 1152–73. 0002764213487340.

Wong, Carol A., Jacquelynne S. Eccles, and Arnold Sameroff. 2003. "The Influence of Ethnic Discrimination and Ethnic Identification on African American Adolescents' School and Socioemotional Adjustment." *Journal of Personality* 71 (6): 1197–232.

Immigrant Children and Children of Immigrants in American Schools

Shifting Demographics

EDELINA M. BURCIAGA, UNIVERSITY OF COLORADO, DENVER

EDITORS' NOTE

School is one of the first sustained points of contacts between immigrant children, as well as between the children of immigrants and the societies into which they've immigrated. As a result, school has long played an important role in the immigrant incorporation process, providing immigrant children and the children of immigrants with the opportunity to learn English as well as to learn about American culture and society. In fact, part of the reason Horace Mann's nineteenth-century arguments for the construction of "common schools" were so successful was because Mann's supporters saw these schools as a tool to help "Americanize" newcomers from Ireland, Italy, and eastern Europe.

For a long time, sociologists who were interested in immigration used the word **assimilation** to describe the immigrant incorporation process. For them, assimilation was an inevitable process in which immigrants slowly took on the characteristics of natives in their adopted countries. However, in an insight that mirrors intersectionality, some contemporary immigration scholars argue that this assimilation process is **segmented** and that in the United States, black and Latino immigrants may be particularly unlikely to incorporate into white American culture. Others, meanwhile, point out that the legal apparatus and the structure of schooling may shape immigrant incorporation trajectories, restricting undocumented students' access to equal educational opportunities and limiting their chances to gain full membership in American society.

KEY POINTS

- In the past, sociologists were confident that immigrants to the United States became more thoroughly assimilated into American society over time. Today, however, scholars are less confident about this pattern, worrying in particular that black and Latino immigrants are less likely to be assimilated into American society.
- While immigrant children often have high hopes for educational success, their experiences in school are highly variable.
- Even though the US Supreme Court holds that all children have a right to attend US public schools, regardless of their immigration status, undocumented immigrant youth face particular challenges in US schools.

INTRODUCTION

Immigrants and the immigrant experience are a foundational topic of study in American sociology. Continuous immigration flows over the twentieth and twenty-first centuries provide a rich source for understanding the social processes that shape integration into American society. In 2014, more than 42 million immigrants were living in the United States, including people from an array of countries across the globe, such as India, China, Mexico, Canada, and the Philippines (Zong, Batalova, and Hallock 2018). There are currently 2.1 million first-generation immigrant children living in the United States, and another 15.4 million children live with at least one immigrant parent (Zong, Batalova, and Hallock 2018). In the sociology of immigration, adults who move to the United States are considered first-generation immigrants. In order to completely understand the educational experiences of immigrant children, it is important to distinguish between the second generation (United States–born children of immigrant parents), the 1.5 generation (immigrant children who arrived as babies or very young children), and recently arrived immigrant children (children born in another country who enter school in the United States upon arrival).

While immigrant children arrive in the United States under a variety of circumstances, these newcomers share one central experience: participation in school. For immigrant children, school isn't just a place to learn academic knowledge: it is also a key socializing experience. In school, immigrant children develop their first relationships beyond their families in their new home country. Through day-to-day interactions with their teachers and peers, immigrant children begin to acquire the educational, language, and cultural skills that will help them navigate their lives in the United States (Suarez-Orozco, Suarez-Orozco, and Todorova 2008). This chapter's central questions focus on various aspects of the immigrant experience in schools in the United States: How have immigrant children fared in US public schools over time? What policies and practices affect immigrant children and children of immigrants? Finally, how does immigration status shape immigrant children's educational opportunities and experiences?

TODAY'S IMMIGRANT STUDENTS

Immigrant children and their families are a diverse group. They arrive in the United States with various educational, economic, and social resources. While previous research shows that, in general, immigrants are a highly motivated and self-selective group (Feliciano 2006), the political and legal context in which immigrants arrive significantly shapes immigrant children's educational aspirations and expectations.

Immigrant children can arrive in the United States with visas, as refugees, without legal permission (undocumented), and as unaccompanied minors. These categories are known as "immigration status"; and as researchers have demonstrated, children's status matters for educational outcomes. A discussion of undocumented immigrant children will highlight the role of legal status in shaping educational experiences.

Immigration laws and policies, in addition to educational policies, are crucial to understanding the schooling experiences of immigrant children. For example, studies show that for undocumented immigrant children, the legal uncertainty they face when graduating from high school lowers educational expectations for some and not for others (Gonzales 2015). Regardless of immigration status, immigrant children must, upon arrival, acclimate to a broad array of new social experiences. This may include learning a new language and a new culture, getting used to a different classroom experience, and meeting new teachers and peers. This process of socialization has been a primary focus of immigration scholars (Alba and Nee 2003; Portes and Rumbaut 2014) and is called assimilation and/or integration.

For both immigrant children and the children of immigrants, the integration process happens primarily in school, both inside and outside of the classroom. Theories of immigration integration provide a way for us to understand if and how immigrants are becoming a part of the United States and whether they are "fitting in" (Kao, Vaquera, and Goyette 2013). Sociologists have adopted three approaches for understanding immigrant assimilation: straight-line, or classic, assimilation theory; segmented assimilation theory; and new assimilation theory. Each of these approaches permits key insights into the experiences of both children of immigrants and immigrant children.

THE INTEGRATION OF THE NEW "SECOND GENERATION"

Before 1965, the vast majority of immigrants to the United States were from Europe. While these immigrants encountered challenges when integrating into the American mainstream, the eventual incorporation of this group of primarily white immigrants formed the basis of classic assimilation theory. Sociologists Robert Park and Ernest Burgess are credited with applying the concept of assimilation to describe the experiences of southern and eastern European immigrants in the early twentieth century (Rumbaut 2015). In this theoretical approach, it was assumed that assimilation was inevitable (e.g., with each generation, immigrants became more "American"); zero-sum (e.g., immigrants lost their language, cultural practices, and traditions); and natural (e.g., the process was believed to happen organically through social interaction). As a result, assimilation became synonymous with a process of Americanization; it was an option most readily available to children of European immigrants. Rooted in classic assimilation theory, straight-line assimilation theory proposed that as the children of immigrants adapted to and integrated into American culture, they would experience upward social mobility—a desirable outcome. Straight-line assimilation is described as a linear process of assimilation and was measured both by upward mobility and by a lack of distinction from the white American population. Theories of assimilation often suggest a tendency toward intergenerational progress, predicting that second-generation immigrants (children born in the United States to immigrant parents) will be better assimilated than 1.5-generation immigrants (children who arrived as babies or very young children) and recently arrived immigrant children (children born in another country who enter school in the United States upon arrival).

Classic assimilation and, relatedly, straight-line assimilation theory, as defined by a process of Americanization, have largely fallen out of favor in sociology. Yet sociologists recognize that "this social science concept [assimilation] offers the best way to understand and describe the integration into the mainstream experienced across generations by many individuals and ethnic groups, even if it cannot be regarded as a universal outcome of American life" (Alba and Nee 1997: 827). Contemporary sociological debates focus on the shifting demographics of the immigrant population in the United States and how race and social location shape the integration experiences of adult immigrants and their children. Building on classic assimilation theory, both segmented assimilation theory and new assimilation theory offer a more nuanced perspective on immigrant integration. While both theories account for the shifting demographics of immigration in the twentieth and twenty-first centuries, they differ in their predictions about the trajectories for second-generation immigrants.

Patterns of immigration to the United States changed dramatically after the passage of the Immigration and Nationality Act of 1965, which implemented a new system of immigration quotas that were evenly distributed across all countries. Post-1965 immigration was largely non-European and changed the face of migration to the United States, as most immigrants in this period migrated from Asia and Latin America. This demographic shift invited new ways of thinking about the assimilation of the new second generation, or United States–born children of immigrants. Recognizing this demographic shift, some sociologists argue that black, Asian, and Latino immigrants face vastly different circumstances precisely because of their racial/ethnic background and the ongoing disappearance of working-class occupations in American society at large (Portes and Zhou 1993).

Segmented assimilation theory captures the varied possible outcomes of the adaptation process for immigrants who are associated with stigmatized racial groups. Central to segmented assimilation theory is the acknowledgment that race plays a key role in determining social acceptance in the United States, and that racialized immigrants and their children are subject to the same structural barriers that limit social mobility among established, nonimmigrant minority groups. Just as the second generation can experience upward social and economic mobility, segmented assimilation theory suggests that members of the second generation can experience downward assimilation by, for example, dropping out of school, joining a gang, or entering into the criminal justice system.

Moving beyond the upward- and downward-assimilation binary, segmented assimilation theory suggests that the most beneficial trajectory for immigrant children and children of immigrants is a process of *selective acculturation.* Selective acculturation is characterized by a lack of conflict between immigrant parents and their children, full bilingualism, and preservation of immigrant values and norms. Individuals who have selectively acculturated do better in school, have higher expectations for their futures, and have higher self-esteem (Portes and Rumbaut 2001). While selective acculturation is a worthy ideal, sociologists disagree about the inevitability of downward assimilation for racialized groups.

The most recent iteration of assimilation theory is new assimilation theory, which also examines the integration experiences of the new second generation (the children of post-1965 immigrants) but proposes a more optimistic assimilation trajectory, including gradual social inclusion and upward mobility (Alba and Nee 2003). While segmented assimilation theory suggests that downward assimilation is one possibly trajectory, studies find very little support for second-generation decline or downward assimilation (Kasinitz et al. 2008; Waldinger and Feliciano 2004). Further research distinguishes between three types of acculturation: dissonant, selective, and consonant. Dissonant acculturation occurs when children adopt American ways far faster than their parents, introducing a cultural wedge between generations. This style of acculturation, which is associated with downward mobility in the second generation, "is the exception, not the norm, among the new second generation" (Waters et al. 2010: 1185). Consonant acculturation, which occurs when children and their parents assimilate together, and selective acculturation, which occurs when parents and children learn about American ways but retain ties to their ethnic community, are far more common patterns. This is important precisely because immigrant children and children of immigrants who are able to maintain their home language, culture, and positive relationship with their immigrant parents are poised to thrive in an increasingly globalized world. Nevertheless, what the research about immigrant children shares with research about children of immigrants is the recognition that schools, as social institutions, are integral to creating an environment where immigrant children can adapt to American culture while maintaining valuable aspects of their home and family cultures.

HOW DO RESEARCHERS STUDY THE EDUCATIONAL EXPERIENCES OF IMMIGRANT CHILDREN IN SCHOOLS?

Researchers who examine the school experiences of immigrant children and children of immigrants use surveys, observation, and in-depth interviews to understand their educational outcomes and experiences. In addition to national data sets, researchers have conducted original and long-term studies of immigrant children and children of immigrants, focusing on cities with large immigrant populations. Studies of particular regions or cities are especially useful because they can explore the ways in which assimilation experiences vary between immigrant groups and across different social *contexts*. Studies in this tradition have collected data about immigrant children and children of immigrants in cities and regions across the United States, including Los Angeles and San Diego, California; Miami, Florida; and New York City. In addition, these studies have examined the experiences of immigrant children and children of immigrants from a variety of countries, including Mexico, El Salvador, Guatemala, Honduras, Haiti, the Dominican Republic, China, and Russia.

How Do Immigrant Children Fare in School?

For immigrant parents, the experience of migration can be traumatic as they leave behind family or other social networks and must learn to navigate a new language and culture. Some immigrant parents may experience a significant downward shift in terms of jobs or social status. One way children of immigrants can redeem their parents' sacrifices is by doing well in school, attending college, and eventually securing a good job. This has been referred to as the "immigrant bargain" and may explain why some immigrant children and children of immigrants have high academic and college-going expectations.

Educational research shows that people's academic expectations—that is, what they anticipate achieving in school—are important for how hard they work and what they eventually accomplish in school, or their educational attainment (Domina, Conley, and Farkas 2011; Feliciano 2006). Both children of immigrants and immigrant children tend to develop unusually high educational expectations, motivated in part by the immigrant bargain and in part by the perception of better educational opportunities available in the United States. This sense of optimism is known as the immigrant advantage; it is paradoxical given the likelihood of limited language abilities and knowledge of American schooling that immigrant children and children of immigrants bring with them into the classroom. While there is much less agreement about whether these expectations are fully realized, higher educational ambitions may explain—to some degree—the academic achievement of immigrant children and children of immigrants. As one study shows, when comparing native-born and immigrant children, the latter are more likely to expect to attend graduate school (Feliciano and Lanuza 2015). This same study demonstrates that these higher educational expectations highlight the important cultural resources that immigrant families bring with them to the United States (Feliciano and Lanuza 2015). This is important because immigrant families are often viewed as having limited resources to offer their children, especially in the context of school.

While previous research firmly establishes that children of immigrants have high educational expectations, it is important to understand that not all immigrant children and children of immigrants are "super-achieving." This is due in part to several mediating factors, including family structure, socioeconomic status, immigration status, parents' premigration education, and neighborhood and school contexts. In order to completely understand the educational experiences of immigrant children, it is important to distinguish between the second generation (children of immigrants born in the United States to immigrant parents), the 1.5 generation (immigrant children who arrived as babies or young children), and recently arrived immigrant children (children born in another country who enter school in the United States upon arrival). Unlike the former two groups of students, recently arrived immigrant children who enter school must often contend with a new language as well as a new academic and social culture in school. Often this group of children figures most prominently in the public's imagination when the subject of immigrant children in schools comes up.

For example, one study shows that recently arrived immigrant children generally fall into four groups: declining achievers, low achievers, improvers, and high achievers (Suarez-Orozco, Suarez-Orozco, and Todorova 2008). Similarly, research shows that undocumented immigrant youth fall into two groups: college-goers and early exiters (Gonzales 2015). While these studies examine different groups of immigrant children and children of immigrants, each study concludes that a complex set of factors shapes schooling experiences and outcomes. Among the most important factors, however, are school, neighborhood, and family contexts.

Immigrant children and children of immigrants, like all students, enter schools that vary in quality. Unfortunately, immigrant students who may need the most help acclimating to school life in the United States settle in neighborhoods segregated by race and poverty. As a result, the schools these students enter are characterized by high teacher and staff turnover and a lack of resources. Schools profoundly shape the academic engagement and performance of immigrant children, as school is the institution with which immigrant children have the most sustained interaction. However, research also suggests that a host of premigration and familial factors are also important for understanding the educational experiences and achievement of both immigrant children and children of immigrants.

Sociologists and education scholars agree that family structure, parental education, and parental employment all play significant roles in shaping the educational opportunities and experiences of immigrant children. Immigrant families take many forms, but those children who have both parents in the home and/or access to other adult caregivers can catalyze more resources of support. In addition, premigration status, or the selectivity of immigrant groups before migrating, can also shape the educational expectations of children of immigrants, as research shows that both individual and group premigration status can increase the educational expectations of immigrant children and children of immigrants (Feliciano 2006). As noted earlier in the chapter, educational expectations are a significant predictor of academic achievement. While many immigrant parents, even highly educated parents, experience a downward trajectory upon migration to the United States, those parents who have greater human capital (i.e., better-paying or high-status jobs or access to strategic goods) are better able to facilitate their children's adaptation (Portes and Rumbaut 2001). In the past thirty years, immigration or citizenship status has become a significant factor in shaping the educational experiences of immigrant children and children of immigrants.

Undocumented Immigrant Children

In *Plyler v. Doe* in 1982, the Supreme Court of the United States challenged the implementation of a fee in the state of Texas that was charged only to undocumented immigrants, which, the court ruled, effectively excluded the children of these immigrants from public education. Justice Lewis F. Powell, who wrote the court's opinion, argued that denying undocumented immigrant children access to public education would contribute to the "creation of a permanent caste of undocumented residents" (Lopez 2005: 1401). The opinion reflected a tacit acknowledgment of the importance of education in creating a pathway to upward social mobility; in the case of undocumented children, the ruling aimed to avoid a state-sanctioned downward trajectory. While *Plyler* was a landmark legal decision for undocumented immigrant children, it unwittingly invited the question of what might happen as undocumented immigrant youth graduate from high school.

Most of the research about the lives of undocumented immigrant youth has focused on the transition from high school, which marks the end of a long period of legal protection. After high school, undocumented young people may face diminishing returns because there is no guarantee that when they graduate from college they will be able to use their degree to work. In addition, undocumented immigrant youth do not qualify for federal financial aid. As a result, tuition policies granting undocumented youth in-state tuition rates are a key policy intervention that can either ease or block college attendance. Currently, seventeen states have laws permitting eligible undocumented students to pay in-state tuition: California, Colorado, Connecticut, Florida, Illinois, Kansas, Maryland, Minnesota, Nebraska, New Jersey, New Mexico, New York, Oklahoma, Oregon, Texas, Utah, and Washington (see figure 7). In addition, four state university systems—Rhode Island, Hawaii, Michigan, and Oklahoma—offer in-state tuition rates to undocumented students. In contrast, six states bar undocumented immigrants from paying in-state tuition: Alabama, Arizona, Georgia, Indiana, Missouri, and South Carolina. Current research suggests that policies that deny undocumented students in-state tuition significantly reduce college-going among this cohort in those states (Bozick, Miller, and Kaneshiro 2015).

While most of the research about the educational experiences of undocumented immigrant youth in the United States focuses on those who are college-bound or are enrolled in college, only about seven thousand to thirteen thousand undocumented youth attend college annually, and an even smaller number graduate. The vast majority are early exiters, undocumented young adults who may graduate from high school yet never make it to college. For these undocumented young people, several factors influence their post–high school pathways, including being pushed out of school, financial responsibilities, and significant legal and cost obstacles to college attendance. In contrast, "college-goers" are able to harness support from teachers, counselors, citizen friends, and other undocumented youth to overcome the barriers to college attendance.

Earning a college degree may set undocumented immigrant youth on a pathway to social mobility, but challenges still remain. In 2012, President Barack Obama announced the Deferred Action for Childhood Arrivals (DACA) program, which allows eligible undocumented young adults to apply for a work permit and avoid deportation. Early research suggests that undocumented young adults benefit in multiple ways from this program in social, economic, and psychological terms, whether it leads to obtaining a driver's license, securing a better job, or lifting the fear of deportation (Wong et al. 2017).

The DACA program does not provide a pathway to citizenship, however, and research suggests that undocumented young adults remain uncertain about their futures (Gonzales and Burciaga 2018). Further driving this uncertainty has been the Trump administration's efforts to end DACA in 2018, reflecting the contentious political climate surrounding immigration and immigration reform efforts such as DACA. There is considerable public and political disagreement about the best solution for the eleven million undocumented immigrants currently living in the United States. However, according to a 2017 news poll by the *Washington Post* and *ABC News,* 86 percent of Americans support "a program that allows an undocumented immigrant to stay in the United States if they arrived here as a child, completed high school or military service, and have not committed a serious crime."

RESEARCH FRONTIERS

There is value in distinguishing between children of immigrants, the 1.5 generation, and recent arrivals. While these children and youth may share the experience of being the children of immigrants, their experiences in American schools are, by nature, different. They will negotiate different opportunities, obligations, and adaptations that are integral for understanding how and why some immigrant children and children of immigrants experience educational success and others do not. Future research should continue to consider the various experiences of first-generation immigrant children and of 1.5-generation and second-generation children of immigrants. Building on the diversity of experiences of immigrant children and children of immigrants, future research should continue to examine how immigrant groups vary by country of origin, premigration family and group status, and across the school spectrum.

As I discuss in this chapter, immigration status—specifically an undocumented status—significantly shapes educational opportunities and challenges. The absence of a comprehensive immigration solution has resulted in a fractured legal landscape. These fractures apply not only to college access policies but also to a number of policies that can make the everyday lives of undocumented immigrant children and their families better—or worse. While preliminary research suggests that laws restricting college access for undocumented students and/or requiring these students to pay out-of-state tuition have negative consequences for their postsecondary trajectories, more research is needed to illuminate the role of local and state laws and policies in influencing the educational experiences and academic achievement of undocumented immigrant children and youth. In addition, much of the research about undocumented immigrant children and youth has focused on high-achieving students who are college-bound or are in enrolled in college. Future research in this area should examine the experiences of middle- and high-school-aged

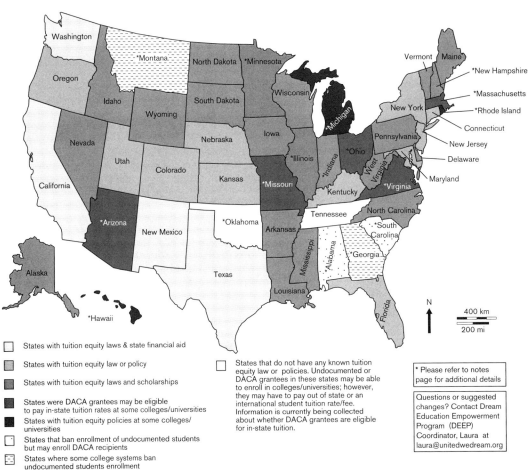

Tuition and State Aid Equity for Undocumented Students and DACA Grantees | Access by State
*Notes|May 2014

States with tuition equity laws & state financial aid

States with tuition equity law or policy

States with tuition equity laws and scholarships

States were DACA grantees may be eligible to pay in-state tuition rates at some colleges/universities

States with tuition equity policies at some colleges/universities

States that ban enrollment of undocumented students but may enroll DACA recipients

States where some college systems ban undocumented students enrollment

States that do not have any known tuition equity law or policies. Undocumented or DACA grantees in these states may be able to enroll in colleges/universities; however, they may have to pay out of state or an international student tuition rate/fee. Information is currently being collected about whether DACA grantees are eligible for in-state tuition.

* Please refer to notes page for additional details

Questions or suggested changes? Contact Dream Education Empowerment Program (DEEP) Coordinator, Laura at laura@unitedwedream.org

Figure 7. Tuition and state aid policy for undocumented students, May 2014. Source: reproduced with permission from United We Dream, http://unitedwedream.org/wp-content/uploads/2012/09/DEEPTuitionEquityMapMay2014merged.pdf.

Tuition and State Aid Equity for Undocumented Students and DACA Grantees | Access by State
*Notes|May 2014

Questions or suggested changes? Contact DREAM Education Empowerment Program Coordinator, Laura laura@unitedwedream.org

	Montana (MT)-Bans the enrollment of undocumented students, however the public university system has declared that it is not bound by the initiative of banning enrollment and intends to admit eligible students regardless of their status **Georgia (GA)-**Bans undocumented students from the top five public universities (Georgia State University, Georgia Institute of Technology, GeorgiaCollege of Medicine, University of Georgia, Georgia College & State University)
	Minnesota (MN)-In-state tuition and private institutional scholarships for students who meet certain criteria, regardless of their status **Illinois (IL)**-Provides in-state tuition and funding (IL Dream Fund)
	Arizona (AZ)-Pima Community College System and Maricopa Community College System enroll DACA recipients at in-state tuition rates **Ohio (OH)**-Board or Regents decision provides in-state to DACA recipients at state colleges and universities **Missouri (MO)**-University of Missouri Kansas City began enrolling DACA recipients at in-state rates fall 2013. Also, community colleges in the Kansas City metro and St, Louis area are enrolling DACA recipients **Massachusetts (MA)**-Undocumented immigrants who qualify for DACA should receive tuition breaks at the 29 public colleges and universities in Massachusetts **New Hampshire (NH)**-University of New Hampshire enrolls DACA recipients at in-state tuition rates **Virginia (VA)**-Virginia Attorney General concluded on 4/29/14 that no provision of state or federal law precludes individuals approved under DACA from forming subjective domiciliary intent to remain in Virginia; they are capable of establishing domicile and qualifying for in-state tuition in accordance with Virginia code §23-7.4
	Michigan (MI)-University of Michigan's (UM) Board of Regents decision provides in-state tuition to undocumented students at UM and their flagship Ann Arbor campus and satellites in Flint and Dearborn. Some of these universities may also provide financial aid. Eastern Michigan University and Wayne State are also providing in-state tuition to undocumented students. **Hawaii (HI)**-University of Hawaii's Board of Regents decision provides in-state tuition and financial assistance to eligible students regardless of status **Rhode Island (RI)**-Board of Governors decision provides in-state tuition at State colleges and universities
	Alabama (AL)-Bans the enrollment of undocumented students, however, enrolls DACA recipients at in-state tuition rates at community colleges and the following universities: University of Alabama in Huntsville, University of AL in Birmingham, University of AL in Tuscaloosa, University of Montevallo, University of Troy in Dothan, University of Troy in Troy. Auburn University at Montgomery and Auburn University at Auburn **South Carolina (SC)**-Bans the enrollment of undocumented students, however, enrolls DACA recipients. In-state tuition rates have yet to be resolved
	Indiana (IN)-In 2011, the state passed HB 1402 that requires that students be lawfully present to receive in-state tuition benefits at state colleges and Universities. In 2013, SB 207 passed which ensures that those students who had already been enrolled before implementation of HB 1402 would still have access to in-state tuition. Thus, SB 207 states that students enrolled in State postsecondary educational institutions as of July 1, 2011 are eligible to pay in-state tuition rates without needing to verify status. Due to both of these laws Indiana denies in-state tuition to a *majority* of undocumented students, particularly new students.

NOTE: The above listings are some but not all of the states/institutions that make in-state tuition rates available to students with DACA. Information is still being gathered; if you have any questions, changes or additions to make please contact DEEP Coordinator (information above).

undocumented youth across the achievement spectrum to better understand the educational pathways of undocumented immigrant children.

IMPLICATIONS FOR PRACTICE AND POLICY

As I have discussed throughout this chapter, the integration of immigrant children and children of immigrants depends on a complex set of factors. While many of the influences that shape the educational experiences and academic outcomes of these children occur outside the schoolhouse doors, schools are integral institutions in the lives of this group. It is in school that immigrant children and children of immigrants learn the formal and informal norms of schooling in the United States. There are key policies and practices that schools can implement and which facilitate a process of selective acculturation, assisting in the maintenance of language and other valuable characteristics and qualities that immigrant families bring with them to the United States.

Dual-Immersion and Language Maintenance Programs

While immigrant children and their parents are eager to learn English, in an increasingly globalized world the ability to speak a language other than English is an asset. Schools should strive to support the English-language development of immigrant children, especially recent arrivals, but not at the expense of their native language. Dual-language immersion programs—programs in which students who speak primarily English are placed in the same classroom with students who primarily speak another language—offer a promising model for considering how students can be a resource for each other. Dual-immersion and language maintenance programs, with supplemental support for developing English proficiency for immigrant children, are pragmatic approaches to an often emotionally charged issue.

Promoting Selective Acculturation

In the twenty-first century, immigrant children and children of immigrants experience "transnationalism of the heart" (Suarez-Orozco, Suarez-Orozco, and Todorova 2008: 371). They maintain ties to their home countries either through connection to family who remain there or by visiting regularly. Despite these sustained connections, immigrant children and children of immigrants are also deeply connected to the United States. Much like language maintenance, facilitating the development of a hybrid identity is a realistic approach to an uncommon benefit that immigrant children and children of immigrants have: the ability to navigate an increasingly multicultural world.

Understanding the Role of Immigration Status

Approximately 5.5 million children in the United States have at least one undocumented parent, and another 1 million children (under the age of eighteen) are undocumented themselves. Because of the *Plyler v. Doe* decision, K–12 schools are a legal, safe haven for undocumented immigrant children and children with an undocumented parent. In this regard, school staff and teachers are often the primary point of contact for these families. While it is crucial that policy makers regularize the status of undocumented students, we must also work to increase educators' knowledge of the role that an undocumented status plays in the day-to-day educational experiences of young people. Furthermore, we need to provide better information to undocumented young people about the educational opportunities they do have. In states like California, which has had in-state tuition laws for nearly ten years, undocumented youth still report that they are told that they cannot attend college because of their undocumented status. Helping students and their teachers better understand the challenges—as well as the opportunities—facing undocumented young people has the potential to narrow one of the most important axes of inequality in contemporary America.

CHAPTER 5 REVIEW

Discussion Questions

1. How do straight-line assimilation, segmented assimilation, and selective acculturation differ? Why do sociologists of education propose that selective acculturation is the most beneficial process of integrating immigrant children and children of immigrants?

2. Why is it important to distinguish between the educational experiences of the second generation (children born in the United States and who have at least one immigrant parent) and first-generation immigrant children (those who migrate to the United States and enter school)?

3. What is paradoxical about the high educational expectations of immigrant children and children of immigrants? How does the "immigrant bargain" shape educational expectations?

4. How does being undocumented influence the schooling experiences of immigrant children?

5. Undocumented immigrant youth face legal uncertainty; consider how living with this type of uncertainty might shape your educational experiences.

Suggestions for Further Reading

Feliciano, Cynthia, and Yader R. Lanuza. 2015. "The Immigrant Advantage in Adolescent Educational Expectations." *International Migration Review* 50 (3): 758–92.

Gonzales, Roberto G. 2015. *Lives in Limbo: Undocumented and Coming of Age in America.* Berkeley: University of California Press.

Kasinitz, Philip, John H. Mollenkopf, Mary C. Waters, and Jennifer Holdaway. 2008. *Inheriting the City: The Children of Immigrants Come of Age.* New York: Russell Sage Foundation.

Portes, Alejandro, and Rubén G. Rumbaut. 2001. *Legacies: The Story of the Immigrant Second Generation.* Berkeley: University of California Press.

Suarez-Orozco, Carola, Marcelo M. Suarez-Orozco, and Irina Todorova. 2008. *Learning a New Land: Immigrant Students in American Society.* Cambridge, MA: Harvard University Press.

References

Alba, Richard, and Victor Nee. 1997. "Rethinking Assimilation Theory for a New Era of Immigration." *International Migration Review* 31 (4): 826–74.

———. 2003. *Remaking the American Mainstream: Assimilation and Contemporary Immigration.* Cambridge, MA: Harvard University Press.

Bozick, Robert, Trey Miller, and Matheu Kaneshiro. 2015. "Non-citizen Mexican Youth in U.S. Higher Education: A Closer

Look at the Relationship between State Tuition Policies and College Enrollment." *International Migration Review* 50 (4): 864–89.

Clement, Scott, and David Nakamura. 2017. "Survey Finds Strong Support for Dreamers." *Washington Post,* September 24. www.washingtonpost.com/politics/survey-finds-strong-support-for-dreamers/2017/09/24/df3c885c-a16f-11e7-b14f-f41773cd5a14_story.html?utm_term=.8167c8775603.

Domina, Thurston, AnneMarie Conley, and George Farkas. 2011. "The Link between Educational Expectations and Effort in the College-for-All Era." *Sociology of Education* 84 (2): 93–112.

Feliciano, Cynthia. 2006. "Beyond the Family: The Influence of Pre-migration Group Status on the Educational Expectations of Immigrants' Children." *Sociology of Education* 79 (4): 281–303.

Feliciano, Cynthia, and Yader R. Lanuza. 2015. "The Immigrant Advantage in Adolescent Educational Expectations." *International Migration Review* 50 (3): 758–92.

Gonzales, Roberto G. 2011. "Learning to be Illegal: Undocumented Youth and Shifting Legal Contexts in the Transition to Adulthood." *American Sociological Review* 76 (4): 602–19.

———. 2015. *Lives in Limbo: Undocumented and Coming of Age in America.* Berkeley: University of California Press.

Gonzales, Roberto G., and Edelina M. Burciaga. 2018. "Segmented Pathways of Illegality: Reconciling the Coexistence of Master and Auxiliary Statuses in the Experiences of the 1.5-Generation Undocumented Young Adults." *Ethnicities* 18 (2): 178–91.

Kao, Grace, Elizabeth Vaquera, and Kimberly Goyette. 2013. *Education and Immigration.* Malden, MA: Polity Press.

Kasinitz, Philip, John H. Mollenkopf, Mary C. Waters, and Jennifer Holdaway. 2008. *Inheriting the City: The Children of Immigrants Come of Age.* New York: Russell Sage Foundation.

Lopez, Maria. 2005. "Reflections on Educating Latino and Latina Undocumented Children: Beyond *Plyler v. Doe.*" *Seton Hall Law Review* 35 (4): 1373–1406.

Portes, Alejandro, and Rubén G. Rumbaut. 2001. *Legacies: The Story of the Immigrant Second Generation.* Berkeley: University of California Press.

———. 2014. *Immigrant America: A Portrait.* Berkeley: University of California Press.

Portes, Alejandro, and Min Zhou. 1993. "The New Second Generation: Segmented Assimilation and Its Variants." *Annals of the American Academy of Political and Social Science* 530: 74–96.

Rumbaut, Rubén. 2015. "Assimilation of Immigrants." In *International Encyclopedia of the Social and Behavioral Sciences,* 2nd ed., edited by James D. Wright, 2:81–87. Oxford: Elsevier.

Suarez-Orozco, Carola, Marcelo M. Suarez-Orozco, and Irina Todorova. 2008. *Learning a New Land: Immigrant Students in American Society.* Cambridge, MA: Harvard University Press.

Waldinger, Roger, and Cynthia Feliciano. 2004. "Will the New Second Generation Experience 'Downward Assimilation'? Segmented Assimilation Re-assessed." *Ethnic and Racial Studies* 27 (3): 376–402.

Waters, Mary C., Van C. Tran, Phillip Kasinitz, and John H. Mollenkopf. 2010. "Segmented Assimilation Theory Revisited: Types of Acculturation and Socioeconomic Mobility in Young Adulthood." *Ethnic and Racial Studies* 33 (7): 1168–93.

Wong, Tom K., Greisa Martinez Rosas, Adam Luna, Henry Manning, Adrian Reyna, Patrick O'Shea, Tom Jawetz, and Philip E. Wolgin. 2017. *DACA Recipients' Economic and Educational Outcomes Continue to Grow.* Washington, DC: Center for American Progress.

Zong, Jie, Jeanne Batalova, and Jeffrey Hallock. 2018. *Frequently Requested Statistics on Immigrants and Immigration in the United States.* Washington, DC: Migration Policy Institute. www.migrationpolicy.org/article/frequently-requested-statistics-immigrants-and-immigration-united-states# Numbers.

Sexualities in Education

1

C. J. PASCOE, UNIVERSITY OF OREGON

TONY SILVA, NORTHWESTERN UNIVERSITY

EDITORS' NOTE

We often think of schools as places where kids learn to read and write, and we often conceptualize their consequences in economic terms. But it's clear that they are more than that. In chapter 3, Riegle-Crumb provided examples of how schools help shape students' conceptions of what it means to be a boy or a girl. In chapter 4, Eschmann and Payne told us about how schools help create race and perpetuate racial hierarchies.

University of Oregon sociologist C. J. Pascoe and Northwestern sociologist Tony Silva point out that schools are also profoundly sexual institutions. Intentionally or not, schools often reinforce the idea that heterosexual relationships are the norm, and that same-sex relationships are abnormal or even deviant. Schools do so via both **hidden** and **explicit curricula.** Can you think of explicit lessons—perhaps in sex education or literature classes— that you've been exposed to that conveyed ideas about what hetero- or homosexuality is? Can you think of instances in which you learned similar lessons, not via classroom instruction, but by the way your school was organized or by means of things you heard teachers say (or not say) in offhand remarks?

You might also notice in this case study that Pascoe and Silva use evidence very differently than many of the authors you've encountered so far. What can these qualitative data tell you that the quantitative data you encountered in the tables elsewhere in the book cannot?

KEY POINTS

- Educational institutions are a key part of the heterosexualizing process.
- Formal and informal curricula, institutional practices, and students' peer groups socialize students into (hetero)sexual meanings.
- Schools can be hostile environments for sexual- and gender-minority students.

SCENES FROM A HIGH SCHOOL

I recently visited River High School, a working-class suburban school in Northern California, on National Coming Out Day.[1] In preparation for National Coming Out Day, which happened to fall on the same day as the school's homecoming football game and a related schoolwide pep rally, several of the students from River High's Gay/Straight Alliance created shirts that read "Nobody Knows I'm a Lesbian" or "Nobody Knows I'm Gay" to wear to the homecoming assembly.

The rally consisted of six homecoming princesses competing in skits to be elected as that year's homecoming queen. The final skit of the homecoming rally, titled "All for You," featured seven girls in tight jeans and black tank tops dancing suggestively, and each grabbing a boy, as Janet Jackson sang, "How many nights I've laid in bed excited over you / I've closed my eyes and thought of us a hundred different ways / I've gotten there so many times I wonder how bout you. . . . If I was your girl / Oh the things I'd do to you / I'd make you call out my name." The girls walked up behind the boys and ran their hands down the fronts of the boys' bodies. They turned the boys around and made them kneel in front of them so that the boys were facing the girls' crotches, took the boys' heads in two hands, and moved them around as the girls wiggled their hips into the boys' faces. This skit followed two others featuring homecoming princesses performing similar, slightly less sexually explicit, dances.

After the homecoming rally and its celebration of heterosexuality, Lacy, Genevieve, and Riley, all members of River High's Gay/Straight Alliance, ran up to me wearing all black with rainbow pins and belts. Given the alliance's preparations leading up to National Coming Out Day, I was wondering why they were not wearing their special gay pride T-shirts. I didn't have time to ask where their shirts were as they tumbled over each other, indignantly explaining to me what had happened. Lacy angrily unbuttoned her sweater, revealing her black-and-white "Nobody Knows I'm a Lesbian" T-shirt, and said, "Mr. Hobart [the school principal] came up to me and said I have to cover this shirt up. I couldn't wear it!" Riley and Genevieve, equally resentful, cried, "He made me take mine off, too!" Riley unfolded the shirt she had painted in rainbow colors. Lacy, incensed, cried, "And look what they can do up there! All grinding against each other and stuff! And I can't wear this shirt!"

---

1. Adapted from C. J. Pascoe's book *Dude, You're a Fag: Masculinity and Sexuality in High School, with a New Preface* (Berkeley: University of California Press, 2011).

When I asked Genevieve later why the girls could not wear the shirts, she explained,

'Cause this school says that if you are wearing a shirt saying that you're a lesbian, that says that you are supposedly having sexual acts with the same sex. I find that stupid, because what if someone was walking around saying, "Hey, I'm a heterosexual"? Does that mean that you're sexually active? I was very, very, very angry that day. 'Cause that was the homecoming assembly day, my God! Did you see what those girls were doing? Not that I was complaining, but I did have a complaint toward the authority of the school. The school will let chicks rub their crotches and shake their asses in front of all these students in the school. Like, nastiness; but my girlfriend can't wear a "Nobody Knows I'm a Lesbian" shirt.

While the principal may have argued that the problem was not homosexuality but sexual activity, the explicitly sexual displays in the homecoming skits indicated that something more than concern over sexual activity was at play. It seemed, given this incident, that the school had very little problem with students addressing sex as long as they focused on heterosexuality. Explicit expressions of heterosexual sexuality, such as sensual dance moves, skits that tell stories about heterosexual relationships, and in fact an entire homecoming ritual based on male and female pairings, were sanctioned, whereas expressions that challenge such an order, like T-shirts expressing alternative identities, were banned.

This situation is not unique to River High School. This case study explores the way that schools in the United States set up particular sexual orders that typically affirm heterosexuality and normative masculinity and femininity.

INTRODUCTION

While we tend to focus on schools' academic functions, schools are also fundamentally sexual institutions. In the West, most schools—public, private, and religious—promote specific sexual practices and relationship forms, particularly heterosexual penetrative sex within the confines of a committed monogamous relationship (preferably sanctioned by marriage). The ways in which schools promote normative sexual practices, identities, and expressions are often so mundane, everyday, and taken-for-granted that children and adolescents do not realize that schools are helping create their frameworks for understanding and expressing sexuality.

Schools promote particular forms of sexual identities, practices, and norms through interrelated processes of homophobia, heterosexism, and heteronormativity. *Homophobia* refers to prejudice and discrimination against lesbian, gay, bisexual, transgender, and queer (LGBTQ) individuals (Bridges and Pascoe 2016; Doan, Loehr, and Miller 2014). *Heterosexism* is the ideology that heterosexuality is the only normal sexuality. Both reinforce practices and policies that institutionalize *heteronormativity,* the assumption that individuals are straight and that their gender identity matches up with their assigned biological sex. All these create particular expectations for, and demands and constraints on, how individuals identify and express their sexuality and gender. Schools set up formal and informal sexual practices through school rituals, pedagogical practices, and disciplinary procedures that reflect definitions of masculinity and femininity as opposite, complementary, unequal, and heterosexual, in what Judith Butler calls the "heterosexual matrix" (Butler 1993). Schools convey and regulate sexual meanings organized in ways that are heteronormative and homophobic. The heterosexualizing process organized by educational institutions from elementary school through high school cannot be separated from, and is central to, the development of masculine and feminine identities.

Gender and sexuality are distinct—and this case study focuses on sexuality—but institutional and individual practices often regulate gender normativity and heterosexuality simultaneously. They do so in part by encouraging the development of purportedly opposite and complementary gender practices—resulting in expressions of normative femininity for girls, and normative masculinity for boys—central to which are expressions of heterosexuality: girls should be interested exclusively in boys, and boys should be exclusively interested in girls, and the way they express these interests should be shaped by femininity and masculinity, respectively.

Educational institutions regulate sexualities through formal and informal curricula, including heteronormative framings of animal or human biology and sex education; institutional practices such as school disciplinary measures; bullying policies; school rituals; student-adult interactions; and decisions about the degree to which they permit and/or promote the Gay/Straight Alliance and other student groups concerned with equal rights.

There are some important terms to know for this case study. *Sex* refers to individuals' biological characteristics, such as chromosomes, genitalia, reproductive organs, and hormones. *Gender* is the set of social expectations about behavior, ideology, appearance, and disposition that are assigned to people of a given sex. In the West, gender is shaped by the cultural expectation that there are two purportedly opposite and complementary types of people—men and women—who should express themselves in masculine or feminine ways, respectively, depending on the sex they were assigned at birth. *Heterogender* is the way in which heterosexuality operates differently for men and women: for example, men should be aggressive, dominant, and highly interested in (heterosexual) sex; and women should be passive, submissive, and not nearly as interested in sex. *Hegemonic masculinity* is the dominant form of masculinity at a given time and place that guarantees the reproduction of patriarchy (Connell 1987).

EMPIRICAL FINDINGS

To date there has been relatively little research on the role of schools in shaping child and adolescent sexuality, but what research does exist points to the enforcement of heteronormativity and heterosexism through curricula, institutional practices, and students' social worlds. Studies use diverse research methods, including semistructured interviews, content analysis, ethnographies, and surveys. Much of the nationally representative survey research uses the National Longitudinal Study of Adolescent to Adult Health and its related study, the Adolescent Health and Academic Achievement Study, as well as the Youth Risk Behavior Survey.

Curricula

Schools reinforce heteronormativity and heterosexism through both informal and formal curricula. See chapter 9 by Patricia Bromley and Daniel Scott Smith for a more detailed discussion of the multiple forms of curricula. Formal curricula include educational goals, explicit messages in textbooks, learning objectives, and class assignments. It is what we think of as the work that occurs in schools. Informal curricula, also known as hidden curricula, are the norms, values, attitudes, and ideologies that children learn at school but that are not an official part of schools' lesson plans (Martin 1976).

Formal Curricula   Formal curricula emphasize heteronormativity and normative sexual practices, especially through sex education. Given the anemic and shifting federal regulation of sex education, it is highly varied and inconsistent across American states. As table 1 demonstrates, only twenty-four states and Washington, DC, require sex education in public schools; only thirty-three states and Washington, DC, require education about HIV/AIDS; and only twenty states require that sex education be medically accurate (NCSL 2016). Given such limited coverage and irregular standards, few youth are exposed to comprehensive sex education: among those aged fifteen to nineteen in 2011–2013, only 55 percent of men and 60 percent of women were taught about contraception, only 58 percent of men and 50 percent of women were taught how to use a condom, and fewer than half were taught where to access contraception (Lindberg, Maddow-Zimet, and Boonstra 2016; see also Guttmacher Institute 2016). The proportion of teens who receive comprehensive sex education actually declined between 2006 and 2013, especially in rural areas.

Currently most sex education curricula employ one of three main approaches:

1. Abstinence-only education, which teaches that abstinence is the only morally correct option for teenagers; it censors information about condoms and contraception.
2. Abstinence-plus education, which includes information about condoms and contraception in the context of strong abstinence messages.
3. Comprehensive sex education. which teaches about abstinence as the best method for avoiding sexually transmitted infections (STIs) and unintended pregnancy, but also teaches about condoms and contraception to reduce the risk of unintended pregnancy and of infection with STIs, including HIV. Comprehensive sex education also often teaches interpersonal and communication skills and helps young people explore their own values, goals, and options.

Since the 1980s, the federal government has provided hundreds of millions of dollars to abstinence-only-until-marriage education programs. Today, tens of millions of dollars per year are allocated under Title V of the Temporary Assistance for Needy Families Act, which requires that states contribute three dollars for every four federal dollars they receive (for a history of sex education in the United States, see SIECUS n.d.).

Until recently, to be eligible for funding, sex education programs had to follow an eight-point abstinence model, as outlined in section 510(b) of Title V of the Social

Table 1 State Policies on Sex Education in Schools

State	Be Age Appropriate	Be Culturally Appropriate and Unbiased	Cannot Promote Religion	Notice	Consent	Opt Out
Alabama	X					X
Arizona	X			HIV	Sex	HIV
California	X	X	X	X		X
Colorado	X	X		X		X
Connecticut						X
Delaware						
DC	X			X		X
Florida	X					X
Georgia				X		X
Hawaii	X					X
Idaho						X
Illinois	X					X
Indiana						
Iowa	X	X		X		X
Kentucky						
Louisiana	X		X	X		X
Maine	X					X
Maryland						X
Massachusetts				X		X
Michigan	X			X		X
Minnesota						X
Mississippi	X			X		X
Missouri	X			X		X
Montana						
Nevada	X			X	X	
New Hampshire						X
New Jersey	X	X		X		X
New Mexico						X
New York	HIV					HIV
North Carolina	X					
North Dakota						
Ohio						X
Oklahoma				X		X
Oregon	X	X		X		X
Pennsylvania	HIV			X		HIV
Rhode Island	X	X				X

Table 1 *(continued)*

State	Be Age Appropriate	Be Culturally Appropriate and Unbiased	Cannot Promote Religion	Notice	Consent	Opt Out
South Carolina	X			X		X
Tennessee	HIV					X
Texas	X			X		X
Utah		X		X	X	
Vermont	X					X
Virginia	X			X		X
Washington	X	X		X		X
West Virginia				X		X
Wisconsin				X		X
TOTAL	26+DC	8	2	22+DC	3	36+DC

SOURCE: "State Policies on Sex Education in Schools," National Conference of State Legislatures, December 21, 2016, www.ncsl.org/research/health/state-policies-on-sex-education-in-schools.aspx.

Security Act. This meant a program that "(A) has as its exclusive purpose, teaching the social, psychological, and health gains to be realized by abstaining from sexual activity; (B) teaches abstinence from sexual activity outside marriage as the expected standard for all school age children; (C) teaches that abstinence from sexual activity is the only certain way to avoid out-of-wedlock pregnancy, sexually transmitted diseases, and other associated health problems; (D) teaches that a mutually faithful monogamous relationship in [the] context of marriage is the expected standard of human sexual activity; (E) teaches that sexual activity outside of the context of marriage is likely to have harmful psychological and physical [side] effects; (F) teaches that bearing children out-of-wedlock is likely to have harmful consequences for the child, the child's parents, and society; (G) teaches young people how to reject sexual advances and how alcohol and drug use increases vulnerability to sexual advances; and (H) teaches the importance of attaining self-sufficiency before engaging in sexual activity."[2]

Even though this type of abstinence program is widely taught, research indicates it is ineffective. While comprehensive sex education programs increase youths' contraceptive use and delay their first sexual experience, abstinence-only-until-marriage programs do not (Kirby 2008). Indeed, comprehensive sex education helps reduce unintended pregnancy and rates of STI transmission (UNESCO 2015). Most female youth who pledge abstinence break their pledges. Moreover, they are likelier to contract the human papillomavirus than their peers who do not pledge abstinence, and more likely to experience unintended pregnancy (Paik, Sanchagrin, and Heimer 2016; see also Brückner

---

2. "Separate Program for Abstinence Education," Compilation of the Social Security Laws, Social Security Administration, https://www.ssa.gov/OP_Home/ssact/title05/0510.htm.

and Bearman 2005). Abstinence-only education is in fact associated with a *higher* likelihood of teenage pregnancy, not lower (Kohler, Manhart, and Lafferty 2008; Stanger-Hall and Hall 2011). Teen pregnancy has declined dramatically since 1990. However, this is attributable to both delaying sex and greater contraceptive use (Kearney and Levine 2014; Patten and Livingston 2016). The most widely used federally funded abstinence-education curricula contain pervasive errors and misinformation (US House of Representatives 2004). Indeed, many underestimate the effectiveness of condoms and other contraceptives, make false claims about the physical and psychological risks of abortion, misinform youth about the incidence and transmission of STIs, and replace scientific facts with religious views and moral judgments. This helps explain why the United States has one of the highest teen pregnancy rates in the West and high rates of sexually transmitted infection among youth. In countries with comprehensive sex education, in contrast, youth have far lower rates of teen pregnancy and STI transmission, and more egalitarian views of sexuality (Schalet 2011). While many comprehensive sex education programs discuss the dangers of sexuality, few explore its pleasures. Similarly, most programs do not stress gender egalitarianism in sex, contributing to an "orgasm gap" in female-male sexual encounters in which women are far less likely to orgasm than men (Armstrong, England, and Fogarty 2012: 454).

Regardless of gender or sexual identity, in general youth in the United States are ill-informed and ill-prepared when it comes to making safe and healthy decisions about sexual activity; but this is especially exacerbated among LGBTQ and gender-nonconforming youth. Indeed, only 12 percent of millennials report having received education about same-sex relationships in sex education (Jones and Cox 2015). Many of the schools that do offer sex education neglect discussions of sexual health in relation to LGBTQ populations, promoting penile-vaginal sex within the context of a monogamous other-sex relationship (often marriage). Overall, the typical contemporary sex education curriculum—or its lack—often reinforces inequalities on the axes of sexuality, gender, race, and class (Fields 2008).

Informal Curricula   Informal curricula are a set of implicit beliefs and behaviors that are rewarded by dominant institutions and instilled in children (Vander Zanden 1993). In contrast to the "curriculum proper," or what is openly intended that students should learn (Martin 1976), hidden curricula include the lessons students learn from the ways in which schools organize bodies and from offhand comments by teachers, among other sources. It may be that students learn more from the informal sexuality curriculum than from the formal one.

In terms of sexuality, the hidden curriculum can be seen in the images that accompany nonsexual topics, examples used by teachers to illustrate a variety of concepts, or the language used to teach nonsexual topics. The vast majority of parental images in literature provided by schools, for example, show a mother and a father, rather than two mothers or two fathers, reinforcing the belief that heterosexuality is the only normal sexuality, and monogamy is the only acceptable relationship form. The way science is framed and communicated to students underscores heteronormativity (Letts 2001).

Many biology textbooks explain animal behavior using Western understandings of heterosexuality and normative masculinity or femininity, ignoring the extensive diversity of sex, gender, and sexuality in the animal kingdom (Roughgarden 2013). Human biology textbooks explain the merging of eggs and sperm using frameworks that reflect the centrality of physicality and aggression to normative masculinity, erroneously framing sperm as active and eggs as passive, just waiting to be fertilized (Martin 1991). These textbooks ignore the fact that the egg moves, saying instead that it "is swept" or "drifts," whereas they describe sperm as "strong and efficiently powered," active penetrators who rescue the passive egg from certain death (Martin 1991: 489).

Such examples are not limited to biology lessons, however: as the following lesson plan indicates, teachers can illustrate that the letters Q and U always go together by planning a mock wedding between "Queen Q" and "Quarterback U" (or some variation of these names).[3] The lesson plan includes a wedding story that reads: "Their wedding was the happiest day of their lives, and from that day forward they were known as Q and Quarterback U of Alphabet Land blissfully working together to make the /qu/ sound." The story is accompanied by drawings of a female stick figure with pigtails who is dressed in a formal gown, with a gold crown on her head, next to a male stick figure who is wearing a football uniform, complete with helmet, cleats, and football in hand. Also included in the lesson plan are invitations for students to attend the wedding event in which the pair is "to be joined forever in marriage to make new words together." The invitation further reads: "Boys are invited to come dressed as quarterbacks while girls are invited to come as queens." A wedding guestbook sign-in and a quilt activity for the wedding gift are also part of the lesson plan. This lesson is not explicitly about gender or heterosexuality, but at a young age children are learning about how these two types of people—male and female—"are joined together in marriage" on "the happiest day of their lives."

The way schools organize children—often by gender—also points to a hidden curriculum reinforcing a binary gender order and heteronormativity. Schools require youth to identify as male or female; schools also develop institutional practices, as well as organize physical building layouts (e.g., locker rooms and restrooms), to separate them by gender. Separate facilities for boys and girls teach youth that there are only two sexes that are opposite and complementary in social and sexual practice.[4] In childhood, children are organized by gender daily in activities ranging from lining up to competing in contests; this continues in young adulthood, during which time youth are separated by gender for sports teams and graduation events. Segregation by gender affects how children understand themselves as gendered and sexual beings. Girls and boys are taught to identify and express themselves in distinct and purportedly complementary ways—which become so normalized they feel natural, when in fact they are the products of learning—and this reinforces heteronormativity.

---

3. Variations of this lesson can be found in multiple places. This particular one is quoted from Growing Kinders on the Teachers Pay Teachers website: www.teacherspayteachers.com/Product/The-Wedding-of-Q-and-U-128393.
4. See biologist Anne Fausto-Sterling's influential work "The Five Sexes, Revisited" demonstrating that there are more than two biological sexes. People who are neither male nor female are "intersex."

Institutional Practices

School-sponsored events, student-adult interactions, and disciplinary practices also reinforce heteronormativity, as is evident in our opening vignette that took place at River High School. School rituals do not simply reflect heteronormative gender difference: they affirm its value and centrality to social life.

Prom, in particular, is an iconic school ritual and a rite of passage for adolescents (Best 2000). As a symbol of idealized dating and romance, prom is a central site for the regulation and production of (hetero)sexuality. It valorizes heterosexuality and its centrality to successful adulthood—and with it, normative masculinity for men and normative femininity for women. For example, boys are expected to ask out girls and plan for activities that will take place both before and after the prom, while girls are expected to fantasize about romance and obsess about their appearance. Through discourses of romance and sexuality at prom, inequality between boys and girls is naturalized as a fundamental feature of heterosexuality (Best 2000). Consequently, LGBTQ proms can be a site of resistance (Best 2000), as they challenge the heteronormativity and gender normativity central to heterosexual proms. Other school events perform functions similar to that of high school proms: sports, for instance, feature primarily female cheerleaders who cheer only for males' games, asserting gender differentiation and assigning particular meanings to heterosexuality.

Disciplinary procedures also convey gendered and sexualized meanings. Dress codes, for instance, may be different for boys and girls. Indeed, teachers and administrators may even draw on homophobic sentiments to discipline students, such as in one instance when a principal punished two boys for fighting by forcing them to hold hands in front of the student body. Disciplinary codes regarding sexuality fall more heavily on students of color—black boys are punished for engaging in the same behavior (e.g., sexualized advances toward girls) that white boys engage in with little or no consequence (Ferguson 2000; Pascoe 2011)—and on queer youth.

Student Practices

Messages about gender and sexuality aren't solely transmitted through school regulations, teacher practices, and curricula. Through student practices such as bullying, gendered harassment, or participation in Gay/Straight Alliances, students both reinforce and contest heterosexism in their schools. Boys, for instance, regulate the sexuality and masculinity of male peers through gendered homophobic harassment (Pascoe 2011; Plummer 2001). In her ethnography of a high school, Pascoe (2011) found that boys used this "fag discourse" as an everyday practice to enforce normative masculinity and compulsory heterosexuality. Almost all boys were susceptible to being labeled a "fag," not just gay-identified boys. Key ways boys demonstrated acceptable masculinity to other boys—and repudiated the fag label—were through dominance over girls' bodies, such as through touching, sex, and discussions of sexual dominance over women (Pascoe 2011). Heterosexist and sexist harassment shapes children's frameworks for perceiving what constitutes "normal" masculinity, femininity, and sexuality, as well as how they express their own gender and sexuality.

Rates of harassment of girls and LGBTQ youth may be slowly declining, but harassment still shape these students' educational experiences. Surveys of LGBTQ youth across the United States indicate that the majority hear anti-LGBTQ language or slurs from peers often, and over a third are physically harassed, leading many to feel unsafe at school (Kosciw et al. 2014; see also Greytak et al. 2016). To contest heterosexism and facilitate a welcoming environment in schools, some students form Gay/Straight Alliances (Blumenfeld 2012). Students attending schools that have such alliances—only about half of schools nationwide—hear fewer anti-LGBTQ slurs or remarks, experience less physical harassment, and report feeling safer at school (Kosciw et al. 2014). For girls, peer interaction is often characterized by sexual harassment under the guise of flirtation. Indeed, a majority of girls in middle and high schools experience sexual harassment (Hill and Kearl 2011). In general, schools and peer culture can be hostile places for girls and sexual- and gender-minority students.

UNANSWERED QUESTIONS

The study of sexuality in schools is a relatively new area, and much more research is necessary. Investigation into schools as sexual institutions, not just gendered ones, is critical. More research on transgender and gender-nonconforming students is needed. These students challenge the entire organization of the school—around males and females—itself, calling into question, for example, sports teams, locker rooms, bathrooms, graduation rituals, and senior picture rituals. We also need research on best practices regarding sexual diversity in schools. What works? What does not? Much of this research has been difficult, given the institutional constraints imposed on youth and sexuality research.

IMPLICATIONS FOR PRACTICE

The effects of formal and informal enforcement of gender and sexuality in schools are profound for gender-normative students, but even more so for LGBTQ, or gender-non-conforming, students. Nationally representative studies show that LGB adolescents experience a greater risk of depression, low self-esteem, and substance abuse; often feel less connected to their schools; and have lower rates of advanced-course completion (Wilkinson and Pearson 2009; Pearson, Muller, and Wilkinson 2007). Boys with same-sex sexuality also experience lower grade point averages and higher course failure rates (Pearson, Muller, and Wilkinson 2007). LGB youth are vastly more likely than heterosexual youth to experience physical violence, substance abuse, and risky sexual practices (Kann et al. 2016; Russell, Franz, and Driscoll 2001).

School culture and context also play a large role in the social, emotional, and academic well-being of youth with same-sex sexuality. Both boys and girls report lower well-being in schools that have a greater proportion of boys playing football—a sport tied tightly to hegemonic masculinity and heteronormativity. Girls report lower well-being in schools that have a greater proportion of highly religious students (Wilkinson and Pearson 2009). These findings suggest that there are profound social, emotional, physical, and academic consequences for youths with same-sex sexuality in heterosexist environments, with particular outcomes shaped by youth gender—indicating the different ways in which heteronormativity affects boys and girls.

While many LGBTQ youth form positive views of themselves despite structural heterosexism, a testament to their resilience (Savin-Williams 2005), youth who are outspoken about gender and sexual inequality or who do not embody white, middle-class, gender-normative gay identities face marginalization even in schools with purportedly progressive policies (Elliott 2012). While targeted measures to improve the well-being of LGBTQ youth are imperative, heterosexuality is so institutionalized that efforts aimed at specific populations, in the absence of widespread institutional changes, are likely inadequate.

Legal protections need to be in place to shield LGBTQ and gender-nonconforming students. While male and female students have purportedly been protected from sexual harassment since the passage of Title IX in 1972, its deployment is inadequate and its interpretation is subject to political whim. Boys' sex talk and predatory behavior has become so normalized that teachers don't even recognize it as harassment but, rather, see it as harmless flirting. Teacher training is thus critical: to implement these laws, teachers and administrators must look with new eyes at student interactions, noting the ways in which both homophobic epithets and so-called flirtatious behaviors shore up normative gender and sexual identities and perpetuate unequal gender arrangements.

Our research suggests that educators can take proactive steps to create learning and social environments that are more supportive of LGBTQ and gender-nonconforming youth. Educators need to look seriously at the inclusion (or lack) of LGBTQ and gender-variant people in the school curriculum. LGBTQ students report feeling less isolated when they learn about nonheterosexual and gender-nonconforming people as a part of the regular school curriculum, and experience less homophobic harassment (Kosciw et al. 2014). Learning about LGBTQ, or gender-nonconforming, people also sends a message to straight students about the school's stance on homophobic and sexist teasing. We argue, therefore, that topics about sexuality, gender, and LGBTQ issues should be included in social studies, history, health, family life, and English courses. For instance, history classes should teach about LGBTQ liberation movements and the Stonewall riots, and English classes should discuss gay authors and homoerotic or sexually ambiguous themes in the writings of classic authors. Health and family life classes can discuss a variety of family forms, gender identities, and partnering preferences. Organizations and professionals from a range of disciplines have been mobilizing around issues of harassment, bullying, sexism, and homophobia in schools over the last decade.

A majority of LGBTQ students report experiencing discriminatory treatment by adults at school, such as not being allowed to participate in the same public displays as heterosexual students or being prevented from attending a school function with an individual of the same sex (Kosciw et al. 2014). Relatedly, a majority of schools do not adequately protect LGBTQ students from bullying, harassment, or discrimination. Eighteen states and Washington, DC, have enumerated bullying laws to protect students on the basis of sexual orientation and gender identity; thirteen states and Washington, DC, have laws to protect students from discrimination on the basis of sexual orientation and gender identity; and one (Wisconsin) protects students only on the basis of sexual orientation. Seven states—Utah, Texas, Oklahoma, Louisiana, Mississippi, Alabama, and South Carolina—actually forbid the discussion of LGBTQ people in a positive way; and two states, South Dakota and Missouri, prohibit school districts from enumerating bullying laws to protect LGBTQ students (GLSEN 2016). Whether transgender students have equal access to facilities corresponding to their gender identity under Title IX remains to be seen; there are active court cases at the time of this writing. Mandating bathroom use based on an individual's sex assignment at birth prevents transgender students from engaging in basic human functions and reinforces their marginalization.

Administrators can modify the social organization of schools so that they are less homophobic and more gender normative. Steps include placing affirming posters in classrooms, providing support for Gay/Straight Alliances, sponsoring inclusive assemblies and speakers, and reorganizing highly gendered school rituals. Recognizing LGBTQ issues by noting National Coming Out Day, ensuring that gay and lesbian students are celebrated during multicultural assemblies, and acknowledging the Day of Silence to protest discriminatory treatment of LGBTQ people would be easy ways to incorporate gay and lesbian visibility. Further, schools can rework rituals such as dances, proms, and homecoming to eliminate heterosexism and sexism. The messages conveyed to students through these rituals should not be that the school advocates and in fact demands heterosexualized gender difference. Rituals need to be organized to reflect the diversity of gender and sexual identities of all students. Developing gender-neutral titles instead of *prom king* and *queen,* and allowing same-sex couples to attend, will have a big impact on students, as will not requiring separate dress codes for youth based on gender (e.g., graduation robes or senior photos). Finally, vetting schoolwide performances for sexist or heterosexist content indicates to LGBTQ and gender nonnormative students, as well as straight and normatively gendered students, that school authorities do not tolerate gender- and sexuality-based harassment or violence.

CASE STUDY 1 REVIEW

Discussion Questions

1. What was the formal sex education curriculum at your school?

2. Do you remember bullying or harassment at your school? Was it different from or similar to what is described here?

3. How might schools be designed so that they are welcoming for all students?

4. Think about examples of the informal sexuality curriculum at your school. What did it consist of? What messages were given?

5. How can schools reorganize their curricula, policies, and practices to eliminate heterosexism, homophobia, heter-onormativity, and sexism? How can they operate differently to accommodate LGBTQ, gender-nonnormative youth, and other marginalized populations (e.g., women, youth of color, and marginalized religions).

Suggestions for Further Reading

Connell, Catherine. 2014. *School's Out: Gay and Lesbian Teachers in the Classroom.* Berkeley: University of California Press.

Ferguson, Ann. 2000. *Bad Boys: Public Schools in the Making of Black Masculinity.* Ann Arbor: University of Michigan Press.

Fields, Jessica. 2008. *Risky Lessons: Sex Education and Social Inequality.* New Brunswick, NJ: Rutgers University Press.

Pascoe, C. J. 2011. *Dude, You're a Fag: Masculinity and Sexuality in High School, with a New Preface.* Berkeley: University of California Press.

Wilkinson, Lindsey, and Jennifer Pearson. 2009. "School Culture and the Well-Being of Same-Sex-Attracted Youth." *Gender and Society* 23 (4): 542–68.

References

Armstrong, Elizabeth A., Paula England, and Alison C. K. Fogarty. 2012. "Accounting for Women's Orgasm and Sexual Enjoyment in College Hookups and Relationships." *American Sociological Review* 77 (3): 435–62.

Best, Amy L. 2000. *Prom Night: Youth, Schools, and Popular Culture.* New York: Routledge.

Blumenfield, Warren J. 2012. "'We're Here and We're Fabulous': Contemporary U.S.-American LGBT Youth Activism." In *Sexualities in Education: A Reader,* edited by E. R. Meiners and T. Quinn, 73–83. New York: Peter Lang.

Bridges, Tristan, and C. J. Pascoe. 2016. "Masculinities and Post-homophobias?" In *Exploring Masculinities: Identity, Inequality, Continuity, and Change,* edited by C. J. Pascoe and T. Bridges, 412–23. New York: Oxford University Press.

Brückner, Hannah, and Peter Bearman. 2005. "After the Promise: the STD Consequences of Adolescent Virginity Pledges." *Journal of Adolescent Health* 36 (4): 271–78.

Butler, Judith. 1993. *Bodies That Matter.* New York: Routledge.

Connell, R. W. 1987. *Gender and Power: Society, the Person, and Sexual Politics.* Palo Alto, CA: Stanford University Press.

Doan, Long, Annalise Loehr, and Lisa R. Miller. 2014. "Formal Rights and Informal Privileges for Same-Sex Couples: Evidence from a National Survey Experiment." *American Sociological Review* 79 (6): 1172–95.

Elliott, Kathleen O. 2012. "The Right Way to Be Gay: How School Structures Sexual Inequality." In *Sexualities in Education: A Reader,* edited by E. R. Meiners and T. Quinn, 158–66. New York: Peter Lang.

Fausto-Sterling, Anne. 2000. "The Five Sexes, Revisited." *Sciences* 40 (4): 18–23.

Ferguson, Ann. 2000. *Bad Boys: Public Schools in the Making of Black Masculinity.* Ann Arbor: University of Michigan Press.

Fields, Jessica. 2008. *Risky Lessons: Sex Education and Social Inequality.* New Brunswick, NJ: Rutgers University Press.

Gay, Lesbian, and Straight Education Network (GLSEN). 2016. "State Maps." www.glsen.org/article/state-maps.

Greytak, Emily, Joseph Kosciw, Christian Villenas, and Noreen Giga. 2016. *From Teasing to Torment: School Climate Revisited: A Survey of U.S. Secondary School Students and Teachers.* New York: GLSEN.

Guttmacher Institute. 2016. "American Teens' Sources of Sexual Health Education." Fact sheet. April.

Hill, Catherine, and Holly Kearl. 2011. *Crossing the Line: Sexual Harassment at School.* Washington, DC: American Association of University Women.

Jones, Robert P., and Daniel Cox. 2015. *How Race and Religion Shape Millennial Attitudes on Sexuality and Reproductive Health: Findings from the 2015 Millennials, Sexuality, and Reproductive Health Survey.* Washington, DC: Public Religion Research Institute.

Kann, Laura, E. O. Olsen, T. McManus, William A. Harris, Shari L. Shanklin, Katherine H. Flint, Barbara Queen, et al. 2016. "Sexual Identity, Sex of Sexual Contacts, and Health-Related Behaviors among Students in Grades 9–12—United States and Selected Sites, 2015." *Morbidity and Mortality Weekly Report, Surveillance Summaries* 65 (9): 1–202.

Kearney, Melissa S., and Phillip B. Levine. 2014. *Media Influences on Social Outcomes: The Impact of MTV's 16 and Pregnant on Teen Childbearing.* Cambridge, MA: National Bureau of Economic Research.

Kirby, Douglas B. 2008. "The Impact of Abstinence and Comprehensive Sex and STD/HIV Education Programs on Adolescent Sexual Behavior." *Sexuality Research and Social Policy* 5 (3): 18–27.

Kohler, Pamela K., Lisa E. Manhart, and William E. Lafferty. 2008. "Abstinence-Only and Comprehensive Sex Education and the Initiation of Sexual Activity and Teen Pregnancy." *Journal of Adolescent Health* 42 (4): 344–51.

Kosciw, Joseph G., Emily A. Greytak, Neal A. Palmer, and Madelyn J. Boeson. 2014. *The 2013 National School Climate Survey: The Experiences of Lesbian, Gay, Bisexual, and Transgender Youth in Our Nation's Schools.* New York: Gay, Lesbian, and Straight Education Network.

Letts, Will. 2001. "When Science Is Strangely Alluring: Interrogating the Masculinist and Heteronormative Nature of Primary School Science." *Gender and Education* 13 (3): 261–74.

Lindberg, Laura D., Isaac Maddow-Zimet, and Heather Boonstra. 2016. "Changes in Adolescents' Receipt of Sex Education, 2006–2013." *Journal of Adolescent Health* 58 (6): 621–27.

Martin, Emily. 1991. "The Egg and the Sperm: How Science Has Constructed a Romance Based on Stereotypical Male-Female Roles." *Signs* 16 (3): 485–501.

Martin, Jane R. 1976. "What Should We Do with a Hidden Curriculum When We Find One?" *Curriculum Inquiry* 6 (2): 135–51.

National Conference of State Legislatures (NCSL). 2016. www.ncsl.org/research/health/state-policies-on-sex-education-in-schools.aspx.

Paik, Anthony, Kenneth J. Sanchagrin, and Karen Heimer. 2016. "Broken Promises: Abstinence Pledging and Sexual and Reproductive Health." *Journal of Marriage and Family* 78 (2): 546–61.

Pascoe, C. J. 2011. *Dude, You're a Fag: Masculinity and Sexuality in High School, with a New Preface.* Berkeley: University of California Press.

Patten, Eileen, and Gretchen Livingston. 2016. "Why Is the Teen Birth Rate Falling?" *Pew Research,* April 29.

Pearson, Jennifer, Chandra Muller, and Lindsey Wilkinson. 2007. "Adolescent Same-Sex Attraction and Academic Outcomes: The Role of School Attachment and Engagement." *Social Problems* 54 (4): 523–42.

Plummer, Ken. 2001. "The Quest for Modern Manhood: Masculine Stereotypes, Peer Culture and the Social Significance of Homophobia." *Journal of Adolescence* 24 (1): 15–23.

Roughgarden, Joan. 2013. *Evolution's Rainbow: Diversity, Gender, and Sexuality in Nature and People, Tenth Anniversary Edition, with a New Preface.* Berkeley: University of California Press.

Russell, Stephen, Brian T. Franz, and Anne K. Driscoll. 2001. "Same-Sex Romantic Attraction and Experience of Violence in Adolescence." *American Journal of Public Health* 91 (6): 903–6.

Savin-Williams, Ritch C. 2005. *The New Gay Teenager.* Cambridge, MA: Harvard University Press.

Schalet, Amy. 2011. *Not under My Roof: Parents, Teens, and the Culture of Sex.* Chicago: University of Chicago Press.

Sexuality Information and Education Council of the United States (SIECUS). N.d. "A History of Federal Funding for Abstinence-Only-until-Marriage Programs." https://siecus.org/wp-content/uploads/2018/07/4-A-Brief-History-of-AOUM-Funding.pdf. Accessed on October 27, 2016.

Stanger-Hall, Kathrin F., and David W. Hall. 2011. "Abstinence-Only Education and Teen Pregnancy Rates: Why We Need Comprehensive Sex Education in the U.S." *PLoS One* 6 (10): 1–11.

United Nations Educational, Scientific and Cultural Organization (UNESCO). 2015. *Emerging Evidence, Lessons and Practice in Comprehensive Sexuality Education: A Global Review.* Place de Fontenoy, France: United Nations.

US House of Representatives. 2004. "The Content of Federally Funded Abstinence-Only Education Programs." *Committee on Government Reform—Minority Staff, Special Investigations Division.* Washington, DC: United States House of Representatives.

Vander Zanden, James. 1993. *Sociology: The Core.* 3rd ed. New York: McGraw-Hill.

Wilkinson, Lindsey, and Jennifer Pearson. 2009. "School Culture and the Well-Being of Same-Sex-Attracted Youth." *Gender and Society* 23 (4): 542–68.

6

Social Class and Student-Teacher Interactions

JESSICA CALARCO, INDIANA UNIVERSITY

EDITORS' NOTE

Indiana University sociologist Jessica Calarco continues our discussion of the informal ways schools mirror and reinforce the categories that exist in society at large. Calarco has spent years observing informal interactions between students and teachers and studying how these interactions reinforce socioeconomic inequalities.

Calarco introduces the concept of **cultural capital.** Much like human capital, which we first discussed in chapter 1, cultural capital consists of skills that people employ to advance their interests in the larger society. But while the skills we usually associate with human capital are typically part of schools' explicit curriculum, the skills we associate with cultural capital are often taught informally to students. Calarco describes, for example, the skills and expectations that allow students from relatively affluent families to effectively advocate for themselves in the classroom as a reflection of these students' cultural capital. In fact, as we'll see when we turn to an examination of experiences of first-generation college students in chapter 7, students sometimes need cultural capital to make sense of a school's hidden curriculum and succeed.

As you read this chapter, note the tension between Calarco's findings and the evidence that Downey assembles, in chapter 2, regarding the ways schools compensate for socioeconomic inequality. While Downey illustrates that in-school learning inequalities are narrower than out-of-school inequalities, Calarco's findings provide a powerful reminder of important differences between the ways in which poor students and affluent students experience school.

KEY POINTS

- Parents' income and educational attainment are closely linked to a child's school outcomes.
- Class-based inequalities reflect differences both in students' resources and in students' interactions with their teachers at school.
- Teachers tend to have more positive relationships with more-privileged students than they do with less-privileged students.
- Students from different social class backgrounds tend to approach interactions with teachers in different ways. More-privileged students tend to be more comfortable seeking support from teachers, voicing their needs and opinions, and advocating for themselves at school. Those differences are apparent as early as preschool and persist through college.

INTRODUCTION

We know that social class matters in school. Of course, students' experiences with social class are intersectional—they differ for boys and girls and for children from different racial and ethnic groups. Across those groups, however, research shows that parents' income and education are the best predictors of a child's school performance. Certainly, mobility is possible—some students from less-privileged families do well in school, earn college degrees, and get high-paying, high-status jobs. More often, though, class-based inequalities are reproduced from one generation to the next. On average, students from more-privileged families earn higher grades, do better on standardized tests, are more likely to graduate from high school and college, and get better jobs than do their less-privileged peers.

Social class matters, in part, because of its relationship to differences in students' material and financial resources. Privileged students, for example, typically have more resources at home—food on the table, high-quality health care, books on the shelves, computers in their rooms. Privileged students also tend to have more resources at school—lots of Advanced Placement classes, science labs stocked with plenty of books and new equipment, small classes, and teachers with master's degrees. The resources available to privileged children at home matter for brain development, affecting their chances even before they set foot in school. Resources also matter for learning, shaping how children respond to the information and opportunities they encounter in school.

Social class also matters because of its relationship to differences in students' cultural resources. Those cultural resources include the language, habits, skills, styles, knowledge, and beliefs that people use in social interactions. Considering how class-based cultural resources matter in the classroom, my research has shown that more-privileged and less-privileged students interact with teachers in different and highly consequential ways. Considering the popular image of schooling—with teachers instructing from the front and students working silently at their seats—we might assume that student-teacher interactions play only a limited role in schooling. In recent decades, however, the influence of progressive philosophies in education has led to a dramatic shift in the nature of classroom instruction, and interactions between students and teachers are now commonplace (Cuban 2004; Tyack and Cuban 1995). Unfortunately, those interactions also create real opportunities for inequality.

Now, student-teacher interactions also vary by gender and by race, and those variations are important. Nevertheless, in the interest of clarity and brevity, this chapter focuses on social class, looking primarily at positive student-teacher interactions (e.g., support and engagement); chapter 12 goes into detail about school discipline and other negative student-teacher interactions.

INTELLECTUAL ROOTS

To understand how social class matters in student-teacher interactions and how those interactions contribute to inequalities, it is helpful to first unpack a number of relevant concepts and theories. These include social class, cultural capital, the hidden curriculum, teacher bias, the self-fulfilling prophecy, and resistance theory.

Social class has been defined in various ways but is essentially a measure of the resources a person has and the status attached to those resources by society as a whole. In research on education and inequality, a student's social class is generally determined by his or her parents' income, educational attainment, and occupational status. Those statuses, however, are also closely linked to differences in class cultures. Annette Lareau (2011), for example, compares children in poor and working-class families to those in middle- and upper-middle-class families and finds that children's lives vary dramatically across these two groups. Parents in the more-privileged group regularly solicit their children's thoughts and opinions and try to guide their children's behavior through reasoning and negotiation. They also enroll their children in numerous organized activities and tend to be heavily involved in their children's schooling. Parents in the less-privileged group use directives to guide children's behavior at home. They also encourage their children to spend most of their time in free play, and they take a more hands-off approach to education, trusting that teachers will ensure that their children's academic needs are met at school. Other scholars have also linked these differences in parenting styles to children's school outcomes, suggesting that class cultures pattern family life and interactions, and that they do so in consequential ways (DiMaggio 1982; Domina 2005; Dumais 2002; Lee and Bowen 2006).[1]

---

1. It is important to note, however, that the parenting styles common in more-privileged families are equally or more beneficial when they are used by less-privileged parents (Domina 2005; Lee and Bowen 2006).

While much of the research on social class and schooling has focused on parent-teacher interactions, there is also evidence to suggest that social class matters in student-teacher interactions as well. Research on teacher bias, for example, shows that teachers tend to underestimate the abilities of less-privileged students (Kozlowski 2015; Ready and Wright 2011), and that, as a result, less-privileged students are disproportionately assigned to lower academic tracks and ability groups (Oakes 2005; Rist 1970). Such findings suggest that teachers may be biased against less-privileged students, or at least the behaviors and orientations that less-privileged students exhibit in school. Consistent with that view, qualitative studies find that less-privileged students receive less time and attention from teachers than do their middle-class peers (Calarco 2011; Nelson and Schutz 2007; Streib 2011).

Two key questions, however, are: why does social class matter in student-teacher interactions, and why do those interactions contribute to inequality in school? Drawing on cultural capital theory and research on the hidden curriculum of schooling, existing research typically treats the middle-class advantage as the result of a cultural matching process. From that perspective, schools evaluate students on their knowledge of both the academic curriculum and the "hidden" curriculum of behavioral norms—that is, stay in your seat, raise your hand. Because the hidden curriculum is not taught overtly to students, those who learn such behaviors at home—namely, more-privileged students—have an advantage in school. Essentially, those students come to school equipped with "cultural capital"—knowledge and skills that can be activated to generate rewards in those settings, including better grades, higher praise, and more opportunities for learning.

That said, there is also reason to question whether cultural matching is the only mechanism by which more-privileged families secure advantages in school. Research shows, for example, that teachers often feel compelled to comply with more-privileged parents' requests, even when they would prefer not to, and even when they know that doing so will disadvantage less-privileged students (Lewis and Diamond 2015). Similarly, and as I will discuss in more detail, my research suggests that middle-class students do not always stay in their seats, raise their hands, or defer to teachers' authority. Instead, they gain advantages, at least in part, by calling out, getting up from their seats, challenging their teachers, and persisting in their requests, even when teachers try to say no. Taken together, such findings suggest that more-privileged families might secure advantages not just by complying with school norms and expectations (as cultural capital theory predicts) but also by compelling teachers to comply with their expectations instead.

RESEARCH METHODS

Much of the research on social class and student-teacher interactions is ethnographic in nature. That means researchers spend an extended period of time—

often six months or more—observing in classrooms and getting to know students and teachers. My own research, for example, followed a group of students from third grade through seventh grade. The group included more-privileged (middle- and upper-middle-class white and Asian American) and less-privileged (poor and working-class white and Latinx) students, and they all attended the same school. Focusing on students in one school allowed me to isolate the importance of social class in shaping student-teacher interactions. If I had instead observed more privileged students in one school and less privileged students in another, it would have been difficult to say whether any differences I observed were really the result of social class, or whether they instead reflected differences in school environments, teaching styles, or peer cultures. During the active phases of the project, I observed the students (and their teachers) at least twice a week, for about three hours per visit, and kept detailed field notes (including notes about dialogue, facial expressions, and context) that described the student-teacher interactions I observed. As I will discuss in more detail, those observations revealed how students interacted with their teachers, how those interactions varied along social class lines, and how those interactions contributed to inequalities in school.

In-depth interviews are also useful for studying social class and student-teacher interactions, particularly as a supplement to ethnographic research. In my own research, I conducted interviews with the students (after fifth grade and seventh grade) and with teachers and parents. Those interviews revealed how students and teachers perceived classroom roles and expectations and how those perceptions varied along social class lines. The interviews with parents also helped illuminate the origins of social class differences in student-teacher interactions, showing how more-privileged and less-privileged students learned to behave in different ways.

While interviews and observations can describe the nature and content of student-teacher interactions, highlight the mechanisms that produce social class differences in student-teacher interactions, and reveal the consequences those interactions have for students in school, qualitative data are not designed to quantify these patterns or assess their impact on student outcomes. Those questions are better addressed with survey research. Quantitative data can be used to more precisely measure relationships between social class, student-teacher interactions, and student outcomes. Robert Crosnoe and colleagues (2004), for example, used data from a nationally representative survey to examine how student-teacher relationships in secondary school (measured by student reports of how well they get along with their teachers and whether their teachers are caring and fair) vary across groups and predict student achievement and student behavior. Similarly, Chandra Muller (2001) examined how teachers' and students' investment in their relationship (measured by students' perceptions of teachers' caring and teachers' perceptions of student effort) both contribute to student achievement in secondary school. These quantitative data say little about the nature or content of actual interactions between students and teachers, but they are useful for showing that the quality of those relationships (at least as perceived by the students and teachers in them) matters for students and contributes to inequalities between more-privileged students and their less-privileged peers.

KEY FINDINGS

Social Class and Student-Teacher Interactions

Research has shown that the quality of student-teacher relationships tends to vary along social class lines. Crosnoe and colleagues (2004), for example, found that, on average, secondary school students whose own parents have more education tend to report higher-quality relationships with their teachers. They view their teachers as more caring and report getting along better with their teachers overall (Muller 2001). Those social class differences in the quality of student-teacher relationships may reflect the fact that teachers tend to treat more-privileged and less-privileged students in different ways (Brophy and Good 1974; Oakes 2005; Rist 1970). In general, studies have shown that teachers interact more positively with privileged students and more negatively with students from less-privileged backgrounds. While privileged students often receive praise from teachers, less-privileged students tend to receive criticism. Teachers often do more to encourage the contributions of more-privileged students, are less likely to punish those students (even when they misbehave), and rate those students as having greater potential (regardless of their actual ability).

This focus on teachers and their treatment of students is important, but it often overlooks the agency that students have in their interactions with teachers. In an effort to address this limitation, some scholars have begun to consider how social class matters in student-initiated interactions. My own research, for example, examines social class differences in students' requests for assistance, accommodations, and attention from teachers (Calarco 2011, 2014a, 2014b). I found that more-privileged students see interactions with teachers as opportunities for reward. As a result, those students seem to be very comfortable seeking support from their teachers and do so frequently, proactively, and persistently (i.e., calling out with questions and continuing to ask for assistance or accommodations or attention, even when teachers deny their requests). Less-privileged students tend to see interactions with teachers as opportunities for reprimand instead. As a result, they prefer to deal with problems on their own or with help from peers. Furthermore, when those students do seek support from teachers, they tend to do so patiently and politely (i.e., raising their hands and backing down quickly if teachers say no) so as to avoid upsetting teachers with their requests.

Those social class differences in student-initiated interactions start early and persist over time. Jessi Streib (2011), for example, found that even preschool-aged

Figure 8. A teacher meets with her students in New York City, 1911. Source: New York Public Library, New York Public Library Archives.

children exhibit class-based strategies in their interactions with teachers. Observing more-privileged and less-privileged children in one preschool classroom, Streib discovered that children from more-privileged families dominate classroom interactions. They "have larger vocabularies, speak more often, interrupt more, and feel more entitled to speak to teachers" (341). As a result, children from less-privileged families have few opportunities to interact with teachers. Anthony Jack (2016), meanwhile, found that class-based patterns of student-initiated interactions with teachers continue even into college. Through interviews with black and Latino students at an elite college, Jack learned that more-privileged students have a sense of "ease" interacting with authority figures, regularly seek out professors during office hours, and feel comfortable "advocating" for themselves in those interactions (by, for example, asking for grade changes or extensions on assignments). Less-privileged students, on the other hand, "lack the skill set or desire to engage faculty, even as they perceive their peers reaping the benefits of forging relationships" (8).

Students are clearly active agents in their interactions with teachers, but teachers and schools also play important roles in translating students' class-based styles and strategies into unequal opportunities in school. Streib (2011: 343), for example, found that because teachers do not stop their more-privileged students from dominating conversation, less-privileged students rarely have a chance to talk. Similarly, my own research shows that even when teachers are frustrated with the constant requests they receive from more-privileged students, and even when they worry that too much support from teachers might undermine students' development of responsibility and respect and resourcefulness, they rarely deny students' requests.

Why are teachers so reluctant to say no? One possibility is that schools are middle-class institutions with middle-class norms, and that those norms subconsciously bias teachers' expectations of students (Stephens et al. 2012). Another possibility is that teachers are responding to structural constraints. My research suggests that teachers are faced with large class sizes, mountains of paperwork, and more curriculum than they can cover in a year, and that they rarely have time to check in with students one-on-one. Thus, they rely on students to voice their own needs (ensuring that more-privileged students, who are more comfortable speaking up, get most of the support). Furthermore, even in situations where teachers might want to deny more-privileged students' requests, they worry about the costs of saying no, which can include both time wasted on back-and-forth negotiations with students and even the threat of retaliation from privileged parents, who often hold positions of power within the school.

The Consequences of Stratified Interactions in School

Regardless of why teachers interact with more-privileged and less-privileged students in different ways, those differences are important because they contribute to larger patterns of inequality in school. In the classroom, for example, class-based styles and strategies seem to give more-privileged students a leg up, in relation to their less-privileged peers. My own research shows that, by seeking assistance, accommodations, and attention from teachers, and by doing so proactive and persistently, more-privileged students get extensions on assignments, extra hints on tests, hands-on help with projects, clearer explanations of directions, and more opportunities to express their ideas and demonstrate their creativity. Similarly, Streib (2011: 342) found that proactively engaging with teachers gives more-privileged preschoolers "the power both to direct classroom events and to further improve their own language skills."

Through their impact on students' experiences in school, social class differences in student-teacher interactions may also contribute to inequalities in student learning and achievement. They may do so, in part, by shaping students' commitment to schooling and their sense of academic aptitude. We know that students do better in school and feel more attached to school when they have teachers whom they perceive as friendly, caring, and supportive (Hallinan 2008). Similarly, students who experience a stronger sense of connectedness to teachers and others at school tend to be more engaged in learning and more successful in school, and they experience fewer behavior problems (Crosnoe,

Johnson, Elder 2004). Having teachers who care also seems to be particularly important for less-privileged students, as it helps reduce the likelihood of negative outcomes for students who are perceived to be academically at risk (Muller 2001).

Social class differences in student-teacher interactions may also contribute to achievement gaps through their influence on teachers' perceptions of students and their abilities. As Streib (2011: 342) suggests, more-privileged students may be seen by their teachers "as more engaged, smarter, and better able to make connections" with academic material. Those perceptions may lead teachers to offer more praise to more-privileged students, which has been shown to improve students' achievement over time (Cohen and Lotan 1995). Teachers may also invest more time and energy in and set higher expectations for students whom they perceive as more committed to success. Research shows, in turn, that students do better in school when they have teachers who actively engage them in learning. High academic expectations, especially when coupled with support and encouragement from teachers, also have a positive impact on learning and achievement.

The Origins of Stratified Interactions in School

If less-privileged students recognize the advantages that teachers and their support can provide, why do those students not act more like their more-privileged peers? Research suggests that class cultures are deeply ingrained and difficult to set aside. They are often learned from parents at home and reinforced by the class-based circumstances that shape children's lives. In my research, for example, I found that parents coach their children to interact with teachers in class-based ways. More-privileged parents stress that teachers are resources—their children learn to feel entitled to support and accommodations. Less-privileged parents emphasize responsibility and respect for authority, instead—their children learn not to rely on others for help and not to expect special favors. Children internalize those lessons (albeit with some pushback) and learn to perceive themselves and their teachers through their parents' eyes. The lessons that children learn from their parents are also reinforced by the class-based circumstances of children's lives. Jack (2016: 9), for example, describes the case of Shaniqua, a young black woman whose experience with poverty and homelessness made it hard for her to advocate for herself with faculty at her elite college. As Shaniqua notes, "When you're poor and you're homeless, you get used to [taking] what is given. You don't complain. Someone gives you a shirt, even if it's ugly, you wear it. Of course you'll be grateful. It's made it hard for me to advocate for myself. Part of me is like, 'I've been given enough.'" Thus, even when less-privileged students recognize the potential benefits of interacting with teachers, they often find it difficult to ignore the cultural voices that push them the other way.

UNANSWERED QUESTIONS AND RESEARCH FRONTIERS

As scholars have highlighted the importance of social class in shaping student-teacher interactions, educators and policy makers have often responded by looking for ways to make less-privileged students look and act more like their more-privileged peers. Charter schools in the Knowledge Is Power Program, for example, explicitly teach less-privileged students to sit up, listen, ask and answer questions, nod, and track the speaker (or "SLANT"). Elite prep schools and colleges also tend to have special preenrollment programs for less-privileged students, and those programs are often designed to equip less-privileged students with the cultural knowledge and skills they need in order to feel at ease in an elite environment.

Those efforts, however, tend to ignore three very important questions: (1) can students learn new class cultures? (2) how do we teach those class cultures? and (3) is teaching less-privileged students to act like more-privileged students really the best way to reduce inequality?

A few studies offer tentative answers to these questions, but there is still much to be learned. With respect to the first question, research suggests that cultural mobility is possible, but that it is a difficult and often emotionally challenging process. Behaviors and orientations learned early in life tend to persist over time. Even less-privileged students who graduate from elite colleges, and even those who go on to marry individuals from more-privileged backgrounds, often struggle to emulate the habits of their more-privileged peers. That experience of upward mobility can also be deeply isolating, leaving less-privileged students feeling alone and out of place both in college and for years after.

With respect to the second question, it seems that class cultures are most malleable when students are young, when they are deeply immersed in new cultural contexts, and when they are supported throughout that immersion process by others who are like them. Research shows, for example, that early childhood education is particularly beneficial for less-privileged children (Barnett 1995; Lee et al. 1990), and that early experiences in school have lasting consequences for students (Alexander, Entwisle, and Olson 1997). Research on elite preparatory schools, meanwhile, shows that attending those total institutions—where students spend twenty-four hours a day with privileged peers—does (in most cases, at least) lead less-privileged students to think and act more like their more-privileged peers (Jack 2016; Khan 2011). While we know little about how those elite institutions teach class cultures, such findings suggest that simple skill-building programs for less-privileged students are unlikely to produce the same results.

Regardless of whether it is possible for students to learn new class cultures, however, and with respect to the third question, emerging research suggests that there may be real drawbacks to encouraging what might be called "entitlement for all." Certainly, it is important for less-privileged students to feel comfortable voicing their needs and seeking support from teachers when they need it. At the same time, there is reason to question whether the interactional styles of more-privileged students are really as beneficial as they seem. In my own research, for example, teachers (and less-privileged parents) were quick to point out the problems that arise when students are overreliant on teachers' support. Those students, they suggested, would struggle with the work ethic, respectfulness, and responsibility. Consistent with that view, a number of high-profile books and news articles have raised concerns about the "me" generation and the entitlement and overdependence they display in college and in the workplace. While more research is needed to assess the validity of these claims, it seems that an entitlement-for-all approach might create as many problems as it solves.

IMPLICATIONS FOR TEACHERS, SCHOOLS, AND POLICY MAKERS

Of course, the situation is not hopeless. Rather, there are things that schools and teachers can do to level the playing field and alleviate both social class differences in student-teacher interactions and their contributions to inequalities in school. In my own research, I have found that small actions on the part of teachers can go a long way in making less-privileged students feel more comfortable voicing their concerns and seeking support when they need it. First, teachers can explicitly encourage students to seek help and support when they are struggling. I find that when teachers' expectations are more explicit, students are less inclined to rely on class-based habits they have learned at home. Second, teachers can look for signs of silent struggle (body language, facial expressions, and even off-task behavior), approach students, and offer unsolicited assistance. When teachers take that first step, less-privileged students are much less likely to worry that they might bother teachers or disrespect them by asking for support. Third, teachers can extend the benefits of individual requests to the class as a whole. If one student asks for an extension of time on an assignment or for clarification on a test or even for a reprieve for misbehavior, there are probably others who would benefit from such accommodations, even if they are reluctant to ask. Teachers need resources and time and support to make these changes, but they are do-able.

Unfortunately, however, helping less-privileged students feel comfortable speaking up for themselves is not enough. History has shown that as those with less privilege move toward equal footing, those with more privilege find new ways to stay one step ahead. Alleviating those inequalities requires that teachers be willing to say no to more-privileged students (e.g., denying requests for extensions on assignments or extra hints on tests or reprieves from punishment for wrongdoing), and it also requires that more-privileged parents be willing to part with their own relative privilege (e.g., supporting teachers rather

Figure 9. A teacher addresses his students in a contemporary classroom. Source: Photograph by Victoria Choi, USAG Humphreys Public Affairs Officer, reproduced under a Creative Commons license.

than pushing back or demanding special accommodations and exemptions from rules). At the policy level, these findings call into question the common, deficit-oriented approach to tackling inequalities. They suggest that policy makers should focus not just on supplementing what some people lack but also on reducing the (often unfair) advantages that others are able to create for themselves.

These findings also call into question the popular practice of blaming teachers for inequalities in school. Certainly, we know that teachers—and especially their subconscious biases—play an important role in stratifying students' experiences and outcomes. At the same time, research on social class and student-teacher interaction reveals that students have real agency in shaping their own experiences and outcomes. Students come to school with different class cultures, and those cultures lead students to activate different strategies when navigating problems and interacting with teachers at school. Teachers help translate those different strategies into unequal outcomes, but they seem to do so inadvertently and in response to structural constraints (e.g., large class sizes, expanding curricula, accountability pressures, and pushback from privileged parents). Such findings suggest that, to fix inequalities in school, we will need to look beyond the classroom and focus more on families and society as a whole.

CHAPTER 6 REVIEW

Discussion Questions

1. Why do students from more-privileged families tend to outperform their less-privileged peers?
2. How do interactions between students and teachers contribute to social-class-based inequalities in school?
3. Why do students from different social class backgrounds tend to interact with teachers in different ways?
4. What steps can schools take to alleviate inequalities that result from social class differences in student-teacher interactions?

Suggestions for Further Reading

Calarco, J. M. 2018. *Negotiating Opportunities: How the Middle Class Secures Advantages in School.* New York: Oxford University Press.

Domina, Thurston. 2005. "Leveling the Home Advantage: Assessing the Effectiveness of Parental Involvement in Elementary School." *Sociology of Education* 78 (3): 233–49.

Dumais, Susan A. 2002. "Cultural Capital, Gender, and School Success: The Role of Habitus." *Sociology of Education* 75 (1): 44–68.

Lareau, Annette. 2011. *Unequal Childhoods: Class, Race, and Family Life.* Berkeley: University of California Press.

References

Alexander, Karl L., Doris R. Entwisle, and Linda S. Olson. 1997. *Children, Schools, and Inequality.* Boulder, CO: Westview Press.

Barnett, W. Steven. 1995. "Long-Term Effects of Early Childhood Programs on Cognitive and School Outcomes." *Future of Children* 5 (3): 25–50.

Brophy, Jere, and Thomas Good. 1974. *Teacher-Student Relationships: Causes and Consequences.* New York: Holt, Rinehart, and Winston.

Calarco, Jessica McCrory. 2011. "'I Need Help!' Social Class and Children's Help-Seeking in Elementary School." *American Sociological Review* 76 (6): 862–82.

———. 2014a. "Coached for the Classroom: Parents' Cultural Transmission and Children's Reproduction of Educational Inequalities." *American Sociological Review* 79 (5): 1015–37.

———. 2014b. "The Inconsistent Curriculum: Cultural Toolkits and Student Interpretations of Ambiguous Expectations." *Social Psychology Quarterly* 77 (2): 185–209.

Cohen, Elizabeth G., and Rachel A. Lotan. 1995. "Producing Equal-Status Interaction in the Heterogeneous Classroom." *American Educational Research Journal* 32 (1): 99–120.

Crosnoe, Robert, Monica Kirkpatrick Johnson, and Glen H. Elder Jr. 2004. "Intergenerational Bonding in School: The Behavioral and Contextual Correlates of Student-Teacher Relationships." *Sociology of Education* 77 (1): 60–81.

Cuban, Larry. 2004. "The Open Classroom." *Education Next* 4 (2).

DiMaggio, Paul. 1982. "Cultural Capital and School Success: The Impact of Status Culture Participation on the Grades of U.S. High School Students." *American Sociological Review* 47 (2): 189–201.

Domina, Thurston. 2005. "Leveling the Home Advantage: Assessing the Effectiveness of Parental Involvement in Elementary School." *Sociology of Education* 78 (3): 233–49.

Dumais, Susan A. 2002. "Cultural Capital, Gender, and School Success: The Role of Habitus." *Sociology of Education* 75 (1): 44–68.

Hallinan, Maureen T. 2008. "Teacher Influences on Students' Attachment to School." *Sociology of Education* 81:271–83.

Jack, Anthony Abraham. 2016. "(No) Harm in Asking: Class, Acquired Cultural Capital, and Academic Engagement at an Elite University." *Sociology of Education* 89 (1): 1–19.

Khan, Shamus Rahman. 2011. *Privilege: The Making of an Adolescent Elite at St. Paul's School.* Princeton, NJ: Princeton University Press.

Kozlowski, Karen Phelan. 2015. "Culture or Teacher Bias? Racial and Ethnic Variation in Student-Teacher Effort Assessment Match/Mismatch." *Race and Social Problems* 7 (1): 43–59.

Lareau, Annette. 2011. *Unequal Childhoods: Class, Race, and Family Life.* Berkeley: University of California Press.

Lee, Jung-Sook, and Natasha K. Bowen. 2006. "Parent Involvement, Cultural Capital, and the Achievement Gap among Elementary School Children." *American Educational Research Journal* 43 (2): 193–218.

Lee, Valerie E., Jeanne Brooks-Gunn, Elizabeth Schnur, and Fong-Ruey Liaw. 1990. "Are Head Start Effects Sustained? A Longitudinal Follow-Up Comparison of Disadvantaged Children Attending Head Start, No Preschool, and Other Preschool Programs." *Child Development* 61 (2): 495–507.

Lewis, Amanda E., and John B. Diamond. 2015. *Despite the Best Intentions: How Racial Inequality Thrives in Good Schools.* New York: Oxford University Press.

Muller, Chandra. 2001. "The Role of Caring in the Teacher-Student Relationship for At-Risk Students." *Sociological Inquiry* 71 (2): 241–55.

Nelson, Margaret K., and Rebecca Schutz. 2007. "Day Care Differences and the Reproduction of Social Class." *Journal of Contemporary Ethnography* 36 (3): 281–317.

Oakes, Jeannie. 2005. *Keeping Track: How Schools Structure Inequality.* New Haven, CT: Yale University Press.

Ready, Douglas D., and David L. Wright. 2011. "Accuracy and Inaccuracy in Teachers' Perceptions of Young Children's Cognitive Abilities: The Role of Child Background and Classroom Contexts." *American Educational Research Journal* 48 (2): 335–60.

Reardon, Sean F. 2011. "The Widening Academic Achievement Gap between the Rich and the Poor: New Evidence and Possible Explanations." In *Wither Opportunity? Rising Inequality, Schools, and Children's Life Chances,* edited by Greg J. Duncan and Richard J. Murnane, 91–116. New York: Russell Sage Foundation.

Rist, Ray. 1970. "Student Social Class and Teacher Expectations: The Self-Fulfilling Prophecy in Ghetto Education." *Harvard Educational Review* 40 (3): 411–51.

Stephens, Nicole M., Stephanie A. Fryberg, Hazel Rose Markus, Camille Johnson, and Rebecca Covarrubias. 2012. "Unseen Disadvantage: How American Universities' Focus on Independence Undermines the Academic Performance of First-Generation College Students." *Journal of Personality and Social Psychology* 102 (6): 1178–97.

Streib, Jessi. 2011. "Class Reproduction by Four Year Olds." *Qualitative Sociology* 34:337–52.

Tyack, David, and Larry Cuban. 1995. *Tinkering toward Utopia: A Century of Public School Reform.* Cambridge, MA: Harvard University Press.

First-Generation College Students

LISA M. NUNN, UNIVERSITY OF SAN DIEGO

EDITORS' NOTE

The previous two chapters provided rich examples of processes that often lead to the reproduction of social inequality. Because affluent students are at ease in the classroom, they often feel comfortable advocating for themselves and customizing their educational experiences in a way that poor students do not—as Jessica Calarco demonstrates in chapter 6. The peer dynamics that William Carbonaro documents in chapter 8 may compound these advantages, since hanging out with affluent peers may further advantage students. In both cases, these informal processes increase advantaged students' odds of succeeding in school and enjoying the rewards associated with school success, while decreasing the odds that poor students experience that same school success.

That said, **socioeconomic mobility** certainly occurs in American schools. University of San Diego sociologist Lisa Nunn describes the experience of one set of socioeconomically mobile students, students who are the first in their families to attend higher education.

As you read this chapter, note the challenges that these first-generation college students encounter. Note also how other student characteristics—including race, gender, and nativity—can intersect with a person's status as a first-generation college student to influence students' college experiences. Do any of these challenges resonate with your own college experience or that of your class peers? What do you think colleges and universities can do to improve first-generation college students' educational experiences?

KEY POINTS

- Social reproduction is the most prominent pattern that we see in the United States across generations, and education is a key element in the process.
- First-generation college students are in a position to break the cycle of social reproduction and become upwardly mobile by obtaining a four-year degree, something their parents do not hold.
- First-generation students overall do not fare as well academically as continuing-generation students, which limits their ability to actually become upwardly mobile after all.
- First-generation students are likely to be lower-income and ethnoracial minorities, and from immigrant families, which are identities that intersect with first-generation status, creating compounding disadvantages in education.
- First-generation students bring many valuable qualities, such as determination, self-reliance, and rich life experiences, to the college environment.

INTRODUCTION

First-generation college students are in a position to live out the epitome of the American Dream because, as the name "first-generation college student" suggests, they are the first in their families to earn a college degree. The American Dream is the idea that with hard work and possibly some talent, anyone can be successful. If you were born into a family that struggled financially, you can build a better life for yourself than your parents had by getting a good education and working hard toward a successful career (Hochschild and Scovronick 2003). We call this upward mobility: moving upward in socioeconomic status over your lifetime. The dream promises that if you work hard enough to achieve upward mobility, then your own children will be born into circumstances that are more financially secure than the ones into which you were born. In this way, generation after generation, the same family can continue on this upward path, achieving higher and higher socioeconomic positions. Thus, when first-generation students succeed in college, it is an important first step toward upward mobility.

Unfortunately, the dream does not come to fruition as easily as we often think it does. Recent research shows that upward mobility has sharply declined in the United States. Where 92 percent of adults born in 1940 earned more than their parents, that number dropped to 50 percent of Americans born in 1984; researchers refer to this as "the fading American Dream" (Chetty, Grusky, et al. 2017). The reality is even more complicated because, by and large, Americans' incomes, on average, follow the same patterns as their parents' incomes (Chetty, Friedman, et al. 2017). Children who grew up in households with the lowest incomes earn, on average, the lowest incomes among adults their age. Similarly, children who grew up in households with the highest incomes end up with the highest incomes themselves among people their age. The pattern holds across the entire spectrum of households. Children who grew up in the middle, land in the middle. So, even though half of American adults today still earn more than their parents, we find that they are, on average, in the same socioeconomic position as their parents when we compare them to people their age.

Sociologists and others have rightly debunked the American Dream as a myth because, while success is available to some who work hard, it is simply not available to all who do so. Nonetheless, the myth is appealing. The dream allows us to believe that no one in America is doomed to remain in a low socioeconomic position he or she happened to be born into. If you are willing to work hard enough, you can "make it." The problem is that the deck is stacked against a large segment of the population: our education system, our labor market opportunities, and a whole host of other systematic obstacles stand in the way of those who have few resources to start with.

Upward mobility is not impossible; indeed, we see examples all the time of people who have risen to great heights from humble roots. However, those examples are much more rare than we tend to believe. According the Equality of Opportunity Project,[1] Americans born into families in the lowest 20 percent of incomes have less than a 10 percent chance of reaching the top 20 percent as adults. In fact, it is even less likely for a poor child to rise to such great heights than it is for a wealthy child to drop from the top 20 percent down to the bottom 20 percent as an adult. We call the latter downward mobility, and the chance of such a decline is about 12 percent in America today (Chetty, Friedman, et al. 2017).

Instead, the pattern in the United States is what we call social reproduction. Social reproduction happens when a person, as an adult, remains in a socioeconomic position similar to the one he or she was born into, as I described earlier when I noted the circumstance of children's incomes following the patterns of their parents' incomes. Then, the next generation is born into that position, reproducing the existing social order in which one family occupies a top position in society generation after generation, and another family remains at a lower position generation after generation. While there is certainly some movement up and down the economic ladder between parents and children, it is not nearly as dramatic as it would be if the American Dream were coming true for most of us. This is why first-generation students are such an important population of college students: when they succeed in college, they are breaking the cycle of social reproduction.

We can see why social reproduction is such a strong pattern when we think about upper-middle-class and wealthy families. We expect the children born

---

1. The Equality of Opportunity Project uses big data to learn about how the American Dream is playing out around the nation: www.equality-of-opportunity.org/.

into these families to become upper-middle-class and wealthy adults themselves, and the majority of them do. On this path, they attend expensive, excellent schools, where they become well qualified to be admitted to top universities, which in turn set them up well to qualify for elite professional careers. Even if children from such families were to be troublemakers or unmotivated, the family's resources and safety nets would likely ensure that they would live out their adult lives in the same high socioeconomic position without dropping very far in socioeconomic status, if at all. If we lived in a truly fair, meritocratic society, where an individual's hard work and talent were the only keys to success, then we would see a great deal of both upward mobility among ambitious and motivated lower-income youth and downward mobility among unmotivated youth born into more prosperous families. But by and large, we do not.

The myth of the American Dream is a powerful ideology in US culture. It clouds our ability to see the social reproduction happening around us all the time. It encourages us to focus on the inspiring—but rare—examples of individuals who have "made it"; and by doing so, it allows us to blame individuals who don't make it for not working hard enough. As this chapter shows, first-generation students must navigate many challenges in order to be successful in college and bring the dream to life. It requires much more than hard work alone.

WHO ARE FIRST-GENERATION COLLEGE STUDENTS?

There is disagreement about when a person counts as a first-generation student. Some institutions count you if neither of your parents ever attended college. By that definition, 24 percent of college students are first-generation, according to a study conducted by the National Center for Educational Statistics (NCES), which is part of the US Department of Education (Redford and Hoyer 2017: 5). Others count you if neither of your parents ever earned a bachelor's degree, which means that if your mom attended college for a year, or even if she earned an associate's degree from community college, that does not disqualify you as first-generation. By that definition another 32 percent are included, so that altogether 56 percent of college students are first-generation (Redford and Hoyer 2017: 5). This latter definition is the one many sociologists, including myself, use, because the sociological dynamics that matter for first-generation students' experiences are present even with those broad parameters.[2]

---

2. To make matters more complex, some agencies, such as Free Application for Federal Student Aid, use an intermediary definition: "parents have not earned any post-secondary degree." By this definition you are considered first-generation if one of your parents attended college without earning a degree, but you are not first-generation if your parent earned a two-year degree such as an associate's degree from a community college.

Table 2   Selected Data on First-Generation Students from National Center for Education Statistics Study

	First-Generation Students		Continuing-Generation Students
	Neither parent attended college (%)	At least one parent has some college experience but neither parent holds a bachelor's degree (%)	At least one parent holds a bachelor's or higher degree (%)
Household income as a high school sophomore			
$20,000 or less	27	12	6
$20,001 to $50,000	50	43	23
Ethnoracial identity			
White	49	61	70
African American	14	17	11
Latinx	27	14	9
Asian American	5	5	6
High school GPA lower than 3.0	66	62	44
First-attended institution after high school			
Less-than-two-year institution	9	5	2
Nonselective two-year institution	52	46	30
Any four-year institution	40	49	70
Moderately selective four-year institution	16	21	27
Highly selective four-year institution	6	10	28
Degree attained within ten years of being a high school sophomore			
Bachelor's degree	20	26	42
Master's degree or higher	3	5	13

SOURCE: US Department of Education, National Center for Education Statistics, *Education Longitudinal Study of 2002*. Adapted from Redford and Hoyer 2017.

While 56 percent is the majority, this figure includes everyone enrolled in postsecondary education, including those in community college, for-profit private colleges, and trade schools. First-generation students attend four-year institutions at much lower rates. While 70 percent of continuing-generation students enroll in four-year institutions after high school, 40 percent of students whose parents have never attended college do so—60 percent of them attend community college or trade school (Redford and Hoyer 2017: 10). That number increases to 49 percent among students who have a parent with some college experience but who does not hold a bachelor's degree (51 percent of that group attends community college or trade school, see table 2; Redford and Hoyer 2017: 22). Of course, these numbers include only the students who enroll in postsecondary education at all.

These statistics are worrisome if we want upward mobility to be possible like the dream promises. When first-generation students graduate college, it means that higher education is doing what it is supposed to do—namely, providing a pathway to economic success. A bachelor's degree opens doors to better-paid jobs and greater social status, thus these students are set up to be more successful economically than their parents were (see chapter 16, by Eric Grodsky and Julie Posselt).

Also worrisome is that, as a group, first-generation students are not as successful in higher education as we might hope. Getting them enrolled in college is not the only hurdle. Compared to continuing-generation students, they have lower grade point averages (GPAs) and are more likely to leave college before they earn a bachelor's degree. Overall, in higher education in the United States, 55 percent of college students complete a bachelor's degree within six years of enrollment (Shapiro et al. 2017: 2). However, the rate for continuing-generation students is about double the rate for first-generation students, according to the NCES study (which followed high school sophomores over a ten-year period, rather than following students for six years after they enrolled in college). As table 2 shows, the NCES study also found that 3 percent of first-generation students whose parents never attended college, and 5 percent of students who had a parent with some college experience, but not a bachelor's degree, had completed a master's degree or higher during that time (approximately eight years after finishing high school), compared to 13 percent of continuing-generation students (Redford and Hoyer 2017: 22).

Multiple factors contribute to the circumstance that first-generation students experience less educational success. These factors include socioeconomic status, racial dynamics, and immigrant family backgrounds, each of which intersects with first-generation status and produces compounding effects.

SOCIOECONOMICS

First-generation students are likely to come from low-income backgrounds. Of course, not all first-generation students do, but it is a fairly common experience. According to the NCES study, 27 percent of students whose parents have never attended college come from households with very low incomes (less than twenty thousand dollars a year in 2002), as do 12 percent of students who have a parent with some college experience but who lacks a bachelor's degree, compared to 6 percent of continuing-generation students. Even combining the bottom two categories of household income (less than fifty thousand dollars in 2002), 77 percent and 55 percent, respectively, of first-generation students grew up in such households, compared to 29 percent of continuing-generation students (see table 2).

That means they are more likely to have attended modest- or poor-performing K–12 schools, which makes them less likely to be academically prepared for the demands of college. It does not mean that they are less intellectually capable of doing the work, of course: it simply means that they have not been as exposed to critical thinking, critical analysis, writing, and other skills as much as a typical student has who attended high-performing schools, which are often located in more affluent neighborhoods. (See case study 3, by Megan Thiele and Karen Jeong Robinson.) Schools in upper-income neighborhoods tend to offer more Advanced Placement courses, as well as rigorous academic work, whereas as in lower-income neighborhoods the opportunity to learn college-level content is limited (IES 2016a).

The NCES study found that 66 percent of first-generation college students had high school GPAs lower than 3.0 (62 percent among those who had a parent with some college experience), compared to 44 percent of continuing-generation college students (see table 2). This difference does not take into account the fact that a 4.0 GPA at a high-performing, academically rigorous school is more challenging to attain. So, the achievement difference between first-generation and continuing-generation students is likely larger than GPA alone reflects. Regardless, it would be misguided for us to assume that lower GPAs are a sign of lower intellectual capability. It's necessary to understand some of the factors that contribute to how academic performance ends up differing so much between these groups.

For the moment, let's focus on consequences: with lower high school GPAs, first-generation students tend to be less college-ready than continuing-generation students. Lower GPAs, combined with fewer Advanced Placement courses on their transcripts, mean that on college applications they seem less academically competitive. Thus, it makes sense that first-generation students are much more likely to attend nonselective two-year institutions as they start their college trajectories. As table 2 shows, 52 percent of first-generation students whose parents have never attended college, and 46 percent of students who have a parent who has some college experience but not a bachelor's degree, start there, compared to 30 percent of continuing-generation students (Redford and Hoyer 2017: 22). On the opposite end of the college-going experience, continuing-generation students are about three times more likely to head straight to a highly selective four-year institution: 28 percent, compared to 6 percent and 10 percent of the two groups of first-generation students, respectively. Meanwhile 16 percent and 21 percent of first-generation students, respectively, go to moderately selective four-year institutions, compared to 27 percent of continuing-generation students (Redford and Hoyer 2017: 22).

A look at academic preparation not only can help us understand who enrolls where but also helps us understand who leaves college before they have graduated. Of course, not all first-generation students are underprepared for the academic demands of college (Hand and Payne 2008; Reid and Moore 2008). Research shows that college-ready first-generation students return to college after their first year at the same rate as continuing-generation students; however, first-generation students who are not college-ready return at lower rates for a second year (Furquim et al. 2017). This emphasizes both how critical it is to offer students solid K–12 learning opportunities and experiences and the importance of understanding how closely academic preparation is tied to family income.

Having access to tuition-based private schools, which tend to prepare students well for college, costs families money. Even among public schools, which are free to attend, access to excellent schools generally depends on which neighborhood a student's parents can afford to live in, as the quality of public schools tends to be higher or lower in line with the property values of the surrounding homes (Lareau and Goyette 2014). While this is not always the case in every community, by and large in the United States the more expensive a neighborhood is to live in, the higher performing its public schools are. Family finances play an additional role in the patterns of who stays in college all the way through to graduation. The NCES study found that 54 percent (and 53 percent) of first-generation students who left college early reported that they could not afford to continue attending, compared to 45 percent of continuing-generation students who dropped out (see table 2).

Bringing additional financial strain, first-generation students take out student loans more often, and in higher amounts, than continuing-generation students in their first year (Furquim et al. 2017). Although student loans help with tuition and living expenses, lower-income students' budgets are tighter for things like books and lab supplies. They are more likely to simply make do in a class without buying the book, which makes it challenging to earn a grade as high as they might have earned with a copy of the book. First-generation students are also more likely to have to find a job to help support themselves while they are enrolled in college, which takes time and energy away from schoolwork—which also makes it unsurprising that their college GPAs are lower on average than those of their more affluent classmates (Davis 2010; Jehangir 2010).

Financial concerns were front and center in the lives of students in my research study. I interviewed students entering two different highly selective four-year universities, one public and one private, and I followed those students across their first two years in college. All were starting college as first-year students in the fall of 2015. Interestingly, in my study, many continuing-generation students and first-generation students alike held part-time jobs. The difference was that continuing-generation students told me that they wanted to work so that they could have extra money for fun activities and feel somewhat independent from their parents; the extra money was not necessary to make ends meet.

For example, Madison (all names have been changed) worked every summer: "I'm a swim coach at a country club. It's super fun and the finances are fun." Madison was considering working during the school year, too: "I might get a job next semester. . . . [M]y parents give me money, and it's not an issue, but I feel like I should try to make my own money just so I'm not completely relying on them." Many continuing-generation students who were working during the school term said that their parents were clear that if their schoolwork started to slip, the first thing they would have to do is quit their jobs. Madison's parents were similar: "They want me to focus on school and do my schoolwork, but if I said I wanted to get a fifteen-hour-a-week job, I don't think they would be mad."

For first-generation students in my study, on the other hand, working was not a luxury. Kevin is a good example: "This summer I had three jobs, trying to pay for tuition and to help my parents pay off house bills. . . . I was focusing on money so much in the beginning of the year that it took a hit on my grades. I made money during the summer with three jobs, but it was nowhere near enough." Before taking those summer jobs, Kevin had already been working during the school year: "I have federal work-study, which is only three thousand [dollars]. I understand students usually use that as pocket money; but I can't, because I have to save that for tuition next semester. . . . Outside of work-study, I have another job. It's really hard focusing on all these different aspects right now." For many first-generation students in my study, like Kevin, not only did working take their attention away from schoolwork for several hours a week, but also the financial insecurity that drove them to find work in the first place was a source of constant stress, which only made school more challenging.

RACIAL DYNAMICS

First-generation students are more likely to be from ethnoracial minority and mixed-race families, thus they are faced with the issues and realities of racial dynamics both within the system of education and in US society more broadly. Comparing census data (Humes, Jones, and Ramirez 2011) with the NCES study, we see that whites comprise 64 percent of the US population. And while 70 percent of continuing-generation students are white, only 49 percent of first-generation students whose parents have never attended college, and 61 percent of students who have a parent with some college experience but who does not hold a bachelor's degree, are white (Redford and Hoyer 2017: 20). Thus, white students are overrepresented among continuing-generation students and underrepresented among first-generation students.

The reverse is true for African American and Latinx students. According to the same data sources, African Americans make up 13 percent of the US population, and 11 percent of continuing-generation students are African American, as compared to 14 percent of first-generation students whose parents have never attended college and 17 percent of first-generation students who have a parent with some college experience. Sixteen percent of the US population are Latinx, while 9 percent of continuing-generation students are Latinx. However, 27 percent of first-generation students whose parents have never attended college, and 14 percent of students who have a parent with some college experience, are Latinx. By contrast, Asian Americans make up 6 percent of the US population and comprise 6 percent of continuing-generation students and 5 percent of first-generation students.

My research at the two universities took place during the Black Lives Matter movement, which sought to draw attention to police brutality enacted on communities of color, particularly African American communities. The 2016 presidential election was also happening as I interviewed students. Donald Trump's presidential campaign sparked white supremacy displays across the United States. At the two universities in my study, it was commonplace for these political tensions to play out on campus, as was the case for many colleges around the nation. Students I interviewed could not help but be affected by it. Protests and walkouts were organized both for and against black student initiatives. Graffiti popped up routinely, depicting swastikas, portraying the border wall promised by Donald Trump, denouncing Mexico and Mexicans, or demanding restoration of white rights in America. Racial tensions on both campuses were part of the everyday environment. Students of color described it to me as "exhausting," "frustrating," and "scary" to have to navigate those tensions while trying to go to class and get their work done.

African American and Latinx students are underrepresented not just among continuing-generation families but also in the more selective and elite institutions (see chapter 16 by Grodsky and Posselt). It is the lower-ranked, less selective, large, public, two-year and four-year institutions that more often serve students of color. As I noted earlier in this chapter, 55 percent of US college students overall graduate with a bachelor's degree within six years of enrolling. For white and Asian/Pacific Islander students, the national six-year graduation rate is 62 percent and 63 percent, respectively (Shapiro et al. 2017: 2). For African Americans, that rate is only 38 percent. For Latinx students, it is 46 percent. For Native Americans, the rate is 41 percent.

These realities are daunting. Carlos, a student in my study, told me that after a year of struggling both academically and socially at his four-year public university, he found out in a peer-leadership class what the graduation statistics were for first-generation, low-income, Latinx students like himself. He told me that he was so angry he wanted to cry. That's one ugly side of the American Dream: when people discover the extent to which the odds are against them, they feel tricked or worse.

However, dedication is one of first-generation students' most positive attributes. They have a strong motivation to succeed (Beattie 2018). They believe in the power of education to improve not only their own lives but also the lives of their families, by extension.

First-generation students in my study often talked about wanting to stay in college and graduate so they could be strong role models for younger siblings or cousins. Ilana explained what that feels like: "I'm the first one from all of them—all of my older cousins and everything—to go to a college. None of them have gone to community [college] or nothing. They just work." Ilana told me her family saw her as "this girl that's so motivated—and for them I'm super smart—so if I [fail], and I'm back home, . . . they are like, 'What are you doing here?' And if I say, 'Oh, it was hard,' I feel like I will unmotivate them. Because they will say, 'If this girl wasn't able to do it, what makes me think that I'll do it?'" Ilana told me that this responsibility to her family helped her push herself in moments of doubt when she wanted to give up on an assignment or an entire class.

IMMIGRANT FAMILY BACKGROUND

It is not uncommon for the children of immigrant families to be first-generation college students (Jehangir 2010). Several first-generation students in my study had immigrated to the United States during their childhood, or their parents were immigrants. For these students, additional motivation to succeed comes from their sense of obligation to their families. Edelina Burciaga discusses the "immigrant bargain" in chapter 5 of this book. The immigrant bargain is an often-unspoken agreement that children must make good on the sacrifices their parents made in order to come to this new country in hopes of providing a better life for their children, including educational opportunities. Most students I interviewed whose parents were immigrants echoed those ideas.

Ramon is a good example. He told me, "College also is a validation for my parents' hard work and sacrifices. That's what it also serves for me. It shows them it wasn't a waste; it went somewhere." Such students are highly driven, which helps them persist in the face of challenges (Somers, Woodhouse, and Cofer 2004; Stebleton and Soria 2012). For continuing-generation students in my study, the concerns over academic success sounded different. Continuing-generation students were more likely to say they did not want to "waste" their parents' money. Both perspectives show that many college students desire to honor their parents' contributions to their educations by doing well; however, first-generation immigrant students I interviewed seemed to carry their obligation with a graver sense of duty, which created extra anxiety over their grades and other aspects of their performance in school.

However, other dynamics also play out among some students whose parents are immigrants. The parents of two students in my study were in the process of being deported from the United States during their children's first year of college. This added a great deal of stress and uncertainty to these students' lives at the same time that they were trying to adjust to campus life and to the academic demands of college.

Also, some parents who never earned a college degree themselves do not fully support college education as the route their children should take, even though they might believe strongly in education in general. Mai, for example, lived under the obligations of the immigrant bargain, which added obstacles to her academic success. Mai was under great pressure to help in her family's automotive business. Her parents allowed her to move away to attend a four-year university, but while she was there they wanted her to take automotive classes at night school and come home on weekends to work in the shop. All of which Mai dutifully did. However, Mai soon became overwhelmed and found it difficult to cultivate friendships with her roommates and others on campus.

Ultimately the combination of her obligation to meet her parents' wishes and her uncertainty about what major she wanted to pursue led Mai to leave college in her second year and work full time instead while also finishing her night school certificate program. Her parents viewed an automotive certificate as more valuable than a bachelor's degree. According to the NCES study, first-generation students are between two and a half and four and a half times more likely to enroll in trade school rather than college, compared to continuing-generation students (Redford and Hoyer 2017: 22). Mai told me she would like to go back to college in the future, but she was not sure where life would take her.

As in Mai's case, it is common for first-generation students to have responsibilities at home that make it difficult for them to focus their time and energy on their schoolwork, and this is the case whether the student's parents are immigrants or not. First-generation students are likely to be devoted, contributing members of their family households, and going to college does not necessarily release them from their duties. For example, they are more likely to be parents themselves or caretakers of other family and community members (Jehangir 2010).

FIRST-GENERATION IS A STATUS OF ITS OWN

Low socioeconomic status, ethnoracial minority identity, and immigrant family background all are dynamics that are typically part of a first-generation student's complex lived experiences. However, those are each separate from what it means to be a first-generation college student. They are dynamics that intersect with first-generation status. To be first-generation means that your parents do not have wisdom from their own college experiences to pass on to you.

Typically, such parents are not familiar with college applications, financial aid forms, the requirements related to registering for classes, or the important considerations in deciding on a major. This means they are unlikely to step in and facilitate those processes and decisions for you in the way that the parents of many continuing-generation students are well equipped to do (Holland 2018). One student in my study, Zach, was a typical example of continuing-generation students' experiences. When I asked how he decided to major in business, he said, "I talked to both my parents pretty extensively about my major decision, and they have been helpful with that."

Similarly, Grayson, another continuing-generation student, told me that his parents constantly shared their college wisdom: "In terms of life advice like finances or managing my life or applying for something, they're very good at that." Grayson's dad "had a great college experience" and was full of stories. "He tells me all about his professors; and he had one professor that he was obsessed with, and it sounds like one who I'm obsessed with at this point, which is my chem professor. It's kind of a similar story. Yeah, he gives good advice about that." Grayson did not need to rely solely on his dad, either. His mom also bombarded him with information "about her college experiences," even when he felt like he could not relate.

Meanwhile, first-generation students are on their own as they attempt to figure things out. Their parents are not able to guide them. Brianna, a first-generation student in my study, called her parents "clueless" when it came to college advice. And Brandon's explanation is typical among the first-generation students I interviewed. When I asked if he turned to his family for college advice, Brandon said, "No. Not at all. They would not understand. They don't understand anything college-related. If it comes to financial aid, if it comes to academics, if it comes to social life, if it comes to anything. They just don't. Their mind doesn't wrap around college. They're like, 'Well, I wish I could help. I don't know what to say.'" Brandon seemed to accept this as a fact of life, but it also detached him from his family. "When it comes to—they don't know anything. I don't tell my mom or my family anything I'm going through. I just keep it to me."

Rashné Rustom Jehangir (2010) described first-generation students as "strangers without codebooks" to emphasize the feelings of isolation and confusion that are part of navigating the unfamiliar terrain of college. As Grayson and Zach show us, a parent who successfully finished college might remind you to check your syllabi regularly for assignment due dates, or push you to go see your professors during their office hours to ask questions, which will help you. But without college experience, she cannot pass along that wisdom. She may not know what office hours are.

This is why campus programs that target first-generation students' needs—such as Student Support Services, a Federal TRIO program—often provide peer mentors and professional academic advisors to help fill in the gaps in students' information and "college-knowledge." All students benefit from having trustworthy others in their lives who have college experience and insider knowledge to share, and first-generation students cannot access that wisdom from their parents the way that continuing-generation students can.

Combined with college-knowledge are cultural approaches to problem solving, behavior, and modes of interacting with authority figures that are more common among the families of first-generation students, but which are not always aligned well with college norms (see chapter 6 by Calarco and case study 3 by Thiele and Robinson). April Yee (2016: 852) found in her research that "first-generation students believe they are responsible for earning good grades on their own." By contrast, continuing-generation students "believe that they are responsible for reaching out to get help."

First-generation students in Yee's study focused on *strategies of independence,* such as "buckling down" by studying harder and longer when they encountered challenges. On the other hand, continuing-generation students used additional *strategies of interaction,* such as seeking help during office hours, asking professors to allow them to resubmit essays after revising them, and other personalized accommodations.

Yee (2016: 852) concludes that continuing-generation students "are more likely to achieve not because they exert more absolute effort, but because they employ a wider range of strategies." She argues that the system of higher education expects students to engage in learning behaviors that are interactive (not independent), thus the strategies used by continuing-generation students "are recognized and rewarded at the same time that the independent engagement strategies of first-generation students are largely ignored."

I saw this dynamic in my research as well. A positive trait that stood out in the first-generation students I studied is their strong, well-developed sense of self-reliance. They were ready to hold themselves accountable to meet deadlines and accomplish their work. Like all students, they took joy in their successes, but I found that first-generation students also more readily took personal responsibility for their missteps. Unlike continuing-generation students, they did not typically think of asking for permission to turn in an assignment late if they had missed the deadline, or to revise an essay that earned a low grade, or to retake an exam they had bombed. This robust sense of self-reliance leads first-generation students to engage in what Yee calls "strategies of independence."

For example, when Sabrina failed her first two midterms in chemistry and biology, she felt devastated. Then she sat herself down and decided, "Okay. I really need to learn how to study." Her high school had not prepared her well for the demands of college. She had never had to open a science book before; her teachers had always delivered the information during class that she needed to know. She had aced her tests throughout high school and felt proud of her success. So, even though she gave herself a week to study for her first college midterms, she could not absorb all the material in time. She was not used to the expectation that students should read chapters on their own, covering content in addition to the lecture.

As did many other first-generation students in my study, Sabrina felt confused and frustrated by how much material other students in her classes seemed to already know from high school. But, like other first-generation students, she was determined to bounce back from her failures and "do whatever it takes" to pass her classes. She told me, "I was really disappointed with myself, but at the same time: 'Okay, I'll just do better.' . . . I didn't even open my chemistry book, and now I read the entire chapter even though it takes me so many hours."

While these traits of self-reliance and motivation give first-generation students a boost, it is not always possible to come out ahead in a course even when one tries one's hardest. Students have to have the time to develop the skills to master the content as well as work out exactly what the professor wants.

Ironically, self-reliance can be counterproductive for first-generation students if they postpone reaching out for help from teachers during office hours or at tutoring centers, because they are trying to figure things out on their own first. Typical of first-generation students, Marisol told me she had been "scared to go to office hours because they are so smart and so intelligent and . . . I didn't want them to think I'm dumb. . . . I want to do what I can to learn by myself so I won't have to go to them or try to annoy them."

Reaching for resources versus figuring things out alone is one of the key differences between continuing-generation students and first-generation students (Yee 2016). In my research I found that first-generation students like Marisol worried about bothering their professors, while continuing-generation students felt entitled to their professors' time. "That's what they are there for" was a common sentiment among continuing-generation students. They were more comfortable asking for one-on-one attention, asking them to explain assignment instructions again, requesting extensions on due dates, and requesting other accommodations when they made mistakes or misunderstood what was expected of them. Other scholars have found similar dynamics among students from more affluent, well-educated family backgrounds (Calarco 2014, 2018; Jack 2016; Thiele 2015).

When first-generation students in my study did reach for help, they often went to their peers. Lucas offered a typical explanation: "I just reach out to students. Because no one knows better than them, especially for making your schedules; which classes should I take . . . or professor I should take; or 'No way I have time to finish this; what should I tell my professor?' That type of stuff." I asked Lucas if he felt like he got good advice from his fellow students, and he said, "For the most part. They're also kids, too, so I guess nobody has the real right answer. I guess literally no one has the right answer to anything." Lucas and other first-generation students often felt like the details and logistics of college were so vast and mysterious that it was impossible to expect to know it all.

Meanwhile, continuing-generation students in my study felt differently. For example, Lily remembered trying to switch classes on the third day of school: "It was so stressful and I did it all by myself; and I had no idea what I was doing, so I texted my RA [residential assistant] and my first-year mentor, who is also a student. . . . [B]ut I wished I had an adult to give me some advice and show me how to do it." Lily did not know how to get a hold of her academic advisor on such short notice, so she settled for peer advice even though she was not confident that her RA and peer mentor were adequately knowledgeable. She explained, "When you have that adult that has that label, then it gives them more credibility and it makes you trust them more." Continuing-generation students had often relied on high school counselors and parents for advice in the past, so seeking out "adult" resources in college felt comfortable and reassuring.

Indeed, Lily and others are on to something. First-generation students like Lucas would likely be better off if they reached out to university staff and professors for advice in addition to their peers—just as first-generation students such as Marisol would be better off if they went to their professors during office hours for clarification of course material. Yet, for first-generation students the habit of reaching out to authority figures for help can be challenging to develop, because it goes against their desire to show respect for their professors by not "bothering" them and to prove their maturity and good character by figuring things out on their own. Continuing-generation students are much less likely to hold those beliefs.

CONCLUSION

The issues related to first-generation students in higher education are multifaceted. One aspect is that first-generation students are not enrolled in strong numbers at highly selective universities in the United States. As table 2 shows, they are more likely than continuing-generation students to attend trade schools or two-year colleges. This leads to lower overall earnings as adults. According to the Equality of Opportunity Project, students who started college at an elite college have incomes by age thirty-four that are approximately twenty percentile points higher than those who started at a two-year college (Chetty, Friedman, et al. 2017). The good news is that attending college, be it a four-year or a two-year college, promotes upward mobility for students whose parents were in the bottom half of incomes in the United States. However, the type of college matters. Average incomes for thirty-four-year-olds who attended elite colleges hover around the seventieth percentile (among incomes of thirty-four-year-olds only). Since being in the seventieth percentile means that 70 percent of incomes are below yours, that is well above average. Meanwhile, average incomes for those who went to two-year colleges hover around the fiftieth percentile, which is right about average. Non-elite four-year universities land people neatly in between those two, around the sixtieth percentile, according to the research.

It is not uncommon for first-generation students to attend for-profit colleges instead. This is worrisome, because students who attend for-profit colleges amass greater student loan debt than average, default on loans at a higher rate, and have higher unemployment rates after graduating, compared to students at other types of schools (Deming, Goldin, and Katz 2012). For-profit colleges also have a six-year graduation rate of 28 percent for bachelor's degrees, compared to 56 percent for public institutions and 65 percent for private nonprofit schools (Aud et al. 2012). This means that many students who attend for-profit colleges end up with heavy student loan debt but no degree.

It also is not uncommon for first-generation students to start college later than the traditional age of eighteen to twenty (Jehangir 2010). This makes extension programs, adult degree completion programs, and online programs attractive options. While first-generation students benefit from online or distance learning programs (Pontes and Pontes 2012), we know that adult students drop out of school at higher rates than traditional-age students because "life happens" and other priorities are simply more pressing than schoolwork (Bergman et al. 2014). My research study focuses on the experiences of first-generation students in two highly selective nonprofit four-year universities, but that is a small slice of the territory first-generation students occupy in higher education. That said, it is also a critical one, since the chance for the greatest upward mobility in America comes through attending such schools (Chetty, Friedman, et al. 2017). Programs such as the Federal TRIO / Student Support Services specifically target first-generation students with support on college campuses, and a growing number of colleges are creating offices and programs to support first-generation students' needs.

For many advocates, the goal is not simply to make first-generation students become more like their continuing-generation counterparts. The goal is to transform four-year educational institutions so that they accommodate the wider set of life histories and adult responsibilities of the entire student body. Currently, many schools, like the two in my research study, create policies, housing options, class schedules, and grading criteria that assume their students typically fit the mold of the traditional-aged, relatively affluent student whose "only job right now is to focus on school," as many of my continuing-generation informants phrased it. Changing that assumption would make four-year institutions more viable possibilities for first-generation students and would improve their odds of success, in comparison to those who attend adult degree completion programs and for-profit colleges.

Beyond studying the logistical elements of college life, Jeff Davis (2010: 54–55) urges us to recognize that first-generation students "bring vitality and new ideas to the college environment, that they bring a different set of needs and expectations, and that the coming together of the privileged and the non-privileged can be a positive, transformative experience for both first-generation students and institutions." Jehangir (2010: 151) argues that this kind of transformative experience would entail cultivating campus and classroom environments in which ground rules permit "a sense of trust and community" to develop in order "to allow students to engage in thoughtful disagreement" when their life histories and viewpoints are so widely varied that conversations become challenging.

The dialog that Jehangir envisions would take place in campus communities where all students feel a sense of belonging, and where their perspectives are both validated and respected. Jehangir's ideal contrasts with the current experiences of many first-generation students on four-year campuses, who often struggle to feel that they belong and are inclined to hide their backgrounds and circumstances in order to seem more legitimate to their peers and professors (DeRosa and Dolby 2014; Flores 2014; Strayhorn 2012; Stuber 2011). Thus, changing higher education to expect and value the many traits first-generation students bring with them requires much more than simply enrolling first-generation students.

CHAPTER 7 REVIEW

Discussion Questions

1. Do you personally share any of the typical traits, or have you had any of the typical experiences, described in this chapter as common among first-generation students? If so, how has this influenced your college experience?

2. Do you talk with your parents about college life? What are some examples of useful and not-so-useful advice they have given you?

3. Thinking about intersectionality, how might the experiences of a student who is white, low-income, and first-generation compare with those of a student who is Latinx, middle-class, and first-generation? Based on what you learned in this chapter, what might you expect to be different for them?

4. What do you think colleges should do regarding first-generation students? What changes would you suggest?

Suggestions for Further Reading

Davis, Jeff. 2010. *The First-Generation Student Experience: Implications for Campus Practice, and Strategies for Improving Persistence and Success.* Sterling, VA: ACPA College Student Educators International.

Jehangir, Rashné Rustom. 2010. *Higher Education and First-Generation Students: Cultivating Community, Voice, and Place for the New Majority.* New York: Palgrave Macmillan.

Reid, M. Jeanne, and James L. Moore. 2008. "College Readiness and Academic Preparation for Postsecondary Education: Oral Histories of First-Generation Urban College Students." *Urban Education* 43 (2): 240–61.

Yee, April. 2016. "The Unwritten Rules of Student Engagment: Social Class Differences in Undergraduates' Academic Strategies." *Journal of Higher Education* 87 (6): 831–58.

References

Aud, Susan, William Hussar, Frank Johnson, Grace Kena, Erin Roth, Eileen Manning, Xiaolei Wang, and Jijun Zhang. 2012. *The Condition of Education 2012.* NCES 2012–045. Washington, DC: US Department of Education.

Beattie, Irenee R. 2018. "Sociological Perspectives on First Generation College Students." In *Handbook of the Sociology of Education in the 21st Century,* edited by B. Schneider and G. Saw, 171–91. New York: Springer.

Bergman, Mathew, Jacob P. K. Gross, Matt Berry, and Brad Shuck. 2014. "If Life Happened but a Degree Didn't: Examining Factors That Impact Adult Student Persistence." *Journal of Continuing Higher Education* 62:90–101.

Calarco, Jessica McCrory. 2014. "Coached for the Classroom: Parents' Cultural Transmission and Children's Reproduction of Educational Inequalities." *American Sociological Review* 79:1015–37.

———. 2018. *Negotiating Opportunities: How the Middle Class Secures Advantages in School.* Oxford: Oxford University Press.

Chetty, Raj, John N. Friedman, Emmanuel Saez, Nicholas Turner, and Danny Yagan. 2017. "Mobility Report Cards: The Role of Colleges in Intergenerational Mobility." NBER Working Paper No. 23618. National Bureau of Economic Research.

Chetty, Raj, David Grusky, Maximilian Hell, Nathan Hendren, Robert Manduca, and Jimmy Narang. 2017. "The Fading American Dream: Trends in Absolute Income Mobility." *Science* 356:398–406.

Davis, Jeff. 2010. *The First-Generation Student Experience: Implications for Campus Practice, and Strategies for Improving Persistence and Success.* Sterling, VA: ACPA College Student Educators International.

Deming, David, Claudia Goldin, and Lawrence Katz. 2012. "The For-Profit Postsecondary School Sector: Nimble Critters or Agile Predators?" *Journal of Economic Perspectives* 26: 139–64.

DeRosa, Erin, and Nadine Dolby. 2014. "'I Don't Think the University Knows Me': Institutional Culture and Lower-Income, First-Generation College Students." *Interactions: UCLA Journal of Education and Information Studies* 10:1–18.

Flores, Angel D. 2014. *50 Things I Wish Someone Would Have Told Me about College: Straight Talk for First-Generation Students FROM First-Generation Graduates.* San Bernardino, CA: Serolf Press.

Furquim, Fernando, Kristen M. Glasener, Meghan Oster, Brian P. McCall, and Stephen L. DesJardins. 2017. "Navigating the Financial Aid Process: Borrowing Outcomes among First-Generation and Non-First-Generation Students." *Annals of the American Academy of Political and Social Sciences* 671: 69–91.

Hand, Christie, and Emily Miller Payne. 2008. "First-Generation College Students: A Study of Appalachian Student Success." *Journal of Developmental Education* 32:4–6, 8, 10, 12, 14–15.

Hochschild, Jennifer L., and Nathan Scovronick. 2003. *The American Dream and the Public Schools.* New York: Oxford University Press.

Holland, Megan. 2018. *Divergent Paths to College: Race, Class, and Inequality in High Schools.* New Brunswick, NJ: Rutgers University Press.

Humes, Karen R., Nicholas A. Jones, and Roberto R. Ramirez. 2011. *Overview of Race and Hispanic Origin: 2010.* Washington, DC: US Census Bureau.

Institute of Education Sciences (IES). 2016a. *The Condition of Education 2016.* Washington, DC: Institute of Education Sciences, National Center for Education Statistics, Department of Education.

———. 2016b. *Status and Trends in the Education of Racial and Ethnic Groups 2016.* Washington, DC: Institute of Education Statistics, National Center for Education Statistics, US Department of Education.

Jack, Anthony Abraham. 2016. "(No) Harm in Asking: Class, Acquired Cultural Capital, and Academic Engagement at an Elite University." *Sociology of Education* 89:1–19.

Jehangir, Rashné Rustom. 2010. *Higher Education and First-Generation Students: Cultivating Community, Voice, and Place for the New Majority.* New York: Palgrave Macmillan.

Lareau, Annette, and Kimberly Goyette. 2014. "Choosing Homes, Choosing Schools." New York: Russell Sage Foundation.

Pontes, Manuel C. F., and Nancy M. H. Pontes. 2012. "Distance Education Enrollment Is Associated with Greater Academic Progress among First-Generation Low-Income Undergraduate Students in the US in 2008." *Online Journal of Distance Learning Administration* 15.

Redford, Jeremy, and Kathleen Mulvaney Hoyer. 2017. *First-Generation and Continuing-Generation College Students: A Comparison of High School and Postsecondary Experiences.* Washington, DC: National Center for Education Statistics, US Department of Education.

Reid, M. Jeanne, and James L. Moore. 2008. "College Readiness and Academic Preparation for Postsecondary Education: Oral Histories of First-Generation Urban College Students." *Urban Education* 43:240–61.

Shapiro, Doug, Afet Dundar, Faye Huie, Phoebe Khasiala Wakhungu, Xin Yuan, Angel Nathan, and Youngsik Hwang. 2017. *A National View of Student Attainment Rates by Race and Ethnicity—Fall 2010 Cohort.* Signature Report No. 12b. Herndon, VA: National Student Clearinghouse Research Center.

Somers, Patricia, Shawn R. Woodhouse, and James E. Cofer Sr. 2004. "Pushing the Boulder Uphill: The Persistence of First-Generation College Students." *NASPA Journal* 41:418–35.

Stebleton, Michael J., and Krista M. Soria. 2012. "Breaking Down Barriers: Academic Obstacles of First-Generation Students at Research Universities." *Learning Assistance Review* 17:7–19.

Strayhorn, Terrell L. 2012. *College Students' Sense of Belonging.* New York: Routledge.

Stuber, Jenny M. 2011. *Inside the College Gates: How Class and Culture Matters.* Lanham, MD: Lexington Books.

Thiele, Megan. 2015. "Resource or Obstacle?: Classed Reports of Student-Faculty Relations." *Sociological Quarterly* 57: 333–55.

Yee, April. 2016. "The Unwritten Rules of Student Engagment: Social Class Differences in Undergraduates' Academic Strategies." *Journal of Higher Education* 87:831–58.

Peer Sorting, Peer Influence, and Student Outcomes

WILLIAM CARBONARO, UNIVERSITY OF NOTRE DAME

EDITORS' NOTE

Take a second to remember an experience at school that helped define who you are today. For some of us, the first moment that comes to mind might be the moment when a tough idea final started to make sense, or the moment we discovered a fact or idea that sparked our curiosity. But for many of us, that moment probably has nothing at all to do with a teacher, or a classroom, or a textbook. Instead, it probably happened in the lunchroom or the hallway or the playground, and it probably involved our **peers**.

Sociologists of education are fascinated by many different ways our friends, enemies, classmates, and study partners shape our educational experiences. Peers are every bit as important as teachers and school administrators in shaping and conveying the hidden curriculum of schooling. Their expectations, attitudes, and behaviors undoubtedly influence our own. But that influence can be complicated. Which are the peers who mattered for your development? Did all of your school's classmates matter? Just the students you took classes with? Just your closest friends?

Notre Dame sociologist William Carbonaro argues that figuring out how, when, and why peers matter requires careful measurement of youth **social networks.** As you read about the ways sociologists conceptualize and measure social networks, see if you can apply these ideas to your own social worlds.

KEY POINTS

- Peer sorting occurs through both formal and informal processes.
- Formal sorting processes expose students to very different sets of schoolmates and classmates.
- Informal sorting processes involve the creation of status groups and friendship networks based on propinquity (social proximity) and homophily (similarity).
- Peers affect the learning outcomes for a given student because they directly and indirectly shape the resources that students need to succeed academically.

INTRODUCTION

The Breakfast Club was one of the top-grossing films of 1985. The film's poster read, "They were five total strangers, with nothing in common, meeting for the first time. A brain, a beauty, a jock, a rebel, and recluse." The main premise of the film was simple: five high school students from different social cliques are forced to spend their entire Saturday together in detention. The timeline opens with the students arriving at school for detention, and it closes on the very same day, when detention ends. During this time, the school principal gives the students an assignment: Write an essay answering the question "Who do you think you are?" Most of the "action" (largely, conversations between characters) transpires in the school library, where the students are serving their time in detention. At first, the interactions between the students are tense, awkward, and often antagonistic. However, as the day wears on, stereotypes and assumptions based on group memberships eventually fall away, and ultimately the students realize that none of them can easily be defined by their outward appearances and group memberships. The students recognize that they are more similar than they originally believed, and to everyone's surprise (including the audience's), some meaningful friendships and bonds of camaraderie are formed. The film resonated so strongly with movie audiences because it captures how peer relations are formed and maintained.

I argue that the sorts of peer relationships captured so memorably in *The Breakfast Club* have a crucial impact on students' schooling outcomes. In this chapter, I describe theories and research that focus on *peer sorting* and *peer influence* in education. Together, peer sorting and peer influence are central to scholarship on peers, schooling processes, and student outcomes. Research shows that peers serve as important resources that are unequally distributed across schools, classrooms, and friendship networks, thereby explaining why some groups experience greater educational success than others. Consequently, peer sorting and peer influence are strongly implicated as key mechanisms in creating and maintaining educational inequality. At the end of the chapter, I will discuss the many challenges that "peer effects" pose for policy makers who are interested in equalizing opportunities and reducing inequality in learning outcomes among students.

PEERS AND PEER INFLUENCE IN SCHOOLS

"Peers" are fellow students who occupy the same social space, such as the school, the classroom, the neighborhood, and/or the friendship network. Peer sorting is the process that determines how a given student is matched with a given set of peers, and it is driven by both formal and informal processes. Formal processes sort students into peer groups on the basis of a clearly defined set of rules, procedures, and guidelines. These formal processes are created, monitored, and enforced by gatekeepers, who possess the organizational authority to directly affect how peer sorting occurs. Two important types of peer groups—schoolmates and classmates—are largely shaped by formal sorting processes in the educational system.

For example, in the United States, a student's schoolmates are largely determined by his or her family's residence. The rules of school assignment are established by state and local officials, and they are largely enforced by school districts. Families possess agency, meaning that they have freedom to make choices about where to live, and some families may choose to send their children to either private schools or public schools of choice (e.g., magnet or charter schools). However, these are strategic choices made under the constraints of the formal processes that are in place. Families who lack the resources to move to a given area, or who cannot afford private school tuition, face greater constraints than families who possess these resources, and peer sorting reflects these differential constraints.

Some peer sorting, however, is driven by informal processes, where formal rules and procedures for determining membership in a peer group are absent. For example, there are no formal criteria or rules that determine which students belong to a given friendship group. In addition, the "gatekeepers" of friendship networks do not have formalized roles and authority, unlike the individuals who make school and classroom assignments. Instead, the sorting process is informal, and it is largely created, monitored, and enforced by peers themselves. A familiar example is the prototypical "mean girl" who uses cultural and behavioral cues to determine who can enter a friendship network and who cannot. As with formal processes, informal processes are driven by both self-selection and gatekeeping. Students can make strategic choices regarding which peer groups to join, and which friendships to form, but peers also have the autonomy to reject or accept students as group members and/or friends.

Propinquity and *homophily* are two driving forces that affect informal peer sorting. Propinquity describes the tendency for people to form relationships with peers with whom they regularly interact. Accordingly, friendships are more likely to form among classmates than nonclassmates simply because classmates spend more time with one another than nonclassmates. Thus, the formal sorting of peers into different classes based on ability sets the stage for friendships in which friends are more similar in academic ability than would be the case in a mixed-ability classroom. Homophily is the tendency for people to form relationships with others who share traits similar to their own. The adage that "birds of a feather flock together" is largely accurate in predicting that students with shared interests, similar backgrounds, and comparable visions of the future will select each other as friends and accept each other as members of the same social groups.

The Breakfast Club shows how formal and informal sorting creates the peer groups that appear in the film. While the five students belong to different informal groups within the school, they are all white, which is likely due to formal sorting processes. That is, these five white students all attend a largely racially homogeneous high school because they live in the same geographic area. However, propinquity and homophily also work together to drive informal peer-sorting processes. The film makes clear that the five students rarely interact with each other because they are enrolled in different classes and participate in different extracurricular activities. Lacking propinquity, they have a low chance of forming friendships. However, once they are forced to interact with one another in detention, the principle of homophily keeps them apart: as members of different social groups, with different social identities, the students initially have little interest in forming friendships. It is only *after* the students look beyond those group identities and find some shared similarities that they begin to form friendships.

Peer influence is the effect of a peer (or a peer group) on an individual student's behavior, attitude, or learning outcome. Consider the example of a student who has a classmate who regularly misbehaves in class. If a student decides to emulate this student in class (perhaps as an attempt to impress this student or other classmates), this would be an example of direct peer influence: that is, the peer is directly shaping the student's behavior. Imagine another student in the same class who chooses not to emulate either of the two misbehaving students. While the third student has not been directly affected by the two misbehaving students, the students' disruptions in class make it difficult for the teacher to cover the required material and teach effectively. This is an example of indirect peer influence, because the peer group (in this case, classmates) affects a key learning resource (the quality of instruction), thereby inhibiting learning for the class.

Peer influence generally stems from the fact that peers affect the quality of learning resources that students experience in school. At the level of schoolmates, peers can shape how resources are allocated to different schools. For example, teacher quality is a critically important component of student learning, and more-experienced teachers prefer to teach in schools with children who are more advantaged (Lankford, Loeb, and Wyckoff 2002). In addition, parents from more affluent families tend to be more involved in their children's schools, and this involvement can spill over and help children whose parents have low levels of involvement (Ho and Willms 1996; Lareau 2000).

Classmates also affect the learning resources that students receive, because peers affect both the cognitive and the behavioral climate of the classroom. Teachers generally teach to the middle of the ability distribution in a given class, which means that the pace and rigor of instruction varies, depending on the ability levels of a student's classmates. In addition, students can learn directly from each other in the classroom: when classmates use new words or share important new ideas in class, students have opportunities to learn from them. As noted, peers can affect the behavioral climate in a classroom, which affects the quality of instruction that students receive. Finally, peer characteristics can affect a teacher's expectations for his or her students, which can either negatively or positively affect student performance.

Friendship networks can also provide students with learning resources by providing social capital through their social ties with each other (Coleman 1988). Social ties are useful for transmitting important information: friends can share knowledge and information about class requirements and assignments and can help each other with their schoolwork outside of the classroom. Social ties are useful for communicating expectations and providing mutual support. Friends can also provide encouragement and support to each other, and they can reinforce behaviors and attitudes by expressing their approval or disapproval. Finally, friends can serve as behavioral models that either reinforce or undermine norms and expectations associated with school success. Since homophily is an important basis of friendships, friends will often try emulate each other as a way to affirm and strengthen their bonds.

Flashman (2012) constructed a useful conceptual diagram that describes how peer sorting and peer influence are mutually reinforcing processes (see figure 10). This illustration shows that formal sorting processes allocate students to different schools and classes, which creates differing "opportunities" for students to form friendships on the basis of propinquity. Informal sorting processes are driven by students' "preferences" for friends, whereby students select friendship ties based on shared similarities (homophily). These friendship ties create peer effects on "behavior," which in turn reinforce students' "preferences," creating a cycle in which students' friendship networks become increasingly homogenous over time.

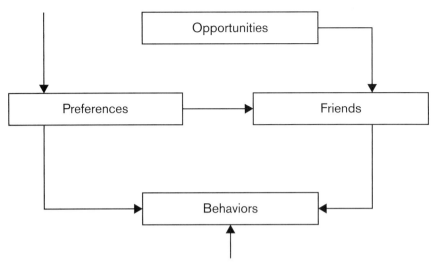

Figure 10. A conceptual model of the relationship between peers and student behavior. Source: adapted from J. Flashman, "Academic Achievement and Its Impact on Friend Dynamics." *Sociology of Education* 85, no. 1 (2012): 61–80.

RESEARCH METHODS

There are many methodological challenges involved in measuring both peer sorting and peer influence. The crux of the problem is that peer sorting can be easily mistaken for peer influence; in practice, it is difficult to separate the two processes empirically from each other when analyzing data. For example, consider a school where students with low academic grades tend to have friends who also have low grades. Is it reasonable to conclude that a student's low grades were *caused* by his or her friendship ties with low-achieving friends? While this is one plausible explanation for the relationship, it is equally plausible to argue that students form their friendship ties based on their shared characteristics, and the relationship between students' grades and their friends' grades are driven by a process of *self-selection*. Thus, if low-achieving students are more likely to befriend other low-achieving students based on shared interests, shared identity, or some other shared trait, it is difficult to know whether students are affecting each other or simply selecting each other as friends.

Likewise, students are not randomly sorted into schools. Family background and a family's residence strongly shape which students attend which schools, so it is difficult to know whether variables like school composition actually affect student outcomes, or whether they are merely correlated with other variables (resources in the family and neighborhood) that matter for educational achievement and attainment. Once again, peer sorting and peer influence are difficult to disentangle when we estimate the effects of school composition.

One way to disentangle peer sorting and peer influence is to collect and analyze data at multiple points in time, known as longitudinal data. With longitudinal data, researchers can examine whether peer characteristics at one point in time are related to student outcomes at a later point in time. Since time flows in only one direction (from the past to the future), longitudinal data allow researchers to make stronger claims regarding how peer sorting and peer influence are related to student outcomes. Unfortunately, most research on peers and friendships analyzes data from one point in time, which makes it impossible to distinguish between peer sorting and peer influence.

A scarcity of high-quality data is another important challenge in estimating the effects of peers and student friendships on student outcomes. Consider two hypothetical students who are friends. Each student can reliably and accurately report his or her own grades in a math class. However, if each student is asked to report his or her friend's math grades, this information will likely be less accurate than the student's report of his or her own grades. Indeed, research suggests that students tend to overestimate the similarity between their friends' characteristics and their own characteristics. Unfortunately, most studies that examine the effects of students' friends' characteristics analyze data from students' reports of their friends' characteristics, and this data likely overstates the effects of friends' characteristics on student outcomes.

Increasingly, researchers are using social network data to study peer sorting and peer influence. Network data include information about both individual respondents and their social ties with other members in the sample. For example, some network data sets sample all of the students in a given school and then ask each student to "nominate" each other student in the school that she or he considers a friend. Social network data allow researchers to embed individual respondents within their social networks and, thereby, conduct rich and sophisticated analyses of both peer sorting and peer influence processes (e.g., Carbonaro and Workman 2013, 2016; Moody 2001; Flashman 2012).

EMPIRICAL FINDINGS

There is an abundance of empirical evidence that shows that (a) peer sorting is pervasive in our educational system, and (b) peer influence is an important mechanism that drives educational inequality in the United States. Certain key studies document peer sorting and influence in the US school system.

Peer Sorting in American Education

Other chapters in this text review the research on formal sorting processes that affect students' schoolmates and classmates (see chapter 10 and chapter 13). I focus instead upon research that documents pervasive informal peer sorting within American schools. In his classic study *The Adolescent Society* (1961), sociologist James Coleman found that schools were divided into several informal but distinct social groups with different norms, attitudes, values, and educational aspirations. Each school had a "leading crowd" that was rarely dominated by the highest-achieving students; rather, athletic success, social class, and physical attractiveness predicted which students were the social elite of the school. Thus, while racial, economic, and academic segregation across schools meant that students did not attend schools with equivalent sets of peers, Coleman's study pointed out that *peers within schools* were differentiated into subgroups of students with differing norms, values, identities, and social memberships.

Subsequent research by Lawrence Steinberg (1996), a developmental psychologist, built on Coleman's study and pointed to further subdivisions of schoolmates into qualitatively different categories of peers. Steinberg examined the informal peer sorting within schools, and he found three meaningful clusters of peers: best friends, cliques, and crowds. At the most intimate level, students typically have one or two intense friendships with peers whom they consider best friends. Students spend a great deal of time with these peers, and these ties are strong and enduring. Best-friend ties are typically nested within a larger network of friendship ties that constitute a clique. Cliques include peers with whom students regularly interact and socialize, but these ties are neither as enduring nor as intimate as best-friend ties.

Finally, students are also members of larger social groups called crowds. These larger social groupings are similar to subgroups that Coleman observed in *The Adolescent Society,* and Steinberg emphasized that students draw upon these crowds in forming their social identity and, in particular, their orientation toward school. Steinberg found several different types of crowds in the schools that he studied, and each crowd tended to have different labels and orientations toward schooling: "populars," "jocks," "burnouts," "brains," and so on (Eckert 1989). Of these groups, only one ("nerds") outwardly embraced school success and the academic ethos of the school. This crowd was the highest academically performing group, but it was also typically the smallest (roughly 5 percent) in the school. When taken together, Steinberg concluded, the different crowds within schools generally supported a prevailing norm of "getting by" rather than pursuing academic excellence (Bishop 1999). Overall, Steinberg described a social landscape of peer groups that is remarkably similar to those described in *The Breakfast Club.*

Steinberg also found that 15 percent of students belonged to "racially identifiable" crowds. Asian friendship groups had "pro-school" norms, which valued hard work and academic success. In contrast, Steinberg found (as did some other researchers) that low-performing racial/ethnic minorities tended to create an "oppositional culture," which devalued school success and opposed pro-school norms (Fordham and Ogbu 1986; Fordham 1996). Researchers have not reached a consensus regarding whether minority peer groups differ in terms of their orientation toward school; some scholars argue that "oppositional culture" is either rare or limited to specific academic contexts (Ainsworth-Darnell and Downey 1998; Tyson, Darity, and Castellino 2005).

Researchers have consistently found that students form friendships based on both propinquity and homophily. Most adolescent friendships occur within schools (Harding 2008), and student friendships are more common among classmates than nonclassmates (Frank et al. 2008). Curricular tracking within schools, as well as extracurricular participation, tends to reinforce racially homogenous friendship ties (Moody 2001). Thus, the formal processes that sort students into the schools and classrooms indirectly shape the informal peer-sorting processes. Regarding homophily, research consistently shows that students are similar to their friends in terms of family background and, especially, academic ability (e.g., Flashman 2012).

Peer Influence on Student Outcomes

Informal peer groups create status inequalities within schools, but research indicates that they are also important for schooling outcomes. Steinberg (1996) examined whether crowds, cliques, and close friendship ties affected students' academic performance over time. A major advantage of Steinberg's study was that he observed the same students over a three-year period. By collecting longitudinal data, he could compare peer associations and performance at the beginning and the end of the study and, thereby, account for self-selection into peer groups. Overall, he found that students who began the study with higher-achieving peers performed better academically (relative to their own baseline scores) at the end of the study; conversely, students with lower-performing peers did worse. Steinberg found that the same pattern of peer effects extended to delinquency and deviance. The effects of peers in Steinberg's study were sizable, rivaling the effects of parenting practices on students' outcomes.

These findings are consistent with other studies that analyzed different data sets with students who were studied at multiple points in time (e.g., Carbonaro and Workman 2013, 2016; Flashman 2012; Kandel 1978). A colleague and I found that having a friend at high risk of dropping out in middle or high school makes you more likely to drop out of high school, even after controlling for other risk factors (Carbonaro and Workman 2013, 2016). Flashman (2012) analyzed changes in student friendship patterns over time, and she found that (1) students were more likely to form friendship with students with grades similar to their own, and (2) a student's friends' grades affected that student's own grades. This study is an excellent example of how peer sorting and peer influence are mutually reinforcing: they work together to sustain and exacerbate educational inequality.

IMPLICATIONS FOR POLICY AND PRACTICE

The research on peer influence indicates that peers—whether schoolmates, classmates, or friends—serve as important resources for learning. Research on peer sorting also shows that students in America's schools interact with very different sets of schoolmates, classmates, and friends as they progress through the K–12 system. Students who are socioeconomically disadvantaged and/or low achieving tend to interact with students who share those same characteristics, which ultimately makes it more difficult for them to succeed in school. Together, these conclusions pose some important challenges for policy makers who want to equalize educational opportunities and reduce educational inequality.

Historically, policy makers have tried to remedy inequalities driven by formal peer sorting through two main reform initiatives: racial and socioeconomic desegregation (designed to diversify students' schoolmates), and curricular "de-tracking" (intended to expose students to more diverse classmates academically). Although both of these reform efforts have had their share of successes and failures, it is noteworthy that both have triggered strong political resistance, particularly from parents of more advantaged students. Because such reforms can be politically risky, elected officials are hesitant to implement these policies. Resolving these political conflicts is a major barrier that must be overcome in order to reduce the segregating effects of peer sorting.

A potentially more perplexing question for policy makers is: What, if anything, can be done regarding informal peer sorting in schools? Perhaps "burnouts" might benefit from interacting with and befriending "brains," but one cannot legislate friendships. This is true, but *The Breakfast Club* provides a few useful lessons that might foster greater diversity among peers. First, in in the film, "Saturday detention" serves as a *shared social space* for the five students who would otherwise rarely interact. Schools might consider providing more shared social spaces where students from different groups can regularly interact and possibly form friendship ties that are more heterogeneous. For example, schools could have more service clubs and activities that are less dependent on student identity and more focused on students' shared interests and values. Peer-tutoring programs could also create additional shared social (and academic) spaces in schools that might foster more diverse friendships.

A second lesson for schools might be that they can devote more attention to promoting *shared identities* among students. In the film, the students overcome their narrow group identities because they find a set of common enemies: adult authority figures (namely, the school principal and their own parents). Obviously, shared identities based on animus should be discouraged. Rather, schools could be more deliberate about promoting shared identities that help bring students together and encourage them to recognize their commonalities.

Finally, as research by Coleman and Steinberg indicates, academically successful students do not enjoy high social status in most schools, and the norm of "getting by" generally prevails for most. There is no simple solution to this problem, but schools need to recognize this mismatch between their organizational goals (promoting academic excellence) and peer culture and to generate some countervailing forces that better align academic success and social status for their students.

CHAPTER 8 REVIEW

Discussion Questions

1. Were there crowds in your high school? If so, how many were there, and did they have labels associated with them? Were they consistent with the crowds that Steinberg identified in his research?

2. List your close and distant friends during high school. Does your list provide support for the importance of propinquity and homophily for friendship formation?

3. Are strategies and policies that are designed to diversify students' peer groups more or less important than other strategies designed to equalize educational opportunities? Explain.

Suggestions for Further Reading

Flashman, Jennifer. 2012. "Academic Achievement and Its Impact on Friend Dynamics." *Sociology of Education* 85:61–80.

Milner, Murray. 2004. *Freaks, Geeks, and Cool Kids: American Teenagers, Schools, and the Culture of Consumption.* New York: Routledge.

Moody, James. 2001. "Race, School Integration, and Friendship Segregation in America." *American Journal of Sociology* 107:679–716.

Steinberg, Lawrence. 1996. *Beyond the Classroom: Why School Reform Failed and What Parents Need to Do.* New York: Simon and Schuster.

References

Ainsworth-Darnell, J. W., and D. B. Downey. 1998. "Assessing the Oppositional Culture Explanation for Racial/Ethnic Differences in School Performance." *American Sociological Review* 63:536–53.

Bishop, J. 1999. "Nerd Harassment, Incentives, School Priorities, and Learning." In *Learning and Earning: How Schools Matter,* edited by Susan Mayer and Paul Peterson, 231–80. Washington, DC: Brookings Institution Press.

Carbonaro, William, and Joseph Workman. 2013. "Dropping Out of High School: Effects of Close and Distant Friendships." *Social Science Research* 42:1254–68.

———. 2016. "Intermediate Peer Contexts and Educational Outcomes: Do the Friends of Students' Friends Matter?" *Social Science Research* 58:184–97.

Coleman, J. S. 1961. *The Adolescent Society.* New York: Free Press.

———. 1988. "Social Capital in the Creation of Human Capital." *American Journal of Sociology* 94 (supplement): S95–S120.

Eckert, P. 1989. *Jocks and Burnouts: Social Categories and Identity in the High School.* New York: Teacher's College Press.

Flashman, J. 2012. "Academic Achievement and Its Impact on Friend Dynamics." *Sociology of Education* 85 (1): 61–80. www.jstor.org/stable/41507148.

Fordham, S. 1996. *Blacked Out: Dilemmas of Race, Identity, and Success at Capital High.* Chicago: University of Chicago Press.

Fordham, S., and J. Ogbu. 1986. "Black Students' School Success: Coping with the 'Burden of "Acting White."'" *Urban Review* 18:176–206.

Frank, K. A., C. Muller, K. S. Schiller, C. Riegle-Crumb, A. S. Mueller, R. Crosnoe, and J. Pearson. 2008. "The Social Dynamics of Mathematics Coursetaking in High School." *American Journal of Sociology* 113 (6): 1645–96.

Harding, D. 2008. "Neighborhood Violence and Adolescent Friendships." *International Journal of Conflict and Violence* 2 (1): 28–55.

Ho, E. S., and Willms, D. 1996. "Effects of Parental Involvement on Eighth-Grade Achievement." *Sociology of Education* 69:126–41.

Kandel, D. B. 1978. "Homophily, Selection, and Socialization in Adolescent Friendships." *American Journal of Sociology* 84 (2): 427–36.

Lankford, H., Loeb, S., and J. Wyckoff. 2002. "Teacher Sorting and the Plight of Urban Schools: A Descriptive Analysis." *Educational Evaluation and Policy Analysis* 24:37–62.

Lareau, A. 2000. *Home Advantage: Social Class and Parental Intervention in Elementary Education.* 2nd ed. Lanham, MA: Rowman and Littlefield.

Milner, Murray. 2004. *Freaks, Geeks, and Cool Kids: American Teenagers, Schools, and the Culture of Consumption.* New York: Routledge.

Moody, J. 2001. "Race, School Integration, and Friendship Segregation in America." *American Journal of Sociology* 107 (3): 679–716.

Pope, Denise C. 2001. *"Doing School": How We Are Creating a Generation of Stressed Out, Materialistic, and Miseducated Kids.* New Haven, CT: Yale University Press.

Steinberg, L. 1996. *Beyond the Classroom: Why School Reform Has Failed and What Parents Need to Do.* New York: Simon and Schuster.

Tyson, K., W. Darity, and D. R. Castellino. 2005. "It's Not 'A Black Thing': Understanding the Burden of Acting White and Other Dilemmas of High Achievement." *American Sociological Review* 70 (4): 582–605.

2

The "Asian F" and the Racialization of Achievement

JENNIFER LEE, COLUMBIA UNIVERSITY

SEAN DRAKE, NEW YORK UNIVERSITY

MIN ZHOU, UNIVERSITY OF CALIFORNIA, LOS ANGELES

EDITORS' NOTE

The bulk of the research in the sociology of inequality focuses on the consequences of inequality for relatively disadvantaged groups. As you saw in preceding chapters, women's experiences in mathematics and science, the structural challenges facing African American children, and the biases and low expectations that teachers bring to their interactions with students from relatively poor families are all topics of particular resonance for sociologists. This emphasis on the experience of the socially disadvantaged makes sense. It reflects a shared belief that understanding the costs of inequality and the processes that produce those costs is an important step toward making a more just social world.

But as this case study's **ethnographic** treatment of the experiences of Asian American youth illustrates, studying the experiences of relatively advantaged groups can also yield sociological insight. Asian American youth are often considered a "model minority" in American schools, and educators and others often stereotype Asian Americans as high academic achievers. This investigation of Asian American school experiences sheds light on some of the ways these stereotypes translate into real educational advantages for Asian American youth. It is revealing to contemplate, for example, the degree to which schools that assume that virtually all Asian students should take advanced courses can be thought of as **meritocratic.** But these high academic expectations carry a hidden price, particularly for Asian American youth who do not excel academically.

As you read this case study, you'll notice that it is formatted very differently from the chapters and the earlier case study. Where the chapters have "key points," this case study has an "abstract," a "data and methods" section, a "findings" section, and a "discussion and conclusions" section. That's because this case study advances a goal very different from those of the others. The others synthesize theory and research in order to introduce you to their topics. This case study, in contrast, is a research paper, which presents the findings of a single research project. Research papers like this one are the primary way sociologists of education—and indeed other social scientists—communicate their research findings with one another.

Try to read this paper as a social scientist might. Ask yourself: What are the authors' research questions? Why do these questions matter? What sorts of data do the authors use to answer these research questions? Are their answers convincing? What are the limitations of the evidence they present? What questions does this study leave unanswered? What new questions does it raise?

ABSTRACT

Asian Americans make up 6 percent of the US population but account for more than one-fifth of the entering classes in the country's Ivy League universities. In prestigious public universities like the University of California, Berkeley, they constitute more than 40 percent of the student body. No longer the province of whites only, academic achievement has become racialized as "the Asian thing"; moreover, grades have been recalibrated on an Asian scale, so that an A minus is regarded as an "Asian F." The racialization of achievement affects both in-group and out-group biases and has social psychological consequences, including "stereotype promise"—the boost in performance that comes with being anointed as smart, high-achieving, and deserving. These biases are reinforced in educational institutions by teachers, guidance counselors, and school administrators who assume that Asian American students will excel, giving them advantages denied to other students and generating a self-fulfilling prophecy of Asian American exceptionalism. The racialization of achievement, however, is a double-edged sword that makes those who are average or low-achievers feel like failures and ethnoracial outliers because they do not meet the perceived norm.

INTRODUCTION

Asian Americans are the fastest-growing racial group in the United States, having increased from 0.7 percent in 1970 to 6 percent in 2015. By 2065, demographers project, the number of Asian Americans will more than double and will account for 14 percent of the US population (Colby and Ortman 2014). Driving the growth is immigration: China and India have passed Mexico as the leading sources of new immigrants to the United States, and demographers project that, by 2065, Asian immigrants will comprise 38 percent of the country's foreign-born population. While their rapid population growth has caught the attention of demographers, it is their discernable presence on college campuses that has caught the imagination of the American public.

At Ivy League universities like Harvard, Yale, and Princeton, more than one-fifth of each year's entering class is Asian American. In elite public universities like the University of California, Berkeley, Asian Americans constitute more than 40 percent of the student body. No longer the province of whites only, academic achievement has become racialized as "the Asian thing." Grades have been recalibrated on an Asian scale so that an A minus is regarded as an "Asian F," meaning that earning anything less than an A is tantamount to failure.

The glaring overrepresentation of Asian Americans as a proportion of the population in the country's top universities has led pundits to speculate about the so-called Asian advantage. In the fall of 2015, *New York Times* op-ed columnist Nicholas Kristof wrote an editorial on the subject, which was so popular that it was later translated into Chinese and Korean for readers. Kristof cited a number of factors that lead to the high educational attainment of Asian Americans, but in the end he pointed to "East Asia's long Confucian emphasis on education," as well as to Asian Americans' "hard work, strong families and passion for education." Like a legion of pundits before him of varying political persuasions, Kristof reduced achievement to Asian cultural traits and values and hailed Asians as America's model minority whom other groups—including native-born whites—would be wise to follow.

We argue that this cultural fallacy fails to acknowledge the role that US immigration law has had in ushering in a steady stream of highly selected, highly educated immigrants from Asia—what Lee and Zhou (2015) refer to as "hyperselectivity." This missing piece is critical because it underscores the fact that the cultural manifestations of Asian American academic achievement have legal and structural roots (see also Fernández-Kelly 2016; Jiménez 2016; Hsin 2016; Tran 2016; Wong 2015). In this case study, we focus on the social psychological consequences of hyperselectivity, including in-group and out-group biases, the racialization of achievement, and "stereotype promise"—the boost in performance that comes with being perceived as smart, high-achieving, and deserving (Lee 2014). These biases are reinforced in educational institutions by teachers, guidance counselors, and school administrators who assume that Asian American students will excel, giving them advantages denied to other students and generating a self-fulfilling prophecy of Asian American exceptionalism. The racialization of achievement, however, is a double-edged sword that makes Asian Americans who are average or low-achievers feel like failures and ethnoracial outliers because they do not meet the perceived norm.

DATA AND METHODS

We use two data sources for this case study. First, we draw on in-depth interview data from a random sample of Chinese and Vietnamese respondents who participated in the Immigration and Intergenerational Mobility in Metropolitan Los Angeles study.[1] Second, we include rich ethnographic data from a Southern California high school, dubbed Pinnacle—the flagship high school in an affluent suburb, dubbed Valley View.

---

1. For a description of this study, see "Immigration and Intergenerational Mobility in Metropolitan Los Angeles (IIMMLA)," n.d., Russell Sage Foundation, www.russellsage.org/research/Immigration/IIMMLA.

Immigration and Intergenerational Mobility in Metropolitan Los Angeles

The Immigrant and Intergenerational Mobility in Metropolitan Los Angeles study has two components: a telephone survey; and face-to-face, in-depth interviews. The survey includes forty-eight hundred randomly selected 1.5- and second-generation residents in the greater Los Angeles metropolitan area between the ages of twenty and forty. It includes a number of different ethnic groups, such as Mexicans, Chinese, Vietnamese, Filipinos, Koreans, Guatemalans, and Salvadorans, as well as native-born whites and blacks in Los Angeles.

The second phase of the study includes 162 face-to-face, in-depth interviews with a randomly selected group of survey respondents, spearheaded by Lee and Zhou (2015). In conducting these interviews, Lee and Zhou purposely sampled from three groups—Mexicans, Chinese, and Vietnamese—and added interviews with native-born whites and blacks for comparison. For this case study, we focus on the educational attainment patterns of the Chinese and Vietnamese and explain the implications for Asian Americans more generally. The Chinese are the largest Asian group in the United States and Los Angeles, with the longest history of immigration to the United States. By contrast, the Vietnamese are a relatively recently arrived group, as well as the largest Asian refugee group in the Los Angeles metropolitan area.

Ethnography of Pinnacle

The second data source for this case study is an ethnographic study of Pinnacle High School conducted by Sean Drake. The ethnography includes participant observation and nonparticipant observation and both formal and informal face-to-face, in-depth interviews of teachers, students, and parents. The observations and interviews were conducted over the course of twenty months during the school year (between October 2013 and November 2015), resulting in 111 hours of observation and nearly six hundred pages of single-spaced, typed field notes and analytic memos.

Drake observed multiple high school spaces and events, including classes, athletic events, luncheons, assemblies, conferences, department meetings, back-to-school nights, and graduations. During each of these event types, Drake engaged in informal conversations with teachers, administrators, students, and parents in accordance with the interviewing-by-comment technique of qualitative data gathering (Snow, Zurcher, and Sjoberg 1982). Themes emerged inductively in a manner conforming with a grounded-theory approach (Charmaz 2001), including the ways in which Pinnacle supports and reinforces the racialization of achievement, encourages the philosophy that an A minus is an Asian F, and promotes Asian American exceptionalism.

FINDINGS

The Hyperselectivity of Contemporary Asian Immigration

The 1965 Immigration and Nationality Act—which privileged foreign-born applicants with high levels of education and skills—changed the socioeconomic profile of Asian immigrants. Despite their ethnic and class diversity, Asian immigrants who immigrated after the 1965

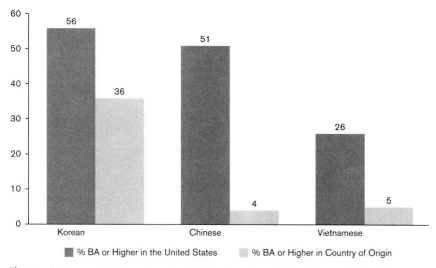

Figure 11. Hyper and high immigrant selectivity, by national origin. Source: adapted from Jennifer Lee and Min Zhou, *The Asian American Achievement Paradox* (New York: Russell Sage Foundation, 2015).

Immigration and Nationality Act are, on average, highly educated and highly selected (Pew Research Center 2012). For example, if we look at the three largest East Asian immigrant groups in the United States—Chinese, Vietnamese, and Koreans—we find that each is highly selected from its country of origin. More than half (56 percent) of Korean immigrants in the United States have a bachelor's degree or higher, compared to only 36 percent of adults in Korea, meaning that US Korean immigrants are more than one and a half times as likely to have graduated from college than their ethnic counterparts who did not immigrate.

The degree of selectivity among Vietnamese immigrants is even higher. More than one-quarter (26 percent) of Vietnamese immigrants have at least a bachelor's degree, but the comparable figure among adults in Vietnam is only 5 percent (see figure 11). Chinese immigrants are the most highly selected: 51 percent have graduated from college, compared to only 4 percent of adults in China, meaning that US Chinese immigrants are more than twelve times more likely to have graduated from college than Chinese adults who did not immigrate.

In addition, some Asian immigrant groups—such as Chinese and Koreans—not only are highly selected but also are more highly educated than the general US population, 28 percent of whom have graduated from college. This dual positive immigrant selectivity is what Lee and Zhou (2015) refer to as "hyperselectivity."

The Consequences of Hyperselectivity

The Racialization of Achievement　　Hyperselectivity affects the educational attainment of the children of immigrants in ways that defy the status attainment model—

meaning that socioeconomic class matters less for these immigrant children than others. We argue that this is, in part, because hyperselectivity affects in-group and out-group perceptions of these groups and has social psychological consequences that affect academic performance. For an illustration of this, consider the fact that US Chinese immigrants are, on average, more highly educated than the general American population, and as a result Chinese Americans are stereotyped as smart, competent, hardworking, and high achieving. Moreover, because of the racialization that occurs in the context of the United States, ethnic stereotypes about Chinese extend to East Asians as a group, regardless of migrant selectivity and socioeconomic status (Tran et al. 2018).

These so-called positive stereotypes affect the way that teachers, guidance counselors, and school administrators perceive and treat Asian American students. Identified by their teachers as bright, competent, hardworking, better prepared, and more willing to put effort into their schoolwork (Hsin and Xie 2014), Asian American students are more likely to be given the benefit of the doubt regarding their academic ability. In addition, they also are subject to higher academic expectations than non-Asian students, including non-Hispanic white students, by their teachers, guidance counselors, and peers (Jiménez and Horowitz 2013).

These out-group perceptions have had consequences for the educational opportunities of Asian American students. For example, teachers' and guidance counselors' perceptions of Asian Americans affected the grades that Asian American students received, which led to their likelihood of being placed into rigorous academic programs and tracks like GATE (Gifted and Talented Education), Advanced Placement (AP), and honors. Teachers and guidance counselors also encouraged Asian American students to apply to prestigious four-year universities. For example, while some of the Chinese and Vietnamese respondents recalled that they tested high enough to qualify for an honors or Advanced Placement track, others did not remember taking a placement exam in junior high school, and still others admitted that, although their junior high school grades were mediocre, they were nevertheless tracked into high school honors and AP courses.

An illustrative case is that of Nam, a twenty-four-year-old second-generation Vietnamese woman. She was placed into the Advanced Placement track in high school even though, as she admitted, she was an average junior high student. She recalls having received a mix of As, Bs, and Cs in her classes. Even more surprising is that Nam does not recall having taken an exam for this placement and has no idea how she was chosen. However, once Nam was placed into the honors track, she began taking her schoolwork more seriously and spent more time doing her homework and studying for tests in order to keep up with her high-achieving peers. Nam graduated high school with a grade point average (GPA) above 4.0 and was admitted to all the University of California schools to which she applied.

Perhaps one of the most striking cases of the symbolic capital afforded to Asian American students is that of Ophelia, a twenty-three-year-old second-generation Vietnamese woman who described herself as "not very intelligent" and recalled nearly failing the second grade because of her poor academic performance. By her account, "I wasn't an exceptional student; I was a straight C student; whereas my other siblings, they were quicker than I was, and they were straight A students." Despite her lackluster grades in elementary and junior high schools, Ophelia took an AP entrance exam at the end of junior high school. Yet although she failed the exam, she was still placed into the AP track in her predominantly white high school. Once there, something "just clicked," and Ophelia began to excel in her classes. When we asked her to explain what she meant by something "just clicked," she explained, "I wanted to work hard and prove I was a good student. . . . I think the competition kind of increases your want to do better." She graduated from high school with a GPA of 4.2 and was admitted into a highly competitive pharmacy program.

Stereotype Promise   Social psychologists have shown that individuals have powerful, largely unconscious tendencies to remember people, events, and experiences that confirm their expectations (Fiske, Lin, and Neuberg 1999; Lee and Fiske 2006). So strong is this tendency that individuals often fail to see disconfirming evidence; or, if they do see it, they often reinterpret it in stereotype-confirming ways, ignore it, or dismiss it altogether as the exception (Ridgeway 2011). Teachers are more likely to notice Asian American students who excel and to overlook or ignore those who do not. So even when teachers come into contact with average-performing Asian American students, they tend to reinterpret the evidence in stereotype-confirming ways, as Nam and Ophelia's cases demonstrate.

Asian American students benefit from "stereotype promise"—the boost in performance that comes with being perceived as smart, hardworking, and deserving (Lee 2014; Lee and Zhou 2015). When placed in a context where Asian American students are anointed as high-achieving—where the expectations of teachers, guidance counselors, and peers are elevated—they put more effort into their schoolwork to meet those expectations. As a result of their increased effort, their academic performance improves, confirming teachers' expectations. Critical to add is the fact that because the students' outcomes matched their teachers' expectations, the teachers can point to these students' stellar academic achievement as proof of their initial assessment about all Asian American students—that they are highly intelligent and hardworking, and deserve to be placed into the most competitive academic tracks—all the while unmindful of their role in generating a self-fulfilling prophecy (Merton 1948).

The Reproduction of Advantage: A Case Study of Pinnacle High School

In this section, we provide a case study of the effects of hyperselectivity in a high school in Valley View, an affluent suburb in Southern California, where the median household income is $92,663 and 66 percent of its adult residents have earned at least a B.A. degree. Valley View is predominantly populated by whites (45 percent) and Asians (39 percent), but also has a fair share of Latinos (9 percent) and a small share of African Americans (2 percent). Pinnacle is the flagship high school in Valley View and consistently ranks among the top fifty public high schools in the nation. Pinnacle's top ranking is reflected in its high school exit exam scores, graduation rates, and percentage of seniors who attend four-year universities immediately following graduation. Ninety-six percent of Pinnacle's graduates enroll in postsecondary institutions, and 60 percent attend four-year colleges and universities. That Pinnacle enrolls nearly twenty-five hundred students each year, with class sizes routinely approaching forty students, makes its top-fifty national ranking especially impressive.

Praise of Pinnacle's academic prowess is prominently affixed to its architecture. Flanking the school's name on the entrance archway are two permanent markers of distinction: "California Distinguished School" and "National Exemplary School." Beyond the archway, one finds fifty-five sprawling acres of clean pathways and manicured lawns adorned with neatly pruned maple and pine trees that frame the school's well-maintained structures. Pinnacle boasts an auditorium, gymnasium, baseball field, football field, all-weather track, swimming pool, tennis courts, and separate buildings that house its math, science, humanities, arts, and athletic departments.

Academic exceptionalism is Pinnacle's central institutional identity, and its culture is reinforced by students who enroll in multiple honors and Advanced Placement classes, earn grade point averages that exceed 4.0, achieve high (and in some cases perfect) SAT scores, and gain admission to multiple prestigious colleges and universities. Here, an A minus is an Asian F. Markers of academic excellence bring high status, and at this school the high achievers are the "cool kids." So normalized is high academic achievement that students who do not measure up feel like failures and outliers within an institution that promotes an exacting definition of success.

"Don't Be All Asian about It"   At Pinnacle High School, different racial groups are associated with particular talents, and Asian American students—most of whom are the children of Chinese and Korean immigrants—are hailed as the academic pacesetters. They consistently attain the highest GPAs and test scores, and make up about 80 percent of the honors and AP classes at Pinnacle, regardless of subject. According to Mr. Holt, an assistant principal at Pinnacle for nearly a decade, the Korean and Chinese students are the ones to thank for the school's competitive national academic ranking and for contributing to the studious classroom culture at Pinnacle. Mr. Holt explained, "They are what keeps our school rank high. They improve our test scores. If you are a teacher that wants order and you don't want to have to deal with problems, and you want the kids that come in and know their stuff, you want the Chinese and Korean kids. They will study probably hours and hours without ever raising a finger saying anything."

Pinnacle's teachers, like Ms. Tanaka (a Japanese American English teacher with a law degree from Stanford University), concurred with the assistant principal and had even higher expectations of their Asian American students. She candidly admitted, "I don't necessarily look at my classroom and treat a kid differently because they are Asian, but I know that if I have an Asian student in my classroom that I can count on that student. That student will probably work hard and be engaged. I can rely on that kid, and the parents, more so than I can for other [racial] groups."

The racialization of achievement has become deeply embedded in Pinnacle's institutional culture, to the extent that teachers have leveraged it as a pedagogical tool. For example, on the first day of school, Ms. Watson (a white, middle-age teacher of AP US history and psychology) distributed to her psychology class a few handouts that provided details about the class curriculum. In her class, twelve of the twenty students were Asian, six were white, and two were Latino. "Don't be alarmed by all of the handouts," she stated. before adding, "It's not like you need to read every word, okay? Relax. Don't be all Asian about it." Some students smiled, while others laughed quietly at these instructions, but none were offended by Ms. Watson's casual racialized instruction. Furthermore, for these students, there was a tacit understanding of what it means "to be all Asian" about one's study habits: enrolling in challenging classes, studying for hours on end, and achieving at least a 4.0 GPA.

The racialization of achievement at Pinnacle did not go unnoticed by students of other ethnoracial backgrounds, such as Caroline, an African American junior. Caroline was an exceptional student: she maintained a 4.1 GPA, had achieved nationally competitive test scores, and was active in extracurricular activities such as sports, student government, and community service. Nevertheless, Caroline noticed the stark difference in the advice that Pinnacle's guidance counselors gave her and that which they gave her Asian American friends—even those with lower grades, less impressive test scores, and little involvement in school or their community. Caroline noticed that the school's counselors encouraged her Asian American friends to apply to the most prestigious colleges and universities in the nation. And that, when Caroline mentioned the same schools to her counselors, they steered her away from her "dream schools" and encouraged her to apply to what she deemed her "safety schools"—colleges with applicant pools that were far less competitive.

These out-group biases manifested not only among the school's guidance counselors but also among its teachers. As a freshman, Caroline found that her test scores won her a place in the honors academic track for math. As she explained, "Most of the students in the class were Chinese, [as was] the teacher. There were only a small handful of us that weren't Chinese." Caroline added that the math teacher would take extra steps to make sure that the Chinese students understood the material: "The teacher would sometimes speak in Chinese, so only the Chinese students could understand her. This would usually happen during exams, or when the Chinese kids were struggling. It's like she took it personal that they would struggle, and she wanted to help them out. I felt really left out, and I know others did, too." Within this classroom, the Chinese students—some of whom Caroline referred to as "average students at best"—excelled with the help of the math teacher who often spoke to them in Chinese, thereby giving these students an advantage denied to others.

The Racialized Burden of Academic Excellence   Although Asian American students at Pinnacle accrue institutional benefits from the racialization of achievement, these benefits come at a cost. Combined with Pinnacle's exacting success frame, the racialization of achievement places a heavy burden on all Asian American students to meet the perceived norm. The Asian American students at Pinnacle candidly admitted that they jammed as many AP classes as they could into their schedule and often stayed up into the early morning hours to keep up with their schoolwork. Ryan, a sixteen-year-old

Chinese-American junior who enrolled in AP biology, AP chemistry, AP US history, and AP Chinese, admitted to being constantly exhausted from staying up well past midnight and "sometimes until 2 a.m. if there's a test the next day."

Although Ryan's AP course load and 4.2 GPA would have propelled him to the top of many US high schools, at Pinnacle his academic performance was not the stellar exception. In fact, even the most academically successful Asian American students—like Ryan—felt as though they were failing to meet their academic potential. Ryan, for example, spoke at length about how parents push their children to excel by comparing them to their other high-achieving classmates. He revealed that "parents talk to each other, and they know who the smartest kids are and what grades they get. I remember I got a 96 [percent] on my honors chemistry final last year. I told my mom, but she already knew about a girl who had gotten a perfect score, so she told me to work harder and do better." Ryan's experiences were not unique; rather, they reflect the sentiments and experiences of the Asian American high achievers at Pinnacle.

The pressure to academically excel falls even more heavily on Asian American students who are not in AP classes, who do not attain high SAT scores, and who cannot boast of academic records that will win them admission to an elite university (Drake 2017). These Asian American students feel like ethnoracial outliers because their performance diverges from the perceived norm. For example, Arata, a senior whose parents emigrated from Japan to Valley View two years before he was born, took four honors-level classes during his freshman year. Despite studying for hours every night, he admitted to struggling and barely earning a 3.0 GPA in his honors classes. Arata's inability to get As in his classes left him feeling "inadequate and left back, left alone," because, in his view, "all my friends and everyone around me was succeeding." Compounding his feeling of inadequacy was his inability to attain a competitive score on the SAT exam, which he took six times in order to achieve a score that would appease his parents. Envying his Asian American peers who aced the SAT exam on their first try, Arata conveyed that he wished he could be more like them.

Arata's feelings of failing were magnified when several of his Asian American friends and classmates gained admission into one or more Ivy League universities. He, on the other hand, was not admitted to any, leading him to doubt his intelligence. He remarked, "I wish I could be smart, but I'm just not. Maybe I could be smart at another high school, but at Pinnacle I'm probably below average. It sucks, but those other [Asian American] kids deserve it more than me." Arata recognized that because Pinnacle's highest achievers set the bar for academic excellence, those who fell below it (and even those who met it) could feel like failures and ethnoracial outliers and question their ability, talent, and intelligence.

DISCUSSION AND CONCLUSIONS

Though they comprise only 6 percent of the US population, Asian Americans constitute more than 20 percent of the student body at Ivy League universities and are a discernible presence on elite campuses. Unable to explain this outcome, Americans often point to Asian culture as the driver of achievement. This cultural fallacy fails to acknowledge the role of US immigration law in determining the class and educational selectivity of US Asian immigrants. With the change in immigration law in 1965 came a change in the selectivity and socioeconomic profiles of Asian immigrants, who are, on average, both more highly educated than those who do not immigrate and more highly educated than the general US population. Lee and Zhou (2015) refer to the dual positive immigrant selectivity as *hyperselectivity.*

The hyperselectivity of contemporary Asian immigrants has intersectional spillover effects, one of which is that Asian Americans—regardless of ethnicity, nativity, or class—are perceived and stereotyped as smart, hardworking, and deserving (Hsin 2016). Perceptions have consequences: these so-called positive stereotypes affect the way that teachers and guidance counselors perceive and treat Asian American students. In our research, Chinese, Korean, and Vietnamese interviewees consistently related the fact that their teachers expected them to do well in school and offered extra help with college applications, financial aid forms, and even on assignments when they had trouble with certain subjects.

Moreover, Asian American students related experiences of having been placed into the AP track despite not having tested for it and, in some cases, even after having failed the placement test. However, once these students were placed into the most competitive academic track, they worked hard to meet others' high expectations and picked a new reference group against whom they measured their success. These are benefits of "stereotype promise"—the boost in performance that results from being perceived as intelligent and capable. These benefits did not go unnoticed by non-Asian friends and classmates, who often felt that their Asian American peers received the benefit of the doubt and an unfair advantage in school because they were perceived as naturally more intelligent.

But there are also negative consequences associated with sky-high ethnoracial expectations. At Pinnacle High School, the racialization of achievement, which links Asian American identity with academic success, prompts students who are low or even average achievers to feel like failures and outliers. Those who earn an A minus feel that they have failed, which has led to the pithy phrase "An A minus is an Asian F." And even the high achievers feel as though they could, and should, do better. In educational institutions like Pinnacle, where there is an exacting institutional success frame that intersects with a racialized success frame, Asian American students who do not meet the perceived norm question their intelligence, talents, and ability (Drake 2017).

Our findings have several important implications for policy and practice in schools. First, as the ethnoracial diversity of America's youth continues to increase with steady flows of immigration, the ethnoracial makeup of America's schools will follow suit. Hence, it is critical that teachers and administrators seek a comprehensive understanding of the ways in which their student populations are changing, so that they may better respond to the specific needs of their students. Educators would be wise to promote activities and events at school that reflect and celebrate the ethnoracial and cultural diversity of their campuses. Moreover, it is vital that educators gain a better understanding of the tremendous cultural and socioeconomic diversity among Asian Americans. Perceiving all Asians as members of a homogenous group promotes ethnoracial and cultural stereotypes that place an undue burden on Asian American students, pushing some to sacrifice their health for academic achievements, and making others feel like ethnoracial outliers and failures. This perception also affects non-Asian minority groups, who are too often cast as culturally deficient.

Second, teachers can counter the rigid success frames espoused by hyperselected immigrant parents and students by stressing the importance of adequate sleep, mental health, and participation in extracurricular activities at school, such as sports and community service. While our research shows that many of these families are fixated on lofty grades and test scores in high school, it also shows that colleges, universities, and employers evaluate the well-roundedness of an applicant and prioritize creativity, critical thinking, and the ability to work together in a team. Therefore, educators should strive to broaden students' and parents' conception of success beyond achieving the highest of grades and test scores, and work to develop both hard and soft skills among students to better prepare them for success beyond high school.

Third, our data indicate that ethnoracial and cultural biases and stereotypes in schools have important consequences for all students' academic engagement and achievement. Some stereotypes and biases benefit some groups of students while harming others. As a result, educators should be trained in teacher credentialing programs and professional development workshops to recognize and challenge these deterministic notions of student ability and potential. Doing so is vital in the effort to support all students and to work toward making education more equitable. And in light of the changing terrain of race and ethnicity in American schools, it will become increasingly important in the coming years.

CASE STUDY 2 REVIEW

Discussion Questions

1. What role do US immigration law and the hyperselectivity of Asian immigration have in contributing to the high academic achievement of Asian Americans?

2. What are some social psychological consequences of hyperselectivity, including stereotype promise?

3. How do institutions support and maintain ethnoracial stereotypes of academic ability? Describe the ways in which these stereotypes advantage Asian American students, as well as the ways in which these stereotypes may be detrimental to Asian American students and their peers of other ethnoracial backgrounds.

4. How might elite institutions serving diverse student populations work to create more inclusive environments?

Suggestions for Further Reading

Jiménez, Tomás R., and Adam L. Horowitz. 2013. "When White Is Just Alright." *American Sociological Review* 78 (5): 849–71.

Lee, Jennifer. 2014. "Asian American Exceptionalism and Stereotype Promise." In *Color Lines and Racial Angles,* edited by Douglas Hartmann and Christopher Uggen. New York: W. W. Norton.

Lee, Jennifer, and Min Zhou. 2015. *The Asian American Achievement Paradox.* New York: Russell Sage Foundation.

Tran, Van C., Jennifer Lee, Oshin Khachikian, and Jess Lee. 2018. "Hyper-selectivity, Racial Mobility, and the Remaking of Race." *Russell Sage Foundation Journal* 4 (5): 188–209.

References

Charmaz, Kathy. 2001. "Grounded Theory." In *Contemporary Field Research: Perspectives and Formulations,* edited by Robert M. Emerson, 335–52. Prospect Heights, IL: Waveland.

Colby, Sandra L., and Jennifer M. Ortman. 2014. *Projections of the Size and Composition of the U.S. Population: 2014 to 2060.* Current Population Reports, P25–1143. Washington, DC: US Census Bureau. www.census.gov/content/dam/Census/library/publications/2015/demo/p25–1143.pdf.

Drake, Sean. 2017. "Academic Segregation and the Institutional Success Frame: Unequal Schooling and Racial Disparity in an Integrated, Affluent Community." *Journal of Ethnic and Migration Studies.* http://dx.doi.org/10.1080/1369183X.2017.1315868.

Fernández-Kelly, Patricia. 2016. "Fixing the Cultural Fallacy." *Ethnic and Racial Studies.* http://dx.doi.org/10.1080/01419870.2016.1200744.

Fiske, Susan T., Monica Lin, and Stephen Neuberg. 1999. "The Continuum Model: Ten Years Later." In *Dual Process Theories in Social Psychology,* edited by S. Chaiken and Y. Trope. New York: Guilford.

Hsin, Amy. 2016. "How Selective Migration Enables Socioeconomic Mobility." *Ethnic and Racial Studies.* http://dx.doi.org/10.1080/01419870.2016.1200742.

Hsin, Amy, and Yu Xie. 2014. "Explaining Asian Americans' Academic Achievement over Whites." *Proceedings of the National Academy of Sciences* 111 (23): 8416–21.

Jiménez, Tomás R. 2016. "Bringing Culture Back In: The Class Origins and Ethnoracial Destinations of Culture and Achievement." *Ethnic and Racial Studies.* http://dx.doi.org/10.1080/01419870.2016.1200739.

Jiménez, Tomás R., and Adam L. Horowitz. 2013. "When White Is Just Alright." *American Sociological Review* 78 (5): 849–71.

Kristof, Nicholas. 2015. "The Asian Advantage." *New York Times,* Sunday Review, October 10. www.nytimes.com/2015/10/11/opinion/sunday/the-asian-advantage.html.

Lee, Jennifer. 2014. "Asian American Exceptionalism and Stereotype Promise." In *Color Lines and Racial Angles,* edited by Douglas Hartmann and Christopher Uggen. New York: W. W. Norton.

Lee, Jennifer, and Min Zhou. 2015. *The Asian American Achievement Paradox.* New York: Russell Sage Foundation.

Lee, Tiane L., and Susan T. Fiske. 2006. "Not an Outgroup, Not Yet an Ingroup: Immigrants in the Stereotype Content Model." *International Journal of Intercultural Relations* 30:751–68.

Lin, Monica H., Virginia S. Y. Kwan, Anna Cheung, and Susan T. Fiske. 2005. "Stereotype Content Model Explains Prejudice for an Envied Outgroup: Scale of Anti-Asian American Stereotypes." *Personality and Social Psychology Bulletin* 31 (1): 34–47.

Merton, Robert K. 1948. "The Self-Fulfilling Prophecy." *Antioch Review* 8 (2): 193–210.

Pew Research Center. 2012. *The Rise of Asian Americans.* Washington, DC: Pew Research Center.

Ridgeway, Cecilia L. 2011. *Framed by Gender.* New York: Oxford University Press.

Snow, David A., Louis A. Zurcher, and Gideon Sjoberg. 1982. "Interviewing by Comment: An Adjunct to the Direct Question." *Qualitative Sociology* 5 (4): 285–311.

Tran, Van C. 2016. "Ethnic Culture and Social Mobility among Second-Generation Asian Americans" *Ethnic and Racial Studies.* http://dx.doi.org/10.1080/01419870.2016.1200740.

Tran, Van C., Jennifer Lee, Oshin Khachikian, and Jess Lee. 2018. "Hyper-selectivity, Racial Mobility, and the Remaking of Race." *Russell Sage Foundation Journal* 4 (5): 188–209.

Wong, Janelle S. 2015. "The Source of the 'Asian Advantage' Isn't Asian Values." *NBC News,* October 13. www.nbcnews.com/news/asian-america/editorial-source-asian-advantage-isnt-asian-values-n443526.

SCHOOLS AND OTHER EDUCATIONAL ORGANIZATIONS

9

Creating the Canon

The Meaning and Effects of Textbooks and Curricula

PATRICIA BROMLEY, STANFORD UNIVERSITY

DANIEL SCOTT SMITH, STANFORD UNIVERSITY

EDITORS' NOTE

Each of the chapters in part 2 of *Education and Society* focus on student educational experiences. By describing the ways in which gender, race, immigration status, class, family educational backgrounds, and peer groups shape both the educational and the social aspects of schooling, these chapters are designed to give you a better sense of how education interacts with social inequality. This line of inquiry is important, and it is central to the sociology of education. But if we focus our attention exclusively on students, it's easy to forget that the structures in which they learn, interact, and grow are, themselves, social constructions.

In part 3 of *Education and Society*, therefore, we shift our attention. The chapters in this section have been designed with an **organizational** approach to the study of education and society. That is, in the chapters that follow, we are interested in social systems that people create to facilitate educational goals, and in the ways in which these systems operate and change. Schools are perhaps the most prominent organizations in this enterprise. But they aren't the only ones. The chapters in this section also discuss districts, policy-making bodies, academic disciplines, and publishing houses as organizations that comprise education in contemporary societies. The rules, norms, and structures that govern these organizations matter for students' educational experiences and for the construction of social inequality. Furthermore, these organizations and the ways in which they interact can change over time. The study of educational organizations, therefore, provides rich opportunities for understanding the opportunities and challenges that those who would change education and its social role face.

Stanford University education scholars Patricia Bromley and Daniel Scott Smith discuss one of education's most ubiquitous technologies: the textbook. Studying how textbooks shape school **curricula,** or the style and content of the instruction to which students are exposed, sheds light on the habits of mind and values that schools attempt to convey. Further, studying changes in textbook content draws attention to how the content of instruction varies across time and place. As you read this chapter, think back on the textbooks that you used and the ways that your school's curricula structured your education. Were any perspectives absent? How could your textbooks and curricula have been changed to send different messages about what is important in education?

KEY POINTS

- Curricula can be defined as the content and form of schooling—intended curricula, which may differ from implemented or attained curricula, constitute the content and form of schooling officially found in policy documents and in textbooks that make up the standardized public-school "canon."
- Textbooks and curricula are standard features of schooling worldwide, and the common assumption is that the structure and content of the intended curricula function to meet specific needs of a given national society or dominant elites.
- An alternative perspective identifies the emergence and globalization of liberal cultural norms as key drivers of formal national curricula over the last half century. From this perspective, the structure and content of schooling are less the outcomes of a specific labor market demand or elite interests, and more the results of countries complying with global models of education.
- Empirically, textbooks and curricula increasingly standardize many subjects, such as mathematics, science, and the social sciences, and they depict the individual as an empowered, rational, rights-bearing global citizen, over and above an obediently patriotic national citizen.

INTRODUCTION

Many of us have firsthand experience with textbooks; you might still get weighed down while thinking about lugging around giant biology and history books. And all of us have been shaped by curricula, although we may not have heard the term or considered its implications. In the broadest sense, curricula are the plans for what students should learn in school, and textbooks are core tools used worldwide for transmitting curricular goals. Curricula provide a standardized, authoritative narrative, condensing complex knowledge into a more limited, shared set of learning goals. Without this structure, our educational experiences would vary wildly—both in terms of the types of requisite courses and the content required to be covered in those courses.

Textbooks and curricula thus have important consequences for society. The content reflects and defines legitimate knowledge and worldviews. By some accounts, these definitions are relatively unproblematic: the content of schooling prepares students for their roles in society as workers and citizens. In other views, the definitions of what counts as the "most important" or "legitimate" knowledge are contested. As a result some groups are excluded, marginalized, and denigrated through dangerous "lies" in textbook content (Loewen 2008). As a result, heated controversies over what and how to teach arise frequently. Some examples of these include the recent debate in California to rename the historical region that had once covered contemporary India, Nepal, and Pakistan as "South Asia," instead of simply "India," in sixth- and seventh-grade social studies textbooks (Medina 2016). On the one hand, proponents of this change argue that "South Asia" better reflects the region's historically diverse minority cultures that would eventually become today's distinct independent states. Opponents, in contrast, argue that removing the traditional name of the area would erase part of India's larger heritage and would flat out ignore its historical importance in the region. Other recent examples of textbook controversy include textbooks naming the millions of black captives forcefully taken by white Europeans during the three-hundred-year-long African slave trade as "workers" instead of slaves (Wang 2015). Both of these accounts demonstrate the hotly contested terrain of education in society and, importantly, textbooks' central place in these debates.

Curricula and textbooks are important because they give us insight into the society that created them. By looking at the content of curricula and textbooks, we learn about the intended socialization of students—the types of things they are supposed to know and skills they are supposed to develop to become fully participating members of that society. Naturally, there are substantial and interesting differences between countries. For example, Julian Dierkes (2010) found that narratives of national identity differ substantially in World War II discussions in East German, West German, and Japanese history textbooks. Whereas Japanese textbooks emphasize national victimhood in light of the atrocities of the Second World War, East German narratives centrally position the present-day East German nation-state as fundamentally antifascist, and the narratives include few or no mentions of the Holocaust perpetuated by former Germany under the Third Reich. Yet, in further contrast, West German narratives foreground Germany's culpability in the massacres, teaching the nation's history and what it means to be West German. Such examples of variation in conceptions of nationness and nationality are to be expected, given that countries have distinct identities, historical legacies, and political, economic, and cultural systems. What is more surprising, and a central theme of this chapter, is that there are also strikingly similar, often widely agreed upon, curricular changes over time in countries around the world.

The rest of this chapter is organized to shed light on some of the most central questions about the role of education in society: Why are standard curricula taught at all? Who decides what should be taught and learned? Can there be an objective narrative in curricula and textbooks? Moreover, how has it come to be that nearly all students everywhere across the globe are increasingly taught a standard set of "core" subjects, such as mathematics, social science, and history? We approach these questions in three parts. First, we introduce three of the prominent scholarly perspectives on the role of curricula and textbooks in education and society. Second, we give an overview of empirical trends in curricula around the world, using the example of social science textbooks. Last, we consider implications and unanswered questions related to our understanding of the role of curricula in education and society.

APPROACHES TO UNDERSTANDING THE MEANING AND EFFECTS OF TEXTBOOKS AND CURRICULA

Curricula outline the formal teaching and learning that are supposed to occur in school. More specifically, curricula are thought of as having intended, implemented, attained, and even hidden elements (UNESCO 2016; Mullis 2013). The intended curriculum is the form and content of schooling that is officially written out in policy documents and formal teaching materials such as textbooks. These include timetables listing the selected subjects that are supposed to be taught in school; the different academic or vocational programs or tracks, which are "schematic plans," or sequences of courses within or between schools, that students are sorted into or choose to take (Kamens, Meyer, and Benavot 1996); and the explicit academic standards of achievement and guidelines for teaching "common core" subjects, including approved instructional materials such as textbooks and standardized tests (National Governors Association 2016). The implemented curriculum is an adapted form of the intended curriculum: what teachers actually teach to a given class, including the modifications, additions, and exclusions of the official, intended curriculum. The attained curriculum is the measurable knowledge and competences of the intended curriculum that students have actually learned as result of the teaching that occurred in their classes. Finally, in contrast to the intended curriculum, the hidden curriculum is the unintended and implicit personal, social, and cultural lessons—values and ideas—that are taught and learned as a result of different social and cultural processes or "arrangements" in the classroom and school (Anyon 1980; McEneaney and Meyer 2000).

We offer power, progress, and cultural construction as three possible analytic lenses through which to investigate these various goals for curricula and to understand the relationship between schooling and society.

Power

One dominant view in sociological research on the curriculum is that education plays a central role in stratification and inequality (e.g., Blau and Duncan 1967; Arum and Shavit 1995; Shanahan, Elder, and Miech 1997; Caspi et al. 1998). The focus has been less on the actual content of curricula and more on the way variations in schooling are mechanisms to sort people of varying backgrounds into different socioeconomic strata or classes (see McEneaney and Meyer 2000 for more discussion of this point).

Social reproduction, or the persistence of social and economic strata across generations, is theorized to occur through schooling in a number of ways. The first way is through curricular policies that select students for academic success who already have enough "highbrow" cultural familiarity. For example, curricular prescriptions that insist students must master the literary and language arts, including a classical canon, favor the types of "domestically transmitted" knowledge, attitudes, and dispositions, as well as the material possessions, of students who come from families with the economic and cultural capital to purchase literature and literary magazines, attend theater performances, and visit museums and art exhibitions (Bourdieu 2011; Bourdieu and Passeron 1977). In this way, schools are not "culturally neutral" organizations; and as a result, they often "discredit" the different types of knowledge and beliefs possessed by students who come from families with recent migration backgrounds or long histories of low-income, blue-collar work (Lamont and Lareau 1988). Extending the conflict tradition of Marx and Weber, Randall Collins (1979) argued, too, that the content and values of education were not only those of dominant classes but also those of dominant cultural groups. Similarly, Michael Apple (1979) theorized that, as a result, culture operates in curricular production as a system reinforcing economic dominance of some groups over others.

More implicitly, social reproduction is also theorized to occur through a "hidden curriculum," when school personnel teach an ostensibly neutral curriculum differentially, depending on the supposed merit of students (e.g., Gatto 2002). In this process, teachers demand higher-order thinking and offer more challenging content to those students attending schools in privileged neighborhoods or occupying higher tracks. In contrast, they expect more rote memorization and task execution from students in disadvantaged schools or lower tracks (Anyon 1980; for a classic debate about tracking, see Hallinan 1994 and the rejoinder in Oakes 1994). Since powerful cultural elites are assumed to have a monopoly over the content and structure of schooling, power, more than merit, is thought to drive the placement of students in schools and tracks. This perspective thus seeks to explain why individuals have a hard time experiencing social mobility and, instead, inherit their families' standings. It offers an explanation for why society remains more or less stably stratified across time by class: not despite education but, indeed, because of it.

Contemporary educational and sociological research investigates these power dynamics in school curricula in order to identify, explain, and even disrupt the unequal transmission of privilege in society. Postcolonialist researchers, for example, identify the entrenched ethnocentrism of national curricula as part of a past, ongoing, or even emergent empire that systemically disenfranchises minority or formerly colonialized peoples (Kanu 2006). Feminist and queer theorists, as another example, study how curricular narratives and depictions of diversity in gender, sex, and sexuality—or complete erasures of these—perpetuate essentialist or biological misunderstandings of self. Gendered social reproduction, in turn, limits people's freedom of self-determination and provides a rationale for historical and ongoing gender- and sex-based inequality and even oppression (Laslett and Brenner 1989).

With the publication of, and surrounding debate over, Allan Bloom's (1987) *The Closing of the American Mind,* which berates the trend of including non-Western texts in American university curricula, the field of higher education shows an elegant case where these two power dynamics intersect. During the late 1980s and early 1990s in the United States, traditional notions of the classical canon were extensively contested on the basis of their perceived Western, often Anglo-American, classist white-male ethnocentrism. These older visions of "Western civilization" neither reflected the "human faces" of the ever-diversifying university student bodies nor adequately provided future members of pluralistic society with a credible and critical basis of knowledge (see Antonio and Muñiz 2007: 279–82 for a brief discussion). It was during this time that university curricula expanded to include interdisciplinary programs on critical race theory and women's and gender studies.

Common to these veins of research and similar ones is the finding that power plays out in education as ongoing oppression and contest. But curricula, and the power they represent, are also envisioned as centrally located in the future emancipation of nondominant groups in society and, thus, justice for all (McCarthy, Giardina, Harewood, and Park 2003).

Progress

A second widely accepted approach to understanding the meaning and effects of curricula and textbooks assumes that curricula are objective; the standardized curriculum is a straightforward tool for achieving learning goals, which are often tied to the demands of the labor market but could also include societal needs such as social cohesion (a central focus of Durkheim's work in education) or political socialization to support citizen participation in government and civil society. Contemporary research in this vein often focuses on how curricula are associated with academic achievement and educational attainment (e.g., Bishop 1997); it does not ask questions about social inequality or imbalances of power. From this view, curricula transmit concrete skills and knowledge—or "human capital"—that make individuals more productive in the long run (e.g., Schultz 1971; Healy and Côté 2001; Becker 2009). At the aggregated level, when national education systems prescribe a set of lessons that result in the most appropriate skill set for the labor market or proper citizenship skills for the smooth running of democratic government, students prosper from more and better capabilities, and society also benefits in terms of national development.

At times, schools, districts, and even national education systems are criticized for falling short of these goals by failing to provide the proper curricular content (e.g., perhaps in computer science or critical thinking) or to teach classes well enough (e.g., achievement suffers and quality is poor). These criticisms usually generate calls for reform (regarding reforms in higher education, see Arum and Roksa 2011 for a critique of how universities are failing to provide students with appropriate workplace skills). The central argument from this analytic lens is that education at all levels should lead to individual and collective progress, and specific types of courses and content are selected to transmit these skills best.

In figure 12, we illustrate these prominent views of education's two main roles in society. In panel A, we represent the first prominent view of how education is often theorized to function in society. To summarize, when education is envisioned as a form of power and domination, it is assumed that the content of curricula serves the interests of a ruling elite. Most obviously, this would manifest as a "classical curriculum" designed to produce a cultural and economic elite to govern society (Kamens and Benavot 1991); or, more subversively, the content of a supposedly comprehensive (rather than elite) curriculum could serve to reproduce inequality on large scale. Through a national curriculum that both explicitly and implicitly selects students from more privileged backgrounds for success, and that selects students with more disadvantaged standings for placement in lower tracks with limited educational opportunity, the social milieu, or strata of society, is systematically reproduced across generations.

We indicate the possibility of curricular change through the recursive pathway (dashed line) between stratified national society and powerful elites. Through conflict and power struggle among the masses and the elite as a result of perceived and demonstrated educational and social inequity, policy elites are pressured to reform schooling and curricula. In these power conflicts, education is often leveraged for social justice. Some examples of how curricula would change as a result of the conflict predicted here could be increased diversification of, and representation in, the traditional canon, as well as greater emphasis on accessible and critical, culturally relevant, and emancipatory skills and knowledge. This was the case, as we saw above, with the inclusion of critical race theory and gender and women's studies programs in university curricula.

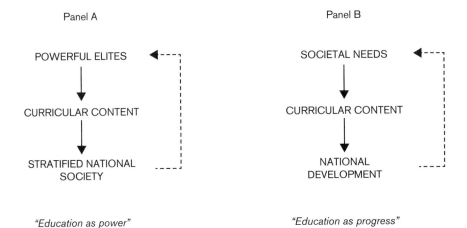

Figure 12. National curricula as functions of powerful elites' interests (panel A) or societal needs (panel B).

In panel B, we present the second view, that functional needs in society determine curricula. A prominent example is that the labor market demands certain knowledge and skills over others, which, in turn, informs how people rationally invest in education. Individuals are incentivized by higher wages to pursue these skills and knowledge through formal higher education, which, in contemporary times, educational economists refer to as the "college wage premium" (Levy and Murnane 2007; Goldin and Katz 2009). Societies, likewise, are incentivized by the prospect of additional national economic development (often indicated by a higher gross domestic product) to institute national curricula that create a workforce with the necessary skills and knowledge to stay competitive and progressively more prosperous in the global market.

Much like in panel A, we indicate the mechanism of curricular change with the recursive arrow that links national development (e.g., economic development) and societal needs (e.g., demands for skilled labor). According to this model, as national economic development ensues, innovation and technological breakthroughs create new and emerging markets. These new markets then demand that members of the national workforce develop more and different skills, which education systems must impart through national curricula. Complementarily, as societies increasingly become diverse and pluralistic, education systems must create a broadly tolerant citizenry. One example of curricular change predicted as a result of the contemporary postindustrial, high-tech service-and-information economy is increased emphases on science, technology, engineering, and mathematics. Another would be university curricula that teach ethnocentric and gender bias in what counts as "Truth" in fields as far apart as biology and comparative literature (Laqueur 1992).

Cultural Construction

In contrast to perspectives that take the functional roles of education in society for granted, we come from an alternative, social constructivist, approach to understanding the origin, spread, and effects of curricula. Using the analytic lenses of power and progress illustrated above, we show the variation in national curricula that occurs as a result of rational actors making deliberate, purposive choices in pursuit of their own interests (e.g., greater prosperity and more power). Others have assumed that societies and individuals alike are agents who precede and react to environmental conditions, whether this entails an evolving economy or the ongoing social protest of illegitimate domination. Our approach instead focuses on the powerful role that the larger social environment has in shaping social identities and interests. This alternative approach focuses on the cultural character of this global context within which national societies and individuals coexist (Meyer et al. 1997). By *cultural character,* we mean worldwide norms, rules, ideas, myths, values, and models—the soft and hard laws that guide and even pressure people, organizations, and institutions to look and act in certain ways, over and above what their unique cultures and histories would have them do. "Culture," in this definition, represents our shared and taken-for-granted assumptions about legitimate ways for "how things are done" and "what makes sense," often objectified and institutionalized in policies, rules, and formal organizational structures.

Contemporary globalized culture arose during the postwar period around liberal, Western values and now provides societies all across the world with the model of the nation-state as the legitimate collective identity replete with a stock set of institutions, central to which is education systems (Meyer et al. 1997; Ramirez 2012). Former collective identities, such as those of empire and patrimonial states, are no longer accepted as legitimate, just as all contemporary nation-states are pressured to provide universal access to high-quality education if they are to be taken seriously. This global culture also distinguishes the rational and rights-wielding human as the legitimate individual identity (Ramirez 2006; Ramirez, Bromley, and Russell 2009). And all individuals, irrespective of birth or origin, have equal dignity, value, and right to self-determination. In terms of social interests and actions, world culture orients both individuals and societies to the universalistic, normative values of progress and justice. It also privileges a certain way of attaining these values. Former traditional or charismatic bases of political and social change are replaced by pressures to be data driven and evidenced based. In other words, individuals, organizations, and societies alike ought to act rationally (Drori et al. 2003) with means-end purposiveness (Bromley and Powell 2012) to solve the problems obstructing the path to greater prosperity and justice for all.

From this perspective, individual and societal investment in education is less a functional need than a cultural rite or ritual. Nation-states "do" education in

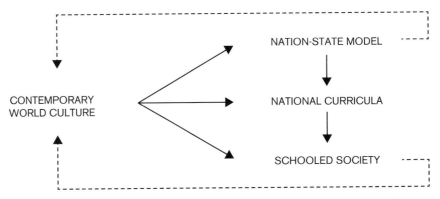

Figure 13. National curricula as part of an enactment of world culture. Source: adapted from J. W. Meyer, J. Boli, G. M. Thomas, and F. O. Ramirez, "World Society and the Nation-State," *American Journal of Sociology* 103, no. 1 (1997): 151.

standardized ways across the world to attain legitimacy among other nation-states who are equally responsive to and partially constructed by world culture (Ramirez 1997). In other words, national curricula are institutionalized and even reformed across the globe in largely standard ways, independent of actual material conditions, in order to conform to the set of broad world-cultural principles of what a "good" or "proper" society looks like and does (Meyer, Ramirez, and Soysal 1992). We illustrate this alternative perspective in figure 13.

To sum up, in figure 13 we depict the perspective that contemporary world culture "constructs" nation-states, their institutions (education systems with national curricula), and their individual members (schooled society). World culture offers blueprints for how national society should be organized, what constitutes a legitimate national curriculum, and what capacities and rights educated, or "schooled," individuals should have.

Curricular change is theorized to occur under certain circumstances: as societies increasingly conform to the model of the nation-state; when they become more closely linked to world culture as they participate in inter- and supranational organizations, such as the United Nations and European Union; and when they ratify international treaties and conventions (Boli and Thomas 1997). Further, as the nation-state system evolves, and as larger proportions of society are schooled, world culture itself can be reconstituted (indicated by the recursive arrows). In this way, individual nation-states' cultures and histories can and do partially mediate the ongoing effect of overarching world-cultural principles on curricular outcomes. Examples of change predicted by this model include the increasing curricular convergence across disparate national contexts, and the increased emphasis on diversity, human rights, and student-centered pedagogies.

Foundational to this approach, and to the value it adds to understanding contemporary trends in education and society, is the fact that the institutionalization of national curricula is theorized to create schooled societies across the whole globe that are prepared to pursue justice and progress. These are the same normative assumptions that underlie the power and progress perspectives depicted in figure 12, and the global consensus about their value enables these perspectives to be applied universally across national contexts to explain the purported functions of education in society.

EMPIRICAL FINDINGS

So how do these theories hold up to observable reality? Do they actually help us answer some of the questions asked earlier in this chapter about the meaning and effects of curricula and textbooks in society?

Curriculum scholars have described the field as in "crisis" because of the lack of empirical research (Young 2013; Baker 2015). The primary challenge for comparative social researchers who study curricula stems largely from the difficulty in constructing large-scale, representative data sets of curricula throughout the world. Collecting this kind of data is difficult because many countries have formally published their official national curricular standards only in recent decades. That means observing trends in these standards in a given country over time would require using a wide array of sources of information on the content and form of schooling—information that might be available for one year and not for the next, or for one country but not another, or in a different format in the same country from one year to the next.

Still, authors of a limited number of studies have tackled assembling curricular details from many countries over time. For example, using surveys sent to ministries of education, as well as historical databases from UNESCO, sociologists have been able to observe the "canon" over time by constructing large cross-national and longitudinal data sets that document the compulsory subjects in school, tracking structures, the hours of instruction formally allocated to these subjects, and more recently, the substantive content intended to be taught within subjects via textbook analyses across several periods (e.g., Benavot et al. 1991). This allows us to see patterns that arise and endure not just over different times but also across diverse national contexts.

Support for Functional Theories of Curricula

Power. In terms of the link between curricula and power, some studies of tracking show that it plays a role in reproducing inequality in society owing to bias in the allocation of students to tracks (e.g., Oakes 2005; Van de Werfhorst and Mijs 2010). The issue, however, is debated. The strongest evidence of tracking as a source of persistent inequality relates to vocational education, which system-atically channels students away from higher education (e.g., Shavit 1984). Tracking students at early ages (e.g., at six years of age) into separate vocational schools with limited upward mobility has been found to be significantly and substantially related to students' language proficiency, migration background, and parents' cultural familiarity and ability to advocate on behalf of their children, not to the students' actual aptitude to study in higher-level tracks (Alba, Sloan, and Sperling 2011).

In some cases, this is certainly true, but as we will discuss, there are also large portions of curricular content that do not seem aimed directly at reproducing national stratification patterns (e.g., content addressing environmentalism, human rights, or global citizenship) and, instead, seem intended to produce empowered individuals. Further, vocational education is declining within national curricula throughout the world (Benavot 1983). For example, since the 1960s, Germany and the Netherlands, long known for their extensive dual system of separated academic and vocational schools, have increasingly implemented comprehensive schools with multiple tracks and programs that offer more opportunities for students to move between tracks, based on their achievement (see Jacob and Tieben 2009 for further discussion of mobility between tracks). Indeed, modern tracking usually entails varying degrees of difficulty of standard subjects (math, science, and so on), rather than an entirely different program of study housed in different buildings terminating in different qualifications. Empirical studies have yet to show how similar subject content with variable degrees of difficulty in high versus low tracks leads to societal-level stratification, absent other, noncurricular factors that generate inequality.

Progress. A core area of research on the link between curricula and progress has been in math and science, where emphasis on these subjects is expected to be tied to national economic growth. In a study of over sixty countries (including forty-three less-developed countries) between 1960 and 1985, Benavot (1992) found that most subject areas of the primary school curriculum (measured in hours of instruction) were unrelated to long-term changes in national economic production. Science education, however, had strong, positive effects; but the number of hours of math and language instruction was unrelated to economic growth, and the number of hours of instruction on prevocational or practical subjects had negative associations with national economic development. At a general level, a greater number of hours of instruction in primary school (as distinct from expanded enrollments or number of hours in specific subjects) has an effect on national economic growth, although as noted earlier, not for all subject areas usually thought to be economically relevant and not across all types of countries. Reviewing decades of cross-national research on education and development, Chabott and Ramirez (2000) found considerable ambiguity in their reviewed analyses of the effects of expanded education on national development and, at the same time, redoubled beliefs in its undoubtedly positive effects and the promise of progress.

Overall, neither the progress- nor the power-oriented view of curricula fully explains their structure and content. In a handful of cases, we saw support for a functional view of curricula as linked to progress or inequality, but these findings emerged unsystematically, appearing in some countries and types of curricula and not in others—with no clear explanation for why this variation exists.

Support for Cultural Theories of Curricula

Convergent curricular structures. Given the great variation in both societal needs and elite power structures among the world's diverse countries—as well as gross disparities in material circumstances, cultures, and histories—curricular structures should be expected to vary considerably. Yet a consistent finding is that, despite national variation in political, economic, or social structures, national curricula are very similar throughout the world (Benavot et al. 1991; Meyer, Ramirez, and Soysal 1992). As a striking example, in response to highly legitimated supranational organizations like UNESCO, many countries structured their education systems according to the standardized model of the six-year primary school, three-year junior high school, and three-year senior high school (Meyer et al. 1997). In course requirements, as well, Wong (1991) found homogeneity: a global transformation occurred after World War II, shifting the focus away from history and geography as separate courses of instruction, and toward a new, integrated subject termed "social studies." Such standardized global trends make it difficult to explain curricula purely as linked to distinct national needs or to the interests of select elites and classes. From progress- or power-oriented viewpoints, it comes as a surprise to observe the comparatively weak influence of national characteristics on national curricular structure: similarities outweigh differences.

Convergent curricular content. Several comprehensive empirical studies of national curricula show that the content of schooling is laid out in widely standardized ways at the national level, relative to what we might expect, given the enormous differences in gender participation, class and/or tribal structures, region or locality, or level of national development (for primary schools, see Benavot et al. 1991; for secondary schools, see Wong 1991 and Kamens, Meyer, and Benavot 1996; for higher education, see Frank and Gabler 2006). A more recent wave of research further examines the intended curricular content of national education systems through analyses of textbooks. Using a data set that included more than four hundred social science textbooks (history, civics, and social studies) published between 1970 and 2010 in roughly seventy countries, scholars have documented worldwide increases in discussions of human rights (Meyer, Bromley, and Ramirez 2010), the environment (Bromley,

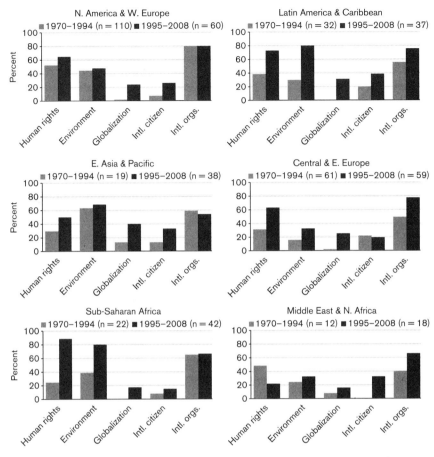

Figure 14. Percentage of textbooks discussing human rights, environmentalism, globalization, international citizenship, and international organizations over time by region.

Meyer, and Ramirez 2011b), global citizenship (Buckner and Russell 2013), and the use of student-centered pedagogical strategies aimed at empowering learners (Bromley, Meyer, and Ramirez 2011a). After controlling for country factors such as level of democracy and gross domestic product per capita, researchers found that these changes occur over time. Drawing on this same textbook data, the bar charts in figure 14 descriptively illustrate the widespread and mainly increasing discussions of human rights, the environment, global citizenship, and international organizations in high school social science textbooks around the world by region (without formal controls for country features).

Illustrations from existing studies show qualitative evidence of the rise of globalist narratives—even in subjects with a traditionally nationalist focus, such as civics. For example, several studies have examined the rise of "international citizenship," identified in figure 14 as increasing over time in most regions of the world. Figure 15 (top) shows an excerpt from a social studies textbook published in 2008 in Kenya that discusses (as reported in Lerch, Russell, and Ramirez 2017: 173) the importance of respecting both human rights (a globalist narrative) and patriotism (a nationalist narrative). Similarly, figure 15 (bottom) shows how a recent civics book from Spain teaches students they are embedded in expanding rings of citizenship. The book states, "We are citizens of the world. . . . [A]s citizens of the world, we are protected by human rights that apply to all humanity. . . . Human rights derive from our human condition, not from our nationality" (as reported in Buckner and Russell 2013: 741). A point of note is that globalized cultural norms do not necessarily replace traditional ideas of national citizenship; rather, globalized cultural norms seem to be layered on top, and the two seem to be depicted as consistent with each other (see also Bromley and Cole 2017).

In contrast to narratives that emphasize international or global citizenship along with national citizenship, a 2002 Pakistan studies textbook for grades 9 and 10 focuses solely on the traditional purpose of education, which is to construct a unified nation-state on the basis of a shared national history, language, and culture (see figure 16). The book explicitly states that although there are regional and group differences within Pakistan, citizens are united by a common language (Urdu) and religion (Islam). The country's technological and cultural accomplishments are celebrated in order to foster a sense of national pride. There is no discussion of how national citizenship relates either to ideas of global citizenship or to universalistic values such as human rights or environmentalism.

It is difficult to explain substantial cross-national similarity—on many fronts and across a wide variety of countries with varied contexts and historical legacies—purely in terms of national economic or political development needs. Furthermore, it is difficult to see how emphases on topics such as universal human rights, environmentalism, or global citizenship—or pedagogical strategies that promote critical thinking and creative, participatory problem solving—serve the interests of national elites in terms of reproducing inequality. Instead, the evolving similarities in curricular content over time seem to be, at least in part, a process of nation-states increasingly participating in and enacting a common culture with a set of universalistic values.

UNANSWERED QUESTIONS AND RESEARCH FRONTIERS

The cultural approach to studying the meaning and effects of curricula and textbooks directs our attention to the remarkable consensus on what is important to teach and learn among our world's wildly diverse societies. Seeing

Elements of Good Citizenship

When we were in class five we learnt about the importance of good citizenship.

Why is good citizenship important?

This year we shall continue to study more on citizenship. When we talk about elements of good citizenship we mean things that a good citizen should have. The elements of good citizenship include the following:

1. *Respect for human rights*
   Good citizenship requires that human rights are respected. For example, we should respect other people's right to life. That is why murder is a very serious crime. Other examples include, the right and the freedom of movement and right to own property.

2. *Loyalty*
   A loyal citizen is one who is faithful to his/her nation and the president of the nation. As Kenyans we must support the president and the government. This will help to promote peace and prosperity. Loyalty includes talking well of our country wherever we are. That will show that you are proud of your nation.

3. *Patriotism*
   Patriotism means total love for our nation. A patriot will die defending Kenya. Patriots put the nation's interests first. For example, our sports people have won numerous prizes for Kenya. These have been at international events like the Olympics games.

Fig. 6.1: Kenyan athletes who are patriotic to Kenya; they bring prestige to our country.

4. *Law abiding*
   Laws are made for our well-being. Obeying them will make our country to develop. Lawlessness causes insecurity.

5. *Respecting symbols of National Unity*
   The National Anthem, the National Flag, the National currency, Coat of Arms and the presidency are symbols of

Figure 15. (*Top*) Blending of national and global citizenship narratives in a Kenyan social studies textbook. Source: Cleophas Ondieki, Naomi Mbugu, and Francis Muraya, *Comprehensive Social Studies* (Nairobi: Longhorn, 2008). (*Bottom*) Blending of national and global citizenship narratives in a Spanish civics textbook. Source: José A. Mario, *Educatión para la Cuidadanía* (Madrid: Ediciones SM, 2008).

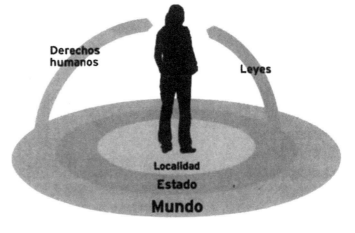

Los círculos de la ciudadanía.

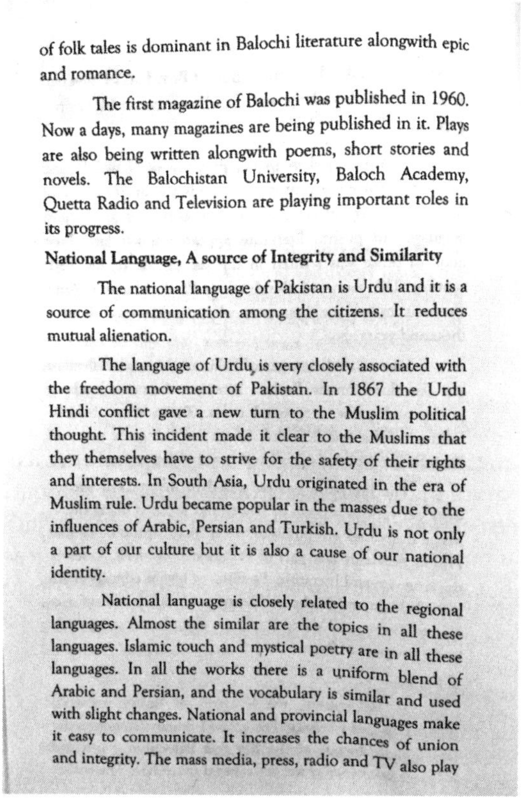

of folk tales is dominant in Balochi literature alongwith epic and romance.

The first magazine of Balochi was published in 1960. Now a days, many magazines are being published in it. Plays are also being written alongwith poems, short stories and novels. The Balochistan University, Baloch Academy, Quetta Radio and Television are playing important roles in its progress.

National Language, A source of Integrity and Similarity

The national language of Pakistan is Urdu and it is a source of communication among the citizens. It reduces mutual alienation.

The language of Urdu is very closely associated with the freedom movement of Pakistan. In 1867 the Urdu Hindi conflict gave a new turn to the Muslim political thought. This incident made it clear to the Muslims that they themselves have to strive for the safety of their rights and interests. In South Asia, Urdu originated in the era of Muslim rule. Urdu became popular in the masses due to the influences of Arabic, Persian and Turkish. Urdu is not only a part of our culture but it is also a cause of our national identity.

National language is closely related to the regional languages. Almost the similar are the topics in all these languages. Islamic touch and mystical poetry are in all these languages. In all the works there is a uniform blend of Arabic and Persian, and the vocabulary is similar and used with slight changes. National and provincial languages make it easy to communicate. It increases the chances of union and integrity. The mass media, press, radio and TV also play

Figure 16. National citizenship narrative in a civic education textbook from Pakistan. Source: M. Hussain, A. Mirza, S. Anees, R. Kharal, S. Haidar, and D. Qais, *Pakistan Studies* (Lahore, Pakistan: Sofi Sons, 2002).

national curricula as the outcomes of world-cultural processes above and beyond their contribution to national needs or their role in reproducing inequality enables us to situate schooling in world-historical social transformations, in particular the emergence of a supranational "human" community deliberately taught and learned about and imagined in the minds of individuals all over globe.

Yet, core questions in the sociology of education remain unanswered and, indeed, arise when one takes the cultural approach. For example, as nation-states increasingly enact world-cultural scripts of individual empowerment and postnational global citizenship through education, are there any observable emerging trends in democracy, peace, and equity in the world? What is the relationship, if any at all exists, between intended curricula as enactments of world culture and their actual implementation in schools? Are there any macro-sociological factors that could help us explain the gaps between official state policies that comply with these world-cultural principles and the actual, on-the-ground practices?

Plausibly, curricula in countries with a more centralized national education system would have more standardized intended and implemented curricula (see Stevenson and Baker 1991 for supporting evidence in math curricula in fifteen countries) and, thus, perhaps more substantial associations with societal outcomes. A worldwide trend toward formalization and standardization of curricula makes curricula an increasingly influential feature of education and, thus, an area of growing importance within the sociology of education.

But even for economic outcomes, the causal mechanisms are unclear. For instance, we know little about why some subjects (e.g., science) are associated with national economic growth but others are not (e.g., math, languages). Related to that, how is variation in the content within a subject (e.g., different topics in, or ways of teaching, science classes) tied to outcomes in terms of either achievement or national measures of progress? In other words, what features of curricula make them more likely to have strong effects on students and/or on society? There has been extensive discussion about the value of "culturally responsive curricula" in terms of improving test scores in the United States (Dee and Penner 2016), but would this approach have similar effects in other times or places?

IMPLICATIONS AND SIGNIFICANCE

Implicitly or explicitly, most of us expect that one of the key ways education shapes society is through curricula. School is thought to transmit actual knowledge about science, math, history, geography, and so on. And we expect this knowledge to be tied to economic, political, social, and cultural outcomes, maybe in terms of progress, or maybe in terms of reinforcing inequality. But there remains a dearth of information about the content actually taught in school—the implemented curriculum. Existing empirical findings suggest there is far more similarity between countries than would be expected if curricular content were aimed primarily at meeting specific national needs or serving elites' goals. Changes in content (e.g., toward discussions of universal human rights or the environment) are also difficult to justify as related to the specific needs of one country but not another. Thus, beyond their role in meeting the needs of specific national societies or class elites, large parts of curricula seem meant to socialize individuals and countries for participation in a supranational community—an interdependent world society with a now-globalized economy and a common culture. Indeed, as countries increasingly move away from policies institutionalizing a distinctly national education and conform to this world model, curricula and textbooks, as we have shown, might be seen as canonizing world culture (Meyer 2007).

CHAPTER 9 REVIEW

Discussion Questions

1. What would education look like if there were no standard curricula? What do you see as the pros and cons of systems that have a central, common national curriculum versus more decentralized systems (either state-level or local-level control)? If there is, in fact, convergence toward the curricular emphases aligned with liberal world cultural values, what are the implications for society (and different societies around the world)?

2. Find examples of contemporary and historical textbooks (there are many available online through publishers or Google Books). Do you see instances of bias or exclusion? Do you see instances where students are being socialized or trained to fill a specifically national need? Do you see instances of content that reflect world norms or values more than national needs or elite domination?

3. Under what circumstances are the progress, power, and cultural explanations of curricula more likely to be true? Design a study that would allow you to test your arguments.

4. How would a new nation-state's national curriculum be predicted to look, according to the cultural approach described above? (Hint: Look at that of South Sudan.)

5. Take a look at your university's course requirements or the syllabi of particular courses (both the front section and the reading list). In what ways do they conform to a standard national or global model? In what ways do they reproduce inequality? In what ways do they serve functional needs in society?

Suggestions for Further Reading

Benavot, A., and C. Braslavsky, eds. 2007. *School Knowledge in Comparative and Historical Perspective: Changing Curricula in Primary and Secondary Education,* vol. 18. Dordrecht, Netherlands: Springer Science and Business Media.

FitzGerald, F. 1979. *America Revised: History Schoolbooks in the Twentieth Century.* Boston: Little, Brown.

Loewen, J. W. 2008. *Lies My Teacher Told Me: Everything Your American History Textbook Got Wrong.* New York: New Press.

References

Alba, R., J. Sloan, and J. Sperling. 2011. "The Integration Imperative: The Children of Low-Status Immigrants in the Schools of Wealthy Societies." *Annual Review of Sociology* 37:395–415.

Antonio, Anthony I., and M. Muñiz. 2007. "The Sociology of Diversity." In *Sociology of Higher Education: Contributions and Their Contexts,* edited by P. J. Gumport, 266–94. Baltimore: Johns Hopkins University Press.

Anyon, J. 1980. "Social Class and the Hidden Curriculum of Work." *Journal of Education* 162 (1): 67–92.

Apple, Michael W. 1979. *Ideology and Curriculum.* London: Routledge.

Arum, R., and Y. Shavit. 1995. "Secondary Vocational Education and the Transition from School to Work." *Sociology of Education* 68:187–204.

Arum, Richard, and Josipa Roksa. 2011. *Academically Adrift: Limited Learning on College Campuses.* Chicago: University of Chicago Press.

Baker, D. 2015. "A Note on Knowledge in the Schooled Society: Towards an End to the Crisis in Curriculum Theory." *Journal of Curriculum Studies* 47 (6): 763–77.

Becker, G. S. 2009. *Human Capital: A Theoretical and Empirical Analysis, with Special Reference to Education.* Chicago: University of Chicago Press.

Benavot, A. 1983. "The Rise and Decline of Vocational Education." *Sociology of Education* 56 (2): 63–76.

———. 1992. "Curricular Content, Educational Expansion, and Economic Growth." *Comparative Education Review* 36 (2): 150–74.

Benavot, A., Y. K. Cha, D. Kamens, J. W. Meyer, and S. Y. Wong. 1991. "Knowledge for the Masses: World Models and National Curricula, 1920–1986." *American Sociological Review* 56 (1): 85–100.

Bishop, J. H. 1997. "The Effect of National Standards and Curriculum-Based Exams on Achievement." *American Economic Review* 87 (2): 260–64.

Blau, P., and O. D. Duncan. 1967. *The American Occupational Structure.* New York: Wiley.

Bloom, A. 1987. *The Closing of the American Mind: How Higher Education Has Failed Democracy and Impoverished the Souls of Today's Students.* New York: Simon and Shuster.

Boli, J., and G. M. Thomas. 1997. "World Culture in the World Polity: A Century of International Non-governmental Organization." *American Sociological Review* 62 (2): 171–90.

Bourdieu, P. 2011. "The Forms of Capital." In *Cultural Theory: An Anthology,* edited by I. Szeman and T. Kaposy, 81–93. Malden, MA: John Wiley and Sons.

Bourdieu, P., and J.-C. Passeron. 1977. *Reproduction in Education, Society and Culture.* London: Sage

Bromley, P., and W. Cole. 2017. "A Tale of Two Worlds: The Interstate System and World Society in Social Science Textbooks, 1950–2011." *Globalisation, Societies and Education* 15 (4): 425–47.

Bromley, P., J. W. Meyer, and F. O Ramirez. 2011a. "Student-Centeredness in Social Science Textbooks, 1970–2008: A Cross-National Study." *Social Forces* 90 (2): 547–70.

———. 2011b. "The Worldwide Spread of Environmental Discourse in Social Studies, History, and Civics Textbooks, 1970–2008." *Comparative Education Review* 55 (4): 517–45.

Bromley, P., and W. W. Powell. 2012. "From Smoke and Mirrors to Walking the Talk: Decoupling in the Contemporary World." *Academy of Management Annals* 6 (1): 483–530.

Buckner, E., and S. G. Russell. 2013. "Portraying the Global: Cross-National Trends in Textbooks' Portrayal of Globalization and Global Citizenship." *International Studies Quarterly* 57 (4): 738–50.

Caspi, A., B. Wright, T. Moffitt, and P. Silva. 1998. "Childhood Predictors of Unemployment in Early Adulthood." *American Sociological Review* 63 (3): 424–51.

Chabott, C., and F. O. Ramirez. 2000. "Development and Education." In *Handbook of the Sociology of Education*, edited by M. T. Hallinan, 163–87. New York: Kluwer Academic/Plenum.

Collins, R. 1979. *The Credential Society: An Historical Sociology of Education and Stratification*. New York: Academic Press.

Dee, T., and E. Penner. 2016. "The Causal Effects of Cultural Relevance: Evidence from an Ethnic Studies Curriculum." NBER Working Paper No. 21865. National Bureau of Economic Research.

Dierkes, J. 2010. *Postwar History Education in Japan and the Germanys: Guilty Lessons*. London: Routledge.

Drori, G., J. W. Meyer, F. O. Ramirez, and E. Schofer. 2003. *Science in the Modern World Polity: Institutionalization and Globalization*. Stanford, CA: Stanford University Press.

Frank, D. J., and J. Gabler. 2006. *Reconstructing the University: Worldwide Shifts in Academia in the 20th Century*. Stanford, CA: Stanford University Press.

Gatto, J. T. 2002. *Dumbing Us Down: The Hidden Curriculum of Compulsory Schooling*. Gabriola Island, BC: New Society.

Goldin, C. D., and L. F. Katz. 2009. *The Race between Education and Technology*. Cambridge, MA: Harvard University Press.

Hallinan, M. T. 1994. "Tracking: From Theory to Practice." *Sociology of Education* 67 (2): 79–84.

Healy, T., and S. Côté. 2001. *The Well-Being of Nations: The Role of Human and Social Capital; Education and Skills*. Paris: Organisation for Economic Cooperation and Development.

Jacob, M., and N. Tieben. 2009. "Social Selectivity of Track Mobility in Secondary Schools: A Comparison of Intra-secondary Transitions in Germany and the Netherlands." *European Societies* 11 (5): 747–73.

Kamens, D. H., and A. Benavot. 1991. "Elite Knowledge for the Masses: The Origins and Spread of Mathematics and Science Education in National Curricula." *American Journal of Education* 99 (2): 137–80.

Kamens, D. H., J. W. Meyer, and A. Benavot. 1996. "Worldwide Patterns in Academic Secondary Education Curricula." *Comparative Education Review* 40 (2): 116–38.

Kanu, Y. 2006. *Curriculum as Cultural Practice: Postcolonial Imaginations*. Toronto: University of Toronto Press.

Lamont, M., and A. Lareau. 1988. "Cultural Capital: Allusions, Gaps and Glissandos in Recent Theoretical Developments." *Sociological Theory* 6 (2): 153–68.

Laqueur, T. 1992. *Making Sex: Biology and Gender from the Greeks to Freud*. Cambridge, MA: Harvard University Press.

Laslett, B., and J. Brenner. 1989. "Gender and Social Reproduction: Historical Perspectives." *Annual Review of Sociology* 15:381–404.

Lerch, J. C., S. G. Russell, and F. O. Ramirez. 2017. "Wither the Nation-State? A Comparative Analysis of Nationalism in Textbooks." *Social Forces* 96 (1): 1–27.

Levy, F., and R. Murnane. 2007. "How Computerized Work and Globalization Shape Human Skill Demands." In *Learning in the Global Era: International Perspectives on Globalization and Education*, edited by Marcelo Suarez-Orozco, 158–74. Berkeley: University of California Press.

Loewen, J. W. 2008. *Lies My Teacher Told Me: Everything Your American History Textbook Got Wrong*. New York: New Press.

McCarthy, C., M. Giardina, S. J. Harewood, and J. K. Park. 2003. "Afterword: Contesting Culture: Identity and Curriculum Dilemmas in the Age of Globalization, Postcolonialism, and Multiplicity." *Harvard Educational Review* 73 (3): 449–65.

McEneaney, E., and J. W. Meyer. 2000. "The Content of the Curriculum: An Institutionalist Perspective." In *Handbook of the Sociology of Education*, edited by J. T. Hallinan, 189–211. New York: Kluwer Academic/Plenum.

Medina, J. 2016. "Debate in California over Curriculum on India's History." *New York Times*. May 4. www.nytimes.com/2016/05/06/us/debate-erupts-over-californias-india-history-curriculum.html.

Meyer, J. W. 2007. "World Models, National Curricula, and the Centrality of the Individual." In *School Knowledge in Comparative and Historical Perspective: Changing Curricula in Primary and Secondary Education*, edited by A. Benavot, C. Braslavsky, and N. Truong, 259–71. Dordrecht, Netherlands: Springer.

Meyer, J. W., J. Boli, G. M. Thomas, and F. O Ramirez. 1997. "World Society and the Nation-State." *American Journal of Sociology* 103 (1): 144–81.

Meyer, J. W., P. Bromley, and F. O. Ramirez. 2010. "Human Rights in Social Science Textbooks Cross-National Analyses, 1970–2008." *Sociology of Education* 83 (2): 111–34.

Meyer, J. W., F. O. Ramirez, and Y. N. Soysal. 1992. "World Expansion of Mass Education, 1870–1980." *Sociology of Education* 65 (2): 128–49.

Mullis, I. 2013. Introduction to *TIMSS 2015 Assessment Frameworks*, edited by I. V. S. Mullis and M. O. Martin, 3–9. Chestnut Hill, MA: TIMSS and PIRLS International Study Center, Boston College. http://timssandpirls.bc.edu/timss2015/downloads/T15_FW_Intro.pdf.

National Governors Association. 2016. "Common Core State Standards Initiative." www.corestandards.org/about-the-standards/.

Oakes, J. 1994. "More Than Misapplied Technology: A Normative and Political Response to Hallinan on Tracking." *Sociology of Education* 67 (2): 84–91.

———. 2005. *Keeping Track: How Schools Structure Inequality.* 2nd ed. New Haven, CT: Yale University Press.

Ramirez, F.O. 1997. "The Nation-State, Citizenship, and Educational Change: Institutionalization and Globalization." In *International Handbook of Education and Development: Preparing Schools, Students, and Nations for the Twenty-First Century,* edited by William K. Cummings and Noel F. McGinn, 47–62. New York: Pergamon.

———. 2006. "From Citizen to Person? Rethinking Education as Incorporation." In *The Impact of Comparative Education Research on Neo-institutional Theory,* edited by D. Baker and A. Wiseman, 367–88. Amsterdam: Elsevier.

———. 2012. "The World Society Perspective: Concepts, Assumptions, and Strategies." *Comparative Education* 48 (4): 423–39.

Ramirez, F.O., P. Bromley, and S.G. Russell. 2009. "The Valorization of Humanity and Diversity." *Multicultural Education Review* 1 (1): 29–54.

Schultz, T.W. 1971. *Investment in Human Capital: The Role of Education and of Research.* New York: Free Press.

Shanahan, M., G. Elder, and R. Miech. 1997. "History and Agency in Men's Lives: Pathways to Achievement in Cohort Perspective." *Sociology of Education* 70 (1): 54–67.

Shavit, Y. 1984. "Tracking and Ethnicity in Israeli Secondary Education." *American Sociological Review* 49 (2): 210–20.

Stevenson, David Lee, and David P. Baker. 1991. "State Control of the Curriculum and Classroom Instruction." *Sociology of Education* 64 (1): 1–10.

UNESCO. 2016. *Different Meanings of "Curriculum."* Geneva: International Bureau of Education. www.ibe.unesco.org/en /geqaf/annexes/technical-notes/different-meanings-%E2%80% 9Ccurriculum%E2%80%9D.

Van de Werfhorst, H.G., and J.J.B. Mijs. 2010. "Achievement Inequality and the Institutional Structure of Educational Systems: A Comparative Perspective." *Annual Review of Sociology* 36 (1): 407–28.

Wang, Y. 2015. "'Workers' or Slaves? Textbook Maker Backtracks after Mother's Online Complaint." *Washington Post,* October 5. www.washingtonpost.com/news/morning-mix /wp/2015/10/05/immigrant-workers-or-slaves-textbook-maker-backtracks-after-mothers-online-complaint/.

Wong, S.Y. 1991. "The Evolution of Social Science Instruction, 1900–86: A Cross-National Study." *Sociology of Education* 64 (1): 33–47.

Young, M. 2013. "Overcoming the Crisis in Curriculum Theory: A Knowledge-Based Approach." *Journal of Curriculum Studies* 45:101–18.

Sorting Students for Learning

Eight Questions about Secondary-School Tracking

SEAN KELLY, UNIVERSITY OF PITTSBURGH

EDITORS' NOTE

Contemporary schools are, in many ways, **bureaucratic organizations**. They are formal structures in which power is distributed hierarchically (for example, principals have power over teachers, who in turn have power over students) and people have specialized organizational roles (for example, English teachers teach English while math teachers teach math). They keep detailed written records. And, above all else, they prize **rationality**.

Academic tracking is an excellent example of the rationalization of instruction in contemporary schools. As University of Pittsburgh education professor Sean Kelly argues, educators sort students for instruction because they think this is an efficient way to match instruction to students' interests and needs.

However, tracking is a controversial practice, and many educators and scholars worry that it contributes to the reproduction of inequality in schools. Dr. Kelly encourages you to consider, as you progress through this chapter, the ways in which you've been tracked during the course of your educational career and the consequences of those tracking decisions.

KEY POINTS

- Tracking frequently undermines learning and engagement among low-track students.
- In high school, different tracks set students up for different futures: the workplace, the military, or two-year or four-year colleges.

- Students in high-track classes learn more material than students in low-track classes.
- Students from privileged families are placed in high tracks more often than students from less-privileged families.
- Tracking magnifies educational inequality, because students who have early success in school gain access to more effective classes, allowing them to move further and further ahead academically.

INTRODUCTION

The sorting of students into differentiated curricular tracks is a rational approach to tailoring instruction to match students' learning needs. Yet research in the sociology of education explains how, among low-track students, tracking frequently undermines student engagement and learning. Some research has even questioned whether tracking might be best understood as a school-organizational response to status competition: is tracking really about the optimal tailoring of instruction, or is it about creating distinction and advantage for select students? This chapter begins with a discussion of research on the common effects of tracking on students. Tracking systems vary from school to school in important ways, however, including the number of levels offered in each subject, opportunities for upward mobility, and the policies used to assign students to tracks. To guide research and improve school policies, the final section presents eight questions about how tracking is implemented.

SECONDARY-SCHOOL TRACKING AS A RATIONAL/ TECHNICAL RESPONSE TO STUDENTS' LEARNING NEEDS

In elementary school, students are frequently grouped for instruction so that tasks and assignments can be better tailored for a given skill level. Such grouping is particularly common in reading instruction and is widely considered to constitute a "best practice" in elementary education. The idea is that both low- and high-achieving students tend to learn more when reading instruction is differentiated than when it is not (Slavin 1987). Reading development proceeds in stages, and it is important that the complexity of texts and lessons matches students' readiness level. For example, according to the Common Core State Standards, third-grade students reading "at grade level" might use a text such as *Charlotte's Web* or *Sarah, Plain and Tall* in a lesson, while students behind grade level might still be working with a picture book like *Frog and Toad Together*. In one effective school reform program targeting achievement growth in early reading, Success for All, students are removed from their regular age-graded class for a block of reading instruction targeted to their performance level (Borman et al. 2007).

In middle and high school, the logic of curriculum differentiation is similar to that of grouping for reading instruction in elementary school. The situation, however, is much more complex. First, differentiation involves multiple subject areas (English, math, social studies, etc.). Second, curriculum differentiation anticipates students' destinations after high school: the workplace, the military, or a two- or four-year college. In other words, differences in course-taking pave the way to disparate outcomes in the labor market. In the 1960s and 1970s, high school tracks were often all-encompassing, with students differentiated by "college-bound" versus "workforce prep" courses of study, in which they took virtually all of their courses at the same level. Today, curriculum differentiation is somewhat more fluid, and it is common for students to take courses at different levels (e.g., an honors math course but a regular-track English course). Yet it is still the case that, from year to year, many secondary students are "tracked," taking the majority of their classes at the same level with the same students.

As in the case of elementary school reading instruction, there are many reasons why curriculum differentiation might be beneficial to secondary school students. First, by the time students reach secondary school, they vary considerably in both achievement and interest in particular subject-areas. In fact, as students begin to develop specialized interests and skills, variation can often exist within one student, as is the case for the student who loves math but struggles in English. While achievement and interest are themselves the products of students' earlier schooling, the reality is that a given student may be more likely to succeed in some advanced classes than in others. Second, for non-college-bound students, a one-size-fits-all emphasis on preparation for college can feel impractical and offers little incentive to exert effort on schoolwork (Rosenbaum 2001). While there are many more professional, managerial, and technical positions in today's workforce than in previous generations, there are still many jobs that do not require a four-year college degree (Kalleberg 2011). Third, while there are surely students who would benefit from a stronger "academic press" and exposure to high-achieving peers in advanced courses, other students might find such pressure counterproductive. Research has shown that, for some students, the social-psychological effects of being the little fish in the big pond offsets some of the benefits of enrolling in advanced classes or more competitive schools (Van Houtte and Stevens 2009). Fourth, some teachers are especially good at working with students who do not identify readily with school, while other teachers are good at working with advanced students who have an affinity for academic material. A differentiated curriculum offers the possibility of matching teachers effectively with students.

Tracking is a ubiquitous practice in the United States and other countries. Table 3, from a study of North Carolina public high schools in 2007–2008,

Table 3 Percentage of North Carolina High Schools Reporting a Given Number of Track Levels in Each Subject in Tenth Grade, 2007–2008 School Year

Subject Matter	Number of Track Levels									Total[a]
	0	1	2	3	4	5	6	7	8	
English	—	6	62	24	9	—	—	—	—	100
Math Geometry[b]	—	8	75	15	2	—	—	—	—	100
Math Sequences	—	2	—	1	—	14	63	16	5	100
Science[c]	—	6	22	35	25	11	1	—	—	100
Social Studies	—	12	73	12	4	—	—	—	—	100
Foreign Language	1	39	35	15	5	5	—	—	—	100

NOTE: $N = 128$.
SOURCE: Reprinted with permission from Kelly and Price (2011).
[a]Values may not add up to 100 owing to rounding error.
[b]Two different measures of differentiation in math are presented: the number of levels of geometry (e.g., regular, honors, etc.), and the combination of math classes taken in freshman and sophomore years (which determines the highest level of mathematics-course-taking that a student can attain).
[c]For freshman year.

shows the number of different levels of school courses. While there is much variability across schools in how differentiated the curriculum is, virtually all schools differentiate students to some extent, and this is especially true in mathematics, which typically has five or more different levels. At the time of this study, the state department of education in North Carolina recommended, but did not require, that students follow one of three programs of study: career prep, college tech prep, or college/university prep. When schools link course-taking policies to a particular program of study, so that all or nearly all students in a given program of study take the same academic courses, it is called an "overarching" tracking system. Alternatively, programs of study may be used only as guidance tools (as in most North Carolina schools), in which students are assigned to individual courses based on grades in previous courses, test scores, teacher recommendations, or other requirements (Kelly and Price 2011).

Whether a school employs an overarching system, uses programs of study as guidance tools, or treats course-taking in each subject as a flexible, individual decision, schools are usually tracked is some shape or form. Even in states such as California and Massachusetts, where there was a strong push in the 1990s to de-track, students still continued to be differentiated to some extent, particularly in math (Loveless 1999). Tracking is also widely used internationally, with many countries choosing to track students into entirely separate secondary schools and to use concurrent school- and work-based programs for upper-secondary students (OECD 2015).

THE SHORTCOMINGS AND UNINTENDED CONSEQUENCES OF SECONDARY-SCHOOL TRACKING

Even though curriculum tracking is widely used, educational researchers, and especially sociologists of education, have long been concerned that tracking, in practice, falls far short of its promised benefits. In *Making Inequality,* James Rosenbaum studied the graduating class of 1971 at Grayton High School. Rosenbaum found that administrators and guidance counselors conceptualized curriculum tracking at Grayton according to the traditional functional ideal: tracking was seen as a logical response to differences in student achievement. Moreover, school personnel believed that track placements were meritocratic— that is, the highest-achieving and hardest-working students could be readily identified and encouraged to take high-track courses. According to this logic, the students themselves made the ultimate decisions about course-taking. In practice, however, Rosenbaum found several glaring discrepancies between this ideal and students' actual experiences. First, despite the fact that students' talents and interests often differ, students were likely to be placed in the same track in disparate subjects (e.g., in math and in English). Second, students almost never moved up the tracking hierarchy; they only moved down. In a truly meritocratic system, hardworking students in lower tracks should have the opportunity to move up to higher courses. To Rosenbaum, Grayton seemed less a meritocracy than a high-stakes tournament. To make matters worse, few of the students who entered Grayton as tenth graders (it was a three-year high school) understood the ramifications of their initial course selections. Rosenbaum concluded that "choice" and meritocracy at Grayton were more illusory than real.

In the 1980s, an increasing amount of research critiqued the meritocratic view of tracking. Jeannie Oakes's *Keeping Track* (1985) provides perhaps the most comprehensive critique. Studying differences in opportunity to learn across tracks in twenty-five schools, she found some modest but important differences in the use of basic instructional time between low- and high-track classes. Teachers of low-track classes spent less time actively instructing students and assigned less work. The biggest differences between high- and low-track classes, however, manifested in student behavior and expectations. Students in low-track classrooms were substantially less engaged in learning and less positive about their academic ability than their peers in high-track courses. Teachers in low-track classrooms often felt that their authority was not respected or that students responded only to highly structured tasks.

Additional research supports Oakes's overall portrait of instruction in low-track classrooms (Northrop and Kelly, forthcoming). Low-track classrooms present fundamental problems of student engagement and lead to deteriorating teacher-student relationships. Even considering that many low-track students begin the school year with a history of underachievement and low academic self-concept and motivation, assignment to a low-track class seems to make matters worse. The effect of tracking on the classroom learning environment is likely due to a complex mix of effects, including a lack of incentives for high performance, negative peer pressure, and deteriorating relationships between students and teachers (Kelly and Covay 2008).

To understand these impacts on the learning environment, first consider that many high school students, especially those who do not see themselves as competing for admission to elite colleges, have what Rosenbaum (2001) has labeled "no penalty" beliefs. Such students, in other words, don't believe it really matters whether they get an A, a B, or even a C. In contrast, students in advanced and honors classes compete fiercely for high grades. This requires paying attention in class, completing assignments, and participating in class discussions. Now consider the fact that tracking concentrates all the students with the least incentive to succeed (and least confidence that they can do well even if they do put forth effort) in the same classes. Without a doubt, students tend to gravitate toward and select as friends students from the same academic track (Hallinan and Kubitschek 1998). Thus, in low-track classrooms, disidentification from school becomes a collective activity of entire peer groups (Berends 1995). Faced with this situation, one created by the existence of the tracked system itself, it's no wonder individual teachers struggle to create learning environments that are as intellectually rich and engaging as those in high-track classrooms.

Consistent with sociologists' growing concerns about tracking, Adam Gamoran's (1987) research on the net effect of curriculum tracking reveals pronounced differences in learning between high- and low-tracked students. For example, in mathematics, the students in college preparatory courses learned more than twice as much in mathematics as their peers in vocational courses over the final two years of high school. The differences are so large that Gamoran concluded that, by the end of high school, tracking in some cases may have a greater impact on student achievement than school attendance.

FLAWED IN PRACTICE OR IN PRINCIPLE?

By the beginning of the 1990s, sociologists of education had amassed substantial evidence that, while tracking in secondary schools benefits those in the highest track, it disadvantages those in the lower tracks in terms of school engagement and the learning trajectory. This evidence includes advanced statistical analyses of nationally representative data (e.g., Gamoran and Mare 1989); close ethnographic studies of teachers, students, and classroom instruction (e.g., Page 1991); and large-scale observational studies like Oakes's *Keeping Track* and Gamoran and Martin Nystrand's (1992) studies of instruction in tracked English and language arts classrooms. Yet disagreement about the fundamental nature of tracking remains, as captured by an exchange between Maureen Hallinan and Jeannie Oakes in the journal *Sociology of Education* (Oakes 1994).

Hallinan argued that secondary-school tracking was flawed primarily in practice, not in principle. Her position was supported in the literature by research comparing tracking in public schools and in private schools. In particular, studies of Catholic schools have found evidence that students are encouraged to "stretch" and take the most challenging classes offered. Even lower-track classrooms displayed a strong emphasis on rigorous academic content (for an overview of this research, see Carbonaro and Covay 2010). Likewise, Gamoran (1993) showcased effective low-track learning environments where experienced teachers with high expectations for their students provided challenging and engaging instruction. These studies suggest that tracking is not inherently flawed, and that it may be possible to improve tracking as it is currently practiced in many schools.

Oakes, drawing an analogy to school segregation by race, argued that tracking *is* an inherently unequal organizational practice. That is, as long as low-achieving students are separated into different classrooms, the situation will always generate inequality. Oakes viewed tracking as an instrument of the political will of powerful middle- and upper-class (and often white) parents. Middle- and upper-class parents *want* schools to be tracked and for high-track students to have an enriched learning environment, so that their children have an advantage in gaining access to competitive colleges and ultimately succeeding in the labor market. If tracking is fundamentally the product of status competition, how can it ever be in the best interests of all students?

Historically, there is some evidence that, at the beginning of the twentieth century, schools began to differentiate the curriculum precisely to accommodate middle-class competition for developing professional occupations such as law and medicine; such professions required a college education, still a novel requirement within the labor market (Labaree 1986). In contrast, contemporary research has found that meritocratic rationales explain much of the variation between schools' tracking systems (Kelly and Price 2011). The schools with the most highly elaborated tracking policies (e.g., greatest differentiation of students, most rules governing course-taking, etc.) are schools with the largest student bodies and the greatest variability in student achievement levels. It makes sense, from a meritocratic standpoint, that those schools would be the most highly tracked. But tracking systems also respond to social pressures. For example, see California's recent promotion of Algebra for All, a de-tracking effort to increase the enrollment of all students in eighth-grade algebra. In the wake of this statewide policy, algebra enrollments increased among students initially tracked for a less-rigorous math sequence. In practice, however, schools responded by creating new opportunities for high-achieving students to take even *more* advanced math (Domina et al. 2016). It seems appropriate to conclude that even if tracking systems are constructed for instrumental and seemingly value-neutral reasons, they are subject to the influence of status competition both in their design and in their effects.

TRACKING AS A MAGNIFIER OF EDUCATIONAL INEQUALITY

Given the negative effects of tracking on the engagement and achievement growth of low-track students, sociologists of education have carefully examined the track placement process. Is tracking a meritocracy, in which achievement and effort determine placements? Or do the policies and procedures limiting choice and governing placements, and/or informal mechanisms related to choice, mean that students from some backgrounds have a higher likelihood than other students of enrolling in high-track classes? Figure 17 provides a summary of what sociologists have learned about the relationships between race, social class, measured achievement, and track placements.

The figure depicts both meritocratic and nonmeritocratic placement processes. First, the most important predictor of a student's level of secondary school course-taking has been found to be the prior achievements of that student, including test scores and grades. This is not surprising, as these factors are explicitly used as criteria by many schools in their course-taking policies. In addition, though, the social class of the student, as reflected in parental education, parents' occupational attainment, and other family background indicators, predicts track placement. The relationship between tracking and family background sometimes reflects higher levels of school involvement among middle- and upper-class parents: having gone to college themselves, they know how important high school course-taking is in competitive college admissions (Useem 1991).

Race is also linked to track placements, but the relationship is indirect rather than direct, operating through both social class/family background and previous achievement (see chapter 2 in this text for a discussion of the correlation between race, SES, and achievement). Whether the linkages are direct or indirect, however, the gaps in course-taking among students from different family backgrounds and racial groups are substantial. For example, in 1990, students whose parents had a college degree had a 23.4 percent chance of having taken both algebra II and geometry in grades nine and ten, while students whose parents did not graduate high school had only a 6.3 percent chance (Kelly 2004). Only in recent years, as states have raised course-taking requirements and achievement expectations in math and other academic subjects, have these gaps begun to decline somewhat (Domina and Saldana 2012).

Figure 17 summarizes research across a wide range of studies, but targeted studies of particular schools or districts often reveal different mechanisms at work. Roslyn Mickelson has studied the joint effects of segregation between schools ("first-generation segregation") and segregation within schools due to tracking ("second-generation segregation") on the educational outcomes of blacks and whites in North Carolina's Charlotte-Mecklenburg school system. For several decades, the school system had an active school desegregation plan in place, but some segregation between schools remained, as did racialized tracking. Black students were less likely to be enrolled in high-track classes,

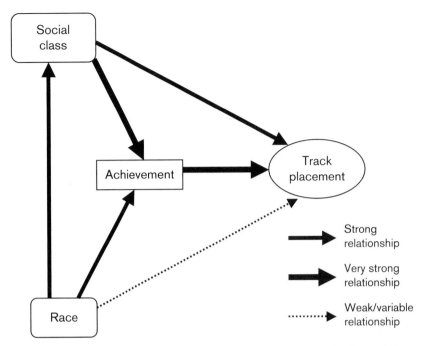

Figure 17. A basic model of the track placement process. Source: reprinted with permission from S. Kelly and E. Covay, "Curriculum Tracking: Reviewing the Evidence on a Controversial but Resilient Educational Policy," in *21st Century Education*, vol. 2, edited by T. Good, 401–9 (Thousand Oaks, CA: Sage Publications, 2008).

because of the mechanisms noted in figure 17 (prior achievement and family background), but there was also a direct effect of race, as well as an effect of attending a segregated, predominantly black elementary school. In fact, whites scoring toward the *bottom* of an elementary achievement test had higher odds of being in the college-prep track in eighth grade than black students scoring toward the top, a glaring example of unequal opportunity (Mickelson 2015).

It is also important to consider the top level of the tracking hierarchy in particular, where Advanced Placement (AP) courses serve as an important credential in selective college admissions. As with tracking more broadly, participation in AP courses differs substantially by student race/ethnicity and social class (Judson and Hobson 2015). And as shown in figure 17, much of the inequality in AP-course-taking by student background is accounted for by measured achievement (Jeong 2009). However, between-school differences in the availability of AP courses make it difficult for some high-achieving students to attain AP-course-taking credentials (Klopfenstein 2004; Yun and Moreno 2006). For example, using data from California, Yun and Moreno (2006) found that the cluster of schools enrolling low-poverty, predominantly Asian and white, students offered 11.6 AP courses on average, compared to fewer than 5 in the cluster of schools enrolling high-poverty Latino and black students and students for whom English was a second language.

Comparing sociological research on the allocation of students to tracks with research on the effects of tracking, a clear picture emerges: even if there were no bias in track placements (which there often is), tracking would magnify educational inequality. This is because smaller initial differences in achievement *increase* among students in tracked schools during the course of their schooling (Gamoran and Mare 1989). Stated differently, tracking appears to contribute to a cumulative advantage process, wherein the students (and sociodemographic groups) who have the most initial success in school gain access to a more effective, high-stakes learning environment and thereby move farther and farther ahead academically (Kerckhoff 1993).

EIGHT QUESTIONS ABOUT TRACKING TO GUIDE RESEARCH AND EDUCATIONAL PRACTICE

To many observers, tracking functions like the practice lanes in a swimming pool—no swim team coach is going to put the slowest swimmers in the same practice lane as the fastest swimmers. Yet, as detailed in this chapter, if tracking fixes one set of instructional problems—how to accommodate diverse levels of academic readiness and aptitude among a heterogeneous student body—it creates another set of problems. At this time, we don't know the ramifications of moving from a highly tracked system to a completely untracked one, in part because such radical reorganizations are rare. However, I offer two conclusions concerning the reform of tracking systems. First, highly differentiated, rigid systems of tracking like the one employed at Grayton High cannot be understood only in terms of instructional utility; indeed, they appear to sharply reduce low-track students' opportunities to learn. Second, research suggests that tracking is a resilient educational practice; incremental change is more likely to occur than complete dismantling. Thus, research should focus on understanding variation in *how* schools track students and in measuring the effects of different policies and practices related to tracking. The organization of the secondary school curriculum does differ substantially across schools, and consequently, we might expect some schools to track students more effectively than others. I pose the following eight questions as if you (the reader) are a school administrator engaged in planning and organizing a secondary-school curriculum.

1. How differentiated is your curriculum?

Does your school offer a minimally differentiated curriculum, permitting many students to take classes with a heterogeneous mix of students? Or do you offer a highly differentiated curriculum? Research shows that even in a school with three or more levels of a subject, most classes are likely to be heterogeneous in terms of students' achievement levels (Hallinan 1992). When was the last time you collapsed course offerings to fewer levels? Or increased the number of levels? What was the rationale?

2. How much does course-taking overlap across subject matter areas?

To what extent do students take all of their courses at the same track level? Do you have explicit programs of study used to structure course-taking (e.g., "college prep"); is this a strict policy or just a guidance technique? What other policies, if any, link classes across subject-matter areas (e.g., corequisite requirements)? How much does the daily schedule factor into course overlap—is it even possible for a student to take courses at a different level? Research suggests that more students are taking courses at different levels in different subjects than in the past (Lucas 1999), and that this is consistent with disparities in achievement or interest for the same student.

3. What role do test scores play in determining course enrollments? Grades? Teacher recommendations?

It is easy to think of test scores and grades as being "objective" measures of student aptitude, and of teacher recommendations as being more subjective. Yet for any given student, it's really not clear which of these indicators predicts most accurately how the student might do in a more rigorous course. These criteria can also be used in different ways, to limit or restrict access to demanding courses or, alternatively, to identify promising students who might not choose a specific course. How do your guidance team and teaching staff use these policies?

4. How much upward mobility is there in curricular tracking in your school?

Can you think of students who, say, started ninth grade in low-track classes but later moved into high-track classes? How often does this happen? What policies or practices are in place to help identify students who would benefit from a more challenging course of study?

5. What policies/programs do you have in place to support course-taking decisions made by potential first-generation college students?

Because of their own school success, parents who went to college themselves often can supply their children with adequate information about how to navigate a stratified school curriculum. In contrast, students from working-class and low-income backgrounds may have no idea that a seemingly small course-selection decision will affect their opportunity to go to college. Beyond informational differences, middle- and upper-class parents are acutely attuned to opportunities that might give *their* students an advantage. Working-class parents value education as much as any other parent, but they may not necessarily see schooling as an arena of status competition, where their students must get ahead at any cost. Potential first-generation college students need extra support in selecting courses.

6. How do you match teachers to classes?

Like other schools, you offer courses in some subjects that vary by student achievement level. You also have a set of (hopefully highly qualified) teachers to teach those courses. How tracked is your teaching staff? To what extent do some teachers teach primarily high-track, and some primarily low-track, classes? What criteria are used to determine which track level of courses the different teachers teach? How does this matching process affect learning opportunities for low-track students?

7. Does your school employ grade weighting?

Grade weighting schemes are commonly employed by districts, even entire states, and are designed to make grade-point-average calculations more meaningful by giving extra weight to more difficult classes. Qualifying courses might have one or even two points added: for example, a student who earns a C in such a course, with two points added to its weight, would receive the same grade for GPA purposes as a student who scored an A in a regular course. Research suggests, however, that grade-weighting schemes produce a "double-disadvantage" for low-track students (Attewell 2001). No matter how hard a low-track student tries, he or she will never be able to compete with high-track students for a high GPA, which may erode incentives for effort.

Moreover, while it is true that, for a student of a given achievement level, it is more difficult to earn an A in a class with higher-achieving peers, it may be a myth that grading is more rigorous in high-track courses. There is some evidence that adjusting for student achievement level, grading is actually *easier* in high-track courses, perhaps because high-track teachers assume their students are hardworking and deserving of high marks (Kelly 2008). Finally, it's important to note that weighted grades do not provide colleges and universities with any real additional information, since they already consider course-taking to be an indicator of college readiness.

8. Are your low-track classes engaging and challenging learning environments?

While the system of tracking as a whole works against student engagement in low-track classrooms, this doesn't mean it is impossible for low-track classrooms to offer engaging learning environments. In fact, if a teacher consistently presents students with tasks that are appropriately challenging, in a supportive setting, she or he can engage disengaged students (Shernoff 2013). Do you have teachers who are known for their engaging instruction with low-track students? What do they do with their students? Do vocational- and academic-subject teachers work together to produce a coherent, relevant curriculum? Relatedly, at the school level, what do you do to incentivize students who might not be planning to attend college at this time? Is it clear how hard work in school pays off in the future?

CHAPTER 10 REVIEW

Discussion Questions

1. Recall Kelly's discussion of the exchange between Hallinan and Oakes (Oakes 1994). Does Kelly seem more sympathetic to the position of Hallinan or Oakes? What is your own perspective on this question?

2. You have just been elected to serve on your local school board and have asked the superintendent and director of curriculum to discuss curriculum differentiation in your district at an upcoming board meeting. After reviewing Kelly's eight questions, what issues will you focus on with your superintendent?

3. In the foreword to Alan Kerckhoff's *Diverging Pathways* (1993), the distinguished sociologist James Coleman noted that "inequality is not everything." In designing and implementing an educational system, we should also be concerned with average levels of performance, as well as maximizing the performance of the very-highest-achieving students. Kelly's eight questions were designed primarily to inform concerns with educational inequality. How might a concern with average levels of performance, and/or maximizing the performance of the very-highest-achieving students, make you think differently about Kelly's questions?

Suggestions for Further Reading

Carbonaro, W. 2005. "Tracking, Students' Effort, and Academic Achievement." *Sociology of Education* 78:27–49.

Kelly, S., and H. Price. 2011. "The Correlates of Tracking Policy: Opportunity Hoarding, Status Competition, or a Technical-Functional Explanation?" *American Educational Research Journal* 48:560–85.

Lucas, S. R. 1999. *Tracking Inequality: Stratification and Mobility in American High Schools.* New York: Teachers College Press.

Oakes, J. 1985. *Keeping Track: How Schools Structure Inequality.* New Haven, CT: Yale University Press.

References

Attewell, P. 2001. "The Winner-Take-All High School: Organizational Adaptations to Educational Stratification." *Sociology of Education* 74:267–95.

Berends, M. 1995. "Educational Stratification and Students' Social Bonding to School." *British Journal of Sociology of Education* 16:327–51.

Borman, G. D., R. E. Slavin, A. C. K. Cheung, A. M. Chamberlain, N. A. Madden, and B. Chambers. 2007. "Final Reading Outcomes of the National Randomized Field Trial of Success for All." *American Educational Research Journal* 44:701–31.

Carbonaro. W. 2005. "Tracking, Students' Effort, and Academic Achievement." *Sociology of Education* 78:27–49.

Carbonaro, W., and E. Covay. 2010. "School Sector and Student Achievement in the Era of Standards Based Reforms." *Sociology of Education* 83:160–82.

Domina, T., P. Hanselman, N. Hwang, and A. McEachin. 2016. "Detracking and Tracking Up: Mathematics Course Placements in California Middle Schools, 2003–2013." *American Educational Research Journal* 53:1229–66.

Domina, T., and J. Saldana. 2012. "Did Raising the Bar Level the Playing Field? Mathematics Curricular Intensification and Inequality in American High Schools, 1982–2004." *American Education Research Journal* 49:685–708.

Gamoran, A. 1987. "The Stratification of High School Learning Opportunities." *Sociology of Education* 60:141–55.

———. 1993. "Alternative Uses of Ability Grouping in Secondary Schools: Can We Bring High-Quality Instruction to Low-Ability Classes?" *American Journal of Education* 102:1–22.

Gamoran, A., and R. D. Mare. 1989. "Secondary School Tracking and Educational Inequality: Compensation, Reinforcement, or Neutrality?" *American Journal of Sociology* 94:1146–83.

Gamoran, A., and M. Nystrand. 1992. "Taking Students Seriously." In *Student Engagement and Achievement in American Secondary Schools*, edited by F. M. Newmann, 40–61. New York: Teachers College Press.

Hallinan, M. T. 1992. "The Organization of Students for Instruction in the Middle School." *Sociology of Education* 65:114–27.

———. 1994. "Tracking: From Theory to Practice." *Sociology of Education* 67:79–84.

Hallinan, M. T., and W. N. Kubitschek. 1998. "Tracking and Students' Friendships." *Social Psychology Quarterly* 61:1–15.

Jeong, D. W. 2009. "Student Participation and Performance on Advanced Placement Exams: Do State-Sponsored Incentives Make a Difference?" *Educational Evaluation and Policy Analysis* 31:346–66.

Judson, E., and A. Hobson. 2015. "Growth and Achievement Trends of Advanced Placement (AP) Exams in American High Schools." *American Secondary Educator* 43:59–76.

Kalleberg, A. L. 2011. *Good Jobs, Bad Jobs: The Rise of Polarized and Precarious Employment Systems in the United States, 1970s to 2000s.* New York: Russell Sage Foundation.

Kelly, S. 2004. "Do Increased Levels of Parental Involvement Account for the Social Class Difference in Track Placement?" *Social Science Research* 33:626–59.

———. 2008. "What Types of Student Effort Are Rewarded with High Marks?" *Sociology of Education* 81:32–52.

Kelly, S., and E. Covay. 2008. "Curriculum Tracking: Reviewing the Evidence on a Controversial but Resilient Educational Policy." In *21st Century Education,* vol. 2, edited by T. Good, 401–9. Thousand Oaks, CA: Sage Publications.

Kelly, S., and H. Price. 2011. "The Correlates of Tracking Policy: Opportunity Hoarding, Status Competition, or a Technical-Functional Explanation?" *American Educational Research Journal* 48:560–85.

Kerckhoff, A. C. 1993. *Diverging Pathways: Social Structure and Career Deflections.* New York: Cambridge University Press.

Klopfenstein, K. 2004. "Advanced Placement: Do Minorities Have Equal Opportunity?" *Economics of Education Review* 23:115–31.

Labaree, D. F. 1986. "Curriculum, Credentials, and the Middle Class: A Case Study of a Nineteenth-Century High School." *Sociology of Education* 59:42–57.

Loveless, T. 1999. *The Tracking Wars: State Reform Meets School Policy.* Washington, DC: Brookings Institution.

Lucas, S. R. 1999. *Tracking Inequality: Stratification and Mobility in American High Schools.* New York: Teachers College Press.

Metz, M. H. 1978. *Classrooms and Corridors: The Crisis of Authority in Desegregated Secondary Schools.* Berkeley: University of California Press.

Mickelson, R. A. 2015. "The Cumulative Disadvantages of First- and Second-Generation Segregation for Middle School Achievement." *American Educational Research Journal* 52:657–92.

Northrop, L., and S. Kelly. Forthcoming. "Who Gets to Read What? Tracking, Instructional Practices, and Text Complexity for Middle School Struggling Readers." *Reading Research Quarterly.*

Oakes, J. 1985. *Keeping Track: How Schools Structure Inequality.* New Haven, CT: Yale University Press.

———. 1994. "More Than Misapplied Technology: A Normative and Political Response to Hallinan on Tracking." *Sociology of Education* 67:84–89.

Organisation for Economic Cooperation and Development (OECD). 2015. *Education at a Glance 2015: OECD Indicators.* Paris: OECD Publishing. http://dx.doi.org/10.1787/eag-2015-en.

Page, R. N. 1991. *Lower-Track Classrooms: A Curricular and Cultural Perspective.* New York: Teachers College Press.

Rosenbaum, J. E. 1976. *Making Inequality: The Hidden Curriculum of High School Tracking.* New York: Wiley.

———. 2001. *Beyond College for All: Career Paths for the Forgotten Half.* New York: Russell Sage Foundation.

Shernoff, D. J. 2013. *Optimal Learning Environments to Promote Student Engagement.* New York: Springer.

Slavin, R. E. 1987. "Ability Grouping and Student Achievement in Elementary Schools: A Best-Evidence Synthesis." *Review of Educational Research* 57:293–336.

Useem, E. 1991. "Student Selection in Course Sequences in Mathematics: The Impact of Parental Involvement and School Policies." *Journal of Research on Adolescence* 1:231–50.

Van Houtte, M., and P. A. J. Stevens. 2009. "Study Involvement of Academic and Vocational Students: Does Between-School Tracking Sharpen the Difference?" *American Educational Research Journal* 46:943–73.

Yun, J. T., and J. F. Moreno. 2006. "College Access, K–12 Concentrated Disadvantage, and the Next 25 Years of Education Research." *Educational Researcher* 35:12–19.

Special Education and Social Inequality

JACOB HIBEL, UNIVERSITY OF CALIFORNIA, DAVIS

EDITORS' NOTE

In chapter 4, we encountered the idea of **social construction** when Robert Eschmann and Charles Payne discussed race and racism in education. Race isn't the only important social construct that operates in contemporary schools. Sociologist Jacob Hibel of the University of California, Davis, discusses a construct that schools explicitly help create: disability.

American educational policy requires that students receive educational opportunities that are appropriate to their needs, and we suspect that in most cases educators identify students for special education with the very best of intentions. But when they do so, they construct an arbitrary line between the "typically developing" child and the "child with disabilities" who qualifies for special education. Further, if **cultural discontinuities** influence their decisions about which children need special education, students from socially disadvantaged backgrounds may be disproportionately exposed to special education.

Special education is thus an excellent example of a school-based activity that has important implications for social inequality. As you read this chapter, consider the organizational processes that create disproportionate special-education assignments. Can you imagine a system that more fairly provides appropriate learning opportunities to all youth?

KEY POINTS

- Congress passed the Individuals with Disabilities Education Act (IDEA) in 1975, requiring public schools to provide children with disabilities with a "free and appropriate public education" in the "least restrictive environment."
- Most students have a judgmental disability rather than a medical disability. As a result, teacher perceptions of disability are critical for placement in special education.
- In addition to children's own achievement and behavior, their outside-of-school learning environments and school contexts can influence whether they are perceived as having a disability. These factors contribute to disproportional placement of some groups—including boys, students from families with low socioeconomic status (SES), and students of color—in special education.
- Although IDEA represents a significant civil rights victory, there is ongoing debate as to whether it has lived up to its promise.

INTRODUCTION

Since becoming a legally mandated element of public education in the mid-1970s, special education has played an important role in reducing social and educational inequalities experienced by young people with disabilities. However, while special education services are explicitly designed to support youth with special learning needs, the social and institutional processes related to disability identification and special education service provision also have the potential to unintentionally create or magnify inequalities. This chapter begins with background on the history of special education in the United States, followed by a discussion of some of the contemporary debates surrounding special education and inequality, with a focus on important insights produced by sociological research. Last, I highlight a few key avenues for future sociological research on special education and discuss the potential impacts of this work for education policy and practice.

BACKGROUND

Before 1975, not only were US public schools absolved of any legal obligation to provide additional resources or support services to children with disabilities, they also were not even required to accept those children as students. Many states went so far as to enact laws that barred students with certain disabilities (e.g., blindness,

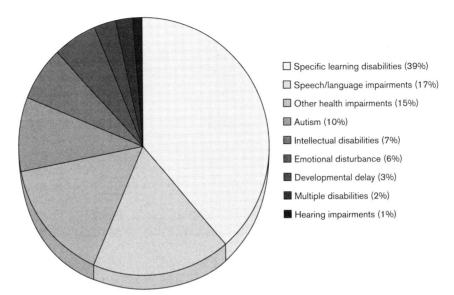

Legend:
- ☐ Specific learning disabilities (39%)
- ☐ Speech/language impairments (17%)
- ◻ Other health impairments (15%)
- ▨ Autism (10%)
- ▨ Intellectual disabilities (7%)
- ▨ Emotional disturbance (6%)
- ▨ Developmental delay (3%)
- ▧ Multiple disabilities (2%)
- ▧ Hearing impairments (1%)

Figure 18. US special education enrollment by disability classification, 2016–17. Note: Fewer than 1 percent of special education students during this period were classified with any of the following disabilities: orthopedic impairments, traumatic brain injury, visual impairments, and deaf-blindness. Source: US Department of Education, Office of Special Education Programs, Individuals with Disabilities Education Act database. www2.ed.gov/programs/osepidea/618-data/static-tables/index.html.

deafness, intellectual impairment, and emotional or behavioral disturbance) from attending public schools. As a result, only 20 percent of the estimated four million school-age youth with disabilities in the United States attended school in 1970, and those who did were all too often educated in under-resourced and completely segregated settings (US Department of Education 2010).

Congress passed the Individuals with Disabilities Education Act (IDEA) (initially known as the Education for All Handicapped Children Act) in 1975, requiring public schools to provide children with disabilities with a "free and appropriate public education" in the "least restrictive environment," which is generally understood to mean being taught within the same general-education classroom as their fellow students to the extent possible (Yell 1998). Following the passage of IDEA, the number of students with disabilities enrolled in public schools began an immediate and continual increase. Today, more than 6.5 million students (13 percent of the total US public school enrollment) receive special education services to help them overcome challenges associated with one or more of the fourteen distinct disability classifications recognized under IDEA (Kena et al. 2016).

Figure 18 presents the distribution of US special education students in the 2016–17 school year by disability type. As we can see, special education services are most often directed toward those with so-called judgmental disability classifications (MacMillan and Reschly 1998). These conditions—learning disabilities, speech/language impairment, and emotional/behavioral disorders—are distinct from "medical disabilities" such as hearing or orthopedic impairments insofar as they do not have a readily identifiable biological or physiological cause. As a result, they are infrequently diagnosed by medical professionals in the preschool years and are instead typically identified only after children have begun formal schooling (Donovan and Cross 2002).

DISABILITIES: INNATE OR SOCIALLY CONSTRUCTED?

The process of judgmental disability diagnosis is most often initiated by a child's classroom teacher. When a child exhibits conduct or learning outcomes that run counter to the teacher's expectations for normal, appropriate student behavior or performance, the teacher begins to consider possible explanations for the student's troubles. One option available to a teacher who is having difficulty pinpointing the cause of a student's challenges is to refer the student for disability assessment. In a large majority of cases (some estimates range as high as 90 percent), this referral results in the student being placed in a special education program (Harry and Klingner 2007). Given this strong link between teacher referral and subsequent special education placement, the circumstances that lead a classroom teacher to suspect that a child may be experiencing disability-related challenges are of the utmost importance. For an individual student, a teacher's subjective expectations for how a student should look, act, speak, or learn can mean the difference between receiving a formal disability label and not. For this reason, many sociologists conceive of disability as socially constructed—that is, defined by a normative understanding of where the line between "typical" and "atypical" is drawn in a given social context.

This notion of social construction is not what many people are used to thinking about in relation to disabilities. For example, it seems clear that students who experience mobility impairment due to cerebral palsy's effects on the motor areas of their brains will be reliably identified as having a physical disability. It is a part of their physiology regardless of where they live or what school they attend. Many people think of learning disabilities or emotional disturbance in the same way, as an innate, permanent characteristic, regardless of social context. And yet, sociology continually reminds us that individuals' lives do not (and indeed cannot) take shape in isolation from their social surroundings. Even something as intimately personal as disability is subject to the influence of social forces.

In the case of judgmental categories, disability is not simply determined by an individual student's innate characteristics. Rather, the major determinant of whether a student is labeled as having a disability is how those characteristics

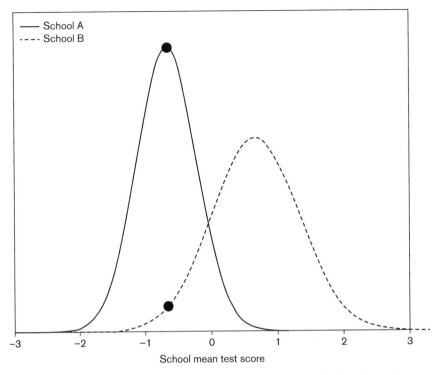

Figure 19. Elementary school test score distributions and average special education student achievement. Source: author's calculations from ECLS-K, 1998–99 data. Adapted from J. Hibel, G. Farkas, and P. L. Morgan, "Who Is Placed into Special Education?" *Sociology of Education* 83, no. 4 (2010): 312–32.

interact with the expectations of key institutional actors (e.g., teachers, counselors, and school psychologists). Because these actors' expectations are rooted in their prior experiences (i.e., their firsthand knowledge of how students are "supposed" to appear), the characteristics of a particular child's schoolmates play an important role. Put in simple terms, disability is not just a matter of who you are; it is also a matter of who happens to sit next to you in class.

To illustrate this phenomenon, consider the two stylized test-score distributions presented in figure 19. These curves reflect the collection of fifth graders' standardized literacy and mathematics scores from two US elementary schools. School B, represented by the dashed line, is a high-achievement school in which the average student scored three-quarters of a standard deviation above the national average (represented by "0" on the horizontal axis). School A, on the other hand, had a much lower level of performance, with an average score approximately three-quarters of a standard deviation below the national average. The point plotted on each curve indicates the average test score of a student receiving special education services in fifth grade across all schools in this nationally representative sample. If disability were a purely innate personal trait, it would be of little consequence whether a student attended school A or school B; she either would or would not have a disability, regardless of the setting. Just as we would not expect a child's eye color or shoe size to change simply because she moved from one school to another, the "innate trait" perspective implies that we should be similarly skeptical about a student suddenly acquiring or being "cured" of a disability because of a change in social setting alone.

But consider the following thought experiment. If you were to picture yourself as a teacher in school B, you might very well imagine that a student demonstrating the level of performance represented by the solid dot would elicit your concern. Compared to the rest of the student body, this student is clearly and conspicuously underperforming, and as a concerned educator acting in the student's best interest, you would likely seek out extra or alternative sources of learning support, including assessment for an underlying disability. Making such a referral opens up the possibility that the student will be identified as having a disability. As we've already seen, once a student is referred for assessment, becoming formally identified as having a disability is the most likely outcome.

If you were a teacher in school A, however, your response to the very same student might look different. In the miniature world that is your classroom, this student is actually a slightly above-average performer. Fully half of the school's fifth graders demonstrate greater achievement difficulties, and you might imagine that those students would be the first to draw your attention and raise concerns about the possibility of disability-related learning challenges. As a result, and given your school's limited pool of resources and capacity to supply special education services to students facing learning challenges, it is relatively unlikely that you would single out the hypothetical student for disability assessment over her more conspicuously struggling classmates. And in the absence of formal assessment, a child cannot be diagnosed as having a disability.

If we consider this scenario from the hypothetical student's perspective, transferring from school A to school B could very well mean transforming from a typical, even above-average student to one who is labeled as having a learning-related disability. Such is the potential power of social context for determining individual outcomes, even one that we often consider as intrinsic to the individual as disability.

While the social construction of disability has clear implications for individual students' career and life-course trajectories, at the aggregate level the subjectivity built into the disability identification and special education placement processes creates a pathway for broader social inequalities to infiltrate special education and thereby reproduce status hierarchies evident in other societal arenas. The presence of ethnoracial, socioeconomic, cultural, linguistic, and gender inequalities in special education forms the basis of the long-running issue of disproportionality.

DISPROPORTIONALITY: PRODUCED BY
SCHOOLS OR BROADER SOCIETY?

The term *disproportionality* is most often used to refer to the presence of a greater proportion of students from a particular population in special education programs than we would expect based on their proportional presence in the overall student body (Harry and Anderson 1994; National Education Association 2007). For example, in the United States in 2015, 14.2 percent of all students between the ages of six and twenty-one were African American. In the absence of disproportionality, we would expect about 14 percent of special education students to be African American as well. However, African Americans made up 18.9 percent of students receiving special education services that year, which constitutes disproportionality, or more specifically, the overrepresentation of African American children in special education.[1] Like African American students, American Indian and Alaska Native and, by some counts, Latino students have historically been overrepresented in special education, as have boys and children from lower-SES and immigrant families.

For decades, scholars, educators, and activists have made tremendous efforts to understand the roots of disproportionate representation in special education, particularly among students of color. Until recently, the prevailing explanation rested on the notion of cultural discontinuity, a concept derived from sociological conflict and critical race theories. This idea suggests that, like other social institutions in the United States, public schooling rewards individuals who possess dominant forms of cultural capital and erects barriers to success for members from nondominant cultural or ethnoracial status groups. Specifically, US public schools are designed to reinforce culturally embedded norms of language (e.g., "standard" academic English), social interaction (e.g., by emphasizing silence and physical and emotional restraint), and knowledge (e.g., by teaching Western literature, art, and history) that, while familiar to European American students, may be comparatively foreign to students from other backgrounds. These culturally embedded expectations, coupled with high levels of ethnoracial homogeneity among American teachers (82 percent of public school teachers employed in the 2011–12 school year were non-Latino white),[2] place students of color at particular risk of violating classroom norms and, therefore, at an increased risk of being labeled with a disability and placed

---

1. Author's calculations based on data reported in US Department of Education, Office of Special Education and Rehabilitative Services, *37th Annual Report to Congress on the Implementation of the Individuals with Disabilities Education Act, 2015* (Washington, DC: US Department of Education, 2015), www2.ed.gov/about/reports/annual/osep/2015/parts-b-c/37th-arc-for-idea.pdf.
2. Source: R. Goldring, L. Gray, and A. Bitterman, *Characteristics of Public and Private Elementary and Secondary School Teachers in the United States: Results from the 2011–12 Schools and Staffing Survey*, NCES 2013–314 (Washington, DC: US Department of Education, National Center for Education Statistics, 2013), http://nces.ed.gov/pubs2013/2013314.pdf.

in special education (Fish 2017). Thus, this perspective suggests, special education disproportionality is one of many symptoms of institutionalized racism in American schools, a privileging of European American cultural norms that is built in to all aspects of US public schooling (Ferri and Connor 2005).

In recent years, new insights have come from sociologists' examinations of large, longitudinal, nationally representative data sets containing information on children, families, classrooms, and schools, allowing scholars to elaborate on the cultural discontinuity perspective. A key advantage of these data sources lies in the measurement of students' academic performance, social-emotional skills, and family socioeconomic resources. These factors are important to consider because, as research in the sociology of education has long demonstrated, ethnoracial inequalities in average family resources are the largest contributor to gaps in academic achievement, particularly those that take shape before children begin formal schooling (Coleman et al. 1966; Condron 2009; Lee and Burkam 2002; see also chapter 2 of this volume). Structural inequalities—which are inherent not just in a single institution but in the entire social order, and which confer advantages and opportunities on individuals based on their ethnic, racial, and socioeconomic backgrounds—create tremendous inequalities in the family resources that support children's early cognitive and social-emotional development.

When my colleagues and I (Hibel, Farkas, and Morgan 2010) examined students' family SES and kindergarten academic performance, we found wide achievement gaps at kindergarten entry associated with inequalities in children's preschool environments. These initial achievement disparities, present at the time children began formal schooling, fully accounted for the patterns of overrepresentation in special education among students of color that we and many other scholars have observed. This line of research suggests that black, Latino, and American Indian students are more likely to be placed in special education than their white peers, primarily because of their higher average levels of early-life educational disadvantage (Hibel, Faircloth, and Farkas 2008; Hibel, Farkas, and Morgan 2010; Morgan et al. 2012; Shifrer, Muller, and Callahan 2011; Sullivan 2013). These findings thus support the conclusion that special education disproportionality is not solely a symptom of institutional racism within public schools, but is also a reflection of deep and durable inequalities in broader society that shape children's educational trajectories before they first set foot inside the classroom.

WHAT PREDICTS SPECIAL EDUCATION RECEIPT: CHILDREN'S OWN CHARACTERISTICS OR THOSE OF THEIR CLASSMATES?

Structural inequalities also influence children's schooling and special education experiences in ways beyond individual development. As implied by our earlier thought experiment, my colleagues and I have found that characteristics of the local comparison group are strong predictors of an individual student's special education placement (Hibel, Farkas, and Morgan 2010). After accounting for individual and family characteristics, we found that attending a school with higher average academic performance or higher teacher-rated classroom behavior increases a student's likelihood of being placed in special education. That is, a child's odds of being placed in special education depend not only on his own learning and behavior characteristics but on those of his classmates as well. In addition, a student's likelihood of receiving special education services declines as the share of nonwhite students enrolled at the school increases. This effect is substantial: if we could hold all other school characteristics constant and move a student from a perfectly ethnoracially integrated school to a school whose ethnoracial composition matches that of the average school attended by an African American student, that student's chances of being placed in special education would decline by an estimated 30 percent. This reflects one enduring and troubling symptom of structural inequality in the United States: dramatic racial segregation across schools (Reardon and Owens 2014; see also chapter 13, this volume). On average in the United States, students of color, especially Latino and African American children (Orfield et al. 2014) and those from lower-SES families (Bischoff and Reardon 2014), are concentrated in schools with high enrollments of demographically similar students. By the same token, non-Latino white and higher-SES students are largely segregated into schools with very few nonwhite or low-SES classmates. The powerful associations among race, ethnicity, family SES, and academic achievement cause students of color and those from lower-SES backgrounds to, on average, attend schools with lower levels of student achievement and teacher-rated classroom behavior (Logan, Minca, and Adar 2012). As illustrated by figure 19, these are precisely the sort of schools in which a given student is least likely to receive special education services. Thus, school segregation is likely to be an important cause of disparities in special education placement and helps explain why sociologists have observed that students of color have lower odds of special education placement than non-Latino white students with comparable levels of academic performance and classroom behavior.

Another intriguing example of contextual effects on the social construction of disability can be observed in the dramatically increasing prevalence of autism spectrum disorder (ASD) diagnoses among children in the United States in recent decades (Weintraub 2011). A group of researchers seeking to understand this trend examined the geographic dispersion of such diagnoses in California, uncovering surprising findings. They found that the diagnoses arose in spatial "clusters," relatively small geographic areas in which diagnosis rates are far greater than average (Mazumdar et al. 2010). For example, children born in one twelve-by-thirty-mile area of Los Angeles exhibited a four times greater risk of ASD than children born anywhere else in the state. These researchers found that neighborhood wealth is a strong predictor of children's odds of being diagnosed with ASD, and that, similar to what occurs when a student moves from a low-achieving school to a high-achieving school, a student whose family made a residential move from a low-income neighborhood to a wealthy one would experience an instantaneously increased risk of ASD identification (King and Bearman 2011). The primary explanation for this contextual effect, the researchers found, lies in the social networks of parents living in ASD cluster communities. These parents possess high levels of interest in, knowledge of, and experience with ASD, and they readily communicate information about ASD symptoms and the benefits of treatment to their friends (Liu, King, and Bearman 2010). Having been exposed to this knowledge, parents of children who exhibit atypical learning and behavior are more likely to pursue ASD evaluation for their children, which consequently increases their children's rates of ASD diagnosis. This "social contagion" effect represents another example of how social contexts—in this case, the network of relationships between a child's parents and other adults who possess knowledge and experience with ASD—shape children's odds of being identified as having a disability even when accounting for their own personal characteristics.

FUTURE DIRECTIONS IN THE SOCIOLOGY OF SPECIAL EDUCATION

Sociological research has revealed numerous ways that the social world influences children's disability and special education experiences. The number of unresolved questions in the field suggests that this area of research has abundant room to continue its development. I highlight just two of these unresolved questions below.

Which type of disproportionality are we facing in contemporary special education: underrepresentation or overrepresentation of students of color? And which situation is worse?

As noted, sociologists who have accounted for inequalities in students' preschool developmental contexts and early learning outcomes find that, among students with comparable individual risk profiles, students of color exhibit lower odds of being placed in special education than non-Latino white students, a finding some scholars have referred to as minority student *under*representation (e.g., Morgan et al. 2015). This finding has proved highly controversial, as other scholars reject the notion that such a comparison is meaningful and, instead, argue that unadjusted baseline differences in special education participation across ethnoracial groups are the relevant, appropriate comparisons to make (Skiba et al. 2016).

Compounding this disagreement is the fact that some researchers conclude that patterns of conditional underrepresentation among students of color imply that they are systematically denied equal opportunities to receive special education supports, and therefore, that the number of students of color placed in special education should increase (Morgan and Farkas 2016). This assertion has been vociferously opposed by those who interpret special education as, at best, a flawed and ineffective method of educational support or, at worst, a tool of social oppression wielded against students from already marginalized populations (e.g., Ford and Russo 2016).

Two types of future research are needed to resolve this disagreement. Those who pursue the first type should aim to determine whether, for whom, and under what conditions special education services provide true educational benefits, producing narrower, as opposed to wider, achievement and attainment gaps between special education participants and nonparticipants. This knowledge is necessary to understand whether special education can more accurately be regarded as a valuable educational resource to which students with disabilities have a constitutional right, or as the bottom rung in a hierarchical system of ability grouping that magnifies preexisting inequalities (see chapter 10, this volume).

Those interested in the second type of research should move toward identifying the appropriate level of special education participation in the school-age population based on rigorous estimates of disability prevalence, rather than simple comparisons across ethnoracial groups. The fact that two or more groups differ with respect to their special education placement rates does not, by itself, indicate which group is disadvantaged. If, for example, an African American student and a non-Latino white student have comparable risk profiles, and the white student experiences a greater likelihood of special education placement, the interpretation that white students experience conditional overrepresentation is equally as plausible as the interpretation that African American students are conditionally underrepresented, absent knowledge of the appropriate level of special education participation. Much contemporary research defines disproportionality by comparing students of color to non-Latino whites. Groups of students who have higher special education placement rates than non-Latino whites are considered overrepresented, and those with lower placement rates are considered underrepresented. However, this approach normalizes non-Latino white students, implicitly regarding their experiences as correct, natural, or expected and those of other groups as aberrant or deviant. Most sociologists would consider this assumption deeply flawed.

Finally, researchers, educators, and policy makers should broaden their approaches to resolving special education placement inequalities by addressing inequalities in children's early learning environments. Recent policies have focused on monitoring and regulating schools' special education placement decisions to ensure ethnoracial proportionality within school districts, an approach that locates the cause and solution to these inequalities within schoolhouse walls (US Department of Education 2016). Yet a long history of sociological research has established that multiple educational inequalities, including disparities in achievement, attainment, student body composition, curricular exposure, school funding, and special-education service receipt, have roots in broader systems of structural inequality (see chapter 2, this volume). Taking a sociological perspective should lead us to ask whether legislatively managing the special education placement process to achieve a particular result while simultaneously ignoring powerful, deeply ingrained social inequalities among America's children is akin to treating a disease's symptoms rather than its cause.

How will contemporary school reform movements affect children with disabilities?

The contemporary education reform era has been marked by efforts to increase accountability and choice (see chapters 14 and 15, this volume). While much research has been devoted to understanding these reforms' consequences for excellence and equity in student performance and educational attainment, comparatively little attention has been given to the specific impacts of current reforms on students with special needs. Education policy scholars have, however, predicted that both approaches to reform may produce unintended negative consequences for members of this sensitive population.

With respect to accountability-focused reforms, the heightened emphasis on standardized test scores that accompanies these approaches may create penalties for students with special needs. For example, Eckes and Swando (2009) find that the failure to improve achievement for students with disabilities is the most common reason that schools incur penalties under the No Child Left Behind Act's test-based accountability system. This situation creates an atmosphere in which teachers may come to view students with special needs as "burdens" or "scapegoats" for an entire school's problems, which compounds the numerous challenges students with disabilities already face (Allbritten, Mainzer, and Ziegler 2004; Shifrer 2013). Further, some scholars have noted that accountability reforms create disincentives for educators and administrators to promote full inclusion among students with disabilities. For example, the strategy of educational triage, which refers to educators' intentional disinvestment in the education of low performers so that they may instead direct attention to students whose achievement is close to proficiency thresholds (Booher-Jennings 2005), works against students whose special learning needs make them less likely than their classmates to produce high scores on standardized tests.

Like pre-IDEA-era public schools, schools of choice (i.e., charter, magnet, and voucher schools) may attempt to minimize their financial costs and pedagogical demands by preventing students with special needs from enrolling (Zollers and Ramanathan 1998). While any efforts to intentionally deny children the opportunity to receive a free and appropriate public education are illegal under federal law, sociologists have described several covert, informal methods that schools of choice have used to selectively screen out students with low achievement, behavior problems, or disability-related needs (e.g., Jennings 2010). These tactics not only disadvantage individual students with special needs by denying them equal access to schools of choice, but they also increase the relative burden on traditional public schools in the surrounding area. The selective "cream skimming" of the highest performing and, in certain important ways, easier-to-educate students by schools of choice directs a proportionately greater share of students who face learning challenges to traditional public schools (Lacireno-Paquet et al. 2002).

CONCLUSION: TACKLING ISSUES OF QUALITY AND INEQUALITY IN SPECIAL EDUCATION

The social and political progress that paved the way for over six million students to currently receive special education services should be celebrated as a major civil rights victory. Yet substantial work remains. While special education programs promise improved equality of educational opportunity for students with special needs, these programs have not yet approached equality of educational outcomes. Compared to students in "mainstream" or "inclusive" education programs, students who participate in special education complete less advanced coursework and experience lower average levels of achievement, lower rates of high school completion, lower earnings as adults, and elevated levels of involvement in the criminal justice system (Donovan and Cross 2002; Losen and Orfield 2002; Shifrer, Callahan, and Muller 2013).

Students who participate in special education differ from mainstream students in numerous, often unmeasured ways, however, which poses a challenge for researchers who endeavor to understand the causal effects of special education programming on student outcomes. For example, it would be impossible to conduct a true randomized control study of special education participation, as doing so would require denying members of the "control" group access to special education services to which they are legally and ethically entitled. However, some researchers have used quasi-experimental methods to analyze observational data on students' special education participation and subsequent schooling outcomes (e.g., Hanushek, Kain, and Rivkin 2002; Morgan et al. 2010; Sullivan and Field 2013). These studies mostly indicate that students who are placed in special education have learning outcomes that are equivalent to or worse than those of similarly challenged students who are not placed in special education. These findings are particularly pronounced for students placed in restrictive special education environments. Given special education's many costs—for example, financial costs to schools, districts, and teacher-training programs; and social-psychological costs to students in the form of stigma and reduced expectations—these findings should be both a cause for concern and a strong call for continued research on approaches to improving special education programming. For special education to fulfill its promise of reducing, as opposed to reproducing, social and educational inequalities, schools must overcome the dual challenges of appropriately identifying students with disabilities and effectively supporting those students' learning needs.

CHAPTER 11 REVIEW

Discussion Questions

1. Chances are that you or someone you know has dealt with educational challenges related to a disability such as attention deficit hyperactivity disorder, speech-language impairment, emotional behavioral disorder, or a specific learning disability. Looking back, can you identify ways that social contextual factors influenced that person's formal identification (or nonidentification) and the types of support resources to which the person had access? How might things have been different if the person had grown up in a different family or attended a different school?

2. Some of the sociological research discussed in this chapter suggests that special-education disproportionality stems largely from inequalities in children's outside-of-school environments. If providing increased special education services to students from historically disadvantaged backgrounds would lead to even more disproportionality, how do you think educators and policy makers ought to address this thorny issue?

3. If you were the parent of a child whose teacher recommended that she be evaluated for a potential learning disability, which factors would be most important to you in considering whether to place her in special education?

4. How do special education inequalities relate to other forms of educational inequality discussed in this book, such as achievement gaps, tracking, and segregation? Does it make sense to consider special education alongside these other axes of inequality, or is there something "special" about special ed.?

Suggestions for Further Reading

Donovan, M. Suzanne, and Christopher T. Cross, eds. 2002. *Minority Students in Special and Gifted Education.* Washington DC: National Academies Press.

Harry, Beth, and Janette Klingner. 2007. *Why Are So Many Minority Students in Special Education?* New York: Teachers College Press.

Losen, Daniel J., and Gary Orfield. 2002. *Racial Inequity in Special Education.* Cambridge, MA: Harvard Education Publishing Group.

Morgan, Paul L., and George Farkas. 2016. "Are We Helping All the Children That We Are Supposed to Be Helping?" *Educational Researcher* 45 (3): 226–28.

Morgan, Paul L., George Farkas, Marianne M. Hillemeier, Richard Mattison, Steve Maczuga, Hui Li, and Michael Cook. 2015. "Minorities Are Disproportionately Underrepresented in Special Education: Longitudinal Evidence across Five Disability Conditions." *Educational Researcher* 44 (5): 278–92.

Skiba, Russell J., Alfredo J. Artiles, Elizabeth B. Kozleski, Daniel J. Losen, and Elizabeth G. Harry. 2016. "Risks and Consequences of Oversimplifying Educational Inequities: A Response to Morgan et al. (2015)." *Educational Researcher* 45 (3): 221–25.

References

Allbritten, Drew, Richard Mainzer, and Deborah Ziegler. 2004. "Will Students with Disabilities Be Scapegoats for School Failures?" *Educational Horizons* 82 (2): 153–60.

Bischoff, Kendra, and Sean F. Reardon. 2014. "Residential Segregation by Income, 1970–2009." In *Diversity and Disparities: America Enters a New Century,* edited by John Logan. New York: Russell Sage Foundation.

Booher-Jennings, J. 2005. "Below the Bubble: 'Educational Triage' and the Texas Accountability System." *American Educational Research Journal* 42 (2): 231–68.

Coleman James S., Ernest Q. Campbell, Carol J. Hobson, James McPartland, Alexander M. Mood, Frederick D. Weinfield, and Robert L. York. 1966. *Equality of Educational Opportunity.* Washington, DC: US Government Printing Office.

Condron, Dennis J. 2009. "Social Class, School and Non-school Environments, and Black/White Inequalities in Children's Learning." *American Sociological Review* 74 (5): 683–708.

Donovan, M. Suzanne, and Christopher T. Cross, eds. 2002. *Minority Students in Special and Gifted Education.* Washington DC: National Academies Press.

Eckes, Suzanne E., and Julie Swando. 2009. "Special Education Subgroups under NCLB: Issues to Consider." *Teachers College Record* 111 (11): 2479.

Ferri, Beth A., and David J. Connor. 2005. "In the Shadow of Brown Special Education and Overrepresentation of Students of Color." *Remedial and Special Education* 26 (2): 93–100.

Fish, Rachel Elizabeth. 2017. "The Racialized Construction of Exceptionality: Experimental Evidence of Race/Ethnicity Effects on Teachers' Interventions." *Social Science Research* 62:317–34.

Ford, Donna Y., and Charles J. Russo. 2016. "Historical and Legal Overview of Special Education Overrepresentation: Access and Equity Denied." *Multiple Voices for Ethnically Diverse Exceptional Learners* 16 (1): 50–57.

Hanushek, Eric A., John F. Kain, and Steven G. Rivkin. 2002. "Inferring Program Effects for Special Populations: Does Special Education Raise Achievement for Students with Disabilities?" *Review of Economics and Statistics* 84 (4): 584–99.

Harry, Beth, and M. Anderson. 1994. "The Disproportionate Placement of African American Males in Special Education Programs: A Critique of the Process." *Journal of Negro Education* 63 (4): 602–19.

Harry, Beth, and Janette Klingner. 2007. *Why Are So Many Minority Students in Special Education?* New York: Teachers College Press.

Hibel, Jacob, Susan Faircloth, and George Farkas. 2008. "Unpacking the Placement of American Indian and Alaska Native Students in Special Education Programs and Services in the Early Grades: School Readiness as a Predictive Variable." *Harvard Educational Review* 78 (3): 498–528.

Hibel, Jacob, George Farkas, and Paul L. Morgan. 2010. "Who Is Placed into Special Education?" *Sociology of Education* 83 (4): 312–32.

Jennings, Jennifer L. 2010. "School Choice or Schools' Choice? Managing in an Era of Accountability." *Sociology of Education* 83 (3): 227–47.

Kena, G., W. Hussar, J. McFarland, C. de Brey, L. Musu-Gillette, X. Wang, J. Zhang, A. Rathbun, S. Wilkinson-Flicker, M. Diliberti, A. Barmer, F. Bullock Mann, and E. Dunlop Velez. 2016. *The Condition of Education 2016.* NCES 2016–144. Washington, DC: US Department of Education, National Center for Education Statistics.

King, Marissa D., and Peter S. Bearman. 2011. "Socioeconomic Status and the Increased Prevalence of Autism in California." *American Sociological Review* 76 (2): 320–46.

Lacireno-Paquet, Natalie, Thomas T. Holyoke, Michele Moser, and Jeffrey R. Henig. 2002. "Creaming versus Cropping: Charter School Enrollment Practices in Response to Market Incentives." *Educational Evaluation and Policy Analysis* 24 (2): 145–58.

Lee, Valerie E., and David T. Burkam. 2002. *Inequality at the Starting Gate.* Washington, DC: Economic Policy Institute.

Liu, Ka-Yuet, Marissa King, and Peter S. Bearman. 2010. "Social Influence and the Autism Epidemic." *American Journal of Sociology* 115 (5): 1387.

Logan, John R., Elisabeta Minca, and Sinem Adar. 2012. "The Geography of Inequality: Why Separate Means Unequal in American Public Schools." *Sociology of Education* 85 (3): 287–301.

Losen, Daniel J., and Gary Orfield. 2002. *Racial Inequity in Special Education.* Cambridge, MA: Harvard Education Publishing Group.

MacMillan, D. L., and D. J. Reschly. 1998. "Overrepresentation of Minority Students: The Case for Greater Specificity or Reconsideration of the Variables Examined." *Journal of Special Education* 32 (1): 15–24.

Mazumdar, Soumya, Marissa King, Ka-Yuet Liu, Noam Zerubavel, and Peter Bearman. 2010. "The Spatial Structure of Autism in California, 1993–2001." *Health and Place* 16 (3): 539–46.

Morgan, Paul L., and George Farkas. 2016. "Are We Helping All the Children That We Are Supposed to Be Helping?" *Educational Researcher* 45 (3): 226–28.

Morgan, Paul L., George Farkas, Marianne M. Hillemeier, and Steve Maczuga. 2012. "Are Minority Children Disproportionately Represented in Early Intervention and Early Childhood Special Education?" *Educational Researcher* 41 (9): 339–51.

Morgan, Paul L., George Farkas, Marianne M. Hillemeier, Richard Mattison, Steve Maczuga, Hui Li, and Michael Cook. 2015. "Minorities Are Disproportionately Underrepresented in Special Education: Longitudinal Evidence across Five Disability Conditions." *Educational Researcher* 44 (5): 278–92.

Morgan, Paul L., Michelle Frisco, George Farkas, and Jacob Hibel. 2010. "A Propensity Score Matching Analysis of the Effects of Special Education Services." *Journal of Special Education* 43 (4): 236.

National Education Association. 2007. *Truth in Labeling: Disproportionality in Special Education.* Washington, DC: NEA Professional Library. www.nea.org/assets/docs/HE/EW-TruthInLabeling.pdf.

Orfield, Gary, and Erica Frankenberg, with Jongyeon Ee and John Kuscera. 2014. *Brown at 60: Great Progress, a Long Retreat and an Uncertain Future.* Los Angeles: Civil Rights Project.

Reardon, Sean F., and Ann Owens. 2014. "60 Years after Brown: Trends and Consequences of School Segregation." *Annual Review of Sociology* 40:199–218.

Shifrer, Dara. 2013. "Stigma of a Label: Educational Expectations for High School Students Labeled with Learning Disabilities." *Journal of Health and Social Behavior* 54 (4): 462–80.

Shifrer, Dara, Rebecca M. Callahan, and Chandra Muller. 2013. "Equity or Marginalization? The High School Course-Taking of Students Labeled with a Learning Disability." *American Educational Research Journal* 50 (4): 656–82.

Shifrer, Dara, Chandra Muller, and Rebecca M. Callahan. 2011. "Disproportionality and Learning Disabilities: Parsing Apart

Race, Socioeconomic Status, and Language." *Journal of Learning Disabilities* 44 (3): 246–57.

Skiba, Russell J., Alfredo J. Artiles, Elizabeth B. Kozleski, Daniel J. Losen, and Elizabeth G. Harry. 2016. "Risks and Consequences of Oversimplifying Educational Inequities: A Response to Morgan et al. (2015)." *Educational Researcher* 45 (3): 221–25.

Sullivan, Amanda L. 2013. "School-Based Autism Identification: Prevalence, Racial Disparities, and Systemic Correlates." *School Psychology Review* 42:298–316.

Sullivan, Amanda L., and Samuel Field. 2013. "Do Preschool Special Education Services Make a Difference in Kindergarten Reading and Mathematics Skills?: A Propensity Score Weighting Analysis." *Journal of School Psychology* 51 (2): 243–60.

US Department of Education, Office of Special Education and Rehabilitative Services. 2010. *Thirty-Five Years of Progress in Educating Children with Disabilities through IDEA.* Washington, DC: US Department of Education.

———. 2016. "Assistance to States for the Education of Children with Disabilities: Preschool Grants for Children with Disabilities." *Federal Register* 81 (41). www.gpo.gov/fdsys/pkg/FR-2016–03–02/pdf/2016–03938.pdf.

Weintraub, Karen. 2011. "The Prevalence Puzzle: Autism Counts." *Nature* 479 (7371): 22–24.

Yell, Mitchell L. 1998. *The Law and Special Education.* Old Tappan, NJ: Merrill/Prentice-Hall.

Zollers, Nancy J., and Arun K. Ramanathan. 1998. "For-Profit Charter Schools and Students with Disabilities: The Sordid Side of the Business of Schooling." *Phi Delta Kappan* 80 (4): 297.

A Sociology of School Discipline

RICHARD ARUM, UNIVERSITY OF CALIFORNIA, IRVINE

E. CHRISTINE BAKER-SMITH, TEMPLE UNIVERSITY

JESSICA LIPSCHULTZ, NEW YORK UNIVERSITY

EDITORS' NOTE

In chapters 6 and 8, we discussed the subtle and not-so-subtle ways that schools socialize students to behavioral norms. If you've ever served a school detention or sat in the principal's office while your parents received a phone call about your behavior at school, you've experienced one of the most direct forms of school-based **socialization**.

Schools discipline students, in part, to maintain order within the building and keep students safe. But sociologists Richard Arum, Christine Baker-Smith, and Jessica Lipschultz argue that by setting rules and punishing students who break those rules, schools teach students how to follow rules and familiarize them with the consequences for failing to do so.

Schools across the United States take very different approaches to school discipline. Some schools take a "zero-tolerance" approach—suspending students and administering other harsh punishments for relatively minor infractions. Other schools take a much less punitive approach to student discipline. In recent years, several schools have adopted "restorative justice" policies that attempt to use the disciplinary process as a place for students to contemplate right and wrong and find ways to repair the harms that others incurred as a result of their behavior.

Arum, Baker-Smith, and Lipschultz point to a growing body of evidence that suggests schools which educate poor, black, and Hispanic students are disproportionately likely to use draconian zero-tolerance disciplinary procedures. Many sociologists worry these tough school disciplinary policies contribute to a **school-to-prison pipeline,** by withholding learning opportunities from disciplined students and socializing them to expect constant policing.

What can you say about the disciplinary approaches that you encountered in school? How did those various approaches shape the way you think about authority and social order? Can you imagine schools in different social contexts taking similar disciplinary approaches? Why or why not?

KEY POINTS

- School discipline is related to a school's culture and climate.
- Durkheim and many others see school discipline as providing a socialization process for students.
- Approaches to, and the purpose of, school discipline have shifted over time and have been shaped by laws governing schools and student rights.
- Zero-tolerance policies were intended to codify disciplinary proceedings but became associated with inequitable outcomes for African American and Latino boys in particular.
- Students who are subject to pronounced school discipline have a greater likelihood of experiencing negative life course outcomes, including higher rates of dropping out of school, becoming unemployed, and interacting with the justice system as adults.
- New trends in school discipline, such as restorative justice, aim to replace exclusionary discipline with approaches in which students and staff meet to repair relationships and reinforce school norms.

INTRODUCTION

School discipline is a topic familiar to anyone who has ever had any contact with a school. Educators, for example, receive formal training in designing engaging curricula or deploying effective behavioral management systems to reduce incidences of disruption, disrespect, and disobedience in the classroom. In spite of educators' best efforts, however, school discipline remains an enduring problem. Over the past decades, school discipline has become such a prominent and contested feature of education and society that the US Supreme Court has regularly weighed-in on cases involving students disciplined for protests that have touched on opposition to war, on civil rights and the promotion of "bong hits for Jesus," on the use of profanity at a school assembly, and on spiking the punch at a school dance.

While educators often think of school discipline as a set of instructional and administrative practices required to maintain order and allow instruction and learning to proceed, sociologists view the matter differently. For sociologists, discipline is not understood as an organizational by-product or as an unpleasant

Figure 20. A schoolboy holds out his hand for flogging in this 1854 illustration. Source: New York Public Library, New York Public Library Archives. https://digitalcollections.nypl.org/items/510d47e1–1d47-a3d9-e040-e00a18064a99.

pedagogical practice peripheral to schooling, but instead as an issue at the very core of what schooling is all about in a society. "The nature and function of school discipline," according to Emile Durkheim ([1925] 1961: 148–49), a founder of modern sociology, "is not a simple device for securing superficial peace in the classroom—a device allowing the work to roll on tranquilly." Instead, for sociologists, school discipline "is essentially an instrument—difficult to duplicate—of moral education." Schools are often the first social institution outside the family, particularly for individuals from nonreligious backgrounds, where youth encounter societal norms, rules, and values. Through these interactions, youth have the opportunity to internalize societal norms, rules, and values as their own—that is, to be socialized for conventional roles in society or to embark on alternative paths associated with deviance, delinquency, and crime. Discipline is understood as being at the core of schooling; and, given the significance of youth socialization, school discipline is also recognized as central to both sociology and society.

Many of the most important sociologists of the past century wrote extensively about school discipline. In the beginning of the twentieth century, Durkheim ([1925] 1961) served in the French Ministry of Education and lectured extensively on how school discipline should be adopted and utilized in productive ways in schools. The role of discipline in schools, according to Durkheim, was to signal clearly that norms had been violated, and that the community expected different behavior from students in the future (see figure 20). Durkheim argued against Hobbesian conceptions of order, where punishment was required to be sure and swift, instilling fear and making unruly subjects cower in compliance. Durkheim's conception of school discipline as being about norms and values served as one of the later building blocks for much of contemporary criminology, including Travis Hirschi's (1969) seminal work on social control.

Durkheim's work on school discipline was also a building block for James Coleman's research in the second half of the twentieth century. Coleman, one of the most prominent US sociologists of the past half century, repeatedly focused on issues related to school discipline. In *The Adolescent Society*, Coleman (1961) examined peer relationships in US high schools and demonstrated how youth were more concerned with peers than adults and were oriented toward peer status systems that typically valued appearances, automobiles, and athletics over academic accomplishments aligned with adult expectations. In a report commissioned by Congress, Coleman and his colleagues (1966) argued that to improve academic outcomes and reduce inequality across racial groups, one had to change peer environments, not simply increase financial investments in schooling. Coleman in the 1980s was still squarely focused on these issues (Coleman, Hoffer and Kilgore 1982; Coleman and Hoffer 1987). He argued that for positive school disciplinary climates to emerge, schools required social capital in their communities—that is, they needed parents to know each other and know each other's kids, so that norms could be agreed upon, monitored, and encouraged.

In the twenty-first century, sociologists have continued to explore many of these original themes in relation to the role of school discipline in youth socialization and social inequality. For example, school discipline has been shown to be shaped by legal environments surrounding schools. In the United States, due process rights were extended to students in public schools in the Supreme Court's *Goss v. Lopez* decision (1974). Students facing minor disciplinary action were granted rudimentary due process rights—that is, the right to know what they were charged with and to tell their side of the story. Students were also granted more formal due process rights (such as the right to a formal hearing, legal representation, and cross-examination) when long-term suspension or other more serious sanctions were applied.

Discipline issues also affect higher education. In the last quarter of the twentieth century, colleges and universities faced pressures, similar to those faced by K–12 schools, to abandon their traditional *in loco parentis* role in regulating student behavior and to honor students' due process rights when applying disciplinary measures. More recently, discipline problems in higher education have focused on both sexual harassment and sexual violence on campus and the institutional regulation of these behaviors. Sexual violence, which includes rape, sexual assault, sexual harassment, and stalking, is considered sex-based discrimination under Title IX of the Education Amendments of 1972, and colleges and universities have thus been required to establish formal procedures for dealing with these issues. Research has demonstrated that 10 to 20 percent of women on college campuses experience sexual assault (Fisher, Cullen, and Turner 2000; Cantor et al. 2015).

Sociologists in recent years have also worked cross-nationally to better understand the relationship between social background and educational achievement, arguing that school discipline is a complex phenomenon that emerged as a joint function of the actions of students and educators: "a product of the actions of teachers and administrators, the cultural beliefs and behaviors of students, and the interactions between students and educators" (Arum and Velez 2012: 2). In this comparative project, in which sociologists analyzed data and educational systems in nine countries, consistent evidence emerged showing that disciplinary problems were strongly associated with lower student achievement. Students attending schools with disciplinary problems had lower test scores and smaller test score gains. In addition, country-level differences in performance on standardized tests were strongly associated with the level of disciplinary problems students and educators reported in the schools they inhabited. In addition, US students were shown to have been afforded explicit legal rights, and litigation in the United States was prevalent to an extent that was significantly greater than in any of the other countries examined.

In this chapter, we review recent research to highlight the extent to which disciplinary practices vary in contemporary US schools; the importance of how disciplinary practices are perceived and experienced by students; the extent to which school discipline is associated with life-course outcomes; and research limitations and areas for additional research.

VARIATION IN DISCIPLINARY PRACTICES: FROM ZERO TOLERANCE TO RESTORATIVE JUSTICE

Public and policy-maker concerns about school shootings, student disorder, and inadequate administrative responses were explicit rationales for the promotion of zero-tolerance policies. The Gun-Free Schools Act of 1994 aimed to ban weapons from school grounds to improve school safety. The resulting policies, such as the increased use of out-of-school suspensions, were labeled "zero-tolerance" policies. These policies have recently come under criticism in general, as well as specifically because of their inequitable implementation within schools, particularly for less severe behaviors (Perry 2014; Nolan 2011). Many studies have found that certain groups of students are most likely to receive discipline under zero-tolerance policies—specifically, students who are black, male, or assigned to special education programs (Fabelo et al. 2011; Gregory, Skiba, and Noguera, 2010; Liu et al. 2013; Losen and Martinez 2013; Mendez and Knoff 2003). As a result, policy makers and school practitioners have been exploring and adopting alternative policies and programs (Civil Rights Project and Advancement Project 2000).

Educators and youth advocates have been promoting classroom management strategies for de-escalating conflict and minimizing the use of suspension and expulsion, as well as introducing several other common techniques, including Positive Behavioral Intervention Systems and *restorative justice circles.* Positive Behavioral Intervention Systems emphasize the development of a positive and proactive method of behavioral support in which expectations are explicitly stated, data are reviewed to make disciplinary decisions, and there is a focus on avoiding disproportionality in discipline (Flannery, Sugai, and

Anderson 2009; Sugai et al. 2000). Restorative justice circles handle infractions through mediated conversation, on the assumption that forming strong relationships among and between adults and students is an effective protective factor against misbehavior (Amstutz and Mullet 2005; Braithwaite 1989). If these relationships are damaged as a result of the infraction, actions designed to restore the relationship, rather than penalize the perpetrator, are taken. Both Positive Behavioral Intervention Systems and restorative justice circles take a holistic approach by aiming to improve school culture by bolstering relationships between teachers and students. The programs are designed to promote perceived fairness through the use of clear guidelines infused into the school's ethos.

Supporting this work, Johnson and Johnson (1996) reported that conflict resolution and peer mediation were effective in reducing the number of school suspensions and improving the school climate. If students were not receiving necessary services to support their emotional well-being, they were more likely to act out as a means of seeking help (Civil Rights Project and Advancement Project 2000). In these cases the explicit training of teachers and other school staff—as opposed to only one staff member—in these techniques was promoted to develop a more cohesive school approach to discipline alternatives. However, one potential problem is that new school initiatives that targeted students' social and emotional well-being were often expected to be led by counselors, who already had heavy, often unmanageable, caseloads (Perusse et al. 2004; Bardhoshi 2012). As a result, guidance counselors struggled to develop close relationships with all of their students and students' mental health needs— needs that, when unmet, were the source of some students' disruptive behaviors (Civil Rights Project and Advancement Project 2000).

Restorative justice practices also face considerable skepticism. They are based on programs developed for adults but are being implemented among youth in schools. Whether such practices will be effective in encouraging stronger relationships among students and between students and teachers remains an open question. Also, given the variation in implementation and practice of these techniques between and within schools, it is unknown whether restorative justice and other alternative practices will be effective in decreasing the number of detentions and suspensions.

LIVED EXPERIENCE AND THE DISCIPLINE LADDER

Understanding how discipline is administered within a school is also an important part of examining school discipline. In general, teachers have only limited authority to administer suspensions. Frequently, a teacher witnesses an event he or she believes requires disciplinary action, and then writes up an incident report detailing what happened and where and when it occurred. From there, an administrator reads the incident report, talks with the student(s) involved, and determines the appropriate disciplinary action. Some options may include an in-school detention, which entails notifying a student's parent and assigning the student to detention during lunch or after school. A conference with parents to discuss the student's behavior and solidify a plan for improvement often follows when students demonstrate repeated problems. The next step is often an in-school suspension, where a student reports to school but spends the day with a staff member or administrator without attending class. Finally, an out-of-school suspension or expulsion is often the result of repeated misbehavior or particularly dangerous student behaviors. Out-of-school suspensions are known as *exclusionary discipline,* which separates the student from his or her peers and is the most punitive. While it is intended to address dangerous behaviors in schools, it is most often used for relatively small behavioral problems as result of disciplinary progression.

Insubordination is one of the most common types of misbehavior in schools and is often the type most commonly noted in out-of-school suspensions. It is a broad term for nonviolent behavior that teachers and administrators perceive as disrespectful. Examples include dress code infractions, speaking while the teacher is delivering a lesson, and bringing a cell phone or other unauthorized object to school. Most of these types of behaviors occur within the classroom. Since they are visible to teachers and fellow students alike, insubordinate behaviors shape perceptions of a school's disciplinary climate and the school's reactions. More severe behavioral problems—especially physical altercations—are considerably less frequent than everyday forms of insubordination. Often, insubordinate behavior is addressed through lower-level sanctions, as noted above, but sometimes it may result in higher-level discipline, such as out-of-school suspension.

It is important to recognize that often it is the administrator who assigns and supervises the discipline, leaving a gap between the teacher who witnessed the event and the disciplinary decision. Such gaps may lead to greater or lesser discipline assignments, depending on the situation and the organizational context, but they clearly create discontinuity between the individual's behavior and the school's response to it. Regardless, the gaps likely affect students' perceptions of school discipline and of the fairness of its assignment. When students feel that discipline is unfairly assigned, or teachers feel that they do not have the authority to assign discipline, the school's disciplinary and overall climate can suffer.

School climate has been defined as "shared beliefs, values, and attitudes that shape interactions between students, teachers, and administrators and set the parameters of acceptable behavior and norms for a school" (Koth, Bradshaw, and Leaf 2008: 96). A positive school climate is considered essential for student engagement and academic achievement (Griffith 1999; Lee, Bryk, and Smith

1993) and results in fewer instances of antisocial behavior (Gottfredson 1986; Hawkins and Lishner 1987; Kupermine, Leadbeater, and Blatt 2001; Welsh 2000; Wilcox and Clayton 2001). One of the earliest studies of high school students, which had almost sixty thousand participants, demonstrated that schools with more cohesive school climates had lower instances of misbehavior (DiPrete and Mueller 1981).

An ineffective school disciplinary climate can result from a clash between a school's behavioral expectations and those of the students. Several studies have found, for example, that expectations for behavior in school align more closely with certain socioeconomic groups' behaviors, leaving nondominant social groups more likely to be disciplined (Ainsworth-Darnell and Downey 1998; Lareau 2011). One study in the state of Texas examined both the types of discipline used and who was disciplined, finding that black students, boys, and those receiving special education services were more likely to be disciplined than their peers. The study also found that the majority of these differences concerned behaviors that were judged by school staff, as opposed to laws (Fabelo et al. 2011). Earlier studies on school discipline often focused on the outcomes associated with being disciplined, but also consistently identified disproportionality in the assignment of this discipline. Linda Raffaele Mendez and Howard Knoff (2003), for example, examined on-time graduation for a 2002 graduation cohort and found that race and gender correlated with suspension likelihood as early as sixth grade. This trend of unequal early assignment of discipline continues in studies today, where even in kindergarten black and male students are more likely to be identified by their teachers as behaving poorly (Garcia 2015).

Statistics related to school discipline identify clear patterns of disproportionality in its application:

- Suspensions and disciplinary problems vary by *grade* (Arum and Velez 2012; Baker-Smith 2017; Diliberti, Jackson, and Kemp 2017).
  - Elementary schools have the lowest levels of suspensions/administered discipline
  - Middle and high schools have the highest
- Boys are more likely to be suspended than girls—nationally, boys receive two out of three suspensions assigned (US Department of Education, Office for Civil Rights 2014).
- Across the United States, African American students have the highest suspension rates (US Department of Education, Office for Civil Rights 2014)
  - 16 percent of African American students are suspended, as compared to 5 percent of white students
  - African American girls are suspended at a higher rate (12 percent) than girls of any other group; in some cases, they are suspended at a rate higher than that for African American boys.

- Students with disabilities are more likely to be suspended than those without this classification (6 percent compared to 13 percent; US Department of Education, Office for Civil Rights 2014).
- The majority of suspensions are those that happen for discretionary infractions as opposed to mandatory suspension required by law (Baker-Smith 2017; Fabelo et al. 2011).

While the causes of these disparities are complex, it is likely that these differences shape individual student understandings of school discipline. Research shows that students' perception of their teachers' use of discipline is particularly important in how they feel about the school's disciplinary climate and the fairness of discipline (Arum et al. 2003). Particularly in the case of discipline for behaviors like insubordination, students are often more likely to be suspended when they are black or male. While this evidence is consistent across all studies, we still do not know the extent to which this happens for truly different behaviors among students or happens because of personal or structural bias in the way discipline is assigned. If a student feels that discipline was unfairly assigned, it is easy to see how a school's disciplinary climate might not feel protective and instead would leave both teachers and students feeling unsafe. Many studies on adolescents suggest that when they feel unfairly treated, teens may respond by explicitly ignoring or fighting against the rules they feel are hurting them. Students who feel unfairly disciplined for minor offenses may disengage from school and begin to exhibit additional problem behaviors. These actions may result in greater misbehavior overall and, particularly relevant in today's discussions of school behavior, may result in bullying and victimization.

LIFE COURSE OUTCOMES

Discipline, warranted or not, can potentially have significant impacts on students' academic success and school relationships. Several studies of Chicago schools highlight the importance of shared trust, clear communication, and consistent enforcement for improved learning and working environments for students and school staff (Bryk et al. 2011; Bryk and Schneider 2002). Friendships also can support or discourage appropriate school behavior and increase or reduce a student's likelihood to be disciplined (Brooks-Gunn et al. 1993; Conger 1976; Kirby 2003; McFarland 2001; Moen and Erickson 1995). Adolescents who form friendship groups that resist school rules often find themselves in a downward cycle as minor infractions compound to change their relationship with school staff and other students (Bryk and Thum 1989; Finn and Rock 1997; Gutman and Midgley 2000; Jessor, Turbin, and Costa 1998; Newman 1992; Weiss 2003; Weiss, Carolan, and Baker-Smith 2010). A suspension may arise owing to a bad relationship, but it also might negatively affect a functional one to the extent that a student may no longer be academically engaged in the school.

There is substantial evidence that school discipline is associated with negative outcomes across the life course (Balfanz, Herzog, and Mac Iver 2007; Gregory, Skiba, and Noguera 2010; Morrison et al. 2001; Skiba et al. 2003). Most of these outcomes have been highlighted by research on what is called the "school-to-prison pipeline." Research shows that out-of-school suspensions are associated with missing multiple days of schools and potentially subsequent course failure or grade retention (Balfanz, Herzog, and Mac Iver 2007; Balfanz and Legters 2004; Eide and Showalter 2001; Hirschfield 2009; Martorell and Mariano 2018). Negative experiences with authority, in the form of school discipline, often are the first link in negative experiences with authority later on, such as the criminal justice system. Advocates of school discipline reform argue that suspensions negatively affect society as a whole because of the lost tax revenue, increased crime costs, and even reduced health, later in life, of those who were suspended (Marchbanks et al. 2013; Rumberger and Losen 2016).

DIRECTIONS FOR FUTURE RESEARCH

Much of the work on the effects of school discipline on sanctioned students shows associations with negative outcomes, but it is also clear when examining institutional outcomes that discipline, when used judiciously, can improve a school's social and academic climate (Arum et al. 2003; DiPrete and Mueller 1981). The relationship between school discipline and student outcomes thus is a complex and not fully settled matter.

School-level discipline analysis has generally suffered from three methodological hurdles that obscure the measurement of school effects on suspensions. First, the majority of scholars engaged in suspension research, at both student and school levels, have had limited access to longitudinal data. This means that we see students or schools at one point in time, as opposed to over several years, so it is hard to disentangle cause and effect in school discipline. Second, the majority of what we know about suspensions at the school level is based on schools or students across the country, state, or district. While these larger discipline policies are certainly important, it is likely that schools even within a particular district use discipline differently (Bryk 1993; Lee 2000; Lee and Loeb 2000). This limitation is particularly true in big districts that have a large number of schools and where schools serve distinctly different student populations with varied disciplinary approaches, even within a larger district policy.

This limitation also brings up the importance of considering other school characteristics when examining school discipline outcomes and policies. For example, the research on discipline shows that students in large urban areas are more likely to have been suspended or charged with a crime and also are more likely to be black and/or poor (Arum and Velez 2012; Liu et al. 2013; Neiman, DeVoe, and Chandler 2009). However, we usually know little about the characteristics of these students' schools beyond the racial composition and poverty status of their students. There might be other things happening in particular schools. For example, a school may be located in a neighborhood where gangs are prominent, or it may occupy a setting where neighborhood organizations are prevalent, engaged, and partnering collaboratively with schools. All of these things have the potential to change how a school implements discipline, regardless of the students served, suggesting that what we know at the school level might not be detailed enough for us to truly understand this relationship (Baker-Smith and Lipschultz 2016).

The biggest puzzle in school discipline research is that it is unclear whether students with greater behavioral problems drive greater use of discipline, or whether greater use of discipline is a result of a different discipline policy and practice. In the first case, student misbehavior would be the driving factor in variations in discipline rates at both the student and the school level. For example, certain schools may enroll harder-to-serve populations who developed higher rates of behavioral problems before even entering the school. In the second case, differences in school-level practices may lead to variation in discipline rates at the student level regardless of student behavior. This variation between schools, in terms of both discipline rates and other characteristics, makes the identification of the origins of disciplinary behavior difficult.

Partially for this reason, the majority of the discipline literature has focused on the impact of exclusionary discipline on students and the variation in discipline assignment to different groups of students overall. These large-scale examinations allow us to see that indeed there are troubling patterns with regard to the use of school discipline, and out-of-school suspensions in particular, for certain students (Liu et al. 2013; Skiba et al. 2002; "Student Safety Act" 2011). Yet because there are few opportunities to distinguish student-level or school-level effects in these studies, this past scholarship does not fully resolve the question of whether these differences in discipline are due to differences in schools' use of discipline or differences in students' behavior.

CHAPTER 12 REVIEW

Discussion Questions

1. How does the study of school discipline relate to other areas of the sociology of education?
2. How did Durkheim challenge the work of Hobbes in his conceptualization of discipline and society?

3. In what ways did Coleman draw on Durkheim's work to advance an understanding of school discipline?
4. What do current patterns in schools look like when it comes to disciplining students? How might discipline contribute to social stratification?

5. Drawing on the idea of norms, what might Durkheim or Coleman say about the use of restorative justice practices in schools? Zero-tolerance policies?

6. In terms of methods, what are some possible research questions and methods that could address the three major school-discipline-related hurdles mentioned earlier in the chapter?

Suggestions for Further Reading

Arum, Richard, Irenee R. Beattie, Richard Pitt, Jennifer Thompson, and Sandra Way. 2003. *Judging School Discipline: The Crisis of Moral Authority in American Schools.* Cambridge, MA: Harvard University Press.

Bracy, N. 2011. "Student Perceptions of High-Security School Environments." *Youth and Society* 43:365–95.

Gregory, Anne, Russell J. Skiba, and Pedro A. Noguera. 2010. "The Achievement Gap and the Discipline Gap: Two Sides of the Same Coin?" *Educational Researcher* 39 (1): 59–68.

Nolan, Kathleen. 2011. *Police in the Hallways: Discipline in the Urban School.* Ann Arbor: University of Michigan.

References

Ainsworth-Darnell, J., and D. Downey. 1998. "Assessing the Oppositional Culture Explanation for Racial/Ethnic Differences in School Performance." *American Sociological Review* 63:536–53.

Amstutz, L., and J. H. Mullet. 2005. *The Little Book of Restorative Discipline for Schools.* Intercourse, PA: Good Books.

Arum, Richard, Irenee R. Beattie, Richard Pitt, Jennifer Thompson, and Sandra Way. 2003. *Judging School Discipline: The Crisis of Moral Authority in American Schools.* Cambridge, MA: Harvard University Press.

Arum, Richard, and Melissa Velez. 2012. "Class and Racial Differences in U.S. School Disciplinary Environments." In *Improving Learning Environments: School Discipline and Student Achievement in Comparative Perspective,* edited by Richard Arum and Melissa Velez. Palo Alto, CA: Stanford University Press.

Baker-Smith, E. Christine. 2017. "Suspensions, Schools and Students: Understanding School Effects on Student-Level Disparities in Suspension Risk." PhD diss., New York University.

Baker-Smith, E. Christine, and Jessica Lipschultz. 2016. "Do Alternatives Matter: Is the Provision of Disciplinary Alternatives Associated with Lower Levels of Low-Level Suspensions in American High Schools?" In *Education and Youth Today,* edited by Yasemin Besen-Cassino and Loretta E. Bass, 281–313. Vol. 20 of Sociological Studies of Children and Youth, edited by Loretta E. Bass. West Yorkshire, UK: Emerald Publishing.

Balfanz, Robert, Liza Herzog, and Douglas Mac Iver. 2007. "Preventing Student Disengagement and Keeping Students on the Graduation Path in Urban Middle-Grades Schools: Early Identification and Effective Interventions." *Educational Psychologist* 42 (4): 223–35.

Balfanz, Robert, and Nettie Legters. 2004. *Locating the Dropout Crisis: Which High Schools Produce the Nation's Dropouts? Where Are They Located? Who Attends Them?* Baltimore: Johns Hopkins University.

Bardhoshi, G. 2012. *The Relationship between Assignment of Non-counseling Duties and Burnout among Professional School Counselors.* Washington, DC: George Washington University.

Bracy, N. 2011. "Student Perceptions of High-Security School Environments." *Youth and Society* 43:365–95.

Braithwaite, John. 1989. *Crime, Shame, and Reintegration.* Cambridge: Cambridge University Press.

Brooks-Gunn, Jeanne, Greg J. Duncan, Pamela Kato Klebanov, and Naomi Sealand. 1993. "Do Neighborhoods Influence Child and Adolescent Development?" *American Journal of Sociology* 99 (2): 353–95.

Bryk, Anthony. 1993. *Catholic Schools and the Common Good.* Cambridge, MA: Harvard University Press.

Bryk, Anthony, Elaine M. Allensworth, John Q. Easton, Penny Bender Sebring, and Stuart Luppescu. 2011. *Organizing Schools for Improvements: Lessons from Chicago.* Chicago: University of Chicago Press.

Bryk, Anthony, and Barbara Schneider. 2002. *Trust in Schools: A Core Resource for Improvement.* New York: Russell Sage Foundation.

Bryk, Anthony, and Yeow Meng Thum. 1989. "The Effects of High School Organization on Dropping Out: An Exploratory Investigation." *American Educational Research Journal* 26 (3): 353–83.

Cantor, David, Bonnie Fisher, Susan Chibnall, Reanne Townsend, Hyunshik Lee, Carol Bruce, and Gail Thomas. 2015. *Report on the AAU Campus Climate Survey on Sexual Assault and Sexual Misconduct.* Rockville, MD: Westat, prepared for the Association of American Universities.

Civil Rights Project and Advancement Project. 2000. *Opportunities Suspended: The Devastating Consequences of Zero Tolerance and School Discipline Policies.* Los Angeles: UCLA, Civil Rights Project. www.civilrightsproject.ucla.edu/research/k-12-education/school-discipline/opportunities-suspended-the-devastating-consequences-of-zero-tolerance-and-school-discipline-policies/.

Coleman, James Samuel. 1961. *The Adolescent Society.* New York: Free Press of Glencoe.

Coleman, James Samuel, Ernest Q. Campbell, Carol J. Hobson, James McPartland, Alexander M. Mood, Frederic D. Weinfield, and Robert L. York. 1966. *Equality of Educational Opportunity.* Washington, DC: National Center for Educational Statistics.

Coleman, James Samuel, and Thomas Hoffer. 1987. *Public and Private High Schools: The Impact of Communities.* New York: Basic Books.

Coleman, James Samuel, Thomas Hoffer, and Sally Kilgore. 1982. *High School Achievement: Public, Catholic, and Private Schools Compared.* New York: Basic Books.

Conger, Rand D. 1976. "Social Control and Social Learning Models of Delinquent Behavior: A Synthesis." *Criminology* 14 (1): 17–40.

Diliberti, Melissa, Michael Jackson, and Jana Kemp. 2017. *Crime, Violence, Discipline, and Safety in US Public Schools: Findings from the School Survey on Crime and Safety: 2015–16;*

First Look. NCES 2017–122. Washington, DC: US Department of Education, National Center for Education Statistics.

DiPrete, Thomas, and Charles W. Mueller. 1981. *Discipline and Order in American High Schools.* Washington, DC: National Opinion Research Center.

Durkheim, Emile. [1925] 1961. *Moral Education: A Study in the Theory and Application of the Sociology of Education.* New York: Free Press of Glencoe.

Edelman, Lauren B. 1992. "Legal Ambiguity and Symbolic Structures: Organizational Mediation of Civil Rights Law." *American Journal of Sociology* 97:1531–76.

Editorial Board. 2014. "Zero Tolerance, Reconsidered." *New York Times,* January 5.

Eide, E. R., and M. H. Showalter. 2001. "The Effect of Grade Retention on Educational and Labor Market Outcomes." *Economics of Education Review* 20 (6): 563–76.

Fabelo, Tony, Michael D. Thompson, Martha Plotkin, Dottie Carmichael, Miner P. Marchbanks III, and Eric A. Booth. 2011. *Breaking Schools' Rules: A Statewide Study on How School Discipline Relates to Students' Success and Juvenile Justice Involvement.* New York: Council of State Governments Justice Center and Public Policy Research Institute, Texas A&M University. https://csgjusticecenter.org/wp-content/uploads/2012/08/Breaking_Schools_Rules_Report_Final.pdf.

Finn, J. D., and Donald Rock. 1997. "Academic Success among Students at Risk for School Failure." *Journal of Applied Psychology* 82 (2): 221–34.

Fisher, B. S., F. T. Cullen, and M. G Turner. 2000. *The Sexual Victimization of College Women: Research Report.* Washington, DC: U.S. Department of Justice.

Flannery, K. B., G. Sugai, and C. M. Anderson. 2009. "School-Wide Positive Behavior Support in High School: Early Lessons Learned." *Journal of Positive Behavior Interventions* 11 (3): 177–85.

Garcia, Emma. 2015. *Inequalities at the Starting Gate: Cognitive and Noncognitive Skills and Gaps between 2010–2011 Kindergarten Classmates.* Washington, DC: Economic Policy Institute.

Gottfredson, D. C. 1986. *An Assessment of a Delinquency Prevention Demonstration with Both Individual and Environmental Interventions.* Baltimore: Center for Social Organization of Schools Report.

Gregory, Anne, Russell J. Skiba, and Pedro A. Noguera. 2010. "The Achievement Gap and the Discipline Gap: Two Sides of the Same Coin?" *Educational Researcher* 39 (1): 59–68.

Griffith, J. 1999. "School Climate as 'Social Order' and 'Social Action': A Multi-level Analysis of Public Elementary School Student Perceptions." *School Psychology of Education* 2:339–69.

Gutman, Leslie Morrison, and Carol Midgley. 2000. "The Role of Protective Factors in Supporting the Academic Achievement of Poor African American Students during the Middle School Transition." *Journal of Youth and Adolescence* 29 (2): 223–49.

Hawkins, J. D., and D. Lishner. 1987. *Etiology and Prevention of Antisocial Behavior in Children and Adolescents.* New York: Plenum.

Hirschfield, P. 2009. "Another Way Out: The Impact of Juvenile Arrests on High School Dropout." *Sociology of Education* 82 (4): 368–93.

Jessor, R., M. S. Turbin, and F. M. Costa. 1998. "Risk and Protection in Successful Outcomes among Disadvantaged Adolescents." *Applied Developmental Science* 2 (4): 194–208.

Johnson, D. W., and R. T. Johnson. 1996. "Conflict Resolution and Peer Mediation Programs in Elementary and Secondary Schools: A Review of the Research." *Review of Educational Research* 6 (4): 459–506.

Kirby, D. 2003. "Risk and Protective Factors Affecting Teen Pregnancy and the Effectiveness of Programs Designed to Address Them." In *Reducing Adolescent Risk: Toward an Integrated Approach,* edited by Daniel Romer, 265–83. Thousand Oaks, CA: Sage.

Koth, C. W., C. P. Bradshaw, and P. J. Leaf. 2008. "A Multilevel Study of Predictors of Student Perceptions of School Climate: The Effect of Classroom-Level Factors." *Journal of Educational Psychology* 100 (1): 96.

Kupermine, G. P., B. J. Leadbeater, and S. J. Blatt. 2001. "School Social Climate and Individual Differences in Vulnerability to Psychopathology among Middle School Students." *Journal of Social Psychology* 39:141–59.

Lareau, A. 2011. *Unequal Childhoods: Class, Race, and Family Life.* Berkeley: University of California Press.

Lee, Valerie. 2000. "Using Hierarchical Linear Modeling to Study Social Contexts: The Case of School Effects." *Educational Psychologist* 35 (2): 125–41.

Lee, Valerie, Anthony Bryk, and J. B. Smith. 1993. "The Organization of Effective High Schools." *Review of Research in Education* 19:171–267.

Lee, Valerie, and Susanna Loeb. 2000. "School Size in Chicago Elementary Schools: Effects on Teachers' Attitudes and Students' Achievement." *American Educational Research Journal* 37 (1): 3–31.

Liu, John C., Ricardo Morales, Ari Hoffnung, Frank Braconi, Jacqueline S. Gold, and Carolyn Karo. 2013. *The Suspension Spike: Changing the Discipline Culture in NYC's Middle Schools.* New York: New York City Comptroller's Office.

Losen, D., and T. E. Martinez. 2013. *Out of School and Off Track: The Overuse of Suspensions in American Middle and High Schools.* Los Angeles: Civil Rights Project.

Losen, D., and R. Skiba. 2010. *Suspended Education: Urban Middle Schools in Crisis.* Montgomery, AL: Southern Poverty Law Center.

Marchbanks, Miner P., III, Jamilia J. Blake, Eric A. Booth, Dottie Carmichael, Allison L. Seibert, and Tony Fabelo. 2013. *The Economic Effects of Exclusionary Discipline on Grade Retention and High School Dropout.* Washington, DC: Civil Rights Project.

Martorell, Paco, and Louis T. Mariano. 2018. "The Causal Effects of Grade Retention on Behavioral Outcomes." *Journal of Research on Educational Effectiveness* 11 (2): 192–216.

McFarland, Daniel A. 2001. "Student Resistance: How the Formal and Informal Organization of Classrooms Facilitate Everyday Forms of Student Defiance." *American Journal of Sociology* 107 (3): 612–78.

Mendez, Linda M. Raffaele, and Howard M. Knoff. 2003. "Who Gets Suspended from School and Why: A Demographic Analysis of Schools and Disciplinary Infractions in a Large School District." *Education and Treatment of Children* 26 (1): 30–51.

Miller, Johanna, and Udi Ofer. 2011. *Education Interrupted: The Growing Use of Suspensions in New York City's Public Schools.* New York: New York Civil Liberties Union.

Moen, Phyllis, and Mary Ann Erickson. 1995. "Linked Lives: A Transgenerational Approach to Resilience." In *Examining Lives in Context: Perspectives on the Ecology of Human Development,* edited by Phyllis Moen, Glenn H. Elder Jr., and Kurt Lüscher, 169–210. Washington, DC: American Psychological Association.

Morrison, Gale M., Suzanne Anthony, Meri H. Storino, Joanna J. Cheng, Michael J. Furlong, and Richard L. Morrison. 2001. "School Expulsion as a Process and an Event: Before and After Effects on Children at Risk for School Discipline." In *Zero Tolerance: Can Suspension and Expulsion Keep Schools Safe?* edited by Russell J. Skiba and Gil G. Noam, 45–72. New Directions for Youth Development, no. 92. San Francisco: Jossey-Bass.

Neiman, Samantha, Jill F. DeVoe, and Kathryn Chandler. 2009. *Crime, Violence, Discipline, and Safety in U.S. Public Schools: Findings from the School Survey on Crime and Safety: 2007–08.* Washington, DC: US Department of Education.

Newman, Fred. 1992. *Student Engagement and Achievement in American Secondary Schools.* New York: Teachers College Press.

Nolan, Kathleen. 2011. *Police in the Hallways: Discipline in the Urban School.* Ann Arbor: University of Michigan.

Perry, Andre. 2014. "Zero-Tolerance Policies Are Destroying the Lives of Black Children." *Washington Post,* July 7.

Perusse, R., G. E. Goodnough, J. Donegan, and C. Jones. 2004. "Perceptions of School Counselors and School Principals about the National Standards for School Counseling Programs and the Transforming School Counseling Initiative." *Professional School Counseling* 7 (3): 152–61.

Rumberger, Russell, W., and Daniel Losen. 2016. *The High Cost of Harsh Discipline and Its Disparate Impact.* Los Angeles: Center for Civil Rights Remedies.

Skiba, Russell, Robert S. Michael, Abra Carroll Nardo, and Reece L. Peterson. 2002. "The Color of Discipline: Sources of Racial and Gender Disproportionality in School Punishment." *Urban Review* 34 (4): 317–42.

Skiba, Russell, Ada Simmons, Lori Staudinger, Marcus Rausch, Gayle Dow, and Renae Feggins. 2003. "Consistent Removal: Contributions of School Discipline to the School-Prison Pipeline." Paper presented to the School-to-Prison Pipeline Research Conference: Harvard Civil Rights Project, May 16–17. www.varj.asn.au/resources/documents/consistent%20removal.pdf.

"Student Safety Act." 2011. New York Civil Liberties Union. www.nyclu.org/schooltoprison/ssa.

Sugai, G., R. H. Horner, G. Dunlap, M. Hieneman, T. J. Lewis, C. M. Nelson, and H. R. Turnbull. 2000. "Applying Positive Behavior Support and Functional Behavioral Assessment in Schools." *Journal of Positive Behavior Interventions* 2 (3): 131–43.

US Department of Education, Office for Civil Rights. 2014. *Civil Rights Data Collection: Data Snapshot: School Discipline.* Civil Rights Data Collection Series: Issue Brief No. 1. Washington, DC: US Department of Education.

Weiss, Christopher C. 2003. "The Neglected Importance of Connections: The Role of Student Engagement in the Transition to High School." Paper presented at the Association for Public Policy Analysis and Management, Washington, DC.

Weiss, Christopher C., Brian Carolan, and E. Christine Baker-Smith. 2010. "Big School, Small School: (Re)Testing Assumptions about High School Size, School Engagement and Mathematics Achievement." *Journal of Youth and Adolescence* 39 (2): 163–76.

Welsh, W. N. 2000. "The Effect of School Climate on School Disorder." *Annals of the American Academy of Political and Social Sciences* 567:88–107.

Wilcox, P., and R. R. Clayton. 2001. "A Multilevel Analysis of School-Based Weapon Possession." *Justice Quarterly* 18:509–41.

Within Elite Academic Walls

3

Inequity and Student Experience on Campus

MEGAN THIELE, SAN JOSE STATE UNIVERSITY

KAREN JEONG ROBINSON, CALIFORNIA STATE

UNIVERSITY, SAN BERNARDINO

EDITORS' NOTE

Selective colleges and universities like to think of themselves as engines of social mobility, institutions that admit diverse students and prepare them socially and economically for elite positions. However, as we learned in chapter 7, first-generation students are half as likely to graduate from college as their peers whose parents have college experience. Sociologists Megan Thiele and Karen Jeong Robinson argue that student experiences at elite colleges and universities often reproduce social inequalities. Students from socially advantaged families often have access to **insider information** that helps them navigate social dynamics on elite college campuses—from the parties in the Greek scene to small talk with a professor during office hours. By contrast, for poor students and students who are the first in their families to go to college, elite college campus life can often feel like a game governed by obscure and unwritten rules.

As you read this case study, see if you can spot similarities between the evidence that Thiele and Robinson have accumulated regarding student life in colleges and universities, and the elementary-school evidence that Jessica Calarco presents in chapter 6, and the high-school evidence William Carbonaro presents in Chapter 8. In addition, consider the **institutional arrangements** that make these classed social dynamics possible. What might elite colleges and universities do differently to help make their campuses more welcoming and accessible to poor and first-generation students?

KEY POINTS

- Students from different social classes, races, and genders draw upon unequal economic, cultural, and social resources during college.
- Privileged students find it easier to leverage their social and cultural capital on highly selective university campuses than do poor, working-class students and students of color.
- The Greek system is a prominent social scene on many campuses. Fraternities and sororities often marginalize poor and working-class students and students of color.
- Poor and working-class students often juggle outside family and work commitments while attending university, which limits their ability to take advantage of university networking opportunities.

INTRODUCTION

Although the characteristics, contexts, and cultures of universities vary greatly, the quintessential college experience is wrought with competition and inequity. Within the United States' system of higher education, there are private universities, online universities, small universities, large universities, rural colleges, urban universities, wealthy universities, resource-lacking universities, public universities, colleges in the desert, colleges in the forest, community colleges, and top Ivy League schools. There are military schools and party schools. Social hierarchies exist in all of them.

The more than five thousand institutions of higher education in the United States enroll twenty million students each year (US Department of Education 2018). With unprecedented rates of college attendance among high school graduates, and more Americans with college degrees than ever before, it might seem that our system is getting more equal. Yet—from beginning to end—our postsecondary schooling system is more highly stratified than ever. Wealthy institutions have resources that enable them to offer a wide array of enriching experiences: free and sponsored events, workshops and travel opportunities, dinners at home with professors, cutting-edge technology such as engineering labs and supercomputer centers, state-of-the-art theater facilities, and ties to professional art, theater, film, and literary houses. Well-endowed universities have powerful and active alumni networks, which can help current students in myriad ways, including regarding job securement. Students graduate at higher rates at elite universities compared to non-elite institutions, and the alumni of highly selective colleges are more likely to marry wealthier partners and earn a higher income—this is particularly true for graduates who are Latinx, black, and first-generation students. Students who attend more modest and low-resource universities have limited-to-no access to this exposure and these opportunities for growth.

As social inequality increases outside of higher education, selective, high-endowment colleges and universities are becoming even more exclusive. Recent research shows that many of these historically and predominantly white institutions enroll more students from families in the top 1 percent of income distribution than from the combined bottom 60 percent (Chetty et al. 2017). In 2015, 15 percent of the college-going age group was black and 22 percent was Latinx, yet black and Latinx students made up just 6 percent and 13 percent of freshmen, respectively, at the nation's top one hundred colleges (Ashkenas, Park, and Pearce 2017). These demographics reflect a number of obstacles in the postsecondary educational experiences of poor, working-class students and students of color. For example, for poor and working-class students, whose parents work in low-income and low-status occupations, college is often a major financial undertaking. Wealthier parents have additional resources to draw upon for the college search process. For example, some high school counselors negotiate with admissions officers on behalf of their students. Counselors in high schools that serve financially well-endowed populations know their students better and will go to bat for them (McDonough 1997). The high schools of upper-class students often have well-established, consistent, and direct connections to elite colleges and universities (Khan 2010; Stevens 2007). And recent college admission scandals reveal just how much these spaces are worth, with some wealthy parents paying half a million dollars through illegal channels to ensure their child's admittance (Chappell and Kennedy 2019). For all of these reasons and more, poor, minority, and first-generation students are often "undermatched," attending less-selective colleges and universities than they qualify for based on their grades and test scores.

Elite universities are competitive not only academically but also in terms of social networking. Elite university campuses include incredibly high-achieving individuals, they also contain students who are immersed in a culture that privileges individuals based on the status they entered into at birth. Those who find themselves at the top of the various social hierarchies within our culture—for example, class, race, and gender—experience a less stressful life course, all else being equal. For example, class-privileged people within all communities hold power over less-privileged members, based on their resources and the status that comes with them. The education system is not without these inequities.

For many students at the top, college is an "absolute blast." Students feel good about themselves as participants in a lively and engaging civic forum, and they receive the benefits of socializing with the elite. For students at the bottom, university life can be grueling as they experience biases based on class, race, and gender on a daily basis. Organizations, mechanisms, and people work to reproduce stratification along the university pipeline, from preenrollment to postgraduation job placement.

Despite all of these challenges, every year thousands of poor, minority, and first-generation students enroll in elite colleges and universities. In this case study, we investigate their experiences, drawing upon data we collected in interviews with students at one elite university to consider how the social lives of students at selective colleges and universities help reproduce social class inequality on campus. In discussing the classed dynamics and interactions of students, we highlight how inequalities at the intersection of class and race/ethnicity connect and reinforce one another.

INTELLECTUAL ROOTS: TRACKED PATHWAYS OF
A HIGHLY STRATIFIED UNIVERSITY

Although many would argue that the acquisition of knowledge and skill is the main purpose of university, social life comprises the experiential core of college for many students (Stevens, Armstrong, and Arum 2008). While socializing during extracurricular activities, at parties, or in other arenas on elite campuses, students form lifelong ties and teach each other how to be elite. The ability to engage with individuals who have elite cultural dispositions is rewarded in the labor market off campus. Unfortunately, not all students are able to engage equally in the social aspects of university life.

Some students come from families where parents and even grandparents went to college and have a wealth of knowledge, stories, and expectations about the culture, traditions, and opportunities available to students. This insider information can influence where a student will live and/or what fraternity or sorority he or she will join, often before the student has even applied to a school. Once on campus, this social and cultural capital gives upper-class students an advantage when it comes to fitting in. Elite students recognize and classify each other based on their clothes, vernacular, and hobbies. In interviews we conducted with students at a highly selective private university, one white, upper-class female student demonstrated the enthusiasm and ease with which she transitioned into university life. "When you come here, it's an oasis practically, the campus is just phenomenal—like the student body, like everyone. Like, it's so easy to just get along with a lot of people. Like, you can just walk, you can walk down the halls and knock on everybody's door and introduce yourself, and be like, 'Hey, I like that guy,' or 'That girl's cool.' You know, just meet all these new people."

Without parents or grandparents to prime them, working-class and minority students may be unaware of or give less weight to the importance of networking with peers. They may not value the social experiences on campus in the same way that class-privileged students do (Stuber 2009); they may prioritize their academics and marginalize socializing on their schedules. Further, many working-class and minority students have less time and/or motivation for extracurriculars and socializing on campus. To keep graduation in sight and their financial aid secure, working-class students must adapt to the high academic standards of an elite private school, which takes time. Moreover, their family and work commitments take up time they might otherwise spend participating in extracurricular activities. From a white, working-class female in our study:

> I hope I can cut my work hours down next year . . . like, [do] ten or fifteen, or make them in the morning instead of the evening so that I can . . . you know, I work during the meetings. I work during the meetings, I forget what they're called—you know, the gay rights organization that is here on campus and that's always been a passion of mine. So, they meet on Monday nights, so hopefully I'll have that time free to go to those meetings. I went to a few at the beginning of last semester, and then I started working a lot and I never have that time free.

THE "GREEK" SYSTEM

The heart of social life on many elite college campuses is the Panhellenic Greek system. Fraternities and sororities tend to be financially exclusive and white, and to dominate the social scene on campus.

A white fraternity member told us,

> The Greek life is very exclusive. I think *exclusive* is the main word. If you're a part of the community, you're a part of it. If you're not a part of it, I think you feel really ostracized by the community. . . . [T]hat exclusivity comes from the fact that it's a very strong, tight-knit organization of people. . . . I think if you're not a part of the Greek system, it's kind of hard to find house parties or things like that to go to. And unless you're part of a house, you can't get involved at all with the Greek community—like, there's no events that are, like, shared, Greek and non-Greek.

Working-class and minority students are largely missing from this elite social scene. These students are tracked away from building relationships and ties with class-privileged peers on campus that could turn into jobs, marriage, and/or children. As an Egyptian student in our study suggested, "Ask any brown girl: there is no ethnicity in sororities. There's, like, five, literally. I was so surprised. I was like, 'Where are all the brown girls?' And that's why the Latinas have their own sororities, and the African Americans—because they're not represented enough in there."

Poor, working-class students and students of color are marginalized or excluded throughout the rigorous selection process known as "rush," in which current fraternity and sorority members handpick new recruits. (See figure 21 for a photograph of rush at one major public university.) The sorting process requires students to have knowledge of the social pecking order on campus and one's place in it; sometimes it requires students to rank potential members by looks. One white, working- and middle-class student at a highly selective private university from our study described the selection and matching process of rush.

> We were taught how to talk, what to say, what to ask about, what to not ask about, what to look for—like, "See how they dress." But it wasn't just, like, a general "See if they are stylish." It was like, "See what their shoes are; see what their purses are." . . . [W]e learned how to judge. We would do a slideshow . . . with all the photos of the recruits, and we would see their pictures. And then we would rank them based on their pictures and if they looked like a good fit for the house. And then the top pictures would be . . . matched with the top girls in our house. So, like, the best talkers or the prettiest girls would be matched with the prettiest pictures and then downward. So you would be matched with a partner based on your attractiveness level and sometimes on your interest or shared region.

As in all socially exclusive clubs, there are both written and unwritten rules and expectations—regarding how to dress, how to speak, how many functions to attend, and how to present oneself—in determining who does and does not belong. Students who are unaware of the rules and expectations are at a considerable disadvantage. At highly selective private institutions, the classism within these organizations is heavily pronounced. The white, middle- and working-class student cited earlier described how a friend helped her prepare for sorority rush.

Figure 21. Students line up for sorority rush at a major university. Source: Huw Williams (Huwmanbeing), Wikimedia Commons, https://commons.wikimedia.org/wiki/File:Alpha_Xi_Delta_sorority_rush.png.

I remember going to my friend's dorm, who was in a sorority, and I was like, "Hey, I'm thinking about going out for spring rush. What should I do?" And I remember, the first day she was like, "Make sure you borrow clothes from me." At the time, I was like, "Oh my gosh, she is so sweet." But what she was really saying was: "You cannot possibly dress the way that you dress and go to sorority rush. If you do, you will be laughed at." And it's not like I wore anything crazy, but I did not own anything outside of Old Navy and Abercrombie; and so she was like, "You have to borrow clothes from me," and I was like, "Okay." And so I borrowed clothes from her. Every day, she would tell me what to wear: "So today, you are going to wear a strap-less, knee-length thing." And I was like, "Okay." I didn't think about it at the time, of why this was important. I was like, "Oh, cool, she's letting me borrow her stuff because she has been through it." And so I joined the sorority.

Non-elite students and students of color are less likely to be familiar with the cultural artifacts, like brand names, that their wealthier, elite counterparts care about. Lacking the appropriate cultural know-how, poor and working-class students and students of color are likely to experience difficulty fitting in, and likely to feel like outsiders at selective and elite colleges, where the dominant social space is elite and white. They become aware of their regional accents and feel inadequate in their linguistic ability. Comparing themselves to their elite peers, students become self-conscious about their modest life-styles, such as where, what, and how they eat. When most students are wealthy and share similar social experiences, such as vacationing in Europe during the summers and ski trips during the winters, it is easy for students from working-class backgrounds to feel excluded and out of place. When working-class students or students of color are not aware of what is expected of them, they are more likely to commit a social faux pas, such as being underdressed at a formal social event or overdressed at a casual one, demonstrating a failure to fit in. Moreover, the elite construct barriers between who is welcome and those who are not; and surface-level stereotypes drive much of the competition in this exclusive social scene. In an erotic marketplace steeped in rewards for objectifying women, there is no room for the LGBTQ community, and eating disorders abound. "I make no bones about the fact that we were not the coolest house. So, we take whoever—we were like, 'Hey, all are welcome, more or less.' . . . I mean, obviously, completely homophobic, and no one is welcome if you are gay, right? . . . And weight is like the number one [cause for] exile from the sorority system."

Beyond the obstacles described above, many of the weekly activities of the Greek system incur mandatory costs for members, and expensive fees make membership difficult for working-class students. Both lower- and middle-class students are not likely to be able to afford participation in the elite social scene, although some take out loans to do so. In sum, classism and racism, among other -isms, marginalize and exclude poor, working-class students, students of color, and others who do not fit into a white, heteronormative, financially elite peer-networking scene.

HOOKING UP

Many elite schools have deep pockets of rituals and cultural artifacts that uphold traditional norms which advantage men, wealthy, and white students. For example, most of the parties are organized by fraternity members; thus, male students are in charge of who enters and who exits the social space. They are notorious for permitting female non-Greeks and denying male non-Greeks entrance. "There are plenty of GDIs, goddamn independents, who are totally just as social [as fraternity members]. They just, for whatever reason, didn't join a fraternity or sorority. And I'd say, as a girl. it's much easier not to be in a sorority. . . . Like, if you still want to be social, you can still go to a fraternity event. But if you're a guy and you're not in a fraternity, you're kind of screwed."

Fraternity members are in charge of more than the guest list. They often also control the alcohol and the transportation. Women wait in lines outside their dorms for men they don't know to pick them up and take them to unknown locations in order to party. In various other ways, men and women exchange status and resources within a field populated with well-established, highly sexist, sexual norms, such as men using women for sex. As one female student explained,

> I see a lot of girls who want serious relationships, but they feel pressured into just, like, playing this little game of hooking up, because they think, "Well, of course, no guys here are, like, looking for a serious relationship. . . . Even if you have a boyfriend, of course he's gonna look at other girls, even." I see and hear a lot of that just walking around campus, and I feel like guys are probably pressured into that role, too. . . . It just seems like they're supposed to be, like, aloof and, like, cannot express deep emotions. . . . I've talked about this with some girls— like the girl I stayed up talking with last night, And she was telling me she had just gone to one of the big parties, . . . and she said, "Girls feel pressured into playing this little game." And I think guys do too, instead of just, like, "Guys just don't care about girls, and all they want is sex, and that's just how it is."

Statistics consistently show that one in four female undergraduates will experience a sexual assault while in school. Not surprisingly, 36.7 percent of students do not trust campus officials to take student charges of sexual assault or sexual misconduct seriously ("AAU Climate Survey" 2015). Nearly all women who attend college are aware that the hookup culture is highly competitive (Armstrong and Hamilton 2013). By exposing powerful experiences of women, sociologists of education have demonstrated how party rape is institutionalized by the Panhellenic system (Armstrong, Hamilton and Sweeney 2006).

Not only are minority and lower-class men and women systematically marginalized and excluded from the privileged white party space, but also, when sorority pledges of color have to defend their desire to participate in the dominant organized social system on campus during the rush process, they may find that it is not for them. Many minority and low-income students do not find the hookup culture attractive (Wade 2017). One white, working-class student whom we spoke to described feeling displeased with the amount of partying on campus. She associated partying with her apathetic former high-school classmates: "I'm just not as interested in the whole, like, college—the college experience where you go out and party every night. And I think, in my high school, it was sort of like: no one really cared about anything and just kind of went out and partied all the time. And I thought that at college there'd be more people into—you know, have different interests and do all these interesting things. But I just didn't really find that here."

The weekend Greek party scene is made for and maintained by wealthy white males. Thus, it is not surprising that wealthier white students are the ones most likely to participate in and enjoy the hookup culture (Wade 2017). While wealthy white students are partying, lower-income students must, as noted earlier, focus on their studies to maintain high GPAs in order to meet their financial aid, grant, and scholarship requirements. Students of color avoid excessive racist penalties by avoiding the dominant, white, hookup culture and party scene on campus. Thus, undermatched minority students are largely missing from the most elite dating scene on elite campuses.

STUDENT-PROFESSOR RELATIONSHIPS

Another stratified relationship is the student-teacher relationship. A positive student-teacher relationship leads to the student's increased ability to navigate institutional procedures, increased satisfaction with self and university, and an improved academic performance. Professors offer meaningful career counseling, letters of recommendation, and important research, mentoring, and employment opportunities. Beyond being sources for objective resources, professors can act as role models for cultural capital, offer new ideas, and inspire. Unfortunately, class, race, and gender influence these relationships as well, which means those at the bottom of the hierarchy are less likely to reap the rewards of such resources.

Building on the findings of sociologists of class and education, we found in our own work—much as Calarco (chapter 6) found regarding students in elementary school classrooms—that upper-class students at a highly selective private university had an easier time developing relationships with their professors than did working-class students. The upper-class students we interviewed knew they needed face time with their professors and were adept at approaching them, both for objective reasons, such as better grades and letters of recommendation, and for abstract purposes, such as general life and career advice. The topics upper-class students and their professors discussed were broad, ranging from class content to favorite authors to how to launch a start-up, and took up time. Upper-class students reported being just as likely to meet up with a professor during office hours as online or for coffee. One upper-class student mentioned a professor who had approached him to discuss business because of the student's family ties. Upper-class students are used to engaging with their teachers as confidants and facilitators of their success. They appreciate their professors generally and strategize to build and maintain relationships with the ones they are particularly drawn to. As one student we interviewed put it, "Professors are very willing to take care, and be concerned, and try to help. . . . The professors have been phenomenal. They really care that you learn and that you better yourself, and not only in the classroom but outside the classroom."

Beyond having to cope with increased family and work commitments that take extra time and energy, many working-class students also do not experience their professors as available. For example, middle-class students were overwhelmingly critical in their comments about their instructors. They were paying large sums for or taking on large debts to finance their education, and they felt entitled to professors who were their for them. They wanted faculty to attend their events and create fun and inventive courses. However, they reported that their professors prioritized their research over teaching and preferred their upper-class peers to them. Not surprisingly, students who felt this way were unlikely to invest much time or energy in these relationships. Rather than seeing their professors as facilitators, role models, or confidants, they evaluated them according to their performance in relation to students. Middle-class students expressed both respect for and resistance to their professors, sometimes in the same sentence. For example, a middle-class female student responded when asked if she had interactions with professors, "Not really. I've had one this year with the second professor that I respect. Everyone else I don't have a feeling for, I don't really like, I don't really appreciate." Later, she added, "I don't feel like faculty here really gives a fuck that you are there. And they don't really, unless you are offering something to them. . . . [For example], if your dad was a founder in the field of something that they can get ahead in. Professors here are too caught up in making money, I think."

Middle-class students' critiques of their professors reflected their internalized sense of weariness about their high-cost education. They expected to be fairly rewarded for their years of schooling, and on campus they faced the reality of an unjust system. As they referenced their upper-class peers, they became cynical and critical of the university and its pillars: their professors. For example, many middle-class students were stressed about their education loan repayments and wanted their professors to focus on them, not the professors' research.

Students from lower-class origins arrive on campus equipped with a different class perspective. Relative to their peers, and given their family history, their arrival on campus signals they have undoubtedly made it and are on the right track. They expect their hard work will continue to be rewarded. Their internalized class status prompts them to defer to authority figures; and, as expected, lower-class students report looking up to and admiring their professors. They minimize their student-teacher interactions out of respect, discomfort, and intimidation, and in response to what they consider appropriate. In turn, their time with faculty is often limited to before or after class and office hours; locations and conversation topics are similarly bounded. "I don't interact a lot with professors one-on-one. I tried to go to study hours for my professors, but they are during the times that I work and during the times I have class, so it's just been very hard. And sometimes I'm not sure what to talk to the professors about, and sometimes I can be super, super awkward with adults. So I don't want to go to office hours and just be super awkward and not know what to talk about with them."

Lower-class students at elite universities often attach a strong sense of meaning to being a college student. They typically come from families in which they are the first to go to college (see Lisa Nunn, chapter 7). They also tend to have been supported somewhere: if not in a high school program, then on campus; and if not in either of these, a community college instructor or other community advocate likely has helped groom them. For example, a working-class Asian American student described how her high school helped prepare her for the work she would do at a highly selective university.

> My high school was very hard compared to my elementary school, so I struggled more with feeling unprepared in high school. I feel like my high school prepared me pretty well. Yeah, the jump from elementary school to high school was very big, because I went to a public elementary school in Chinatown. So, it was very underfunded, and the teachers weren't very strict, and there were a lot of students who didn't take academics seriously. But my mom always pushed me to take academics very seriously, so I studied really hard in elementary school, and then I just tested into a magnet high school. And that high school helped me prepare for here.

Despite the serious efforts of others to transfer cultural and social capital to underrepresented poor and minority students in order to help them fit in on campus, the lower-class students of color in our study who had experienced scaffolding and mentoring programs still, unlike upper-class students, saw professors as traditional authority figures. Some student-mentoring programs are rigorous. These programs work to develop traditionally marginalized students' sense of belonging within an elite and unfamiliar space, one that can present as hostile. At times students attend extra classes for years, all designed to familiarize them with the campus space and climate. Good scaffolding programs invest in cohorts of poor students of color, so they arrive on campus with a group of friends. Similar programs have helped low-income and minority students across the country.

Instructors are part of an important network of cultural and social capital. The race, class, and gender of both the student and the teacher affect the quantity and quality of this relationship. Upper-class white students are best positioned to reap the rewards of this limited resource, compared to students of color and working-class students.

STRATIFIED PATHWAYS OUT OF UNIVERSITY

The competition on campus is stiff because the payoffs are real. A handshake over a cocktail has closed many market deals and trades. Millions of future husbands and wives meet at fraternity parties. In a world where who you know still determines where and how you will make your living, networking well among America's finest can net lifelong returns.

Every year, in perhaps the ultimate competition, approximately two million recently graduated bachelor's-degree holders head into the workforce. Students of color, working-class students, and women are penalized in this marketplace. Working-class students carry a lot of debt, with student loans amounting to, on average, thirty thousand dollars per graduate (Houle and Warner 2017). The prestige of a degree does not shield poor women of color—who are at the bottom of the class, gender, and racial hierarchies—from being presumed incompetent (Muhs et al. 2012). To be clear, the system doesn't work for *most* people after graduation. White men, who are located at the top of race and gender hierarchies, lead the nation in suicide rates. Wealthy white men at highly selective universities are not immune to this reality, but they have more resources compared to their counterparts elsewhere.

Even if one doesn't land a job directly from a friend of a fraternity brother's parent or equivalent, socializing with fraternity members for hours and years on end guarantees that some of the benefits of the collective elite will transfer from university to salary. Evidence of this is found in hiring decisions within the nation's top firms, which are more heavily shaped by applicants' socioeconomic backgrounds than by individual merit. Familiarity with artifacts of elite leisure signal in-group membership to upper-class employers (Rivera 2015). In fact, at some elite firms and corporations, a potential employee's hobbies and self-presentation are more important than job-related competency in hiring decisions.

Members of elite circles are funneled into the most powerful jobs in the finance, consulting, and high-tech industries (Binder, Davis, and Bloom 2015). As students await their first postgraduation jobs, employers are also searching for them. Elite universities have always served as a bridge between the best and the brightest minds and the best companies with the most perks. Since early in the first decade of the twenty-first century, university and corporate partnership programs have thrived. These programs pay annual fees to university career centers in a competition for access to elite university students (Davis and Binder 2016).

And these are all very important avenues by which the elite maintain and reproduce their power. The stakes are high, with members of all classes feeling pressure to maintain status and avoid downward mobility. Many students from working-class and minority backgrounds don't make it to graduation on elite university campuses. Confronted with exclusion and feeling relatively deprived, they leave. For all the students who persist, the competition for postgraduation employment is fierce and structured with persistent patterns of racism, classism, and sexism.

CONCLUDING THOUGHTS

Beautiful college and university campuses serve as a playground for privileged children from wealthy families. Within these privileged, white spaces, elite colleges and universities groom their students for powerful and esteemed positions in society. Students get opportunities to attend talks, luncheons, and receptions with world-renowned scholars and Nobel laureates, famous and wealthy alumni, and guest speakers who are influential political and business leaders. Students learn how to dress, converse, and embody elite status with ease in a variety of forums. Class-privileged white students arrive on campus with more economic, social, and cultural resources than poor and working-class and students of color. All things being equal, they have less to worry about in terms of fitting in, and they are better equipped than their poor and working-class peers and peers of color to take advantage of the many opportunities within and outside the classroom.

Upper-class white students participate in student government, university scholarship committees, campus planning organizations, and off-campus internships more often than, and study abroad more often than, their poor and working-class peers and peers of color. Elite students use extracurricular activities as a means to develop their character, leadership skills, community, and ability to succeed in highly competitive organizations. In addition, participation in these types of activities and in clubs connect them to valuable sources of social capital, such as high-level administrators on campus and local business and political leaders off campus.

Without the financial, cultural, and social resources of their affluent and often white peers, working-class and minority students are less likely to adjust well, are more likely to take a longer time adjusting, and, if successful at fitting in, are less likely to be positioned to reap the many opportunities available on campus. Individuals are unable to change their racial makeup, and young people are often firmly rooted in a class position. Thus, as many researchers suggest, universities should be held accountable for providing an environment where students of all backgrounds have equal opportunities to thrive. We know from research discussed here and elsewhere that scaffolding programs work. These programs empower students so that they are better able to navigate a university, whose culture at times works to subtract from, rather than add to, their dignity. Currently, most scaffolding programs target traditionally at-risk low-income students of color. Universities can implement these programs more broadly to capture all working-class and marginalized students. In short, many more students can benefit from such care.

Universities should also facilitate dialogue about how campus life reproduces inequalities. When campuses marginalize discussions of class, race, and gender, inequality spreads. But the reverse is also true: if campuses prioritize discussions of race, class, and gender, new frontiers can unfold. Universities can model more sustainable practices for their students. Beyond guiding students into high-status, high-wealth careers, campuses can continue to fund and encourage high-impact practices such as investment in student scaffolding programs, race and ethnic studies, women's studies, and the humanities and social sciences.

Further, the university can invest in professors and instructors who are not at the top of these hierarchies. Students of color and working-class students likely feel more at home with professors who come from similar backgrounds. Furthermore, universities can provide professors with the time and resources to focus on teaching and student support. Students of color and students from poor and working-class backgrounds (as well as many middle-class students) may also need direct guidance about how to approach instructors.

The university can work with the Panhellenic Greek system to level the playing field in terms of class, perhaps by providing scholarships to working-class students. By turning a blind eye to the illicit behaviors of those engaging in Greek life, universities ensure that sexism and racism will continue to matter for student discipline. If universities want to follow the law in terms of sexual assault and underage drinking, they must find a way to reorganize Greek life on campus.

The university is in a tough position. To make significant progress on these issues, it would have to disrupt the racial, class-based, and gendered hierarchies and the status quo in direct and powerful ways by, for example, reducing student tuition and increasing student scaffolding programs. Yet the university is steeped in tradition, and it benefits from its location on the privileged side of many hierarchies. It relies on its alumni to donate money to its endowment. In many ways it is coupled so tightly with the status quo that to resist oppression in several areas would lead to such dramatic shifts in how education currently exists that, afterward, the university may not be recognizable to those of us who have benefited from its exclusivity.

There are roots within all of us that we must carefully attend to in order to avoid reproducing a racist, classist, and sexist system. The pressure of the -isms rests on and within all of us, in one way or another. Thus, we must, as the caretakers of the university, its students, and faculty, recognize that the space we occupy has a heavy legacy of wealth, whiteness, and patriarchy. Our stratified sociopolitical economic system, whose status quo has long perpetuated classism, racism, and sexism, permeates our educational system. Because we carry our culture within us, the teachers, students, and university administrators who consciously oppose classism, racism, and sexism, may unconsciously perpetuate expectations and biases based on this system, even when they consciously oppose these -isms. In order to make a new, more equitable system of higher education, we must participate in that new vision. Gathering information is a great way to be ready to do the right thing when the opportunity arises. Existing within a system that regularly disempowers large numbers of individuals based on their in-group status guarantees we will be given opportunities to resist oppression. Change can cause discomfort, especially for those who are accustomed to privilege. That is okay.

CASE STUDY 3 REVIEW

Discussion Questions

1. How is the college experience different for students from different economic and racial backgrounds? Who is more likely to fit in quickly and fit in well at a highly selective university: a student from the upper class or a working-class student? Why? A white student or a nonwhite student? Why?

2. Who is most likely to invite his or her professor to coffee: a student from the lower, middle, or upper class?

3. What microaggressions have you witnessed or experienced on campus? Have they been based on class, race, gender, or some other in group/out group status? What might be done to decrease the presence of microaggressions on campus?

4. How have you knowingly or unknowingly perpetuated one of the top three -isms discussed in this case study?

5. What does it mean to say that race, gender, and class intersect? How might this intersectionality affect the university experience of a working-class female student of color?

6. Using what we have learned about out-group-based oppression, what other sectors of the student body likely suffer from out-group microaggressions? How might out-group slights affect this population's experience on campus?

7. If you were a university policy maker, how might you level the playing field, based on class? On race? On gender? If you had to choose one of the three hierarchies to dismantle first, which would you choose and why?

8. How and why are these -isms allowed to persist? Is there an institutionalization of complicity? If so, are you a part of it? If you are, then how so, and why? If not, what other -isms are institutionalized? How so, and why?

9. Can a class-disadvantaged person be classist? If so, are there limits to this person's ability to disperse classism, compared to the ability of a class-advantaged person? Whose -isms are more powerful systematically? How and why?

Suggestions for Further Reading

Armstrong, Elizabeth A., and Laura T. Hamilton. 2013. *Paying for the Party: How College Maintains Inequality.* Cambridge, MA: Harvard University Press.

Rivera, Lauren A. 2015. *Pedigree: How Elite Students Get Elite Jobs.* Princeton, NJ: Princeton University Press.

Robinson, K. J., and J. Roksa. 2016. "Counselors, Information, and High School College-Going Culture: Inequalities in the College Application Process." *Research in Higher Education* 57:845–68.

Stevens, Mitchell L. 2007. *Creating a Class: College Admissions and the Education of Elites.* Cambridge, MA: Harvard University Press.

Thiele, Megan, and Brian Gillespie. "Educated among Friends? Class Navigations of an Elite Social Scene." Forthcoming. *Sociological Perspectives.*

References

"AAU Climate Survey on Sexual Assault and Sexual Misconduct." 2015. Washington, DC: Association of American Universities. www.aau.edu/key-issues/aau-climate-survey-sexual-assault-and-sexual-misconduct-2015.

Armstrong, Elizabeth A., and Laura T. Hamilton. 2013. *Paying for the Party: How College Maintains Inequality.* Cambridge, MA: Harvard University Press.

Armstrong, Elizabeth A., Laura Hamilton, and Brian Sweeney. 2006. "Sexual Assault on Campus: A Multilevel, Integrative Approach to Party Rape." *Society* 53 (4): 483–99.

Ashkenas, Jeremy, Haeyoun Park, and Adam Pearce. 2017. "Even with Affirmative Action, Blacks and Hispanics Are More Underrepresented at Top Colleges Than Thirty-Five Years Ago." *New York Times,* August 24. www.nytimes.com/interactive/2017/08/24/us/affirmative-action.html.

Binder, Amy J., Daniel B. Davis, and Nick Bloom. 2015. "Career Funneling: How Elite Students Learn to Define and Desire 'Prestigious' Jobs." *Sociology of Education* 39 (1): 20–39.

Chappell, Bill, and Merrit Kennedy. 2019. "U.S. Charges Dozens of Parents, Coaches In Massive College Admissions Scandal." *National Public Radio: Education.* Available at: https://www.npr.org/2019/03/12/702539140/u-s-accuses-actresses-others-of-fraud-in-wide-college-admissions-scandal. Last accessed April 19, 2019.

Chetty, Raj, John N. Friedman, Emmanuel Saez, Nicholas Turner, and Danny Yagan. 2017. "Mobility Report Cards: The Role of Colleges in Intergenerational Mobility." NBER Working Paper Series, TIRNO-16-E-00013. Cambridge, MA: National Bureau of Economic Research. www.equality-of-opportunity.org/papers/coll_mrc_paper.pdf.

Davis, Daniel, and Amy Binder. 2016. "Selling Students: The Rise of Corporate Partnership Programs in University Career Centers." *Research in the Sociology of Organizations* 46:395–422. 10.1108/S0733-558X20160000046013.

Houle, Jason, and Cody Warner. 2017. "Into the Red and Back to the Nest? Student Debt, College Completion, and Returning to the Parental Home among Young Adults." *Sociology of Education* 90:89–108.

Khan, Shamus R. 2010. "Getting In: How Elite Schools Play the College Game." In *Educating Elites: Class Privilege and Educational Advantage,* edited by Adam Howard and Rubén A. Gaztambide-Fernandez, 97–112. Lanham, MD: Rowman and Littlefield Education.

McDonough, Patricia M. 1997. *Choosing Colleges: How Social Class and Schools Structure Opportunity.* New York: State University of New York Press.

Muhs, Gabriella Gutiérrez y, Yolanda Flores Niemann, Carmen G. González, and Angela P. Harris, eds. 2012. *Presumed Incompetent: The Intersections of Race and Class for Women in Academia.* Logan: Utah State University Press.

Rivera, Lauren A. 2015. *Pedigree: How Elite Students Get Elite Jobs.* Princeton, NJ: Princeton University Press.

Stevens, Mitchell L. 2007. *Creating a Class: College Admissions and the Education of Elites.* Cambridge, MA: Harvard University Press.

Stevens, Mitchell L., Elizabeth A. Armstrong, and Richard Arum. 2008. "Sieve, Incubator, Temple, Hub: Empirical and Theoretical Advances in the Sociology of Higher Education." *Annual Review of Sociology* 34:127–51.

Stuber, Jenny. 2009. "Class, Culture, and Participation in the Collegiate Extra-Curriculum." *Sociological Forum* 24 (4): 877–900.

Thiele, Megan. 2016. "Resource or Obstacle?: Classed Reports of Student-Faculty Relations." *Sociological Quarterly* 57: 333–55.

Thiele, Megan, and Brian Gillespie. 2017. "Social Stratification at the Top Rung: Classed Reports of Students' Social Experiences on a Selective University Campus." *Sociological Perspectives* 60 (1): 113–31.

US Department of Education, National Center for Education Statistics. 2018. "Number of Educational Institutions, by Level and Control of Institution: Selected Years, 1980–81 through 2014–15," table 105.50. In *Digest of Education Statistics 2016*. NCES 2017–094. Washington, DC: National Center for Education Statistics, Institute of Education Sciences, US Department of Education.

Wade, Lisa. 2017. *American Hookup: The New Cultures of Sex on Campus.* New York: W. W. Norton.

13

School Segregation by Race/ Ethnicity and Economic Status

ANN OWENS, UNIVERSITY OF SOUTHERN CALIFORNIA

EDITORS' NOTE

Over the last several chapters, you've encountered several educational practices that contribute to the production and maintenance of inequality within schools. While sociologists do not generally think that educators intentionally produce disparities among students, they generally agree that these disparities result from practices like tracking and the disproportionate use of exclusionary discipline. University of Southern California sociologist Ann Owens reminds us that within-school inequalities are only part of the story.

As Owens makes clear, American schools have long been highly **segregated** by both race and socioeconomic status. School segregation has multiple sources. As Eschmann and Payne point out in chapter 4 of this volume, segregation plays an important role in maintaining white students' advantages in American schools. As a result, school segregation feeds off of many of the same long-standing social forces that racist patterns in American life depend on.

But one aspect of school segregation is unique: a defining organizational characteristic of American public education is its highly **decentralized** structure. While many other highly developed countries have a strong tradition of central funding and planning in education, students in the United States traditionally attend neighborhood schools that are funded by local property taxes and governed by local school boards. Social scientists and policy makers have long debated the merits of this structure of schooling. Decentralization and a tradition of local control, advocates argue, allow American schools to serve the disparate needs of diverse student bodies. But all agree that decentralization has historically contributed to segregation and inequality, allowing education leaders to assign students to different schools on the basis of race and providing tools for white leaders to resist federal efforts to desegregate schools.

As you read this chapter, consider the following: Were the schools you attended racially or socioeconomically segregated? If so, what accounts for that segregation, and how might your education have been different had you attended more (or less) racially or socioeconomically diverse schools?

KEY POINTS

- Both minority and white students now attend schools with more minority peers (particularly Hispanic) than in the past, because there are fewer white and more minority students than ever before.
- Evenness measures that take this change in student racial composition into account show that school racial segregation has declined slightly since the 1980s.
- Economic segregation among schools and school districts increased in the 1990s and the decade that followed.
- Minority (black and Hispanic) students attend school with more low-income students than white students do.
- Segregation between school districts, not just schools, is an important source of inequality.
- Racial and economic segregation between neighborhoods is a key contributor to school segregation.
- School segregation contributes to educational achievement gaps.

INTRODUCTION

The US educational system is built on the promise that all children have equal opportunities to learn. Has that promise been kept? Or do children face different barriers and opportunities depending on their racial/ethnic background or on how much money their family earns? One measure of unequal opportunities is segregation—the degree to which students from different racial/ethnic backgrounds or with different family incomes attend different schools. Policies have aimed to integrate schools since even before the famous 1954 *Brown v. Board of Education of Topeka* decision of the US Supreme Court. The first court ruling to outlaw school segregation was California's 1947 case *Mendez v. Westminster School District of Orange County,* which addressed segregation of Mexican American students. *Brown* was the key federal court decision that aimed to stop the practice of separate school systems for black and white students, which was common and legal before 1954, upheld by the *Plessy v. Ferguson* Supreme Court decision in 1896. The *Brown* decision declared that "separate educational facilities are inherently unequal": as long as black and white students were educated in separate schools, black students would receive an inferior education. Despite over sixty years of policies aimed at integrating schools, and research showing the negative consequences of segregation for students' educational success, minority and low-income children today still attend school with a greater proportion of minority and low-income peers than white students do.

This chapter describes segregation by race and by income between schools and school districts in the United States. In doing so, it addresses several key questions: What is segregation, and how do researchers measure it? How has segregation by race and income between schools and school districts changed over time? What factors contribute to segregation? Is segregation harmful to students' educational outcomes? What policies have been put into place to address segregation?

INTELLECTUAL ROOTS

Free public schools were established in the United States in the late nineteenth century to prepare students for the workforce, to socialize students, particularly new European immigrants, into American social norms, and to exert social control over youth. Progressive ideals are reflected in the intended goals of the public education system: the public school system was established to be an equalizing force. All students, regardless of their social background, would have equal access to educational opportunities, which would help them compete on a level playing field for future economic opportunities. The ideal of equal opportunity is tied to values of fairness, self-reliance, and the American Dream—anyone can succeed in the United States, regardless of background, if he or she works hard enough. But the educational system has never truly provided equal opportunities for all. Blacks and other racial/ethnic minorities were initially excluded from schools serving white students, especially in the southern states, and low-income students attended schools that had worse funding and supplies and lower-quality teachers than schools attended by high-income students. School segregation on the basis of race/ethnicity or family income violates the ideal of equal opportunity, because students' social backgrounds determine their access to quality schooling.

The study of school segregation relates to the broader fields of social stratification and inequality. Scholars of stratification study the causes and consequences of inequality in our society. These scholars often investigate social mobility—whether children move up or down the social or economic ladder as they become adults. Segregated schooling limits upward mobility by providing unequal opportunities to students depending on their social backgrounds, maintaining inequality by race and by income. Minority and low-income students lag behind higher-status students in childhood, and they have fewer opportunities to get ahead as they grow up.

Studies of segregation also have their roots in policy studies. Researchers have carefully documented segregation over the past sixty years to trace progress following the *Brown* decision. Did the policies adopted by segregated districts successfully integrate schools? What new aspects of segregation have arisen as the student body population has become more racially diverse? While *Brown* focused on racial segregation, how has economic segregation changed? Concerns about inequality and its solutions have motivated researchers to examine segregation. One critical feature of this research has been how to define and measure segregation.

RESEARCH METHODS

Segregation measures the degree to which student populations from different racial/ethnic backgrounds or with different family incomes attend different schools. Researchers use two main types of segregation measures: exposure indices and evenness indices (Massey and Denton 1988). Exposure indices measure the average makeup of a school attended by a student from a particular racial/ethnic or economic group—the other students he or she is exposed to at school. For example, researchers can report that a black student in the United States attends a school where, on average, 48 percent of other students are also black, or that the average poor student attends a school where 67 percent of other students are also poor, as was the case in 2013. When researchers measure the exposure of a student to other members of his own racial/ethnic or economic group, they call it an isolation index.

The second set of measures, evenness indices, estimates how evenly students are represented in schools or districts, relative to the composition of the population. For example, if a school district's student body is 50 percent white, 15 percent black, 25 percent Hispanic, 5 percent Asian, and 5 percent students of other races, evenness indices measure how much schools deviate from that composition. If there were no segregation (and thus complete integration), every school would have this same makeup. One common evenness measure is called the dissimilarity index. It is measured on a scale from 0 to 1 and can be interpreted as measuring what proportion of students of a certain group would have to be redistributed—that is, would have to change schools—to achieve total integration. For example, if the black-white dissimilarity index were 0.68, it would mean that 68 percent of black students would have to change schools to achieve integration—so that each school's composition matched the racial/ethnic makeup of the district.

Researchers measure segregation at several different geographic or administrative levels. Segregation is measured between schools and also between school districts. Segregation can be measured within the entire United States, states, cities, metropolitan areas, or, in the case of segregation between schools, within districts. For example, a researcher could examine the degree to which students were segregated by race between districts in the state of California, or the degree to which students were segregated by race between schools in the Los Angeles Unified School District.

To measure segregation, researchers rely on data collected by the US Department of Education. Schools report information about the racial/ethnic and economic characteristics of their students each year. The classification of students' racial/ethnic backgrounds has changed over time as the United States has become more racially and ethnically diverse. Today, students are identified as non-Hispanic white, non-Hispanic black, Hispanic, Asian, Hawaiian Native/Pacific Islander, American Indian/Alaska Native, or members of two or more races. Segregation can be calculated between two groups, such as between blacks and whites, or among many or even all groups.

The only economic information schools report about students is whether they are eligible to receive free or reduced-price lunches. Eligibility is based on their family incomes; families with incomes that are less than 130 percent of the poverty threshold for their family size qualify for free lunches, and families with incomes that are less than 185 percent of the poverty threshold qualify for reduced-price lunches. For example, in 2016, the federal government determined that the poverty threshold for a family of four was $24,300, so students whose family incomes were less than $24,300 × 130 percent, which is equal to $31,590, qualified for free lunches. Researchers can also measure segregation between school districts using data collected by the Census Bureau. The Census Bureau collects data on family income in more categories than free-lunch eligibility, so researchers can examine segregation between, for example, the very rich and the middle class.

KEY EMPIRICAL FINDINGS

Racial Segregation: Early Years

In the first years after the *Brown* decision in 1954, school segregation was slow to change. *Brown* abolished de jure segregation—segregation established by law: in this case, separate school systems for whites and minorities. It did little to address de facto segregation—segregation in existence "by fact" but not supported or mandated by law. The court ruling did not require districts to implement strong policies for achieving integration, instead merely creating the option for black students to move to white schools. Schools remained segregated de facto because blacks and whites lived in separate neighborhoods that fed into different schools, and because whites did not want to send their children to school with black children. As a result, segregation changed little from

1954 to the late 1960s (Coleman, Kelly, and Moore 1975; Welch and Light 1987; Orfield 2001; Clotfelter 2004). The majority of black students, especially in the South, continued to attend schools where virtually all students were black.

Beginning in 1968, several subsequent Supreme Court and local court cases required segregated school districts to undertake desegregation and put school assignment policies into place to achieve a racial mix. In particular, in *Green v. County School Board of New Kent County,* the Supreme Court ruled that the school board was required to develop a specific plan and take steps toward achieving an integrated system, rather than put the onus on individual black families to enroll in white schools. Many other districts where legal action was not undertaken voluntarily developed desegregation plans. The plans varied; some common examples were to combine formerly all-black and all-white schools at the elementary, middle, and high school levels, or to consider student race when determining which students enrolled in which schools. As a result, school segregation began to decline. Nationwide, in 1968, blacks attended school where 22 percent of students were white, on average, and this increased to 33 percent by 1972 (Coleman, Kelly and Moore 1975). In 1968, over 50 percent of black students attended schools that were 90–100 percent black; by 1980, only one-third of black students attended such hypersegregated schools (Orfield 1983; Welch and Light 1987). The within-district black-white dissimilarity index declined from .81 in 1968 to .48 in 1990 (Logan and Oakley 2004). Racial segregation declined substantially from 1968 through the mid-1970s and continued to decline, at a slower rate, through the 1980s.

Although considerable desegregation progress was made following *Brown* and *Green,* it did not come easily. In the late 1950s, the National Association for the Advancement of Colored People (NAACP) helped register black students in white schools in the South, but these students faced fierce opposition to their attendance. One famous case was that of Ruby Bridges, a black kindergartener who enrolled in a formerly all-white school in New Orleans in 1960 (see figure 22). An angry white mob met this six-year-old girl with racial slurs and thrown objects, and when she did make her way inside, both teachers and parents boycotted the school, refusing to teach or send their children there. Another famous case was the Little Rock Nine, nine black students who, in 1957, were physically blocked from entering their white high school by the Arkansas National Guard—called up by the state's governor—as well as by white students and parents.

There was also fierce opposition to specific school integration plans in many cities, mainly by white parents and students. In Boston in the mid-1970s, white activists led marches and protests against the plan to bus white students to schools in black neighborhoods and vice versa. Some of the opposition turned violent, including white teenagers attacking a black civil rights attorney, creating a memorable image of the youths hitting him with an American flag. White parents also protested the school integration plans by sending their children to

Figure 22. Federal marshals accompany Ruby Bridges in 1960 as she becomes the first African American student to attend William Franz Elementary School in Louisiana. Source: uncredited US Department of Justice photographer.

private schools, or they moved out of districts undergoing integration to avoid sending their children to racially integrated schools. In the South, private schools known as "segregation academies" were created specifically so parents had such an option, since *Brown* does not apply to private schools. Often, state laws helped parents create these schools at minimal cost, using state grants to cover tuition.

Racial Segregation Trends in Recent Years

Conclusions about school segregation since the 1980s depend on what measure is used (Reardon and Owens 2014). Measured with exposure indices, segregation has increased (Orfield 2001; Orfield and Lee 2007). Figure 23 shows the average composition of schools attended by students of different races in 2013–14. The far right bar in figure 23 shows the racial composition of the US public school student body; so if there were no segregation, the average school

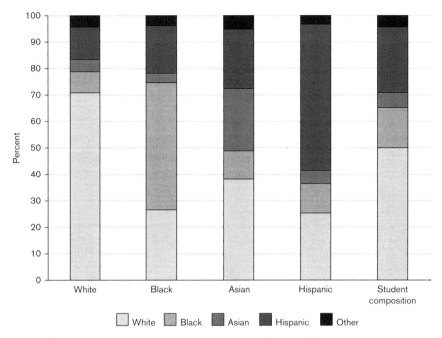

Figure 23. Average school composition experienced by students of different races, compared to composition of all students, 2013–14. Sources: Common Core of Data, *Public Elementary/ Secondary School Universe Survey Data*, National Center for Education Statistics, 2013–14; and National Center for Education Statistics, table 203.50 in *Digest of Education Statistics*, 2016.

composition for students of each race should match this bar. As the other bars in the illustration demonstrate, this is not the case. In the 2013–14 school year, the average black student attended a school that was 27 percent white, compared to 36 percent in 1988 and 32 percent in 1970. The average Hispanic student attended a school that was 26 percent white, compared to 30 percent in 1990 and 44 percent in 1970. The proportion of black and Hispanic students attending schools that are 90–100 percent minority (black or Hispanic) also increased in the first decade of the twenty-first century (for Hispanic students, this proportion has been steadily increasing since 1968). Overall, exposure measures indicate that, since the mid-1980s (or earlier, for Hispanics), school segregation has been increasing. Minority students attend school with fewer white and more minority students today than in the past.

Why do black and Hispanic students attend school with fewer white students today than in the mid-1980s? Demographic changes are the key reason. Over time, the US population, particularly the public school population, has become more racially diverse. The proportion of schoolchildren who are white declined from 80 percent in 1970 to 50 percent in 2013. In contrast, the proportion of schoolchildren who are Hispanic increased fivefold, from 5 percent in 1970 to 25 percent in 2013. The Asian population also increased, from less than 1 percent to over 5 percent during this time, while the black population remained stable at about 15 percent. Because the Hispanic student population has increased and the white population has declined substantially, it is not surprising that black and Hispanic students attend school with fewer white and more minority students. White students, too, attend school with fewer white and more minority students than in the past.

While exposure indices indicate that segregation has increased since the mid-1980s, evenness measures do not. Remember that evenness measures compare school composition to the composition of the broader population. Therefore, evenness measures take the dramatic change in student body racial composition into account and examine whether students are sorted across schools more unevenly, in comparison to the overall racial composition, than in the past. Dissimilarity indices and other evenness measures show that racial segregation did not increase from the mid-1980s through the 2010s (Logan 2004; Stroub and Richards 2013). Students have become slightly more evenly distributed across schools—segregation has declined slightly in large metropolitan areas. This is true of black-white segregation, as well as segregation between white and all nonwhite students and segregation among nonwhite students—black, Hispanic, and Asian students have become more integrated with each other. Although segregation has declined, it remains high—the overall black-white dissimilarity index, taking segregation between both districts and schools into account, was about 0.66 in 2012.

Evenness indices can measure segregation between *schools* or between *districts* within the same city, region, state, or the entire country. As desegregation orders or voluntary integration plans were put into place in districts in the late 1960s, some white parents chose to move out of their school districts to avoid school integration. This "white flight" contributed to rising segregation *between* school districts—school districts were becoming homogenously white or homogenously minority, often reflecting city-suburban divides. In 1974, the Supreme Court ruled in *Milliken v. Bradley* that school desegregation orders did not apply *across* districts—districts are not required to enroll students from outside their own district to achieve integration. In the first decade of the twenty-first century, racial segregation between school districts in large metropolitan areas declined slightly, but less so than segregation between schools within school districts. Segregation between districts contributes more to overall school segregation today than in the past. That is, racially homogenous districts are a key reason that many schools are racially homogenous. For example, the Los Angeles Unified School District is about 75 percent Hispanic, while the nearby Beverly Hills Unified School District is nearly 75 percent white. Even if there were no segregation between schools within the

Los Angeles district—if all schools had the same racial composition—each school would be 75 percent Hispanic. Segregation between that district and surrounding districts is a key reason why Los Angeles Unified schools are majority-minority.

Economic Segregation Trends

Estimates of economic segregation between schools have been available only since around 1990. Exposure and evenness measures support the same conclusion: since 1990, economic segregation has increased between schools and between school districts. I estimated that, measured with an evenness index, segregation between schools on the basis of free-lunch eligibility increased by 40 percent from 1991 to 2012 in the one hundred largest districts, with a sharp increase following the Great Recession in 2008 (Owens, Reardon, and Jencks 2016). In 1993, the average student eligible for free lunch attended school where 52 percent of students were eligible for free lunch. By 2013, that figure increased to 67 percent—the average student eligible for free lunch attended a school where over two-thirds of his or her classmates were also from low-income families.

My research shows that income segregation also increased between school districts from 1990 to 2010 in the one hundred largest metropolitan areas, by over 15 percent (Owens, Reardon, and Jencks 2016). For school districts, income data beyond free-lunch eligibility are available, so we can examine whether rich, middle-income, or poor families are the most segregated. From 1990 to 2010, high-income families were the most segregated from all others—students from high-income families were most likely to enroll in districts with peers from families like theirs. Like racial segregation, economic segregation between schools is driven in large part by economic segregation between districts. Many large urban school districts enroll student bodies whose majorities are composed of students from low-income families. Without integration between richer and poorer districts, economically diverse schools are hard to achieve.

Overall, rising income segregation between schools and between school districts means that, since at least 1990, low-income students attend school with more low-income peers, and high-income students attend school with more high-income peers. No Supreme Court decision requires school districts to adopt economic-integration plans, though a growing number have created voluntary student-assignment policies aimed at socioeconomic integration. In 2007, the Supreme Court ruled in the *Parents Involved in Community Schools v. Seattle School District No. 1* that districts voluntarily using school integration plans (those not under mandatory desegregation orders after *Brown*) cannot assign students to schools on the basis of individual students' racial/ethnic backgrounds. Considering students' socioeconomic backgrounds is permitted,

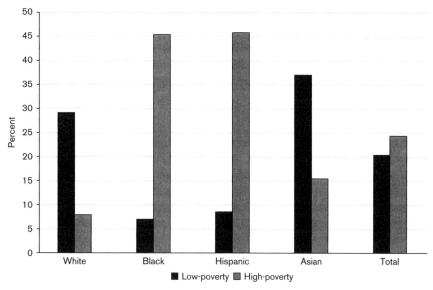

Figure 24. Percentage of students by race attending low-poverty and high-poverty schools, fall 2014. Source: National Center for Education Statistics, table 216.60 in *Digest of Education Statistics*, 2016.

so many districts have changed their policies as a result. For example, in Cambridge, Massachusetts, students do not simply attend their neighborhood school. Instead, parents and students rank their school choices, but the student assignment procedure balances these preferences with the district's goal of enrolling an equal proportion of students who are free-lunch eligible at each school.

The Connection between Race and Income

Because black and Hispanic families in the United States tend to have lower incomes, on average, than white or Asian families, the high levels of racial segregation experienced by black and Hispanic students means they attend school with more low-income peers than white or Asian students (Orfield, Kucsera, and Siegel-Hawley 2012; U.S. Government Accountability Office 2016). In 2014, as figure 24 shows, nearly 30 percent of white students and 40 percent of Asian students attended low-poverty schools—where 25 percent of students or fewer are eligible for free or reduced-price lunch. In contrast, only 7 percent of black students and 9 percent of Hispanic students attended low-poverty schools. Black and Hispanic students are overrepresented in high-poverty schools, where more than 75 percent of students qualify for free or reduced-price lunch. The gray bar on the far right of figure 24 indicates that, nationwide,

24 percent of all students attended high-poverty schools. Nearly twice that figure, over 45 percent, of both black and Hispanic students attended high-poverty schools, compared to 8 percent of white and 15 percent of Asian students.

The poverty composition of schools attended primarily by Hispanic students and, particularly, black students has increased more than that of schools attended primarily by white and Asian students. From 2003 to 2013, the proportion of students eligible for free or reduced-price lunch in the average white student's school increased thirteen points, from 27 to 40 percent, while the poverty rate in the average black student's school increased fifteen points, from 53 to 68 percent. Overall, black and Hispanic students attend school with more poor students than white students do.

Factors Contributing to School Segregation

Why are schools and districts so segregated? A key reason is because neighborhoods in the United States are also highly segregated by race and by income. In most places, public school attendance is determined by where a child lives; most schools' attendance zones, or catchment areas, serve the local community. Over time, this link between where a family lives and where a child goes to school has been weakened. In recent years, some districts have adopted open enrollment policies, allowing students to attend any school in the district, and some districts include magnet schools or charter schools, which typically do not serve specific geographic attendance zones. However, as of 2007, 75 percent of children still attended their neighborhood public school (Grady and Bielick 2010). Neighborhood residence remains tightly linked to district enrollment: less than 1 percent of public school children attended school in a district other than the one serving their neighborhood. Therefore, segregated schools reflect segregated neighborhoods. And, in turn, school options contribute to neighborhood segregation because many parents take schools into account when deciding where to live.

Parents' enrollment choices also contribute to school segregation. Some parents may choose to enroll their children in a private school, magnet school, or charter school if they consider their neighborhood school unsatisfactory. White and higher-income parents are particularly likely to make this choice, meaning that public neighborhood schools have higher rates of poor and minority students than the populations found in the area served by the school (Saporito 2003; Saporito and Sohoni 2007). Parents often (consciously or unconsciously) associate minority students with low test scores or a lack of school safety, citing these nonracial reasons for preferring one school over another. Explicitly racial preferences also exist, and recent research shows that, taking into account school characteristics like test scores to compare similar schools, white parents avoid enrolling their children in schools with larger minority populations (Billingham and Hunt 2016). These decisions reduce the number of higher-income and white students in public neighborhood schools, limiting minority and lower-income students' exposure to white or higher-income students. Although the majority of Americans express support for school integration (Boser and Baffour 2017; *Phi Delta Kappan* 2017), student assignment policies that aim directly or indirectly to mix students by race are often met with fierce parental opposition. For example, New York City officials recently proposed rezoning school attendance boundaries so students living in a public housing development would be integrated into predominantly affluent, white schools, which set off months of protests, petitions, and heated hearings, mainly among high-income white parents. In addition to their opposition to changes in the school composition and community, some also noted potential damage to housing values if test scores in the local school were to decline.

Magnet schools were created in the 1970s as a tool for reducing racial segregation. Magnet schools are public schools, but they enroll students from across geographic boundaries—they are one effort to overcome neighborhood segregation being replicated in schools. Magnet schools often have special curricula (e.g., math and science or the arts), and they are often designed to draw high-income, white, and/or suburban students into urban schools. Evidence on the role of magnet schools in reducing segregation is mixed. On the one hand, magnet schools tend to be more diverse than traditional public schools, so they provide minority students with exposure to more white students. On the other hand, magnet schools may attract many higher-income or white students, or students with highly educated, involved parents, to a district, pulling these students out of traditional public schools in the rest of the district.

RESEARCH FRONTIERS

New technology and data availability allow researchers to investigate links between neighborhoods, school-attendance boundaries, and district boundary lines. Advances in collecting geospatial data permit researchers to understand how neighborhoods are connected to schools and districts so they can answer questions about the relationship between neighborhood and school segregation, or about how school options affect parents' residential choices. National data on students' test scores at the school and district levels are also becoming available, owing to the continued use of accountability tests, and researchers are taking advantage of these data to track inequalities on the basis of race and income.

Researchers continue to investigate the consequences of school segregation for children's educational outcomes. *Why* segregation is harmful for low-income and minority peers is particularly of interest. What role does unequal school funding play? Does interacting with higher-income peers make a difference? How are white and high-income students affected by segregation, if at all?

Researchers also continue to study what types of policies are effective at creating integrated schools. Many of the desegregation orders that were put into place in the early 1970s are now ending, and researchers are monitoring what happens in these school districts. Preliminary evidence suggests that schools are resegregating once no policy is in place that requires integration. For example, in Charlotte-Mecklenburg, North Carolina, the race-based school choice plan was abolished in 2002. Since then, the black-white dissimilarity index has increased substantially, and economic segregation has also increased (Mickelson, Smith, and Nelson 2017). This resegregation has increased achievement gaps between black and white students. Court-ordered desegregation ended in Nashville, Tennessee, in 1999, followed by increased segregation. However, achievement gaps between black and white children have not increased there, perhaps because Nashville provided extra resources to high-poverty, minority schools (Gamoran and An 2016). This raises an important question: Is integration necessary, or can policy makers instead increase resources in majority-minority, high-poverty schools? Does this go against the conclusion in *Brown* that separate can never be equal?

Evaluating socioeconomic integration policies is of particular interest, given that economic segregation has been rapidly rising, that the school poverty rate (as measured by the proportion of students eligible for a free or reduced-price lunch) seems to be a key reason why racial segregation is detrimental for minority students, and that the 2007 Supreme Court ruling in the *Parents Involved in Community Schools v. Seattle School District No. 1* case permits voluntary student assignment plans only on the basis of socioeconomic status, not race. Districts are continuing to develop creative ways to achieve socioeconomic integration; and as of 2016, 8 percent of students attended a school in which socioeconomic status was considered in enrollment policies (Potter, Quick, and Davies 2016).

Finally, the concept of school segregation will continue to change as the US population becomes more racially diverse. In the 1950s, whites were the predominant racial group, and black Americans were the most sizeable minority group, so most research focused on black-white segregation. As of 2014, the majority of US schoolchildren were nonwhite, with Hispanics comprising the largest and fastest-growing group. By 2026, the population of US schoolchildren is projected to be 45 percent white, 29 percent Hispanic, 15 percent black, and 6 percent Asian. Concepts of segregation must accommodate this increasingly diverse population.

IMPLICATIONS

Why does school segregation matter? School segregation contributes to inequality in educational outcomes between white and minority students and between high- and low-income students. Black high school students who attended integrated schools in the 1960s and 1970s after *Brown* were more likely to graduate from high school, attend college, and find good employment as adults, compared to black high school students who attended segregated schools (Johnson 2019). Integrating schools narrowed the black-white educational attainment gap by benefiting black students while not affecting the outcomes of white students. Poor students who attend schools with higher-income peers perform better on achievement tests, earning higher math and reading scores, compared to poor students who attend schools with many other poor students. In Montgomery County, Maryland, the test score gap between high- and low-income students was reduced by 30 percent when low-income students attended school with higher-income peers (Schwartz 2012). School poverty also contributes to the racial achievement gap. Minority students attend school with more poor classmates, and students in high-poverty schools tend to have lower test scores. Integrated schools are beneficial not only for minority and low-income students but also for white and high-income students. White and high-income students in integrated schools develop better critical thinking skills, benefit from better classroom discussion, are more likely to have interracial friendships, and develop cross-cultural competency, all key skills in our increasingly diverse society.

More than sixty years after the landmark *Brown v. Board of Education* decision, school segregation by both race and income remains troublingly high. The Supreme Court ruled that "'separate but equal' has no place," and that integration was necessary for providing equal opportunity. Decades of research document large achievement gaps between white and minority students, and between high- and low-income students, owing in part to their education in often highly separate contexts. To truly provide equal opportunity for all students, regardless of where they were born or who their parents are, policy makers must consider strategies for promoting integration. Researchers can support policy makers by continuing to study why segregation matters and the most effective policies for creating diverse schools. Alternatively, researchers can also investigate what policies can help students achieve even if they attend a high-poverty, hypersegregated school. Because segregation has roots in broader economic inequality and neighborhood segregation, policy makers in other arenas, like housing, welfare, and the labor market, must join forces with educational policy makers. School inequalities are shaped by the larger social context. In turn, school inequalities today will shape inequalities in society in the next generation. Without policy changes, the future success and social mobility of minority and low-income students will be in doubt.

CHAPTER 13 REVIEW

Discussion Questions

1. Think about your own elementary or high school. Did you attend school with students from a background similar to yours? How do you think your school's composition affected your learning experience?

2. What do you think are the most effective policies for reducing racial/ethnic or economic segregation in schools? In what ways can these plans be implemented to avoid resistance from parents, teachers, and students?

3. What is the difference between exposure and evenness measures of segregation? Does one capture inequality better than another? Would you say racial segregation has increased or decreased since the 1980s?

4. Do you think racial/ethnic segregation or economic school segregation is a more pressing issue? Why?

Suggestions for Further Reading

Civil Rights Project (UCLA). https://civilrightsproject.ucla.edu/research/k-12-education/integration-and-diversity.

Reardon, Sean F., and Ann Owens. 2014. "60 Years after Brown: Trends and Consequences of School Segregation." *Annual Review of Sociology* 40:199–218. www.annualreviews.org/doi/abs/10.1146/annurev-soc-071913-043152.

US Government Accountability Office. 2016. *K–12 Education: Better Use of Information Could Help Agencies Identify Disparities and Address Racial Discrimination.* GAO-16-345. Washington, DC: US Government Accountability Office. www.gao.gov/products/GAO-16-345. This is the Government Accountability Office's 2016 report on school segregation.

Suggested Radio Program

The radio show This American Life produced a two-part series on school segregation, "The Problem We All Live With," 2015. www.thisamericanlife.org/radio-archives/episode/562/the-problem-we-all-live-with.

References

Billingham, C. M., and M. O. Hunt. 2016. "School Racial Composition and Parental Choice: New Evidence on the Preferences of White Parents in the United States." *Sociology of Education* 89 (2): 99–117.

Boser, U., and P. Baffour. 2017. *Isolated and Segregated: A New Look at the Income Divide in Our Nation's Schooling System.* Washington, DC: Center for American Progress.

Clotfelter, C. T. 2004. *After Brown: The Rise and Retreat of School Desegregation.* Princeton, NJ: Princeton University Press.

Coleman, J. S., S. D. Kelly, and J. A. Moore. 1975. *Trends in School Segregation, 1968–73.* Washington, DC: Urban Institute.

Gamoran, A., and B. P. An. 2016. "Effects of School Segregation and School Resources in a Changing Policy Context." *Educational Evaluation and Policy Analysis* 38 (1): 43–64.

Grady, S., and S. Bielick. 2010. *Trends in the Use of School Choice: 1993 to 2007.* NCES 2010–004. Washington, DC: US Department of Education, National Center for Education Statistics, Institute of Education Sciences.

Johnson, R. C. 2019. *Children of the Dream: Why School Integration Works.* New York: Basic Books.

Logan, J. R. 2004. *Resegregation in American Public Schools? Not in the 1990s.* Albany: SUNY Albany, Lewis Mumford Center for Comparative Urban and Regional Research.

Logan, J. R., and D. Oakley. 2004. *The Continuing Legacy of the Brown Decision: Court Action and School Segregation, 1960–2000.* Albany: SUNY Albany, Lewis Mumford Center for Comparative Urban and Regional Research.

Massey, D. S., and N. A. Denton. 1988. "The Dimensions of Residential Segregation." *Social Forces* 67 (2): 281–315.

Mickelson, R. A., S. S. Smith, and A. H. Nelson. 2017. *Yesterday, Today, and Tomorrow: School Desegregation and Resegregation in Charlotte.* Cambridge, MA: Harvard Education Press.

Orfield, G. 1983. *Public School Desegregation in the United States, 1968–1980.* Washington, DC: Joint Center for Political Studies.

———. 2001. *Schools More Separate: Consequences of a Decade of Resegregation.* Cambridge, MA: Harvard University, Civil Rights Project.

Orfield, G., J. Kucsera, and G. Siegel-Hawley. 2012. *E Pluribus . . . Separation: Deepening Double Segregation for More Students.* Los Angeles: Civil Rights Project / Proyecto Derechos Civiles.

Orfield, G., and C. Lee. 2007. *Historic Reversals, Accelerating Resegregation, and the Need for New Integration Strategies.* Los Angeles: Civil Rights Project / Proyecto Derechos Civiles.

Owens, A., S. F. Reardon, and C. Jencks. 2016. "Income Segregation between Schools and School Districts." *American Educational Research Journal* 53 (4): 1159–97. doi: 10.3102/0002831216652722.

Phi Delta Kappan. 2017. "The 49th Annual PDK Poll of the Public's Attitudes toward the Public Schools." Supplement, 99 (1): NP1–NP32.

Potter, H., K. Quick, and E. Davies. 2016. *A New Wave of School Integration.* Washington, DC: Century Foundation.

Reardon, S. F., and A. Owens. 2014. "60 years after *Brown:* Trends and Consequences of School Segregation." *Annual Review of Sociology* 40:199–218. doi: 10.1146/annurev-soc-071913-043152.

Saporito, S. 2003. "Private Choices, Public Consequences: Magnet School Choice and Segregation by Race and Poverty." *Social Problems* 50 (2): 181–203.

Saporito, S., and D. Sohoni. 2007. "Mapping Educational Inequality: Concentrations of Poverty among Poor and

Minority Students in Public Schools." *Social Forces* 85 (3): 1227–54.

Schwartz, H. 2012. "Housing Policy Is School Policy: Economically Integrative Housing Promotes Academic Success in Montgomery County, Maryland." In *The Future of School Integration,* edited by R. D. Kahlenberg, 27–65. New York: Century Foundation.

Stroub, K. J., and M. P. Richards. 2013. "From Resegregation to Reintegration: Trends in the Racial/Ethnic Segregation of Metropolitan Public Schools, 1993–2009." *American Educational Research Journal* 50 (3): 497–531.

US Government Accountability Office. 2016. *Better Use of Information Could Help Agencies Identify Disparities and Address Racial Discrimination.* Washington, DC: US Government Accountability Office.

US Department of Education and Common Core of Data. 2013–14. *Public Elementary/Secondary School Universe Survey Data.* Institute of Education Sciences, National Center for Education Statistics website. School-level data file. https://nces.ed.gov/ccd/pubschuniv.asp.

US Department of Education, National Center for Education Statistics. 2016a. *Digest of Education Statistics.* Table 203.50. Washington, DC: US Department of Education. https://nces.ed.gov/programs/digest/d16/tables/dt16_203.50.asp.

———. 2016b. *Digest of Education Statistics.* Table 216.60. Washington, DC: US Department of Education. https://nces.ed.gov/programs/digest/d16/tables/dt16_216.60.asp.

Welch, F., and A. Light. 1987. *New Evidence on School Desegregation.* Washington, DC: US Commission on Civil Rights.

14

Sociological Perspectives on Leading and Teaching for School Change

SARAH L. WOULFIN, UNIVERSITY OF CONNECTICUT

EDITORS' NOTE

No discussion of schools and their operation can be complete without considering the educators who make them work. As we'll discuss further in chapter 15, sociologists have long thought of schools as **loosely coupled organizations** in which teachers work more or less independently in their classrooms to teach their students and lead their learning, largely buffered from policy makers, parents, and administrators who might want to shape their instruction. Sociologists sometimes call such loosely coupled organizations **"egg-crate schools,"** because they put each group of teachers and students into totally separate classrooms, just like a dozen eggs in an egg crate. In such a setting, discretion and independence are often central to teachers' occupational identities. But the occupation of teaching has begun to change over the last several decades as school accountability policy creates new pressures for schools to standardize instruction and new opportunities for administrators to monitor teachers' practices and performance.

University of Connecticut education scholar Sarah Woulfin describes these shifts in educational occupations, directing special attention to the role that instructional coaches play in contemporary schools. By connecting teachers to one another and facilitating communication between teachers and administrators, instructional coaches are poised to fundamentally change how school works. As you read the descriptions of two instructional coaches at the end of the chapter, think about the different strategies these professionals use and their consequences for the schools in which they work.

KEY POINTS

- Educators in schools play active roles in interpreting and carrying out reform efforts.
- Principals, instructional coaches, and teachers have different connections with and responses to policy.
- Instructional coaches enact policy while also educating teachers about elements of instructional policy.
- Instructional coaches' work is shaped by organizational conditions and includes strategic responses.

INTRODUCTION

Schools face pressure on all sides to improve. Since the standards movement of the 1990s, accountability-oriented policies, systems, and practices have proliferated. These policies hinge on content- and grade-level-specific standards in order to change schools in particular ways, as well as to change the nature of teachers' and leaders' work, relying on standardized tests to measure teacher and student outcomes. Reformers and administrators engage in monitoring that includes comparing results among a variety of states, districts, schools, and groups of students. Educators, ranging from superintendents and district administrators to principals, instructional coaches, and teachers, interpret and respond to the ideas and rules of accountability policy, which has consequences for both teaching practices and students' educational outcomes. Further, the idea of teaching to the test is now ubiquitous, as John Diamond (2007) revealed. Thus, accountability policy now structures multiple dimensions of leaders' and teachers' work. However, we also know that different educators respond to the same policy pressures in very different ways. That is, while some enact ambitious instructional reforms, others teach to the test, game accountability policies, or ignore key elements of policies (Diamond 2007). What explains this variation?

Many sociologists of education are interested in the organizational structures and working conditions that shape educators' work. This research tradition acknowledges that individual beliefs, values, and understandings inform educators' interpretations of and responses to policies and programs. In this way, as opposed to attending to policies and structures, scholars redirect focus to administrators, coaches, and teachers, identifying them as the people actually doing the work of reform. For example, consider the increasingly important role that instructional coaches play in influencing how schools respond to accountability policy pressures. Instructional coaches collaborate with teachers and other educators to promote professional learning and reform efforts. In this chapter, you will learn about this new occupational role in American public schools, which will help you understand the macro-, meso-, and microlevel conditions influencing educators' work and the ways in which education practices shape the effects of school reform efforts. You will also learn how individuals' social interactions within specific organizational conditions influence the path of school reform. Throughout, I highlight when and under what conditions leaders' and teachers' work advances—or impedes—change.

SOCIOLOGY OF WORK

A perspective through the lens of sociology of education can help us see in what ways schools, as complex organizations, either remain stable or change. Until recently, sociologists and scholars treated school districts as bureaucracies that lead the operations of a set of schools. They framed district and school leaders as managers who construct systems and monitor outcomes. Scholars also uncovered how schools attempt to achieve ambiguous, competing goals, treating teachers as isolated from policy and their teaching as largely buffered from reform efforts. Sociologists have also highlighted how the organizational structure of the school system—with schools nested in the district, state, and federal education environment—created a "loosely coupled" system (see chapter 15 for more on this concept) that contributes to schools' slowness to improve or to respond to policy pressures. Sociologists have depicted the success or failure of waves of reform, including shifts in how schools structure classrooms and define effective reading instruction. However, much of this research concentrated on macro- or mesolevel forces, with less attention paid to the people carrying out the everyday work of school reform in the classroom. Filling this gap and addressing crucial questions regarding school reform requires turning to the sociology of work, which treats professions as a type of social organization and as the context for social processes.

As Katherine Kellogg (2014: 914) states, the sociology of work focuses on "the question of how and when reform involving professionals is implemented." In the education field, scholars using this framework have studied features of the teaching profession as well as norms of teachers' work. For example, recent scholarship focuses on how teachers plan units and lessons together, and on how they analyze data on student outcomes. In my own research, I am particularly interested in the ways educators conceptualize their work and how their collaboration shapes their occupational identities, instructional practices, and responses to school accountability policies. This occupational perspective encourages scholars to grapple with facets of an occupation, such as priorities offering "guidelines for specific situations" (Rothman 1997: 53), social norms shaping workplace interaction, and tools used during work. Finally, this perspective encourages analyses of the identities, values, and behaviors of members of an occupation. By applying this occupational, rather than organizational, perspective to the operation of schools, we can reveal key features of leading and teaching that enable—or block—school change. This chapter summarizes the field's understanding of the interplay between policy, occupations, and practice from an occupational perspective. This summary provides context to explore both coaches' and teachers' work inside schools. We treat schools as what Hallett (2010) calls "inhabited institutions," which is a useful concept in understanding how instructional coaches operationalize their role. It provides grist for analyzing and reflecting on schools as complex organizations.

PERSPECTIVES ON THREE OCCUPATIONS

Understanding how educational leaders and teachers play a role in advancing school reform requires a look at three differing occupations in the field of education: those of principals, instructional coaches, and teachers. While conducting work in schools, these individuals hold different types of authority and power, have different connections with educational policy, and carry out different implementation tasks. These three types of educators are affected by external factors, including pressures from the education field. Environmental (or macrolevel) pressures, mesolevel conditions, and microlevel (such as individual and cognitive) processes all influence their daily work.

Principal

The principal holds significant responsibility for leading the entire school to reform goals. As administrators, principals hold formal power over teachers and staff, including recruiting, hiring, and firing educators for their schools. Further, principals can gain authority over different aspects of schooling, including the nature of instruction and methods for managing student behavior. They are also intermediaries between the district and school levels. In particular, they communicate and promote rules and protocols set by the central office to their teachers and staff. Thus, the principal's work affects the path of state and district policy implementation. As leaders, principals balance multiple priorities, ranging from improving instruction and running an efficient building to engaging families and community members and advocating for social justice. Depending on district and school conditions, principals may prioritize different facets of leadership. Finally, they benefit from development and support related to these facets of leadership so they can effectively enact policies and programs.

The ways principals conceptualize their leadership and their policy environment influences the way they approach their work. First, owing to changing ideas regarding school leadership in the educational field, principals' role has shifted from that of manager to that of instructional leader. Before the 1990s, principals primarily attended to technical and logistical work to organize the school; they often worked mainly within their offices. By 2010, principals in most states and districts were expected to serve as instructional leaders, supporting quality teaching and learning, and spending time in classrooms engaging with teachers and students. Second, during the accountability-policy era, district leaders created expectations and procedures requiring principals to strictly monitor classroom practices and closely analyze student outcomes—with principals ultimately being held accountable for meeting (or not meeting) goals. In this way, policies steered leadership activities. Third, principals interpret, prioritize, and frame policy messages about topics ranging from new science programs and assessment systems to new rules on student attendance. Therefore, principals' daily work, including routines for engaging with teachers (Spillane, Parise, and Sherer 2011), reflects current reforms.

Mesolevel factors, such as district and school working conditions, shape the nature of principals' reform efforts. In some districts, principals have opportunities to collaborate with and learn from a network of their colleagues regarding reforms, leadership, and instruction. Additionally, depending on the structure and size of schools, principals work with a team of administrators and/or teacher leaders to create a vision for their school, codesign plans for improvement, and distribute reform-oriented activities. This collaboration entails principals forming a network with other educators at their schools and leading routines to advance change. These leaders' networks influence how principals respond to reforms.

In addition to environmental forces and organizational conditions shaping the nature of this occupation, microprocesses push and pull principals. First, principals' beliefs, values, knowledge, and previous experience all shape how they make sense of current policies and how they interpret reforms and engage with other educators during implementation. For example, a principal who taught middle school math for many years may prioritize a district math reform or may conduct evaluations of teachers' math instruction in a way that differs from how a principal who had a background as a high school history teacher would do. Second, principals' work includes cognitive processes, such as motivating and even persuading teachers to take on reforms. In this way, principals bridge policy and teaching by making sense of reforms and communicating their ideas about reform.

Instructional Coach

In contrast with principals, instructional coaches are not administrators. So, in most contexts, they do not officially evaluate teachers or make personnel decisions. However, coaches can gain authority over teachers regarding issues of instruction, while typically only holding informal power. Instructional coaches are leaders, often based within a single school, who develop and support teachers. Coaches usually specialize in one content area, with, for example, math coaches leading math reforms and literacy coaches leading initiatives on English language arts. They function as intermediaries between state and district reform efforts and classroom teachers. Coaches are expected to facilitate ongoing professional learning opportunities to improve the nature of instruction and the level of student achievement. However, coaches do collaborate with other school leaders and may take on some quasi-administrative duties, such as assisting with student testing or managing bus drop-offs. We'll look at more facets of coaches' work later in the chapter.

From the macro perspective, policies and resources enable coaching and define the nature of coaches' work. More explicitly, policies can include funding for coaching positions so that coaches can promote certain aspects of education reform. For example, in the early to mid-2000s, Reading First, a branch of No Child Left Behind, provided resources for reading coaches in underperforming districts across most states. Policies can also affect the ideas and practices that coaches disseminate and promote. For instance, science coaches play a role in developing teachers' understanding of their state's ambitious science standards and components of the district's new science curriculum. In this manner, coaches' work reflects educational policy.

At the meso level, organizational conditions shape the nature of coaches' work. The culture and norms of collaboration are especially important for coaching. Some districts or educational systems have strong cultures for improvement, embracing coaching, supervision, and the alignment of instructional frameworks with educators' work. This culture permits coaches to conduct an assortment of activities in order to affect instruction and improve outcomes. Other districts or systems have weaker cultures of improvement, where coaches need to define and redefine their role and responsibilities, justify their work with teachers, and/or ignore elements of certain policies or programs. In this case, coaching itself is a weakly implemented reform.

In addition to collaborating with teachers, coaches collaborate with principals and other administrators. In many schools, coaches serve on instructional leadership teams and collaborate in other ways to ensure shared understandings of coaching and reform efforts. This communication keeps principals and coaches on the same page. It is important to note that there is evidence that the coach-principal relationship lays the foundation for reform-oriented coaching. That is, when coaches and principals have shared understandings of reforms, school priorities, coaching activities, teachers with the greatest needs for improvement, and coaching activities, coaches can engage in deeper, more targeted coaching to help the school meet its objectives.

At the micro level, coaches' beliefs and knowledge about reforms, instruction, and coaching influence their work. My own research shows how coaches' conceptions of quality instruction shape the focus of their work with teachers. For example, a coach who believes that vocabulary instruction is a crucial aspect of literacy instruction will design professional learning opportunities related to vocabulary. In addition, the coaches' level of understanding of state or district reforms matters for their reform-oriented activities in schools. If a coach has a deep understanding of multiple branches of a new math curriculum, she or he can support teachers as they take on multiple facets of the curriculum. We will explore coaches' reform-oriented work later in this chapter.

Teacher

Teachers operate primarily within their classrooms, and their primary responsibility is that of planning and teaching lessons for students. Teachers usually collaborate with their grade-level team or department and, in some cases, obtain and use informal power while engaging with other teachers. They engage in multiple forms of professional development offered by district leaders or coaches or by external consultants or trainers. And they may also seek out professional learning opportunities through books and professional publications, online networks (e.g., Twitter), and professional associations and conferences.

At the macro level, teachers' work is structured by numerous policies. First, most states have elaborate credentialing systems and require teachers to both graduate from approved certification programs and pass standardized tests to demonstrate their qualifications and competency. These systems play a gatekeeping role; and recently, scholars have realized how credentialing systems disproportionately sort teacher candidates, contributing to strikingly low numbers of teachers of color in US classrooms. Second, standardized assessments, a pillar of accountability policy used to measure student progress plus teacher and school quality, steer teaching practices. Researchers have determined that teachers devote greater attention to tested course material, or "teach to the test." They also engage in test preparation activities in an attempt to boost scores. Further, teachers focus attention on "bubble students," who are close to meeting the proficiency benchmark on formal tests. In these ways, the principles of accountability policy direct teaching and influence students' experiences.

At the meso level, the norms of teaching and the nature of professional interactions influence teachers' work in reform efforts. In the 1970s, Dan Lortie ([1975] 2002) defined individualism, privatism, and conservatism as the longstanding norms of the teaching profession. The norm of individualism refers to teachers working as individuals with groups of students/children. The norm of privatism is associated with the egg-crate structure of schools, in which teachers operate within the confines of their classroom. (See figure 25 for a visual representation of the egg-crate school.) Finally, the norm of conservatism involves the tendency for teachers to maintain many of the same teaching practices that they themselves experienced as students. These norms continue to define how teachers plan and teach. For example, teachers may use computers

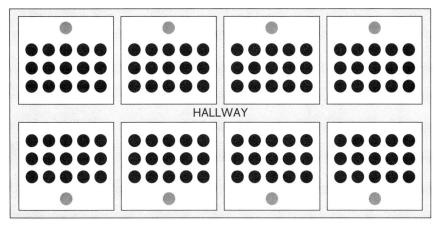

Figure 25. The egg-crate school.

and the internet to find instructional materials or worksheets that replicate how they were taught. In this case, teachers are tinkering with technology, but technology is not altering deeper aspects of their instruction.

In addition to the norms of teaching steering the nature of teachers' work, collaboration conditions and social learning opportunities also influence teachers' role in school change. In some schools, leaders organize opportunities for teachers to leave their egg-crate classrooms to work and learn together. For instance, teachers may meet in grade-level teams (e.g., a group of fourth-grade teachers) or as a department (e.g., all high school math teachers) to analyze data or student work products, plan improvements to instruction, and share areas of strengths and weakness in existing instructional practice. In addition to engaging in this formalized collaboration, teachers also share ideas about policy and pedagogical practice through informal interactions with other teachers in the hallway, in the copy room, at the teacher lunch table, in the parking lot, and when driving to meetings or events. This serves as a reminder that professional learning occurs in spaces not prescribed by the principal and during time not apportioned by the school bell.

Finally, microprocesses influence teachers' work. Coburn (2004) described how each teacher's interpretations of a program, initiative, or new form of instruction are shaped by his or her beliefs, values, and prior experiences. Teachers' race, socioeconomic status, and educational trajectories, as well as their knowledge of reform, steer their conceptualizations of and response to the rules and ideas of reform. For instance, teachers with deeper understandings of literacy instruction may reject ineffectual reading and writing test-prep activities imposed by district leaders. Thus, teachers' knowledge, beliefs, and disposition toward a reform influence whether they change their practices or resist specific aspects of reforms. It is important to note that, within any one school, teachers hold an assortment of beliefs, values, and experiences but often work together during change efforts. As a result, a teacher may spread practical ideas regarding reform.

INSTRUCTIONAL COACHES LEAD REFORM

Instructional coaches' roles and responsibilities illuminate how their work matters in change processes. Focusing upon coaching as one profession in the education sector permits a close exploration of how leaders inside schools influence reform. Moreover, coaching is a good example for understanding the mediation of policy during school reform or change. A look at the background behind coaches' work as intermediaries, along with two vignettes on coaching, will reveal how organizational conditions either enable or constrain coaches' reform-oriented work, shedding light on educators' active, strategic responses to the reforms their schools face.

Role of Coaching in Reform

Across the United States, many districts currently use coaching to promote both individual and system-level instructional change. As the graph in figure 26 illustrates, instructional coaches—or, as they are sometimes called, instructional specialists—represent a new and rapidly growing role in US public schools. Bearing responsibility for building teacher capacity and catalyzing reform, coaches engage in leadership tasks with individual teachers and with groups of educators. This frequently involves developing teachers' mastery of new or different approaches to curriculum and instruction. For example, coaches may meet with teams of teachers, facilitating collective learning while discussing standards-based lesson plans and drafting assessments together. Furthermore, by providing teachers with content-specific instructional expertise, coaches can expand teachers' understanding of standards and curricula to foster reform. They may also analyze data in order to plan professional learning experiences and strive to foster a positive, productive culture among teachers.

Coaches also take on political roles, in many instances. In particular, coaches funnel messages from the district and school levels to teachers, helping them frame instructional policy. For example, in grade-level team meetings, a coach may discuss specific elements of a new curriculum, devoting greater attention to aspects of an initiative that will be strictly regulated and monitored by administrators. These activities can influence teachers' enactment of reforms.

Coaching can catalyze change across systems and schools. In a conceptual piece with Jessica Rigby (2017), I discuss three mechanisms by which coaches, as intermediaries, contribute to school change. First, coaches develop teachers'

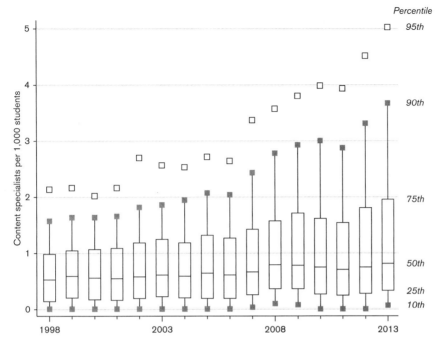

Figure 26. The distribution of instructional-specialist staffing for US public school districts, for the 1997–98 to 2012–13 school years. Source: reprinted with permission from T. Domina, R. Lewis, P. Agarwal, and P. Hanselman, "Professional Sense-Makers: Instructional Specialists in Contemporary Schooling," *Educational Researcher* 44, no. 6 (2015): 359–64.

and leaders' shared understandings of reforms. Coaches' engagement with individuals or groups of teachers and principals helps form common conceptualizations among these educators regarding new initiatives, standards, and instructional methods that, in turn, construct coherence for learning and improvement. Second, coaches model activities and instructional practices in a low-stakes context during their work with teachers. By conducting content-specific classroom observations, providing feedback to teachers, and teaching demonstration lessons related to a teacher's specific goals and districts priorities, coaches can foster learning that is aligned with reform efforts.

Finally, coaches broker ideas about reforms between teachers and leaders. Specifically, coaches can share with principals any evidence they may have on teachers' beliefs, skills, and practices associated with reforms, while also bringing principals' ideas and priorities to teachers. This brokering of ideas on reform, or bidirectional communication among differently positioned educators, helps facilitate communication and enable change. In sum, coaches can advance school change; however, their work is shaped by the organizational culture and working conditions.

Vignettes

Two vignettes illustrate sociological concepts associated with coaches' work. Grounded in qualitative data I collected on instructional coaching systems in a northeastern state, the vignettes provide details on the interplay between structures, leadership activities, and school change.

Vignette 1: Coach as Buffer and Broker

Lindsey has served as an instructional coach at Hamilton Elementary for two years. Hamilton Elementary, an underserved school in a midsized urban district, has adopted numerous initiatives in an attempt to raise achievement on standardized tests. In her role as a coach, Lindsey leads data team meetings and professional development sessions on a range of issues, conducts operational activities, and is a member of the principal's instructional leadership team. Though Lindsey aims to support teachers formally and informally, she spends little time inside teachers' classrooms. Many teachers do not deem Lindsey's classroom observations to be either desirable or helpful.

In the fall of 2016, Hamilton's principal met with Lindsey and shared an observation form he'd received at a recent district meeting. The walk-through form included a chart with points from the teacher evaluation system. He encouraged the coach to begin using this form while visiting teachers' classrooms. However, Lindsey decided that, owing to concerns about the boundaries between coaching for growth and evaluating for accountability, this evaluation form would damage her relationships with teachers. She felt that one of her responsibilities was to buffer teachers from evaluation policy. In response, Lindsey told the principal that, if she engaged in activities like evaluation, teachers would not trust her as a coach, and, therefore, she would not use the form during classroom visits. Lindsey's rejection of the district evaluation form indicates that she prioritized buffering teachers from some aspects of district policy.

Although Lindsey elected to not mirror the evaluation process in her informal walk-throughs, she did plan grade-level-team professional development sessions on elements from the formal evaluation rubric. In this way, she helped teachers learn more about the evaluation system, with the goal of promoting positive responses to this reform. During these sessions, teachers shared their ideas about and experiences with the evaluation system. Subsequently, Lindsey communicated several points about the evaluation process, including some teachers' misconceptions, during leadership team meetings. In this way, this coach functioned as a broker between teachers and administrators. Further, her brokering supported the implementation of the evaluation reform, in a way that helped empower teachers.

Vignette 2: Coach as Definer

In contrast to Hamilton, Fenton Elementary had a stronger coaching system and culture, with organizational conditions enabling coaches' reform-oriented work. Fenton's principal was an enthusiastic proponent of instructional coaching who sometimes led districtwide sessions on the role of coaching in instructional improvement. Fenton's instructional leadership team was composed of the principal, assistant principal, literacy coach, and math coach. Kelvin, the math coach, had served in this role at Fenton for four years. In coordination with the school's literacy coach and assistant principal, and employing the school's coaching model, he facilitated professional development.

Over the course of three staff meetings at the beginning of the 2017–18 school year, the coaches introduced themselves and explained that the underlying goal of coaching was to improve instruction and achievement. They also drafted, on a large piece of paper, a chart of what coaches do and do not do in the context of their school. In this way, the instructional leadership team made clear what coaches would do at Fenton, and they encouraged teachers to reflect on how coaching could be beneficial. Kelvin reported that several teachers shared anecdotes about how coaches provided instructional—as well as personal—support plus mentoring during previous years. Similar to the way Lindsey taught teachers and the principal something about policy, Kelvin developed teachers' understandings of the coaching system itself, with implications for the enactment of coaching at Lincoln. Thus, Kelvin was defining the school's coaching reform in order to promote positive responses to coaching.

Kelvin told me that, after these introductory sessions, several teachers approached him and invited him into their classrooms. He also reached out to teachers after data team meetings to schedule classroom visits during their math-instruction blocks. Further, Kelvin worked inside teachers' classrooms, conducting observation-feedback cycles with teachers targeting various aspects of the math curriculum. These in-classroom coaching activities played a role in shifting the norms of teaching by encouraging teachers to work together on math instruction. In sum, teachers' clarity on coaching played a role in encouraging them to engage in coaching, enabling Kelvin to conduct reform-oriented work within classrooms.

DIRECTIONS FOR FUTURE RESEARCH

Though scholars have illuminated aspects of principals', coaches', and teachers' work in reform, additional research is still needed in this area. One path forward involves using tools from organizational sociology to determine how educators in different positions navigate multiple educational policies. Districts and schools are inundated with reforms, and we need a better understanding of how principals, teachers, and other educators learn about and juggle these pressures. How do educators in different occupations, who have different amounts of power, access ideas about instructional reforms and policies related to state education funding, school choice, teacher credentialing, and student discipline? In addition, there is a dearth of research on how educators are prepared for reform-oriented work, including how teachers understand educational policy and the ways in which it is implemented in schools. While future teachers need not be political science or sociology majors, they would benefit from an understanding of the role of advocates and research in policy making, as well as an understanding of how mandates and monitoring affect implementation. All teachers should gain knowledge about, and skills in comprehending, policies and programs to better ask questions about and advocate for educational policy issues.

Concepts from organizational sociology could be particularly beneficial for analyzing the norms and practices of other occupations in education, such as those of educational consultants, special education teachers, and paraprofessionals. It appears that there has been an expansion of roles in districts and schools, ranging from the roles of district technology administrators to those of behavior consultants. In what ways are these occupations similar to and different from more traditional roles in the education system? And, perhaps more crucially, when and under what conditions do individuals in these roles enact reforms? Finally, social network analysis can be used to ascertain how leaders and teachers interact during change processes. These analyses would map communication about different components of reforms. Furthermore, they could reveal if and how networks vary across systems or at different stages in implementing reforms. In sum, these lines of scholarship would answer important—and intriguing—questions about the people engaging in school change efforts and could also be applied to understanding the work in other occupations.

IMPLICATIONS

Change, particularly within school systems, is complex. Specifically, change takes time and resources, as well as education about the issues being faced. Policy makers, reformers, and educational leaders should find ways to clearly define educators' roles and responsibilities associated with different reforms. In the case of coaches, district and school administrators should be cognizant that most coaches are doing much more than just in-classroom coaching. In fact, many coaches devote the bulk of their time to managerial and operational tasks such as facilitating meetings and completing paperwork. In response to this, administrators should find ways to create supportive working conditions for coaches, protect coaches' time, and build the capacity of principals and coaches to prioritize in-classroom, reform-focused, and content-specific coaching activities.

Further, if reformers and administrators truly understood the intricacies of occupations in the field of education, they could tailor the preparation and ongoing professional learning opportunities of coaches and other instructional leaders. This could result in the creation of professional development for coaches; this professional development would offer guidance to coaches on how they can navigate policy pressures and skillfully engage with teachers. Finally, sociological lenses allow us to see how working conditions matter for the rejection or acceptance of reforms. Teachers, principals, and coaches desire to feel valued, supported, and safe. It continues to be necessary to make both teaching and leading attractive professions. Thus, reformers and administrators should pay close attention to organizational factors, including the distribution of resources, power, and systems for collaboration across districts and schools. Contextualized support, or coaching, for educators at multiple levels of the system could increase job satisfaction and reduce turnover, which, in turn, would promote positive outcomes for children, youth, and families.

CHAPTER 14 REVIEW

Discussion Questions

1. Reflect on a time you've seen an organization change in a significant way. How did people in different roles interpret and respond to new pressures, rules, or ideas?

2. Think about a leader (inside or outside the field of education) whom you've known. How did this person exert power and authority in an organization or group? What were the key practices of this leader? To what extent were they effective? How did this leader communicate with others?

3. Returning to the vignettes on coaching, can you identify the professional norms of teaching and coaching exhibited in the two cases?

Suggestions for Further Reading

Aguilar, Elena. 2013. *The Art of Coaching: Effective Strategies for School Transformation.* San Francisco: Jossey-Bass.

Fullan, Michael. 2014. *The Principal: Three Keys to Maximizing Impact.* San Francisco: Jossey-Bass.

Katz, Michael B., and Mike Rose, eds. 2013. *Public Education under Siege.* Philadelphia: University of Pennsylvania Press.

Spillane, James P., Brian J. Reiser, and Todd Reimer. 2002. "Policy Implementation and Cognition: Reframing and Refocusing Implementation Research." *Review of Educational Research* 72 (3): 387–431.

Woulfin, Sarah L. 2016. "Duet or Duel? A Portrait of Two Logics of Reading Instruction in an Urban School District." *American Journal of Education* 122 (3): 337–65.

References

Coburn, Cynthia E. 2004. "Beyond Decoupling: Rethinking the Relationship between the Institutional Environment and the Classroom." *Sociology of Education* 77 (3): 211–44.

Diamond, John B. 2007. "Where the Rubber Meets the Road: Rethinking the Connection between High-Stakes Testing Policy and Classroom Instruction." *Sociology of Education* 80 (4): 285–313.

Hallett, Tim. 2010. "The Myth Incarnate: Recoupling Processes, Turmoil, and Inhabited Institutions in an Urban Elementary School." *American Sociological Review* 75 (1): 52–74.

Kellogg, Katherine C. 2014. "Brokerage Professions and Implementing Reform in an Age of Experts." *American Sociological Review* 79 (5): 912–41.

Lortie, Dan C. (1975) 2002. *Schoolteacher: A Sociological Study.* Chicago: University of Chicago Press.

Rothman, Robert A. 1997. *Working: Sociological Perspectives.* 2nd ed. New York: Pearson.

Spillane, James P., Leigh Mesler Parise, and Jennifer Zoltners Sherer. 2011. "Organizational Routines as Coupling Mechanisms: Policy, School Administration, and the Technical Core." *American Educational Research Journal* 48 (3): 586–619.

Woulfin, Sarah L., and Jessica G. Rigby. 2017. "Coaching for Coherence: How Instructional Coaches Lead Change in the Evaluation Era." *Educational Researcher* 46 (6): 323–28.

School Choice

15

Policy and Perspectives

LINDA RENZULLI, PURDUE UNIVERSITY

MARIA PAINO, OAKLAND UNIVERSITY

EDITORS' NOTE

As we argued in the introduction to chapter 13, the decentralization of American public education has organizational virtues, even if it contributes to school segregation. To be effective, centrally controlled organizations need clear agreement about organizational goals and a central vision of how best to reach those mutually agreed-upon goals. Consider, for example, an automobile factory. There, the goal is clear—to maximize profits by making as many cars as rapidly and efficiently as possible. To reach that goal, engineers design assembly lines that break the process of building a car into many steps.

Schooling is different. Neither the goals nor the proper methods to reach those goals are well understood. Do we want our schools to produce efficient and docile workers? Committed citizens? Creative artists and scientists? All of the above? Should teachers lecture? Lead students through hands-on projects? Lead discussions? Facilitate technologically assisted learning? We find it difficult to answer these questions, in no small part because the best answers likely vary from student to student and community to community.

Because of this uncertainty, some sociologists argue, it makes sense to build an educational system that is **loosely coupled.** In such a system, teachers develop their own instructional techniques at their discretion. In the best cases, loose coupling allows for innovative and personalized instruction. Charter school advocates argue that these schools capture many of the benefits of loose coupling, since they are publicly funded but exempt from many of the regulations that govern traditional public schools. As you read this chapter by sociologists Linda Renzulli and Maria Paino, look for evidence regarding both the opportunities and the risks associated with the school choice movement.

KEY POINTS

- Two theoretical approaches examine charter schools: institutional and market.
- Charter schools are created in specific legal contexts determined state by state.
- Charter schools are organizations that follow many of the principles of other organizations.
- Academic achievement in charter schools is not conclusively different from that in traditional schools.
- Accountability may be failing to achieve the goals set for it in the market model.

INTRODUCTION

School choice has been a controversial topic in American education for years. Wealthy (and white) families have always had some sort of choice—for example, they could choose a private school and hire tutors, or choose a residence in one of the better public school districts, enabling them to pick the "best" education for their children. Until more recently, poorer families typically had little choice but to send their children to their neighborhood public schools. Today, a broader array of choices are built into many public education systems. In many settings parents can choose among multiple free public schools within their own districts or even, on occasion, in neighboring school districts. There are several forms of public school choice, including vouchers (money to use toward a private school), magnet schools (public schools with a particular curricular focus designed to attract students), open enrollment (picking a school not in your neighborhood), and charter schools (publically funded but privately run schools).

Each of these forms of choice aims to improve schooling through a market model of reduced monopolization of education. However, each may also have unintended consequences. This chapter briefly discusses vouchers and magnet schools, and it focuses primarily on charter schools, examining in particular how the market model of choice is influencing the form and function of the educational system in the United States.

SCHOOL VOUCHERS

School vouchers, also known as education vouchers, are a type of private school choice because they provide money for students to leave their public school and access a private school. Private schools must be approved by state legislatures and must also accept the school voucher. Owing to the highly decentralized nature of the American public school system, school voucher programs occur on a relatively small scale (Lee, Croninger, and Smith 1996). The first school voucher system emerged in 1869, in the state of Vermont, in order to accommodate students who live in rural areas without a public school in their town. The student can attend any public or approved private school, and the student's hometown pays tuition directly to the chosen school. Maine enacted a similar program a few years later. In more recent years, however, voucher programs have targeted low-income urban children.

Empirical research shows that school voucher programs have had mixed results (Lee, Croninger, and Smith 1996), but that is probably not surprising given the high degree of variability among voucher systems. For instance, a case study of New York vouchers shows an improvement in test scores for black students, but not for nonblack students (Mayer et al. 2002; Peterson et al. 2003). In general, research has found that vouchers are not systematically increasing most academic achievement outcomes for students (Lee, Croninger, and Smith 1996; Smrekar and Goldring 1999), although there is evidence to suggest that graduation rates improve for students who take advantage of vouchers (Wolf et al. 2010), and college enrollment rates are significantly higher among black students who use vouchers. School vouchers remain a small portion of the school-choice market and are not available to all students.

MAGNET SCHOOLS

Magnet schools are operated by school districts, have the same school boards as the public schools, and must adhere to state requirements. Magnet schools *are* public schools and thus cannot charge tuition. Students attending magnet schools were drawn across district or neighborhood lines based on specialized curricula or courses (e.g., fine arts or STEM [science, technology, engineering, and mathematics] courses). Some magnet schools may require an entrance exam, audition, or interview. In cases where there is high demand, but noncompetitive entry, magnet schools will use a lottery system. Developed in the 1960s, and then booming in the 1980s, magnet schools were originally intended to help desegregate the public school system. While magnet schools often more closely resemble their attendance zones with regard to racial diversity, they rarely approximate the distribution in socioeconomic status. But parents hailing from lower socioeconomic or minority backgrounds are less likely to be aware of magnet schools in the first place (Henig 1995). Magnet schools are often criticized for "creaming" the best and brightest students from the surrounding public schools, which creates an academic disadvantage for the remaining public school students and those schools (Smrekar and Goldring

1999). While magnet schools have a reputation for attracting and educating high-quality students, the evidence on how magnet schools affect academic achievement remains quite mixed. For instance, students who entered a Chicago lottery for magnet school enrollment were not more likely to graduate or have greater gains in achievement (Cullen, Jacob, and Levitt 2006).

CHARTER SCHOOLS AND CHOICE IN THE UNITED STATES

Although funded by the public typically on a per-student basis, charter schools operate outside the control of traditional public school districts. Accordingly, charter schools are typically exempt from some of the regulations that govern public schools. Charter school advocates argue that this model results in innovative schools that are uniquely responsive to parents' interests.

Since 1992, forty-three states and Washington, DC, have enacted laws authorizing charter schools (Kentucky, Montana, Nebraska, North Dakota, South Dakota, Vermont, and West Virginia do not have charter school laws). As of fall of 2016, nearly three million children (or more than 6 percent of the nation's public school attendees) attend approximately sixty-eight hundred charter schools. A majority of charter schools are located in urban areas, but suburban areas and rural locations also house charter schools and students. In some cities, such as Washington, DC; Detroit; and New Orleans, at least half of students go to charter schools. States grant charter schools more freedom than traditional public schools to construct their own curricula. However, state and federal policies hold charter schools accountable for student success, financial disclosure, and racial equity, among other educational issues, in the same way they hold traditional public schools accountable.

The demographics of the students who attend charter schools look much different from those of students who attend traditional public schools. Close to one-third of students in charter schools are black, compared to 16 percent nationwide. Latino/Hispanic students make up approximately 27 percent of charter school students, but only a fifth of the traditional school population.

Charter schools are part of a set of options designed to put families and local educators in control of schooling. It is still unclear, however, whether charter schools promote better educational outcomes, as measured by test scores, learning, and college-going. And while advocates of charter schools argue that they are educationally more innovative, it is still unclear to what extent this is true.

While charter schools are required to meet certain national standards—for example, they must employ the lottery system and must report academic achievement data—laws governing the schools can differ greatly by state. For instance, some states place limitations on who can authorize a charter school (e.g., in Alaska, only the state board of education can do so). Moreover, each state may cap the number of charter schools allowed in the state (e.g., Illinois limits the total number of charter schools to 120, and only 70 charter schools can exist in Chicago), limit the total percentage of a district's students that a charter school can educate (e.g., charter schools in Connecticut can enroll no more than 250 students, or no more than 25 percent of the district's total student population), and restrict the number of new charter schools that can open in any given year (e.g., Washington, DC, allows only twenty new charter schools to open in a given year). Other states may require that charter schools demonstrate how they will fill an educational need in the community (e.g., New Jersey requires that mission statements include an outline of the proposed school's intended innovations). As a result of the variation in state laws and policies, the charter school movement can appear vastly different from state to state. The variation in state laws, rules, regulations, and norms also contributes to the difficulty that researchers face when studying charter schools at the national level.

THEORETICAL APPROACHES TO CHARTER SCHOOLS

To understand charter schools in the context of educational policy and practice, it is important to understand theoretical perspectives within the sociology of education, as well as broader concepts associated with school choice: market theory and institutional theory.

Market Theory

Advocates of choice, and in particular charter schools, rely on theories of the market. *Market theories,* derived from and used by economists such as Milton Friedman, suggest that public schools should be paid for by the government but controlled locally, and that school choice will drive school reform through competition. The idea is that school competition—that is, the need to attract and retain students and families—will necessarily inspire both innovation in educational methods and accountability in stakeholders. These models also assume that, in expanding innovation and accountability and placing power directly in the hands of families, schools of choice will ultimately challenge the traditional political structures governing schools.

This all suggests that charter schools should look different from traditional public schools. For example, a market-choice proponent would suggest that freedom and competition will breed diversity and innovation in the market owing to the need to compete for students. Along these lines, we would expect to see charter schools adopt innovative missions and curricula, provide diverse and new opportunities not customarily found in traditional public schools, and develop novel ways of organizing the schools themselves. Finally, the assumption behind this approach is that new and different charter schools will change the overall educational market and spur changes in traditional public schools. Do charter schools exhibit these characteristics? Assessing this question is the key to measuring the success or failure of charter schools and the market model from which they derive their rationale.

Institutional Theory

Schools are workplaces as well as institutions of learning. Thus organizational scholars, particularly those espousing *institutional theory,* have offered a set of suppositions regarding the creation and spread of charter schools, the extent to which these schools differ from traditional public schools, and the structural work relations within the school. The ideas and conclusions about, and prospects of, charter schools and choice that emerge from institutional theory diverge from—and are somewhat at odds with—the market theories discussed above.

Schools are highly bureaucratic, and they operate within a set of rules that have come to be accepted as normal. People tend to accept this uniformity and expect that all schools will essentially have the same parts and structure. These bureaucratic norms exist at the federal, state, local, and school levels. Therefore, parents, teachers, students, and the public at large come to have certain expectations about what each level of the school should do and look like, and how different levels of the school system will interact with one another. For example, we expect the interiors of schools to be organized in a specific way, so that we know how to find the main office, classrooms, the gymnasium, and so forth. We also have a general idea about who will be in each space and what each person's job entails: the math teacher will be in her math classroom teaching math, for example, while the school counselor will be in his office counseling students. Further, we now expect the federal government to pass laws every few years that govern academic achievement standards (e.g., No Child Left Behind, Every Student Succeeds Act). These general rules contribute to our expectations and help us navigate the school system. When schools adopt and embrace these norms, this grants schools legitimacy in the eyes of the public. And in the rare cases when schools *do* look different, we may be slow to consider them legitimate places for public education.

Thus, schools tend to be more alike than different. Organizational scholars refer to this tendency as *isomorphism.* In the charter sector, the notion of institutional isomorphism predicts that charter schools will tend to look much like traditional public schools—contrary to charter school advocates' promises regarding innovation. Our analysis suggests that isomorphism tends to hold. While early charter schools had diverse mission statements, over time those mission statements have converged around a model that largely parallels the traditional public school model (Renzulli, Barr, and Paino 2015).

RESEARCH QUESTIONS AND FINDINGS

Diffusion of Policy Models

How do new charter schools select educational and organizational models? To answer this question, we must first examine how educational policy spreads. Thus, before we can understand why a charter school is created, it is important to consider how the organizational structure became an option in the first place. Institutional theories suggest that policy makers mimic the precedents of nearby states: how these actors adopted charter school legislation and went about creating new charter schools. Internal qualities of states—such as the size of the private school sector, the strength of teachers' unions, the racial composition of districts, the degree of urbanization, and the political balance—all factor into legislation and school creation. Since policy makers are inclined to mimic states and areas around themselves, it is no wonder that forty-three states now have charter laws, and that the number of schools has grown to approximately sixty-eight hundred. Schools play an integral role in our society: they are tasked with educating students over a period of many years. Changes to the landscape of public schools have profound effects on the students who frequent these institutions; thus, this type of information is important for understanding, from both a policy and an organizational standpoint, how and why educational change can happen.

Still, this begs the question of why some states embrace charter schools and others do not. Why, for example, does Kentucky *not* have a charter school law, given the fact that it shares a border and many demographic characteristics with Indiana, a state with a law that provides strong encouragement for the charter school model? These are questions that organizational scholars, economists, and policy scholars still need to consider.

Openings and Closings

Our research has also focused, in part, on charter school failures (Paino, Renzulli, Boylan, and Bradley 2014). Our work maps the existence of charter schools and correlates their opening and closing to other simultaneous events and circumstances in the sociopolitical environment, including educational legislation, school achievement, racial composition, and the existence of competing private schools.

Traditional public schools close only rarely: annually, about 1–2 percent of traditional public schools close. By comparison, approximately 15 percent of the sixty-eight hundred charter schools established to date have now closed their doors. Charter schools can close for many different reasons, including problems with their academics, finances, enrollment, facility, and management. Most charter schools cite financial reasons as the impetus for closure; only about 10 percent cite academic issues as the reason for closing their doors.

Even among schools that close for academic reasons, finances play an integral role in closures, and a mixed-method analytical approach reveals how these two factors are interwoven.

In one sense, a charter school's closure demonstrates accountability: it is an admission that a given school has failed to meet the terms laid out in its charter. This is no doubt cold comfort, however, to the students and families who invested in the failing charter school. Most immediately, families must seek an alternative school in which to enroll their students. Beyond this, charter school failures may negatively influence educational outcomes in a number of possible ways. While there is evidence that charter school closures result in the relocation of students to higher-quality schools (Carlson and Lavertu 2016), educational transitions are often difficult for students and may result in achievement declines. Studies have also found that charter school closures disproportionately affect schools that serve predominantly black students, suggesting a persistent disadvantage for a particular demographic.

How organizationally innovative are charter schools? Organizational research in other arenas suggests that inertia is a strong force in organizational life, and that innovation is difficult to achieve and to maintain. In this light, why would charter schools be different from other organizations?

A key element of charter school policy highlights the importance of innovative and specialized missions or curricula. Charter schools have the autonomy and flexibility to offer innovative and/or specialized curricula to students, and many schools embrace this opportunity. The specialized curricula are designed to attract students with unique needs. For instance, a charter school can offer a fine arts curriculum for students who are especially talented or interested in the fine arts. In doing so, that charter school will serve a clear-cut niche in the educational market and fully meet the needs of some students. Charter schools indicate their specialties and innovative curricula through their publicly available mission statements. Parents and students have access to these mission statements and can choose schools that best suit their interests. Specialized charter schools, in turn, draw on distinct subpopulations of students who are interested in their particular specialties.

The concept of organizational innovation includes something called *market niche innovation.* Market niche innovation occurs when an organization changes, improves, or enhances an existing product, service, or approach. As we have seen, charter schools claim to be market-niche innovators in the realm of education. Innovation can vary depending on the time and circumstances. Innovation also varies across different types of organizations. Some organizations may need to develop a new product or service. Other organizations might need to find a way to make an existing product in a more efficient manner. Still others may choose to specialize in a service or product that is available elsewhere, but one they can offer with more options, greater variety, or higher quality. Let's look at three examples of such processes, all of which revolve around organizations that deal with food. In the first example, grocery stores provide a way for individuals to purchase food; but as lifestyles and habits have changed over time, a new niche in the market has opened up for organizations that provide food delivery services. These services accommodate individuals who want healthy food, at reasonable prices, conveniently (i.e., ingredients and recipes are shipped to people). This new service provides food and the recipes necessary to cook the food, but it packages them in a way that makes cooking more convenient for the consumer. In the second example, fast food restaurants have made innovations by taking existing products (e.g., largely burgers and other sandwiches) and making them available quickly, at a low cost. Innovations that focus on efficiency allow organizations to make large quantities of a given product, at a lower cost or in a faster manner, and consumers can obtain the product cheaply and quickly. Bakeries, the third example, are not a new type of organization, but specialty bakeries have become an increasingly common type of bakery. For instance, bakeries that offer only cupcakes are common now. This innovation allows the bakery to offer a greater variety of cupcakes, compared to bakeries that try to offer a large range of baked goods, and which may have only a few cupcake options.

Media outlets advertise charter schools as innovative schools precisely because they are organized in a new way and, in fact, may be introducing new ways of teaching. Current research has found that some charter school missions—those proclaiming innovation—have become increasingly diverse over time. At the same time, charter schools have *also* come to look traditional, something institutional theory would in fact predict. Although some charter schools are introducing innovations, these make up a small portion of all the charter schools currently running. Compared to traditional schools, charter schools have wide latitude when penning their mission statements. Given their freedom, we may expect to see great diversity and innovation in charter school mission statements, but research on such statements reveals a nuanced picture. Since their inception in 1992, charter schools have increasingly produced generic mission statements; however, when they do write innovative mission statements, those tend to be new and diverse. This has interesting implications for the ways charter school laws (discussed above) are created, and for how they move from law to enactment to create educational innovation.

Unanswered in this line of research is how much freedom teachers have to be innovative in their classrooms. Thus far, research has told us little about how much classroom innovation, or on-the-ground innovation, is occurring. Market theory predicts more innovation, whereas institutional theory predicts less.

From an organizational point of view, this leads to another important dimension of charter school work: what are the structural work relations within the charter school?

Schools Are Loosely Coupled Organizations

In an effort to explain why schools all tend to be structured in much the same way, organizational theorists draw on basic premises of neo-institutional theory; but they also note other organizational features that seem to persist in schools. Their conclusions demonstrate that schools not only look the same but also often employ similar methods of organization that allow different pieces of the schools to function harmoniously, but separately; this characteristic keeps everything running smoothly. Therefore, education scholars have labeled public schools as *loosely coupled organizations,* meaning that the internal parts of the schools are connected but largely independent from one another. Classroom instruction, for example, is loosely coupled in the sense that teachers are rarely subject to direct supervision in the classroom and are, instead, free to develop their own instructional approaches largely independent of one another (despite the fact that their students move from one teacher's classroom to another as they progress through school). What keeps the subparts of an organization linked, yet independent from one another, is the shared vision of the organizational goal rather than constant connectivity or persistent interdependence. When educational scholars refer to the "parts" of an organization, they are often indicating the people who work in the school—the administrators, teachers, and staff. But there are other parts of the school, and these can include governing bodies (e.g., departments of education), policies (e.g., No Child Left Behind or its successor, the Every Student Succeeds Act), and the students and parents.

The relationships and interactions between principals and teachers highlight the loose-coupling model prevalent in schools. We think of teachers as managing and instructing their own classrooms as individualized environments, in which the teachers can adjust their lessons and plans to accommodate students as needed. For a clear example of loose coupling between principals and teachers, consider the following example: A principal may advise his or her teachers on techniques and approaches they should use in their classrooms, but only rarely observe or supervise the actual classroom activities, allowing teachers to symbolically close the classroom doors and run their own classrooms.

States and districts may have standards and/or curricula that dictate parameters for teachers' instruction, which would result in teachers having less autonomy and control over their classroom instruction. If teachers closely adhere to district and state standards, then scholars would label this organizational change as tight coupling. In charter schools, however, the mission statements and curriculum decisions are largely left up to the individual schools (and the teachers within the school). Therefore, we would expect charter schools to look different from traditional schools. Charter schools should enjoy a looser relationship with the other parts of the system—namely, they should expect less oversight and input from the state and district levels of the public education system, since they are released from many procedural and bureaucratic rules that affect traditional public schools. As a result, charter schools have the loosest coupling of the public school options.

The structure of charter schools does appear to differ in significant ways from that of traditional schools, at least in the perception of teachers. Charter school teachers report being more satisfied than public school teachers because of greater autonomy given to them in their workplaces. At the same time, charter school teachers are twice as likely to leave the profession as traditional teachers (Stuit and Smith 2010). Why is this the case? Organizational coupling and commitment might be a reason, but more research is needed in order to answer that question.

Achievement

How does the structure of charter schools affect outcomes such as achievement? Academic achievement is a persistent issue for all types of schools, and charter schools are no exception. To reiterate an earlier point: Market theory anticipates that students enrolled in charter schools will achieve more than their traditional school counterparts because charter schools allow students to find schools that fit their needs. Furthermore, according to this model, competition ensures excellence: if schools fail to meet expectations, students can simply leave for a different school. Indeed, charter school advocates argue that charter schools are uniquely situated to perform well, owing to their greater autonomy and flexibility relative to traditional public schools.

Conversely, institutional theorists suggest that given isomorphism, charter and traditional schools tend to look alike. Thus, students going to charter schools may not have achievement gains above what they would have had in traditional school settings. Moreover, students enrolling in a charter school run the risk—if the school fails—of having to transfer to a different school, a process associated with negative educational consequences.

The jury is still out on which theory is correct in predicting charter school achievement. Research on academic achievement in charter schools, compared to traditional schools, shows mixed results. While some charter schools experience a great deal of success, others do much worse, and still others look no different from their traditional school counterparts. Despite the assertions of advocates, it is unclear why some charter schools succeed academically and others fail. In addition, the research on the latter is dominated by case studies or simple comparisons (Henig 2008).

Another stream of research uses lottery data to measure how successfully charter schools educate students. This is somewhat like a natural experiment. If a charter school is oversubscribed, the school will take the names of all those who applied and then draw the selected number the school can hold. Using lottery data, researchers are able to compare highly motived students who enroll in a given school to highly motived students who are not offered enrollment. Some of this work has demonstrated gains in academic achievement among students who attend charter schools, compared to those who do not. In New York City, for example, students who attended charter schools showed cumulative advantages in math and English that were greater than those of their peers in the city, and which rivaled those of the wealthier suburban students (Dobbie and Fryer 2011). In cases where charter schools are in high demand, such as the Harlem Children's Zone (featured in the popular documentary *Waiting for Superman*), researchers found that students who "won" the lottery were at a much greater advantage. These schools were able to close the race gap in academic achievement. (Similar findings in Boston show that lottery "winners" outperform lottery "losers" in both math and English [Angrist et al. 2012].)

Not all analyses of achievement in charter schools show positive gains. In many studies, analyses show mixed results. In a study that included thirty-six charter schools across fifteen states, researchers found no positive effects on math or reading. Another research study shows that charter schools in charter management organizations (CMOs hold the charters of multiple schools) have diverse outcomes. Across twenty-two schools, half of the schools had positive outcomes in math, one-third of the schools produced negative effects in math, and the final four schools showed neither positive nor negative effects in math. One of the larger studies on charter school achievement looked at charter schools in twenty-seven states and found that students in charter schools and students in traditional public schools experienced similar gains in academic achievement. These researchers concluded that students in charter schools were performing at levels similar to those of their traditional public school peers, but were neither better than nor worse than these students (Clark et al. 2011). Additional studies have found similar results among charter school students. Schools receiving the lion's share of the media attention, such as Harlem Children's Zone and the Knowledge Is Power Program, tend to be the schools that demonstrate the greatest academic achievements, but we need to exercise caution when trying to extrapolate from these outliers. Given such mixed results on academic achievement, researchers should continue to investigate the relationship between the charter school model and academic achievement.

Segregation

How do charter schools affect segregation and desegregation in school districts? At the beginning of this chapter, we highlighted the demographic differences that exist between charter schools and traditional public schools.

Underrepresented minorities are disproportionately more likely to attend a charter school, compared to their white and Asian counterparts. Issues of racial segregation have long plagued our public school system, but the proliferation of charter schools adds a new dynamic to this issue. Unlike magnet schools, charter schools were not originally designed to address the systematic segregation present in public schools. For years, desegregation efforts such as busing and magnet schools ameliorated the dramatic segregation in US schools. But as charter schools began to open their doors in greater numbers, and began attracting students of color in greater numbers, they have primarily served as agents of segregation, rather than forces for desegregation.

Though charter schools serve minority students in disproportionate numbers, and there are instances of remarkably diverse schools, charter schools mostly educate minorities in segregated contexts. According to the Civil Rights Project's analysis of forty states and the District of Columbia, charter schools are more racially segregated than other public schools in most states and large cities. In fact, black students who go to charter schools are much more likely to go to segregated schools than their black counterparts in traditional schools (despite the fact that traditional schools are also highly segregated). This racial segregation is not limited to black students. In fact, half of Latino students in charter schools attend segregated schools as well. Some suggest that this segregation is in fact beneficial to students, providing choice and an alternative education for students who were already in segregated and underachieving schools. Thus, the comparisons of charter schools to traditional schools' demographics nationally may be illogical. The jury is still out on the academic advantages of going to a segregated charter school.

RESEARCH FRONTIERS

Over the last twenty years of this educational experiment, we have learned a lot about the ways charter schools open and close and operate. Yet there is much more to be addressed. In this chapter we have only touched on the racial and stratification effects of charter schools. We know a little about who charter schools educate in the cross-section, but these schools' effect on closing or adding to the segregation gap in public schooling is still unknown. In addition, the effects of charter schools on minorities and the growing number of impoverished children, in relation to their long-term educational attainment, is still unknown.

We have very few analyses that follow students as they transition in and out of charter schools. Recent evidence suggests that students who transfer to charter schools (from their districts' public schools) are academically weaker students. But we know little about the cumulative advantage or disadvantage for these students.

Given recent developments in American educational politics and policy, it seems likely that choice will play an increasingly prominent role in the American educational system. However, the extent to which this development will create new opportunities for America's most educationally disadvantaged students remains to be seen. In the years to come, it will be important for researchers, policy makers, and educators to watch how this market model of choice affects the form and function of the educational system in the United States. Who gets access to the best educational practices in what environment and why?

CHAPTER 15 REVIEW

Discussion Questions

1. How are charter schools different from traditional public schools?
2. How can school choice be positive and/or negative for parents, students, and communities?
3. What is the difference between the market theories and institutional theories of charter schools?
4. Institutional theorists suggest that charter schools will look more and more like traditional schools. Is there evidence to support this? Explain.
5. Why is the market model of school choice compelling? Is there evidence that the market model is successful in creating educational innovation and accountability?

Suggestions for Further Reading

Berends, Mark. 2015. "Sociology and School Choice: What We Know after Two Decades of Charter Schools." *Annual Review of Sociology* 41 (1): 159–80.

Berends, Mark, Ellen Goldring, Marc Stein, and Xiu Cravens. 2010. "Instructional Conditions in Charter Schools and Students' Mathematics Achievement Gains." *American Journal of Education* 116 (3): 303–36.

Bifulco, Robert, and Helen F. Ladd. 2006. "The Impacts of Charter Schools on Student Achievement: Evidence from North Carolina." *Education Finance and Policy* 1 (1): 50–90.

Center for Research on Education Outcomes (CREDO). 2013. *National Charter School Study.* Stanford, CA: CREDO. https://credo.stanford.edu/documents/NCSS%202013%20Final%20Draft.pdf.

Hoxby, Caroline M., Jenny Lee Kang, and Sonali Murarka. 2009. *Technical Report: How New York City Charter Schools Affect Achievement.* Cambridge, MA: New York City Charter School Evaluation Project.

Lubienski, Christopher. 2003. "Innovation in Education Markets: Theory and Evidence on the Impact of Competition and Choice in Charter Schools." *American Educational Research Journal* 40 (2): 395–443.

Paino, Maria, Rebecca L. Boylan, and Linda A. Renzulli. "The Closing Door: The Effect of Race on Charter School Closures." *Sociological Perspectives* 60 (4): 747–67.

Paino, Maria, Linda A. Renzulli, Rebecca Boylan, and Christen Bradley. 2014. "For Money or Grades? Charter School Failure in North Carolina." *Educational Administration Quarterly* 50 (3): 500–36.

Renzulli, Linda A., Ashley Barr, and Maria Paino. 2015. "Innovating Education? A Test of Specialist Mimicry or Generalist Assimilation in Trends in Charter School Specialization over Time." *Sociology of Education* 88 (1): 83–102.

Renzulli, Linda A., and Maria Paino. 2013. "Charter School Accountability and Innovation." *Contexts-Viewpoints* 12 (3): 23–24.

Renzulli, Linda A., and Vincent Roscigno. 2005. "Charter School Policy, Implementation, and Diffusion in the United States." *Sociology of Education* 78:344–65.

References

Angrist, J. D., S. M. Dynarski, T. J., Kane, P. A. Pathak, and C. R. Walters. 2012. "Who Benefits from KIPP?" *Journal of Policy Analysis and Management* 31 (4): 837–60.

Carlson, D., and S. Lavertu. 2016. "Charter School Closure and Student Achievement: Evidence from Ohio." *Journal of Urban Economics* 95:31–48.

Clark, M. A., P. Gleason, C. C. Tuttle, and M. K. Silverberg. 2011. "Do Charter Schools Improve Student Achievement? Evidence from a National Randomized Study." Working paper. Princeton, NJ: Mathematica Policy Research.

Cullen, J. B., B. A. Jacob, and S. Levitt. 2006. "The Effect of School Choice on Participants: Evidence from Randomized Lotteries." *Econometrica* 74 (5): 1191–230.

Dobbie, Will, and Roland G. Fryer Jr. 2011. "Are High-Quality Schools Enough to Increase Achievement among the Poor? Evidence from the Harlem Children's Zone." *American Economic Journal: Applied Economics* 3 (3): 158–87.

Henig, J. R. 1995. *Rethinking School Choice: Limits of the Market Metaphor.* Princeton, NJ: Princeton University Press.

———. 2008. *Spin Cycle: How Research Gets Used in Policy Debates—the Case of Charter Schools.* New York: Russell Sage Foundation.

Lee, V. E., R. G. Croninger, and J. B. Smith. 1996. "Equity and Choice in Detroit." In *Who Chooses? Who Loses?* edited by Bruce Fuller and Richard F. Elmore, with Gary Orfield, 70–94. New York: Teachers College Press.

Mayer, D. P., P. E. Peterson, D. E. Myers, C. C. Tuttle, and W. G Howell. 2002. *School Choice in New York City after Three Years: An Evaluation of the School Choice Scholarships Program.* Final report. Princeton, NJ: Mathematica Policy Research; Cambridge, MA: Harvard University.

Paino, Maria, Linda A. Renzulli, Rebecca Boylan, and Christen Bradley. 2014. "For Money or Grades? Charter School Failure in North Carolina." *Educational Administration Quarterly* 50 (3): 500–36.

Peterson, P., W. Howell, P. J. Wolf, and D. Campbell. 2003. "School Vouchers: Results from Randomized Experiments." In *The Economics of School Choice,* edited by Caroline M. Hoxby, 107–44. Chicago: University of Chicago Press.

Renzulli, Linda A., Ashley Barr, and Maria Paino. 2015. "Innovating Education? A Test of Specialist Mimicry or Generalist Assimilation in Trends in Charter School Specialization over Time." *Sociology of Education* 88 (1): 83–102.

Smrekar, C., and E. Goldring. 1999. *School Choice in Urban America: Magnet Schools and the Pursuit of Equity.* Critical Issues in Educational Leadership Series. Williston, VT: Teachers College Press.

Stuit, D., and T. M Smith. 2010. *Teacher Turnover in Charter Schools.* Research brief. Nashville, TN: National Center on School Choice, Vanderbilt University.

Wolf, P., B. Gutmann, M. Puma, B. Kisida, L. Rizzo, N. Eissa, and M. Carr. 2010. *Evaluation of the DC Opportunity Scholarship Program: Final Report.* NCEE 2010–4018. Washington, DC: National Center for Education Evaluation and Regional Assistance, Institute of Education Sciences, US Department of Education.

16

Higher Education and the Labor Market

ERIC GRODSKY, UNIVERSITY OF WISCONSIN

JULIE POSSELT, UNIVERSITY OF SOUTHERN CALIFORNIA

EDITORS' NOTE

The expansion of higher education is one of the distinguishing characteristics of the **schooled society** that Evan Schofer describes in chapter 1. Today, almost all high school seniors in the United States say that they plan to earn a college degree; nearly 80 percent of high school graduates attend some form of higher education; and the college-for-all ideal shapes nearly every aspect of our education system.

But why do we care so much about higher education in contemporary society? Sociologists Eric Grodsky of University of Wisconsin and Julie Posselt of University of Southern California consider human capital, social reproduction, and credentialist explanations for the value of college degrees. While the first two of those ideas should be familiar to you from earlier chapters, the last idea, **credentialism,** is new. This is the idea that the important part of college is not the skills you learn or the social connections you make but the fact that college provides a signal of the sort of person you are.

A significant part of this theory is the recognition that the American higher education system is extremely **differentiated.** When you transitioned from high school to college, you were faced with a higher-education landscape that included a wide range of schools—from the nonselective community college down the street to the incredibly selective elite institution across the country. The variation in status between colleges and universities explains in part how these institutions help sort young people into a highly unequal American social structure. As you read this chapter, think about the degree to which you see evidence of human capital, social reproduction, and credentialism in your school.

KEY POINTS

- Educational attainment confers powerful advantages across the life course, including career opportunities and other economic benefits, as well as lower health risks, lower rates of criminality, and higher rates of civic engagement.
- The cause of these advantages remains a point for scholarly debate. Human capital theories emphasize the ways in which education teaches skills and improves productivity, while social reproduction theories emphasize processes of social closure.
- The postsecondary system in the United States is highly differentiated, and wider patterns of socioeconomic, racial, and gender stratification manifest in enrollment in—and economic returns to degrees from—different institutional types, including community colleges, elite universities, and for-profit institutions.

INTRODUCTION

Most Americans continue their education past high school and have for some time. Rates of baccalaureate completion among individuals thirty-five years of age climbed slowly for cohorts born between 1880 and 1920, before beginning a steep ascent. Between the birth cohort of 1920 and the cohort of 1975, the share of thirty-five-year-old women with at least four years of college education increased from around 7 percent to almost 40 percent; the share for men over this period increased from about 10 percent to around 30 percent (Goldin, Katz, and Kuziemko 2006). These sharp increases in baccalaureate completion mask even greater increases in postsecondary attendance. By the time the high school class of 1960 graduated, college attendance right after high school had become the rule rather than the exception; 57 percent of those students attended some sort of postsecondary institution by 1961, and 32 percent attended a baccalaureate college (Schoenfeldt 1968). Fast-forward forty-three years to the high school class of 2004, and almost eight of ten (77 percent) would attend a postsecondary institution within two years of completing their high school diploma or GED. As of 2006, 46 percent of those students were enrolled in a baccalaureate college and 32 percent in a community or junior college.

Why do so many people seek higher education? What role does college play in reinforcing or weakening the relationships among socioeconomic background, race/ethnicity, sex, and adult outcomes? This chapter explores these questions, bringing together sociology and economics literatures to explain the role higher education plays in people's lives. We begin by describing what we know about the benefits of college completion, focusing largely on baccalaureate credentials. Next, we discuss dominant theories in sociology and economics that try to account for the positive relationship between college completion and labor market outcomes. We then move past the distinction of college or not to consider different types of postsecondary institutions and the degree to which institutional differentiation and social stratification are intertwined.

THE VARIED ECONOMIC RETURNS TO HIGHER EDUCATION

The economic benefits of higher education tend to dominate both popular discussions and the academic literature on the benefits of higher education. Except during a brief dip in the 1970s, much of the past century has witnessed rising economic returns to a baccalaureate degree (Goldin and Katz 2008). Although some estimates of lifetime earnings benefits are as high as $1.1 million (in 2009 dollars; Carnevale, Rose, and Cheah 2011), recent research suggests that an average net return of $444,000 for men and $346,000 for women is more accurate (Barrow and Malamud 2015). The economic returns to college vary by sex (DiPrete and Buchmann 2005) and race/ethnicity, and they may differ across levels of cognitive and noncognitive skill (Heckman et al. 2014) and across college majors and types of college (Eide, Hilmer, and Showalter 2015; Webber 2016).

The economic value of college is not, however, solely a reflection of college completion. In fact, a large share of the value of completing college comes from the opportunity to earn a graduate or professional degree. This is known as the continuation or option value of education (Heckman et al. 2014). Over the 1980s and 1990s the rate of growth in the baccalaureate wage premium over the wage of those who completed only high school declined appreciably; the rate of growth in the college-only advantage was about zero between 2010 and 2015. In contrast, the rate of economic return to graduate or professional degrees relative to college degrees increased steadily between 1980 and 2010 before declining slightly (Valletta 2016). Much of what we commonly refer to as growth in the "college wage premium" over the past quarter century is actually growth in the economic returns to postgraduate training.

Associate's degrees and vocational certificates also confer advantages in the labor market, though recent estimates suggest that the net value of an associate's degree is less than half that of a baccalaureate degree. There is some evidence of growth in the economic returns to associate's degrees over time (Belfield and Bailey 2011), but the evidence for trends in returns at the subbaccalaureate level is less conclusive than for the baccalaureate level.

In addition to economic benefits, those who complete college experience a range of noneconomic benefits (Hout 2012). Educational attainment is a critical social determinant of health, for example. Education in general, and college in particular, also contributes to the "diverging destinies" of American families (McLanahan 2004), with patterns of marriage, marital timing and longevity, and fertility closely bound to college attendance and completion. College graduates are markedly less likely to be convicted of a crime or experience incarceration (Lochner 2011; Oreopoulos and Salvanes 2009) and are more likely to vote and show other evidence of civic engagement (Dee 2004; Milligan, Moretti, and Oreopoulos 2004).

WHY DOES COLLEGE MATTER SO MUCH?

Sociologists and economists have developed a variety of theories to account for the importance of postsecondary education to adult outcomes. The dominant theory in economics since the 1960s has been human capital theory, which asserts that education transmits skills to students that increase their productivity in the labor market. Sociological theories, in contrast, are often based on symbolic relations of power and exclusion. Theories of cultural and social reproduction inspired by the work of Pierre Bourdieu highlight how education helps youth from advantaged families retain their social advantage by conferring and rewarding high-status knowledge and behavior. Credential theory, meanwhile, suggests that education both pays off by restricting access to high-paying and high-status jobs and creates a shared identity among the individuals who hold these roles. Finally, institutional theory posits that what schools actually teach is largely unrelated to their power to produce hierarchy. From the institutionalist perspective, schools are simply chartered by society to produce social distinctions. These theories vary in scope, with human capital and reproduction theory, in particular, striving to account for a range of social phenomena. We will focus primarily on how each perspective accounts for the economic returns to education in general and postsecondary education in particular.

Human Capital and Productivity

Introduced in economics in the late 1950s and early 1960s (Becker 1962; Schultz 1961; Weisbrod 1962), human capital theory expands the realm of productive assets from material resources like land and machinery to include attributes of people that enhance or reduce their productivity. These attributes include their general cognitive skills; their understanding of and capacity to perform specific sets of tasks; their health; and their social skills, among other things. According to human capital theory, we are all capitalists. We make investment decisions about our own stores of productive resources, subject to the intrinsic and extrinsic constraints we face, and as a result encounter highly varied labor market experiences. Although investments in human capital by individuals and society may produce benefits beyond the individual (Weisbrod 1962), we focus here only on those benefits that accrue directly to students. The productivity of those who possess greater amounts of human capital improves their employment prospects and results in earnings greater than those of others who have lesser stores of human capital.

Gary Becker (1962) distinguishes between general human capital, which enhances productivity across a broad range of settings, and firm-specific human capital, which enhances productivity in a particular organizational setting. Through a variety of means, schools cultivate general human capital, including numeracy, literacy, and analytic skills. At each point in their educational career, students, along with their parents, confront a choice either to continue on in school or to enter the labor market. If students choose school, they forego earnings and the opportunity to accrue labor market experience in favor of accruing more human capital.

Human capital theory assumes that the choice to continue in school is informed not only by the opportunities students confront but also by students' varying tastes, preferences, and endowments of cognitive and noncognitive skills. Those with greater stores of cognitive skills find school less challenging but also face steeper costs of attendance in terms of foregone earnings, since they, presumably, would be more productive (and thus successful) in the labor market than those with fewer cognitive skills, all else being equal. The combination of differential selection into higher levels of education based on prior skills, and the differential economic returns to education, accounts for the skewness in the distribution of earnings. Those who begin with the most human capital are also able to accrue more, a phenomenon known as comparative advantage (Carneiro, Heckman, and Vytlacil 2011).

Cultural Reproduction

In contrast to human capital theorists, Bourdieu (1984) emphasized the role of education in rewarding and producing cultural capital and not necessarily skills directly relevant to productivity in the workplace. Early analyses in the US context operationalized cultural capital as "highbrow" cultural consumption such as museum and classical music concert attendance (DiMaggio 1982; Kalmijn and Kraaykamp 1996), but others argued for a broader view of cultural capital that includes any resources people deploy to satisfy "evaluative norms favoring the children or families of a particular social milieu" (Lareau and Weininger 2003). Bourdieu's own conceptions have perhaps been most important to empirical analyses of higher education. He highlighted three forms of cultural capital: *embodied*, one's accumulated cultural dispositions and knowledge; *objectified*, material objects such as art, clothing, and books that are laden with cultural value; and *institutionalized*, the qualifications and credentials that represent competence in a cultural domain.

In students' ascension through grades and degree programs in the French educational system, Bourdieu argued, schools and colleges reward forms of social capital (i.e., resources available through group and network membership) and cultural capital (i.e., high-status cultural knowledge, attitudes, and behaviors) that are disproportionately found among economic elites. In contrast to the vision of an opportunity structure open to anyone with the cognitive skills and willingness to invest in education, cultural reproduction theory asserts that social and cultural capital suffuse even the apparently socially neutral academic standards through which educational opportunities are allocated (Bourdieu and Passeron 1979; Lamont and Lareau 1988). Academic distinctions, including the prestige of the college or university one attends, the status of one's field of study, and even one's grades in school, disguise what are in fact social distinctions. By endorsing and reinforcing the cultural capital of the privileged, schools and postsecondary institutions reproduce social class within their walls and in society more widely (Bourdieu and Passeron 1990).

Students themselves participate in this process of selection and reproduction, according to Bourdieu. People's tastes and actions are shaped by unconscious processes, cultivated through childhood socialization, that manifest in what he called *habitus.* A student's habitus primes her to opt into and out of environments that, in the long run, may confer disparate economic returns. Both families (Grodsky and Riegle-Crumb 2010) and organizations (McDonough 1997) have habitus that help shape students' dispositions and preferences, which makes college attendance more a fait accompli than a conscious, utility-maximizing choice as assumed in human capital theory.[1]

In credential-based economies, social, embodied, and institutionalized forms of cultural capital are also central grounds for hiring in elite professional sectors. Unless one displays ease in high-status cultural activities and has a degree from one of a small handful of elite universities, one's chances for securing a job in a top investment firm are slim at best (Rivera 2016). From this perspective, college degrees matter to future earnings because they signal competence and membership in high-status networks that can be exchanged for elite professional opportunities.

The voluminous literature applying this theory to educational systems outside France indicates limits to its transferability. Bethany Bryson (1996) found that higher education attainment in the United States is negatively correlated with cultural exclusivity and positively correlated with political tolerance, suggesting that US elites have broader cultural tastes than the French. Studies of undergraduate- and graduate-level admissions suggest that advanced educational opportunities in the United States not only tend to be defined by class-related capital but also tend to be located at the intersections of class, gender, and race/ethnicity (Karabel 2005; Posselt 2016; Stevens, Armstrong, and Arum 2008; Yosso 2005).

---

1. A common misinterpretation of Bourdieu's theory pins inequality on lower-SES students' lack of social and cultural capital. More accurate is to emphasize that this theory explains how elites represent and reproduce their power and economic advantages by narrowly defining what counts as valued social and cultural capital.

Credentialism and Credential Inflation

Whereas Bourdieu explained the value of college degrees in terms of institutionalized cultural capital, others have examined how postsecondary education credentials—including degrees, licenses, and certifications—can facilitate professional closure. Although the formal, or manifest, function of credentials may be to certify an individual's qualifications, the demands on those who would obtain them also reduce the supply of workers in a particular field and therefore legitimize higher salaries and greater status (Weeden 2002). Credentials effectively enable some workers to claim a monopoly over a given service or professional jurisdiction. Credentialism may be especially important for understanding the value of graduate and professional education. The economic returns to licensure are estimated to be between 11 and 18 percent, and greater shares of people who hold graduate and professional degrees are in occupations that require licensure, compared to those with lower levels of education (Kleiner and Krueger 2013).

Blending the insights of Bourdieu and Weber, Randall Collins (1979) argued that credentials like the baccalaureate degree certify status cultures rather than technical skills or knowledge. He did not deny that students gain knowledge and skills on the way to earning a degree, but asserted that knowledge and skills were incidental—not essential—to the mission of higher education. Cultural currency permeates Collins's views of social stratification, serving as the means to secure economic and political power in organizations (including firms and businesses). This currency is produced by schools at the secondary and postsecondary levels. As competition for secure and lucrative positions increased over the twentieth century, according to Collins, competition for status via higher levels of educational credentials also intensified, leading to credential inflation. David Brown (1995) extends Collins's work to evaluate the rise of colleges and universities in the United States, arguing that status competition among towns led to a proliferation of postsecondary institutions that was peculiar to the United States and contributed to the rise of credentialism and its spread across the professions.

Charters and the Logic of Confidence

Underlying both cultural reproduction and credentialism is an acknowledgment that higher education has meaning in society over and above the job-relevant skills that postsecondary students obtain. This view has its origin in the "old institutionalist" view of education, advanced first by John Meyer. Building on the work of early social theorists (e.g., Parsons 1964; Sorokin 1959), Meyer argued in a series of prominent papers that education serves not only the function of socializing individual students to particular roles but also the function of allocating (i.e., sorting and selecting) social status (Meyer 1970, 1977). He writes, "Educational allocation rules, that is, give to the schools a social charter to define people as graduates and therefore possessing distinct rights and capacities in society. Thus the schools have power as an institutional system, not simply as a set of organizations processing individuals" (Meyer 1977: 59). The power of colleges as social institutions is rooted in broad-based public acceptance that what they do prepares people for what society needs; therefore, we see an especially close tie between mission-specific colleges and universities (i.e., military academies, professional schools, seminaries) and specific occupational categories (Kamens 1974).

In less narrowly defined colleges and universities, prestige may similarly affect students' professional destinations, albeit indirectly, by "indicating the kinds of careers into which [the college's] graduates are expected to move" (Kamens 1971: 272). Colleges may participate in promoting these social contracts, developing organizational sagas to account for their distinctive characters and unique contributions to higher education and society (Clark 1970). What society believes about high-prestige universities, beyond their ability to offer a superior education, explains the allocation of graduates from high-prestige universities to high-status careers. Although this theory is now more than forty-five years old, recent evidence about the process by which students at Harvard and Stanford are "funneled" into finance and consulting careers suggests its continued relevance in explaining higher education's economic returns (Binder, Davis, and Bloom 2016).

WHO GOES WHERE AND WHY?

Social scientists have devoted substantial attention to understanding not only who goes to college but also what types of colleges students attend. Figure 27 displays the differentiated postsecondary landscape in the United States. Among the 4,600 degree-granting institutions in 2015 were 710 public baccalaureate colleges, 910 community colleges, almost 1,600 private, nonprofit baccalaureate colleges, and 1,262 private, for-profit institutions (National Center for Education Statistics 2016). Like the institutions themselves, the processes by which students choose colleges and colleges choose students (Grodsky and Jackson 2009), the experiences students have while attending college (Kuh et al. 2011), and their likelihood of completing a degree and their economic benefits for doing so (Andrews, Li, and Lovenheim 2014; Carneiro, Heckman, and Vytlacil 2011), vary across and to some degree within institution types.

With their frequent focus on social stratification, sociologists of education have written extensively on three types of institutions: community colleges, elite colleges, and more recently, for-profit colleges. Researchers have sought to answer two basic questions for each of these institution types: who attends them and what benefits do graduates enjoy as a consequence of attending? We briefly summarize this work below.

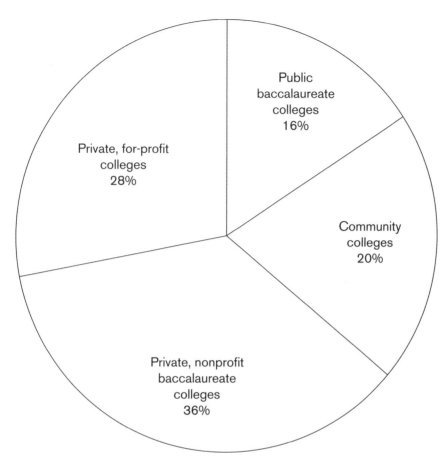

Figure 27. Types of postsecondary institutions in the United States in 2015. Source: National Center for Education Statistics, table 317.10 in *Digest of Education Statistics,* 2016.

Community Colleges

Burton Clark (1960) set the stage for much of the scholarship on community colleges, borrowing a phrase from Erving Goffman (1952) to suggest that community college faculty and staff "cool out" students they serve, diverting them from a baccalaureate pathway when they lack the resources to successfully complete a baccalaureate degree, at least in the eyes of the community college. Steven Brint and Jerome Karabel further develop this theme of managing ambitions, tracing the historic rise of community colleges from their origins as junior colleges—providing the first two years of baccalaureate education when elite four-year colleges preferred not to do so—to their development as institutions that primarily provide vocational education and serve as a means of diverting students from more elite and rewarding baccalaureate programs (Brint and Karabel 1989b).

This critical appraisal set up what has been an enduring debate in the community college literature: are community colleges *democratizing,* providing opportunities to students who would not otherwise participate in higher education, or are they *diversionary,* siphoning off less-advantaged students from the baccalaureate pathway and its status and material rewards? Brint and Karabel recognized the tensions between these theses early on, tempering their critique of the community college by writing, "We wish to make our position clear: in the absence of community colleges, many highly motivated and able individuals, among them workers, immigrants, minorities, and women, would never have entered, much less graduated from an institution of higher education" (Brint and Karabel 1989a: 10).

The empirical evidence on the diversionary effects of community colleges is ambiguous. While there have always been some who have negotiated the community college pathway to reach even the most elite colleges and universities (Neumann and Riesman 1980), transfer from the community to the baccalaureate college remains the exception rather than the rule. Among those starting at a two-year college in 2008, about one in five transferred to a baccalaureate college by 2014 (Shapiro et al. 2015). Not all of those who attend a community college do so in hopes of transferring, but most do: in 2011, among students enrolled in public two-year institutions for the first time, 77 percent expected to earn at least a bachelor's degree, and 35 percent expected to earn an advanced degree (Radford et al. 2016). These are unlikely to be the outcomes they experience, though some recent work suggests a reduction in the baccalaureate penalty associated with attending a community college conditional on high school achievement, social background, and other covariates.[2]

Elite Colleges

Elite colleges and universities include those with relatively low acceptance rates (typically around 25 percent or less) and very high levels of academic achievement among incoming students as measured by entrance exam scores, high school grades, and high school class rank. The set of institutions that count as "elite" in the sociology of higher education varies to some degree based on the measure the researcher employs (e.g., mean SAT/ACT scores of admitted students, selectivity categories created for *Barron's Profile of American Colleges,* and institutions' rankings in the top tier by US News and World Report).

---

2. K. Voss, K. George, and M. Hout, "College Dropout in the United States, 1980–2010: Persistent Problems and Inequalities," Population Studies Center, Institute for Social Research, Brown Bag Seminar, April 9, 2018. For a more comprehensive summary of the democratization/diversion argument and the impacts of community college more generally, see Schudde and Grodsky 2018.

Regardless of the metric one uses, however, the same schools show up near the top of the list—Ivy League universities, the "public Ivies" (e.g., the University of Michigan, the University of Virginia), and a handful of liberal arts colleges (e.g., Amherst, Williams).

Only 5–10 percent of the college-going population attends the most selective colleges and universities, but these institutions have been the subject of considerable research. Baccalaureate completion increases with selectivity (Bowen, Chingos, and McPherson 2009; Long 2008; Small and Winship 2007), and obtaining degrees from elite institutions is associated with a variety of positive postbaccalaureate education and labor-market outcomes, including earnings (Brewer, Eide, and Ehrenberg 1999; Eide, Brewer, and Ehrenberg 1998), continuation to graduate or professional school (Brand and Halaby 2006; Mullen, Goyette, and Soares 2003), and securing an elite position in corporate management (Rivera 2016; Zimmerman 2016). The empirical support for the earnings benefits of elite college attendance is not uniform; some scholars suggest that the observed association between elite college completion and earnings is largely an artifact of who applies to and is accepted by elite postsecondary institutions (Brand and Halaby 2006; Dale and Krueger 2002, 2014).[3]

There is also evidence to indicate varying economic returns to selective college attendance (Hout 2012). Low-income students appear to realize the greatest income gains (Dale and Krueger 2014; Brand and Halaby 2006). On the other hand, elite college attendance may not be enough to overcome other barriers to success. A recent audit study found that black candidates who hold degrees from elite universities do only as well in the labor market as white students with degrees from less selective institutions (Gaddis 2014).

Some of our own work has explored inequities in elite college enrollment, explanations for those inequities, and institutional strategies to redress them. The most selective colleges and universities continue to disproportionately enroll students from high-income families, men, and white and Asian students. Academic preparation for four-year colleges, in the form of advanced-course-taking and grades, has improved among low-income students, black and Latino students, and women. These groups' performance on college entrance exams, however, have shown less improvement, even as test scores and grades have increased in importance over time as predictors of selective college enrollment (Bastedo and Jaquette 2011; Posselt et al. 2012). Combined with the widely held belief that diversity benefits all students, these persistent disparities have contributed to race-based affirmative action (Grodsky 2007; Long 2007) and the adoption of strategies like guaranteeing admission to the top 4 percent to 10 percent of a graduating high school class to enhance institutional diversity (Kain, O'Brien, and Jargowsky 2005; Long 2004).

---

3. For a recent review of postsecondary differentiation under the rubric of "horizontal stratification," see Gerber and Cheung 2008.

For-Profit Colleges

Scholars of higher education are increasingly interested in understanding both the role that for-profit colleges and universities play in providing opportunities for students and the costs that students incur for those opportunities. Although enrollment in for-profit colleges remains a small share of all postsecondary enrollment, at just over 7 percent of all undergraduate enrollment, the sector has expanded appreciably since 1970, when it accounted for only one-quarter of 1 percent of all enrollment (National Center for Education Statistics 2015). Students who attend for-profit institutions are more likely to obtain loans to support their education, and they borrow appreciably more than students at public institutions. They are also more likely to be women, members of racial/ethnic minority groups, or first-generation college students, and they are older on average than students attending other types of postsecondary institutions (Cellini and Darolia 2016).

Are for-profit colleges worth the extra cost? Some evidence suggests that students who attend for-profit certificate and associate's-degree programs are more likely to complete their credentials than those who attend community colleges (Deming, Goldin, and Katz 2012). On the other hand, they are less likely to be employed after completing their credentials or leaving (Cellini and Turner 2018; Deming, Goldin, and Katz 2012), and their chances of being invited to interview for a job are either worse (Deming et al. 2016) or, at best, no greater (Darolia et al. 2015; Deterding and Pedulla 2016) than the chances of students who earned their credentials at public colleges. Finally, while one study reports a small earnings advantage for those who complete a for-profit degree, relative to those who complete their degree at a public college (Cellini and Chaudhary 2012), most research points to either no difference in earnings across college sectors (Denice 2015) or a for-profit earnings disadvantage (Cellini and Turner 2016, 2018; Deming, Goldin, and Katz 2012; Denice 2015).[4]

With these outcomes, why would students bear the substantially greater costs and debt burdens to attend for-profit colleges? The answer, based on several qualitative studies, is enhanced accessibility and customer service. For-profit institutions offer highly structured courses of study (Holland and DeLuca 2016). They schedule classes to meet the needs of returning and part-time students, offering a greater number of evening, weekend, and virtual classes than public baccalaureate or community colleges (Iloh 2016; Rosenbaum, Deil-Amen, and Person 2007). Counselors at for-profit colleges cultivate relationships with student clients and even help them fill out the paperwork to enroll and to secure financial assistance (Rosenbaum, Deil-Amen, and Person 2007). Thus for-profit institutions offer several organizational advantages that lead some students to favor them over seemingly comparable public institutions.

---

4. Denice (2015) shows no difference in earnings by sector for those completing a bachelor's degree, but shows a for-profit disadvantage for those earning an associate's degree.

Matching Students and Colleges

Since Charles Manski and David Wise (1983) published their seminal work *College Choice in America,* social scientists have puzzled over the importance of the right match, or "fit," between students and colleges. While students may think of fit as including the political and social feel of a campus, college and community amenities, focus on Greek life or other features of colleges for which they have a preference, social scientists have mostly considered the degree to which students' postsecondary preparation matches that of other students at the college. Students whose grades or (more commonly) entrance exam scores fall far below the college mean are said to be *overmatched,* while those whose academic qualifications are appreciably above the college mean are said to be *undermatched.* Overmatching has most often been invoked in arguments over affirmative action, with opponents of race-based affirmative action asserting that the intended beneficiaries (African American and Latino students) are harmed by affirmative action because they are induced to attend colleges in which they cannot compete academically. Michal Kurlaender and Eric Grodsky (2013) refer to this as a "paternalistic justification" for abolishing race-based affirmative action. Undermatching, on the other hand, is more commonly experienced by low-income and first-generation college students for a variety of reasons related to both information and preferences (Bowen, Chingos, and McPherson 2009; Hoxby and Turner 2015, Radford 2013). Although the empirical evidence for the effect of overmatching is mixed, our reading of that evidence is that students are typically better off attending the most competitive (i.e., highest average achievement) school they can, owing to those institutions' higher rates of college completion, higher rates of graduate school attendance, and perhaps higher levels of earnings associated with completing degrees at such schools. The empirical evidence for undermatching is less ambiguous; students who are undermatched experience worse outcomes than those who match.

CONCLUSION

The theories presented here to explain the value of postsecondary education may also be utilized to understand who enrolls in different types of postsecondary institutions—public versus private, two-year versus four-year, and non-profit versus for-profit. In our own work, we are particularly interested in better understanding access to and outcomes of graduate and professional education. Until recently, and working from data in which education is often top-coded as "college or more," social scientists have poorly distinguished between economic returns to graduate and professional degrees over those to a baccalaureate degree alone (Posselt and Grodsky 2017). Indeed, the diverse sectors of "higher education" have distinct, albeit related, processes of selection and implications for student outcomes.

We have focused here on theories and research that link higher education and social stratification, but other promising areas for inquiry in the sociology of higher education include (a) postsecondary sectors and fields of study as contexts with life-course implications, and (b) the innovation and knowledge-production functions of postsecondary institutions for society. And as the field of higher education changes, along with the population of students who pursue it, we need to confront long-standing sociological theories like those presented here with current evidence, updating the theories accordingly and creating new ones where needed.

CHAPTER 16 REVIEW

Discussion Questions

1. How may the theories presented in this chapter help explain stratification in the types of postsecondary institutions discussed? For example, what aspects of cultural reproduction theory might be used to explain patterns of unequal enrollment in elite colleges?

2. The gainful-employment rule requires that postsecondary degree programs and institutions meet a minimum bar for the average debt-to-income ratio of their graduates, in order for those institutions to be eligible to receive federal financial aid. This rule puts some for-profit colleges in particular at risk, owing to the large debt students incur relative to their employment outcomes. To what extent should the federal government enforce this rule?

3. Social science is fundamentally an empirical pursuit. What evidence might you bring to bear to decide which of the theories presented in this chapter provides the most compelling account for the economic benefits of (a) college education generally, (b) attending an elite college, and (c) receiving a professional degree? What would convince you that one was more true than the others?

Suggestions for Further Reading

Collins, R. 1979. *The Credential Society: An Historical Sociology of Education and Stratification.* New York: Academic Press.

Denice, P. 2015. "Does It Pay to Attend a For-Profit College? Vertical and Horizontal Stratification in Higher Education." *Social Science Research* 52:161–78.

Grodsky, E., and E. Jackson. 2009. "Social Stratification in Higher Education." *Teachers College Record* 111:2347–84.

Grodsky, E., and C. Riegle-Crumb. 2010. "Those Who Choose and Those Who Don't: Social Background and College Orientation." *Annals of the American Academy of Political and Social Science* 627:14–35.

Lareau, A., and E. B. Weininger. 2003. "Cultural Capital in Educational Research: A Critical Assessment." *Theory and Society* 32:567–606.

Manski, C. F., and D. A. Wise. 1983. *College Choice in America.* Cambridge, MA: Harvard University Press.

Posselt, J. 2016. *Inside Graduate Admissions: Merit, Diversity, and Faculty Gatekeeping.* Cambridge, MA: Harvard University Press.

Posselt, J. R., and E. Grodsky. 2017. "Graduate Education and Social Stratification." *Annual Review of Sociology* 43:353–78.

Sorokin, P. A. 1959. *Social and Cultural Mobility.* Glencoe, IL: Free Press.

References

Andrews, R., J. Li, and M. F. Lovenheim. 2014. "Heterogeneous Paths through College: Detailed Patterns and Relationships with Graduation and Earnings." *Economics of Education Review* 42:93–108.

Barrow, Lisa, and Ofer Malamud. 2015. "Is College a Worthwhile Investment?" *Annual Review of Economics* 7 (1): 519–55.

Bastedo, M. N., and O. Jaquette. 2011. "Running in Place: Low-Income Students and the Dynamics of Higher Education Stratification." *Educational Evaluation and Policy Analysis* 33:318–39.

Becker, G. S. 1962. "Investment in Human Capital: A Theoretical Analysis." *Journal of Political Economy* 70:9–49.

Belfield, C. R., and T. Bailey. 2011. "The Benefits of Attending Community College: A Review of the Evidence." *Community College Review* 39:46–68.

Binder, A. J., D. B. Davis, and N. Bloom. 2016. "Career Funneling." *Sociology of Education* 89:20–39.

Bourdieu, P. 1984. *Distinction: A Social Critique of the Judgement of Taste.* Cambridge, MA: Harvard University Press.

Bourdieu P., and J.-C. Passeron. 1979. *The Inheritors: French Students and Their Relation to Culture.* Chicago: University of Chicago Press.

———. 1990. *Reproduction in Education, Society and Culture.* London: Sage.

Bowen, W. G., M. M. Chingos, and M. McPherson. 2009. *Crossing the Finish Line.* Princeton, NJ: Princeton University Press.

Brand, J. E., and C. N. Halaby. 2006. "Regression and Matching Estimates of the Effects of Elite College Attendance on Educational and Career Achievement." *Social Science Research* 35:749–70.

Brewer, D. J., E. R. Eide, and R. G. Ehrenberg. 1999. "Does It Pay to Attend an Elite Private College? Cross-Cohort Evidence on the Effects of College Type on Earnings." *Journal of Human Resources* 34:104–23.

Brint, S., and J. Karabel. 1989a. "The Community College and Democratic Ideals." *Community College Review* 17:9–19.

———. 1989b. *The Diverted Dream: Community Colleges and the Promise of Educational Opportunity in America, 1900–1985.* New York: Oxford University Press.

Brown, D. K. 1995. *Degrees of Control: A Sociology of Educational Expansion and Occupational Credentialism.* New York: Teachers College Press.

Bryson, B. 1996. "'Anything but Heavy Metal': Symbolic Exclusion and Musical Dislikes." *American Sociological Review* 61 (5): 884–99.

Carneiro, P., J. J. Heckman, and E. J. Vytlacil. 2011. "Estimating Marginal Returns to Education." *American Economic Review* 101:2754–81.

Carnevale, A. P., S. J. Rose, and B. Cheah. 2011. *The College Payoff: Education, Occupations and Lifetime Earnings.* Washington, DC: Georgetown University, Center on Education and the Workforce.

Cellini, S. R., and L. Chaudhary. 2012. "The Labor Market Returns to a For-Profit College Education." NBER Working Paper Series. Cambridge, MA: National Bureau of Economic Research.

Cellini, S. R., and R. Darolia. 2016. *Different Degrees of Debt: Student Borrowing in the For-Profit, Nonprofit, and Public Sectors.* Washington, DC: Brown Center on Education Policy, Brookings Institution.

Cellini, S. R., and N. Turner. 2016. "Gainfully Employed? Assessing the Employment and Earnings of For-Profit College Students Using Administrative Data." NBER Working Paper Series, no. 22287. Cambridge, MA: National Bureau of Economic Research.

———. 2018. "Gainfully Employed? Assessing the Employment and Earnings of For-Profit College Students Using Administrative Data." *Journal of Human Resources* (January 30).

Clark, B. R. 1960. "The 'Cooling-Out' Function in Higher Education." *American Journal of Sociology* 65:569–76.

———. 1970. *The Distinctive College.* New Brunswick, NJ: Transaction.

Collins, R. 1979. *The Credential Society: An Historical Sociology of Education and Stratification.* New York: Academic Press.

Dale, S. B., and A. B. Krueger. 2002. "Estimating the Payoff to Attending a More Selective College: An Application of Selection on Observables and Unobservables." *Quarterly Journal of Economics* 117:1491–527.

———. 2014. "Estimating the Effects of College Characteristics over the Career Using Administrative Earnings Data." *Journal of Human Resources* 49:323–58.

Darolia R., C. Koedel, P. Martorell, K. Wilson, and F. Perez-Arce. 2015. "Do Employers Prefer Workers Who Attend For-Profit Colleges? Evidence from a Field Experiment." *Journal of Policy Analysis and Management* 34:881–903.

Dee, T. S. 2004. "Are There Civic Returns to Education?" *Journal of Public Economics* 88:1697–720.

Deming, D. J., C. Goldin, and L. F. Katz. 2012. "The For-Profit Postsecondary School Sector: Nimble Critters or Agile Predators?" *Journal of Economic Perspectives* 26:139–64.

Deming, D. J, N. Yuchtman, A. Abulafi, C. Goldin, and L. F. Katz. 2016. "The Value of Postsecondary Credentials in the Labor Market: An Experimental Study." *American Economic Review* 106:778–806.

Denice, P. 2015. "Does It Pay to Attend a For-Profit College? Vertical and Horizontal Stratification in Higher Education." *Social Science Research* 52:161–78.

Deterding, N. M, and D. S. Pedulla. 2016. "Educational Authority in the 'Open Door' Marketplace: Labor Market Consequences of For-Profit, Nonprofit, and Fictional Educational Credentials." *Sociology of Education* 89:155–70.

DiMaggio, P. 1982. "Cultural Capital and School Success: The Impact of Status Culture Participation on the Grades of U.S. High School Students." *American Sociological Review* 47:189–201.

DiPrete, T., and C. Buchmann. 2005. "Gender-Specific Trends in the Value of Education and the Emerging Gender Gap in College Completion." *Demography* 43:1–24.

Eide, E. R., D. J. Brewer, and R. G. Ehrenberg. 1998. "Does It Pay to Attend an Elite Private College? Evidence on the Effects of Undergraduate College Quality on Graduate School Attendance." *Economics of Education Review* 17:371–76.

Eide, E. R., M. J. Hilmer, and M. H. Showalter. 2015. "Is It Where You Go or What You Study? The Relative Influence of College Selectivity and College Major on Earnings." *Contemporary Economic Policy* 34 (1): 37–46.

Gaddis, S. M. 2014. "Discrimination in the Credential Society: An Audit Study of Race and College Selectivity in the Labor Market." *Social Forces* 93 (4): 1451–79.

Gerber, T. P., and S. Y. Cheung. 2008. "Horizontal Stratification in Postsecondary Education: Forms, Explanations, and Implications." *Annual Review of Sociology* 34:299–318.

Goffman, E. 1952. "On Cooling the Mark Out." *Psychiatry* 15:451–63.

Goldin, C., and L. Katz. 2008. *The Race between Education and Technology.* Cambridge, MA: Belknap Press of Harvard University Press.

Goldin, C., L. Katz, and I. Kuziemko. 2006. "The Homecoming of American College Women: The Reversal of the College Gender Gap." *Journal of Economic Perspectives* 20:133–56.

Grodsky, E. 2007. "Compensatory Sponsorship in Higher Education." *American Journal of Sociology* 112:1662–712.

Grodsky, E., and E. Jackson. 2009. "Social Stratification in Higher Education." *Teachers College Record* 111:2347–84.

Grodsky, E., and C. Riegle-Crumb. 2010. "Those Who Choose and Those Who Don't: Social Background and College Orientation." *Annals of the American Academy of Political and Social Science* 627:14–35.

Heckman, J. J., J. E. Humphries, G. Veramendi, and S. Urzua. 2014. "Education, Health and Wages." NBER Working Paper Series. Cambridge, MA: National Bureau of Economic Research.

Holland, M. M., and S. DeLuca. 2016. "Why Wait Years to Become Something? Low-Income African American Youth and the Costly Career Search in For-Profit Trade Schools." *Sociology of Education* 89:261–78.

Hout, M. 2012. "Social and Economic Returns to College Education in the United States." *Annual Review of Sociology* 38:379–400.

Hoxby, C., and S. Turner. 2015. "What High-Achieving Low-Income Students Know about College." NBER Working Paper Series. Cambridge, MA: National Bureau of Economic Research.

Iloh, C. 2016. "Exploring the For-Profit Experience." *American Educational Research Journal* 53:427–55.

Kain, J. F., D. M. O'Brien, and P. A. Jargowsky. 2005. *Hopwood and the Top 10 Percent Law: How They Have Affected the College Enrollment Decisions of Texas High School Graduates.* Report to the Andrew W. Mellon Foundation. Dallas: Texas Schools Project, University of Texas at Dallas.

Kalmijn, M., and G. Kraaykamp. 1996. "Race, Cultural Capital, and Schooling: An Analysis of Trends in the United States." *Sociology of Education* 69:22–34.

Kamens, D. H. 1971. "The College 'Charter' and College Size: Effects on Occupational Choice and College Attrition." *Sociology of Education* 44:270–96.

———. 1974. "Colleges and Elite Formation: The Case of Prestigious American Colleges." *Sociology of Education* 47:354–78.

Karabel, J. 2005. *The Chosen: The Hidden History of Admission and Exclusion at Harvard, Yale, and Princeton.* Boston: Houghton Mifflin.

Kleiner, M. M., and A. B. Krueger. 2013. "Analyzing the Extent and Influence of Occupational Licensing on the Labor Market." *Journal of Labor Economics* 31:S173–S202.

Kuh, G. D., J. Kinzie, J. H. Schuh, and E. J. Whitt. 2011. *Student Success in College: Creating Conditions That Matter.* Hoboken, NJ: John Wiley and Sons.

Kurlaender, M., and E. Grodsky. 2013. "Mismatch and the Paternalistic Justification for Selective College Admissions." *Sociology of Education* 86:294–310.

Lamont, M., and A. Lareau. 1988. "Cultural Capital: Allusions, Gaps and Glissandos in Recent Theoretical Developments." *Sociological Theory* 6:153–68.

Lareau, A., and E. B. Weininger. 2003. "Cultural Capital in Educational Research: A Critical Assessment." *Theory and Society* 32:567–606.

Lochner, L. 2011. "Non-production Benefits of Education: Crime, Health, and Good Citizenship." In *Handbook of the Economics of Education*, edited by E. A. Hanushek, S. Machin, and L. Woessmann, 188–282. Amsterdam: Elsevier B.V.

Long, M. 2004. "Race and College Admissions: An Alternative to Affirmative Action?" *Review of Economics and Statistics* 86:1022–33.

———. 2007. "Affirmative Action and Its Alternatives in Public Universities: What Do We Know?" *Public Administration Review* 67:315–30.

———. 2008. "College Quality and Early Adult Outcomes." *Economics of Education Review* 27:588–602.

Manski, C. F., and D. A. Wise. 1983. *College Choice in America.* Cambridge, MA: Harvard University Press.

McDonough, P. M. 1997. *Choosing Colleges: How Social Class and Schools Structure Opportunity.* Albany: State University of New York Press.

McLanahan, S. 2004. "Diverging Destinies: How Children Are Faring under the Second Demographic Transition." *Demography* 41:607–27.

Meyer, J. W. 1970. "The Charter: Conditions of Diffuse Socialization in Schools." In *Social Processes and Social Structures: An Introduction to Sociology*, edited by R. W. Scott, 564–78. New York: Holt, Rinehart and Winston.

———. 1977. "The Effects of Education as an Institution." *American Journal of Sociology* 83:55–77.

Milligan, K., E. Moretti, and P. Oreopoulos. 2004. "Does Education Improve Citizenship? Evidence from the United States and the United Kingdom." *Journal of Public Economics* 88:1667–95

Mullen, A. L., K. Goyette, and J. A. Soares. 2003. "Who Goes to Graduate School? Social and Academic Correlates of Educational Continuation after College." *Sociology of Education* 76:143–69.

National Center for Education Statistics. 2015. "Total Undergraduate Fall Enrollment in Degree-Granting Postsecondary Institutions, by Attendance Status, Sex of Student, and Control and Level of Institution: Selected Years, 1970 through 2027." Table 303.70. In *Digest of Education Statistics 2015*. Washington, DC: National Center for Education Statistics, Institute of Education Sciences, US Department of Education. https://nces.ed.gov/programs/digest/d17/tables/dt17_303.70.asp

———. 2016. "Degree-Granting Postsecondary Institutions, by Control and Classification of Institution and State or Jurisdiction: 2015–16." Table 317.20. In *Digest of Education Statistics 2016*. Washington, DC: National Center for Education Statistics, Institute of Education Sciences, US Department of Education. https://nces.ed.gov/programs/digest/d16/tables/dt16_317.20.asp?current=yes.

Neumann, W., and D. Riesman. 1980. "The Community College Elite." *New Directions for the Community College* 8:53–71.

Oreopoulos, P., and K. G. Salvanes. 2009. "How Large Are Returns to Schooling? Hint: Money Isn't Everything." NBER

Working Paper Series. Cambridge, MA: National Bureau of Economic Research.

Parsons, T. 1964. "The School Class as a Social System: Some of Its Functions in American Society." In *Social Structure and Personality*, 129–54. New York: Free Press.

Posselt, J. R. 2016. *Inside Graduate Admissions: Merit, Diversity, and Faculty Gatekeeping*. Cambridge, MA: Harvard University Press.

Posselt, J. R., and E. Grodsky. 2017. "Graduate Education and Social Stratification." *Annual Review of Sociology* 43:353–78.

Posselt, J. R., O. Jaquette, R. Bielby, and M. N. Bastedo. 2012. "Access without Equity: Longitudinal Analyses of Institutional Stratification by Race and Ethnicity, 1972–2004." *American Educational Research Journal* 49:1112–45.

Radford, A. W. 2013. *Top Student, Top School? How Social Class Shapes Where Valedictorians Go to College*. Chicago: University of Chicago Press.

Radford, A. W., E. D. Velez, A. Bentz, T. Lew, and N. Ifill. 2016. *First-Time Postsecondary Students in 2011–12: A Profile*. Washington, DC: National Center for Education Statistics, US Department of Education.

Rivera, L. A. 2016. *Pedigree: How Elite Students Get Elite Jobs*. Princeton, NJ: Princeton University Press.

Rosenbaum, J. E., R. Deil-Amen, and A. E. Person. 2007. *After Admission: From College Access to College Success*. New York: Russell Sage Foundation.

Schoenfeldt, L. F. 1968. "Education after High School." *Sociology of Education* 41:350–69.

Schudde, L., and E. Grodsky. 2018. "The Community College Experience and Educational Equality: Theory, Research, and Policy." In *Handbook of the Sociology of Education in the 21st Century*, edited by Barbara Schneider. New York: Springer.

Schultz, T. W. 1961. "Investment in Human Capital." *American Economic Review* 51:1–17.

Shapiro, D., A. Dundar, P. K. Wakhungu, X. Yuan, and A. T. Harrell. 2015. *Transfer and Mobility: A National View of Student Movement in Postsecondary Institutions, Fall 2008 Cohort*. Herndon, VA: National Student Clearinghouse Research Center.

Small, M. L., and C. Winship. 2007. "Black Students' Graduation from Elite Colleges: Institutional Characteristics and Between-Institution Differences." *Social Science Research* 36: 1257–75.

Sorokin, P. A. 1959. *Social and Cultural Mobility*. Glencoe, IL: Free Press.

Stevens, M. L., E. A. Armstrong, and R. Arum. 2008. "Sieve, Incubator, Temple, Hub: Empirical and Theoretical Advances in the Sociology of Higher Education." *Annual Review of Sociology* 34:127–51.

Valletta, R. G. 2016. "Recent Flattening in the Higher Education Wage Premium: Polarization, Skill Downgrading, or Both?" NBER Working Paper Series, no. 22935. Cambridge, MA: National Bureau of Economic Research.

Webber, D. A. 2016. "Are College Costs Worth It? How Ability, Major, and Debt Affect the Returns to Schooling." *Economics of Education Review* 53:296–310.

Weeden, K. 2002. "Why Do Some Occupations Pay More Than Others? Social Closure and Earnings Inequality in the United States." *American Journal of Sociology* 108:55–101.

Weisbrod, B. A. 1962. "Education and Investment in Human Capital." *Journal of Political Economy* 70:106–23.

Yosso, T. J. 2005. "Whose Culture Has Capital? A Critical Race Theory Discussion of Community Cultural Wealth." *Race Ethnicity and Education* 8:69–91.

Zimmerman, S. D. 2016. "Making the One Percent: The Role of Elite Universities and Elite Peers." NBER Working Paper Series, no. 22900. Cambridge, MA: National Bureau of Economic Research.

4

Importing School Forms across Professional Fields

An Understudied Phenomenon in the Sociology of Education

AMY BINDER, UNIVERSITY OF CALIFORNIA, SAN DIEGO

SCOTT DAVIES, UNIVERSITY OF TORONTO

EDITORS' NOTE

Academic tracking, detention and suspension, neighborhood- or choice-based school assignment practices, institutional selectivity in higher education—each of the topics that you have read about in the last several chapters are organizational characteristics that help define the institution of education. These and the countless other practices that we take for granted when we talk about school make up the **organizational form** of education in contemporary societies.

Given how important schooling is in contemporary societies, it shouldn't be surprising that this organizational form shapes life outside of schools as well. Today, school isn't just a place for kids. Beyond organizations like Greenleaf Elementary and Montana State University, we have traffic school for drivers who received speeding tickets, "Baby College" for expectant parents, and McDonald's Hamburger University for fast-food employees. Sociologists Amy Binder and Scott Davies provide a potent illustration of just how powerful the organizational form of school is in contemporary societies, describing the creation of "schools" for homeless families and others in need of social services.

In Binder and Davies's telling, organizations outside of education adopt the school's organizational form because it conveys **legitimacy.** Why does education have this legitimating power?

INTRODUCTION

We live in a schooled society (Baker 2014) in which virtually everyone on the globe now experiences some type of formal education. Elementary, secondary, and postsecondary enrollments have expanded in nearly all nations (Meyer et al. 1997; Schofer and Meyer 2005). Postsecondary curricula, in particular, have broadened enormously, with university majors and community college programs stretching their offerings far beyond traditional fields and multiplying into new realms of study (Frank and Gabler 2006). Various types of colleges now teach skills that once were learned only on the job, such as security, bartending, and hotel and restaurant management.

These patterns in schooling are relatively new, however, and reflect a shift in how education is understood within American society, what we might label the idea of "schooling for all." Until approximately 1960, higher levels of formal education were considered appropriate for only a limited number of people, largely because older economies required only small cadres of highly educated workers. But as economies globalized and societies have become more technologically advanced and politically intertwined, education has come to be viewed as suitable for virtually everyone in society. Education is increasingly celebrated as having the potential to trigger an unbridled expansion of economic and human potential; modern economies are thought capable of absorbing unlimited amounts of human capital (Schofer and Meyer 2005). Today, virtually everyone is seen as "educable" and capable of benefiting from an academic education (Richardson 2006).

SCHOOLING AS AN ORGANIZATIONAL MODEL: THEORETICAL UNDERPINNINGS

As early as the 1970s, organizational scholars took note of these changes and proclaimed that schooling—as a form of organizing people—had achieved universal legitimacy.[1] Something is considered legitimate if it is seen as proper and authoritative. So, if individuals want to get ahead in life, they look to schooling. If nations want to grow their economies, they talk about having a better educated workforce. When world leaders discuss the global knowledge society, they point to education's key role in producing highly skilled labor. The idea that education is the answer to society's most pressing problems has widespread legitimacy.

Yet this universal legitimacy is a puzzle: Why should schooling—a less-than-efficient organizational form, compared to, say, manufacturing—be celebrated so widely and continue to spread globally? Schools rarely monitor their core process—classroom teaching—and they fight over whether their prime output—student learning—can ever be measured authentically. A group of scholars known as the New Institutionalists recognize that, while forms of schooling can be valuable for achieving some instrumental goals—such as teaching skills that help prepare students for the labor market—the work of schools as organizations is more subtle and complex than this functionalist model suggests. New Institutionalist scholars show that the capacity of schools to socialize people and successfully fuel

---

1. For wide-ranging summaries of this work, see Jepperson 2000; Meyer et al. 1997; Meyer and Ramirez 2002.

modern economies is actually limited. They do not deny the close association between schooling and academic achievement (Hout 2012), but they doubt that schooling plays the causal role in this process. Rather, the New Institutionalists emphasize that modern societies prize schools not only for their instrumental rewards in sparking economies or helping individuals *but also for their broad associations with furthering human rights, social equity, and personal development.* Indeed, New Institutional scholars are more interested in the symbolic importance of schooling than in its measurable effects. In this light, education (as an institution) has helped create widely shared ideas about modern personhood as a platform for individual self-actualization (Nielsen 2015).

Considering how crucial schooling has become in propagating and standardizing universal norms of human rights and personal development, is it possible that schools influence organizational behavior *outside* the context of formal schooling? We argue that this is, in fact, the case: that schooling has influenced behavior *across* society. *School imports,* as we call this phenomenon, describes those educational ideas and forms that actors from fields outside of formal education bring into their own lines of work. These school imports can take many forms. Administrators at a senior-living complex, for example, might create a bird-watching leisure course for residents. The criminal justice system can implement a requirement that offenders attend classes aimed at rehabilitation, in the place of jail time or probation. Corporations like McDonald's create "campuses" for employee training, such as Hamburger University. But what do these imported school forms actually *do* for the populations that are intended to use them, and for the organizations that rely on imported educational models?

First, we expect that when workers from other professions draw on the cultural and normative meanings of education, they will blend them with their own values and practices. Rather than merely replicating school practices—in which it is assumed that students are empty vessels into which knowledge can be poured—instructors are likely to create new hybrid processes that foreground clients' earlier life experiences. For example, at Hamburger University, instructors might ask new adult franchise owners about their past successful business practices before seeking to align them with the McDonald's way.

Second, professionals from other sectors most likely import only the most mutable features of schooling—such as instructor-student roles and assignments—while discarding others, such as those that tightly couple teaching to quantifiable outcomes like program requirements. For example, when leading a class on the pleasures of bird watching, social service providers might ask residents to talk about their experiences photographing or painting the birds they have seen, not use formal tests to see if they have memorized the details of species evolution or anatomy.

Third, we predict that such imports will reflect mostly noninstrumental values: Rather than a building up of concrete skills that are useful for meeting some end, elements imported from schooling will speak to things like human character. For example, we expect instructors in johns schools, which are attended by men who have paid prostitutes for sex and who are often court-ordered to attend, to emphasize both the exploitation of women who are forced into prostitution, and the personal integrity that comes when men change their attitudes and behaviors toward girls and women. Fundamentally, we expect that importers will use school forms to tap the cultural power of schooling, reframing their practices in ways that appear legitimate in the eyes of their clients and other community members, and signaling messages that connect their schooling activities to principal notions of human rights, personhood, and deservingness.

In this case study, we show how school imports operate in the sector of social services. Because professionals in this sector, and in social work in particular, have strongly uniform value commitments, it's an ideal place to examine when, how, and why workers bring in new practices from formal schooling. Indeed, social service professionals have long adopted educational strategies and components in their work. Jane Addams's late-nineteenth-century Hull House, for example, offered classes in citizenship, literacy, and homemaking as part of its mission to "uplift" Chicago's poor immigrant masses (Gordon 1994). Yet contemporary social services rest on newer principles, including the idea of starting where the client is (Heimer and Stevens 1997), fostering self-determination (Meyerson 1994), and respecting diversity of all types while promoting social justice (Hasenfeld 2000). As we can see, these deep value commitments are not identical to those embraced explicitly in formal schooling. Can we propose a relationship between the ideas and forms found in schools and those found in the sphere of social work? How might workers in this sector borrow school forms and adapt them to their own professional purposes?

Building on the theoretical suppositions of the New Institutionalists, we find three patterns that describe the importing process. First, when social service workers draw on the cultural and normative meanings of education, they blend them with their own professional values and practices. That is, rather than merely replicating school practices, in which instructors *teach* students valued content, social service providers are likely to create new *hybrid procedures* that foreground clients' earlier life experiences. Second, social service professionals import only the *most mutable* features of schooling, such as instructor-student roles and assignments; they discard other features of schooling, such as those that tie teaching to quantifiable measures like program requirements or socioeconomic goals. Third, social workers import mostly *noninstrumental values*—that is, those values that not only promote "getting ahead" in life, economically and socially, but also speak to things like the sanctity and human development of those being "schooled." In each of these three ways, we argue, importers use school forms to tap the *cultural power* of schooling. Social workers reframe their practices in terms of human rights ideas that are accepted as legitimate in the eyes of their funders, their clients, and other members of the community.

CASE STUDY: HYBRID SCHOOL FORMS IN PARENTS COMMUNITY

In the Classroom

To understand how professionals import school forms, we studied Parents Community, a nonprofit organization serving the housing, child care, and social service needs of homeless, single parents and their children.[2] At Parents Community, professional staff, including licensed social workers, help low-income parents become self-sufficient (a classic social work theme) by providing them a place to live for two years at a very low cost. To qualify for this benefit, residents must either work in the formal labor force or be enrolled in some form of educational program. Residents must also attend three basic skills classes per month at Parents Community, taught by staff and a corps of community volunteers. As part of our fieldwork, we attended more than fifty basic skills classes and a large variety of other sponsored events. In addition to fieldwork, we conducted semistructured interviews with forty-four residents or former residents, ten volunteer instructors, and virtually all staff and administrators.

Of course, like any case study, our research at Parents Community has limitations with respect to empirical generalization. We cannot claim to have observed a "typical" process of school importing. Nevertheless, our case of school importing is strategic because it illustrates new connections between education and another major field—social work.

"Life skills" classes cover a range of topics, from utilitarian subjects such as cooking, personal finance, and searching effectively for a job, to those conveying fundamental values, such as how to be a good parent or responsible employee. While some classes are taught by staff, more often they are led by volunteers from the community who have expertise in one of these areas.

Our first question in conducting our research was whether Parents Community courses resemble courses offered in conventional classrooms, or whether they look more like hybrid forms of schooling-plus-social-work. We found some classes that were highly school-like. But others were not and instead used mixed forms of pedagogy, foregrounding instruction at some times and clients' life experiences at others.

One example of a class that closely follows school conventions is called "Making Your Kids as Smart as They Can Be: Tips on Early Childhood Education." This class is taught twice monthly by a volunteer named Heather, who, by day, is a special education teacher in the local public school district. Heather's class is usually attended by eight to twelve participants. She is known throughout the organization for setting a concrete agenda for each class, giving lectures and conveying information about parenting that she thinks is important for building up children's educational capital. Annette Lareau (2002) has labeled such middle-class parenting practices, in which parents structure interactions with children as opportunities for building educational capital, as "concerted cultivation"; Heather clearly embraces such ideas about the home as educational laboratory. Here is a glimpse of Heather's class, from our field notes:

> Heather starts the class talking about the "enriched home." She points out, "These are the kinds of things and activities that you have at home that have been proved to make your kid smarter—these can raise your kid's IQ score by ten points!" She mentions books. She asks, "How much time is your TV *off?*" And she talks about drawing and coloring, talking to your

---

2. The names of the organization and of the people associated with it have been changed to protect confidentiality.

kid, listening to your kid, and involving them in "learning activities." "This is not controversial," she says. "It has been demonstrated that these activities make your kid smarter! If your kid sees you reading, and you read to your kid, they will get interested in reading!"

The class continues on the topic of writing books with children. Although Heather encourages participants to ask questions about class materials, she clearly has a number of concepts she wants to get across to them: "Let them come up with the story. Don't let them ask you what comes next. Rather, say to them, 'You tell me! You're the brilliant author of your book! What would you like to write about next?' The only way for them to learn it is to do it."

Heather's instruction closely mirrors teaching in professional education settings. Whether the subject is writing books with children or (as in a different lecture) explaining why parents must establish a cordial (not contentious) relationship with their children's schoolteachers, Heather acts as the authority on the subject. She maintains control of the classroom so that residents learn from her knowledge base. She sees her role as that of an instructor applying an educational model to her work as a volunteer at Parents Community. She imports a lot from schooling.

But Heather's class was the notable exception. Few other staff or volunteer instructors at Parents Community fit the teacher-as-expert, or sage-on-the-stage, model. Instead, most instructors are self-conscious about "coming to Parents Community and telling residents what to do—how presumptuous is that?" as Sally, the instructor of a Women at Work class, told us. During an interview, another volunteer instructor, Laura, who teaches a class on personal finances, identified the challenges of hard-and-fast instructor/student roles: "You know, it's like, how are they going to perceive me? . . . The reason that they are here is because they have had hard, bad things happen to them. You know, I'm walking in there and saying, 'Hi, I am going to teach you how to run your financial lives better'? How is *that* going to be received? It is kind of like, are they going to throw stuff at me and say, 'Oh, you have no idea, lady.'"

Volunteer instructors are aware, as we all are, of what conventional teaching in formal educational settings looks like. But when they import school forms to Parents Community, they do not use many formal educational features. Instead, they choose to meld "teaching" with a more hands-off, therapeutic model. Raul is a volunteer instructor who leads a basic skills class on affordable housing. Here is a look at Raul's instruction:

> During the first ten minutes of the class, Raul has to introduce himself four separate times as residents trickle in. He tells class participants that "[Parents Community staff] say I'm not supposed to let anyone in if they're late," but he does so anyway, bending the organization's rules. A resident named Hayley complains that the organization's rules make "me want kick them in the head; daycare did that to me today." Then she apologizes, saying that she's "very cranky" this evening. When Raul asks if he can do anything for her, Hayley says, "Kill my soon-to-be ex." Some class members laugh and begin a new conversation on that topic: their lousy exes. Two residents roll their eyes, seeming to wish that Raul might get the class back on track.
>
> Later in the class, Raul requests that participants "please write down all the money you spent last week." After a minute he asks, "How did you do?" Someone mentions being short on cash because of her ex, and this leads to a renewed discussion among several residents about ex-boyfriends and husbands, and how they take what's yours, and don't pay support, and don't show up for their meetings with their kids, and how their kids get out of control when they are with their dads, and aren't given their medication. I follow the streams of

conversation but also keep my eye on Raul to see his response. He nods his head at each person's response, and seems to be torn between letting the residents talk about their personal lives and trying to circle back around to his handouts on affordable housing.

In the spirit of social work empathy, Raul, Laura, and Sally give an honored place to clients' lived experiences. Indeed, the vast majority of classes we observed align more closely with the value commitments of social work than those of conventional education, such as the commitment to start where the adult client is, to maintain an emphasis on personal self-improvement, and to defer to clients' adult experiences. Instructors in most classes do not lecture or stick to a set agenda, as Heather does. Rather, they are much more fluid in their presentation and frequently subvert the official content of their classes to the will of the participants in their classrooms, wherever those conversations lead.

Juggling all these concerns leads instructors to run their classes as a kind of hybrid practice: not quite a class, yet not quite a therapy session either. They take attendance, following the Parents Community rule, but always start late, delaying as residents arrive, and never turn participants away. When residents offer advice to one another that instructors clearly find questionable (such as when a participant in Laura's personal finances class spoke of saving enough money to pay for high premiums for her young son's funeral insurance), instructors find themselves in a predicament, wanting neither to support suggestions they regard as dubious nor to question residents directly. They assert authority by starting each class with an opening statement and handing out materials, but then cede the floor to anyone who wants to speak on any topic. This instructional style is part of a larger organizational strategy "not to put themselves above" residents, as Shawn, the volunteer instructor of the Recovering from Domestic Violence class, told us in an interview. Instead, instructors curtail their authoritative roles and show deference to their adult students.[3]

A further example of the hybrid nature of these school imports is residents' strong voice in determining whether volunteers are invited back to teach basic skills classes. This is the case more so than in formal educational settings, where certified teachers enjoy more sovereignty. The head of the volunteer department told us what happens when "negative feedback" about an instructor comes in from residents:

> In this case, the people who were taking a parenting class didn't like the facilitator because she was an older middle-class woman who didn't have children. And "what was she doing, teaching them parenting?" You know: "She didn't know anything about single parents." And so we talked about that issue with the facilitator . . ., [who] felt that it didn't make any difference, that she had been trained by [a local organization to teach low-income parents about parenting]; that they had done an extensive training with her. She knew the curriculum. But basically what we had to say is: "With our resident population, it isn't a good fit."

Although staff acknowledged that this instructor was sufficiently knowledgeable, she did not meet the organization's other normative criteria—namely, fostering residents' self-determination. Thus, far from replicating formal educational settings, most

---

3. While relinquishing authority happens in mainline educational classrooms, too (Arum 2003), we can interpret it there as part of a lax teaching practice. At Parents Community, staff, volunteers, and residents value this style, which is a result of combining practices from schooling with those of social work.

classes at Parents Community were hybrids, occupying an ambiguous location in the lives of residents, who had dual roles as "students" and "social service clients."

Measuring Attainment in a Hybrid Setting

What is the purpose of requiring residents to take basic classes, anyway? Do school imports at Parents Community—in the form of basic classes—operate just as they are depicted in official policy? Do day-to-day practices map perfectly onto the organization's stated mission? In brochures and during events held for potential donors and other community members, Parents Community staff argue that they boost residents' social and economic circumstances by teaching them basic skills in the program's classes. But in our fieldwork, we found that neither the content of the classes nor residents' learning was very strongly tied to clients' eventual life outcomes. Several types of data demonstrate how weakly associated official policy can be with measurable outcomes— a phenomenon the New Institutionalists call "loose coupling."

One type of evidence for loose coupling—when official policy differs from actual practice—comes from conversations we heard about "consequenting" residents when they do not meet program requirements. Caroline, the director of volunteers, told us that several years earlier, the organization had received funding from a donor to compile statistics on whether residents met their obligations for living at Parents Community, including whether they regularly attended basic skills classes. Caroline reported that while the organization's chief program officer, Trish, had been willing to put together a new database to meet the donor's wishes and even to keep track of residents' failures, Trish was unwilling to use the information to bring residents in line with the program. According to Caroline: "So now, we have a great tracking system in place . . . but Trish didn't want to consequent people!"

Another piece of evidence of loose coupling between school imports and the official purpose of classes stems from the fact that few evening classes are actually required of all residents. With the exception of five mandatory "Introduction to the Program" classes that must be taken in their first month, residents are not required to take any other core curriculum. Only under rare circumstances is a resident directed to take a class on a subject in which he or she specifically "needs help." Otherwise, the choice of three basic skills classes per month is completely voluntary, and the content is not cumulative. This suggests that class content is less oriented to building tangible human capital—for example, by boosting skills, improving financial viability, or enabling participants to find stable housing—than to satisfying other organizational interests.

Third, and related to the last point, when residents "graduate" from Parents Community, staff do not measure whether they have acquired knowledge of parenting, financial management, nutrition, or any other subject. Most courses are stand-alone, nonsequenced subjects that lack any tests or grades.

In sum, classes at Parents Community bear little resemblance to tightly coupled school forms that use grading structures to encourage students to align themselves with educational goals. The staff's reluctance to "consequent" residents for nonattendance or to assess students' learning underscores a key point: school imports are often not tightly coupled forms of education. To be sure, sociologists of education have shown that much official schooling, too, is loosely coupled (think of rules against texting in class and how much students *actually* text in class), so we do not wish to hold Parents Community to a higher standard. The point is that, unlike mainline schooling, where tighter coupling has prevailed over the past twenty years (Coburn 2004), social work professionals are far more ambivalent about accountability and differentiated teacher/ student roles. As a result, when they import school forms into their practice, they do not take *all* of the trappings or quantify school forms' impact.

The Legitimating Effects of Imported School Forms

Finally, as New Institutionalist scholars have long pointed out, *education* has a great deal of cultural resonance and can offer legitimacy to any organizational entity that engages it (Meyer and Rowan 1977). These positive meanings are not lost on Parents Community staff. In a fascinating discussion with Trish, the organization's chief program officer, we learned about the origins of basic skills classes. As it turns out, these classes have more to do with donors' wishes than with social workers' hopes for their clients. Without beating around the bush, Trish told us, "We have classes because our funders and our board members want to know that we're doing everything we can to help our residents get out of poverty. So we instituted evening basic skills classes." She continued by saying, "Maybe they shouldn't even be called 'classes,' because *classes* sounds like: 'We're going to give you education! Get ready: Learn now!' . . . It's a middle-class view." Upon further reflection, Trish surmised, "I think those evening classes are more like a 'group.' . . . It's more of a group-process thing, where residents learn more from each other than from the instructor." Laughing as she said this, she concluded, "But whatever you want to call them, they're there for the residents, and the board and the others want to see that."

In this conversation, Trish revealed her ambivalence about the basic skills classes. Evening classes in their educative meaning—where instructors "give you education," or where students are to "Get ready: Learn now!" is not what this enterprise is about. Or it is *less* of what this is about than classes' other intended benefits for residents. Trish and her colleagues at Parents Community have transposed onto the social work practice of "group therapy" the language and ideology of educational forms, in an effort to make the processes of therapy more recognizable to organizational stakeholders, such as donors. Since education is widely viewed as an unmitigated good, it becomes a cultural tool that staff can use to frame and buttress their work. To borrow the words of John Meyer and Brian Rowan (1977), basic skills classes provide some "myth and ceremony" that legitimate social workers' professional practice at Parents Community.

SCHOOL IMPORTS: IMPLICATIONS AND FURTHER RESEARCH

Our analysis of school imports points to a reality that, surprisingly, is tended to only rarely by sociologists. Today, "education," understood broadly, enjoys a societal currency that allows it to expand well beyond its confines in formal schooling realms. However, this process is not one in which certified and rationalistic actors use school forms to simply meet their technical tasks. In our case, importing is led by shrewd social workers, who are outsiders to the education sector. They create new hybridized and loosely coupled practices, which are prized as much for their cultural association with education ideals as with their capacity to get things done, such as improving their clients' socioeconomic prospects. They blend school forms with their own values, such as "meeting the client where she is at," and they mostly drop the idea of strictly complying with rules.

This likely says something about the field of social work, which differs from other fields in which professionals also import school forms. In the schools designed as an alternative to incarceration for convicted criminals, the hybrid is different because it is embedded in a criminal justice setting. Instructors in these johns schools didn't treat their charges like children, but they also did not use a therapeutic model resembling what we saw at Parents Community. Instead, those instructors wielded some authority and applied strict rules for attendance. We also speculate that in a set of organizations such as corporate universities (e.g., Hamburger University, Dunkin Donuts University, and Kettering University, formerly known as General Motors Institute), importers will borrow human-capital elements of school forms, grading their students and issuing formal credits for sequenced courses, while ditching most developmental/therapeutic elements of those courses.

We have found in our work that importers tend to select elements of school forms that align most closely with their own professional expectations and norms, those that meet both instrumental and symbolic needs, while scrapping elements that do not. Social workers select those elements that are most similar to therapy; criminal justice authorities, we predict, would select those elements that resemble their goal of producing corrected behavior; corporations, we suspect, would prioritize those elements that align with the criteria, language, and culture of employee advancement. Imports in each field would have their own form of decoupling and legitimation-seeking, too. We hope that future researchers—like yourselves—will build on these leads and study additional sectors in which professionals import school forms and make our society ever more "schooled" in the process.

CASE STUDY 4 REVIEW

Discussion Questions

1. What do New Institutionalists mean when they argue that modern societies prize schools not only for their instrumental rewards in sparking economies or helping individuals but also for their broad associations with human rights, equity, and personal development? How is that different from arguing that schools play a causal role in helping to expand economies or enhance the social mobility of citizens?

2. Why do staff at Parents Community emphasize to donors and other members of the community that adult clients are taking "classes"? What do classes mean in today's schooled society?

3. Have you participated in any classes outside of the formal education sector? How were those classes run? In what ways were they similar to or different from formal schooling? Why do you think they were organized that way?

Suggestions for Further Reading

Davies, Scott, and Jal Mehta. 2018. "The Deepening Interpenetration of Schooling in Society." In *Education in a New Society: Renewing the Sociology of Education,* edited by Jal Mehta and Scott Davies. Chicago: University of Chicago Press.

Binder, Amy. 2007. "For Love and Money: Organizations' Creative Responses to Multiple Environmental Logics." *Theory and Society* 36 (6): 547–71.

Collins, Randall. (1979) 2019. *The Credential Society.* New York: Columbia University Press.

Scott, W. Richard, and John W. Meyer. 1994. "The Rise of Training Programs in Firms and Agencies: An Institutionalist Perspective." In *Institutional Environments and Organizations: Structural Complexity and Individualism,* 228–54. Thousand Oaks, CA: Sage.

References

Arum, Richard. 2003. *Judging School Discipline.* Cambridge, MA: Harvard University Press.

Baker, David. 2014. *The Schooled Society: The Educational Transformation of Global Culture.* Stanford, CA: Stanford University Press.

Coburn, Cynthia. 2004. "Beyond Decoupling: Rethinking the Relationship between the Institutional Environment and the Classroom." *Sociology of Education* 77:211–44.

Frank, David John, and Jay Gabler. 2006. *Reconstructing the University: Worldwide Shifts in Academia in the 20th Century.* Stanford, CA: Stanford University Press.

Gordon, Linda. 1994. *Pitied but Not Entitled: Single Mothers and the History of Welfare, 1890–1935.* New York: Free Press.

Hasenfeld, Yeheskel. 2000. "Organizational Forms as Moral Practices: The Case of Welfare Departments." *Social Service Review* 74:329–51.

Heimer, Carol, and Mitchell Stevens. 1997. "Caring for the Organization: Social Workers as Frontline Risk Managers in Neonatal Intensive Care Units." *Work and Occupations* 24 (2): 133–63.

Hout, Michael. 2012. "Social and Economic Returns to College." *Annual Review of Sociology* 38:379–400.

Jepperson, Ronald L. 2000. "The Development and Application of Sociological Neoinstitutionalism." Working Paper no. 2001/5. San Domenico di Fiesole, Italy: European University Institute, Robert Schuman Centre.

Lareau, Annette. 2002. *Unequal Childhoods.* Berkeley: University of California Press.

Meyer, John W., John Boli, George M. Thomas, and Francisco Ramirez. 1997. "World Society and the Nation-State." *American Journal of Sociology* 103 (1): 144–81.

Meyer, John, and Francisco Ramirez. 2002. "The World Institutionalization of Education." In *Discourse Formation in Comparative Education,* edited by Jürgen Schriewer, 111–32. New York: Peter Lang.

Meyer, John W., and Brian Rowan. 1977. "Institutional Organizations: Formal Structure as Myth and Ceremony." *American Journal of Sociology* 83:340–63.

Meyerson, Debra. 1994. "Interpretations of Stress in Institutions: The Cultural Production of Ambiguity and Burnout." *Administrative Science Quarterly* 39:628–53.

Nielsen, Kelly. 2015. "'Fake It 'til You Make It': Why Community College Students' Aspirations 'Hold Steady.'" *Sociology of Education* 88:265–83.

Richardson, John G. 2006. "The Variable Construction of Educational Risk." In *Handbook of the Sociology of Education,* edited by Maureen T. Hallinan, 307–23. New York: Springer.

Schofer, Evan, and John W. Meyer. 2005. "The Worldwide Expansion of Higher Education in the Twentieth Century." *American Sociological Review* 70 (6): 898–920.

Index

Founded in 1893,
UNIVERSITY OF CALIFORNIA PRESS
publishes bold, progressive books and journals
on topics in the arts, humanities, social sciences,
and natural sciences—with a focus on social
justice issues—that inspire thought and action
among readers worldwide.

The UC PRESS FOUNDATION
raises funds to uphold the press's vital role
as an independent, nonprofit publisher, and
receives philanthropic support from a wide
range of individuals and institutions—and from
committed readers like you. To learn more, visit
ucpress.edu/supportus.